THE YALE LIBRARY OF MILITARY HISTORY

THE SPARTAN REGIME

Its Character, Origins, and Grand Strategy

Paul A. Rahe

Yale UNIVERSITY PRESS

New Haven and London

Published with assistance from the Kingsley Trust Association Publication Fund
established by the Scroll and Key Society of Yale College.

Published with assistance from the foundation established in memory of
Amasa Stone Mather of the Class of 1907, Yale College.

Maps by Bill Nelson.

Yale University Press books may be purchased in quantity for educational, business,
or promotional use. For information, please e-mail sales.press@yale.edu (U.S. office) or
sales@yaleup.co.uk (U.K. office).

Set in Minion and Trajan Pro types by Integrated Publishing Solutions.
Printed in the United States of America.

Library of Congress Control Number: 2015960096
ISBN 978-0-300-21901-2 (hardcover : alk. paper)

A catalogue record for this book is available from the British Library.
This paper meets the requirements of ANSI/NISO Z39.48-1992 (Permanence of Paper).

10 9 8 7 6 5 4 3 2 1

Paul Anthony Rahe III

The greatest inconvenience associated with my endeavor is that here one sees men who resemble us almost in nothing, who seem to us to be outside of nature—perhaps as much because we are in that state ourselves as because they are in fact there. Their crimes inspire in us horror. Sometimes their virtues themselves make us shiver. Because we are weak and pusillanimous in good times and in bad, everything that bears a certain character of force and vigor seems to us impossible. The incredulity that we parade is the work of our cowardice rather than that of our reason.

—JEAN-JACQUES ROUSSEAU

Contents

List of Maps ix

Introduction: The Allure of Lacedaemon xi

Prologue: The Spartan Enigma 1

1. *Paideía* 7

2. *Politeía* 36

3. Conquest 64

4. Politics and Geopolitics 98

Conclusion: A Grand Strategy for Lacedaemon 121

Appendix 1. Land Tenure in Archaic Sparta 125

Appendix 2. The *Néoi* at Sparta 137

List of Abbreviations and Short Titles 139

Notes 143

Author's Note and Acknowledgments 195

Index of Subjects 199

Index of Persons and Places 205

Maps

Map 1. Mainland Greece xviii
Map 2. Laconia and Messenia 75
Map 3. Sparta in the Mediterranean 78
Map 4. Mount Taygetus and Messenia 107

Introduction

The Allure of Lacedaemon

I N the summer of 425 B.C., the Athenians managed to pull off a coup. They were at war. They had established a base on the western coast of the Peloponnesus at Navarino Bay for the purpose of harassing the foe. Their opponents controlled the mainland; and, in the course of attempting to drive the Athenians from this base, they had landed a small force of heavy infantry, roughly four hundred twenty in number, on the island of Sphacteria—which lay across the entrance to the bay. Although they were far from home and at a distinct disadvantage, the Athenians had then responded by leveraging their strength at sea in such a manner as to isolate the enemy infantrymen and trap them on the island; and, after a time, they attacked this small band with a superior force including light-armed troops and archers far better suited to the island's rugged terrain than the hoplites deployed by their foe. The enemy band they surrounded. Its members they pelted with arrows and stones. Then, they persuaded those who had survived the initial onslaught to give themselves up.[1]

Ordinarily, such a development would not be especially newsworthy. In time of war, some operations succeed, others fail, and small groups of men frequently get cornered and find themselves compelled to surrender. But this particular event, though at first glance it might seem a mere skirmish of minor importance, was different. There was something about it that made the Athenian victory a genuinely memorable achievement of real strategic importance, well worth recording and later recalling to mind and pondering.

Styphon son of Pharax, the man on whom command of the force that found itself isolated on Sphacteria had devolved, was no ordinary man. The same can be said for one hundred twenty of the two hundred ninety-two men under his command who were still alive on the island and who surrendered when he did. They, too, were extraordinary men. At least, they were supposed to be such. For they were all *Spartíatai*—we would say, Spartiates or Spartans —and, according to Thucydides, the news of their surrender left the Hellenic world dumbfounded and anything but satisfied. "Of all the events that took place in the course of the [Peloponnesian] war," he tells us, "this was the one that was most contrary to the expectation of the Greeks. They thought it in-conceivable that a shortage of food or any other necessity could induce Lace-daemonians to hand over their arms. They expected that such men would fight on for as long as they could and die with their weapons in their hands. They were incredulous and could not believe that those who had surrendered were the equals of those who had died." The Athenians and their allies were not alone in their astonishment. The Spartans themselves were taken aback, and they were shaken. In the aftermath, they repeatedly sued for peace; and when, in time, they got what they wanted and succeeded in persuading the Athenians to approve a treaty bringing the struggle to an end,[2] they did not know what to do with the returnees.[3]

As this anecdote suggests, Lacedaemon's allure is nothing new. In their heyday, the Lacedaemonians and the order of *Spartíatai* who ruled that com-plex community were almost universally regarded with awe, just as they are now. Of course, we may prefer the Athenians, regarding them as more like ourselves, and we may well be right not only in that judgment but in our moral and political preferences as well. Our predilections notwithstanding, however, we name sports teams after the Spartans, and it is about them (and not the Athenians) that we ordinarily write novels and make films—which says a great deal about the ancient Lacedaemonians and perhaps also something about the unsatisfied longings that lurk just below the surface within modern bourgeois societies.

This volume, the prelude to a projected trilogy on the grand strategy of ancient Lacedaemon and on the external challenges that polity faced in the late archaic and classical periods, is an attempt to see the Spartans whole. Its subject is the Lacedaemonian *políteía*. The word—which denotes citizenship and the form of government, constitution, and regime that makes it meaning-ful to speak of citizenship—first appears in *The Inquiries* of Herodotus, who tellingly employs it on that occasion solely with regard to what the citizens at Sparta share.[4] The notion was by no means, however, peculiar to him. By the time that he died, if not well before, the concept had become fundamental to political science.[5]

In the fifth century, Herodotus traveled about the eastern Mediterranean and the Black Sea; investigated the *nómoi*—the customs, habits, and laws—of the Hellenes and of the various barbarian peoples within or on the borders of the Persian empire; and attempted to make sense of the *nómoi* of each nation with an eye to the polity and way of life within which those customs, habits, and laws found their place.[6] At the end of that century, Thucydides depicted the great war between the Athenians and the Spartans as an epic contest between two different *politeíai* and used his history to analyze the strengths and weaknesses of each.[7] In the decades that followed, Xenophon employed the same approach in interpreting the Persian monarchy; and in a book he entitled the *Politeía*, which we now know as *The Republic*, Plato pioneered the study of political psychology with regard to the rise and the decay of the different regimes. Soon thereafter, in his universal history of the Greeks and the barbarians from the time of the Return of the Heraclids to the 340s, Ephorus studied the rise and fall of hegemonic powers with an eye to the virtues nourished by particular regimes and the vices associated with their decay.[8] Then, Aristotle brought regime analysis to full maturity, applied it to an assortment of the polities in existence in his time, and left it as a legacy to Theophrastus, Dicaearchus, Sphaerus, Polybius, Diodorus Siculus, Dionysius of Halicarnassus, Cicero, Sallust, Livy, Tacitus, Dio Cassius, Plutarch, Ammianus Marcellinus, and the other great writers responsible for recording so much of the little that we know concerning the ancient world and for making sense of the changes that took place.[9]

Regime analysis was comprehensive. One acute, if anonymous, ancient observer nicely captured what was at stake for these authors when he defined *politeía* broadly as "the one way of life of a whole *pólis*," and Isocrates did the same when he dubbed it "the city's soul."[10] Though much may separate Thucydides, Xenophon, Ephorus, Plato, and Aristotle from one another, on this fundamental point they and those who subsequently followed their lead were agreed: that to come to understand a polity, one must be willing to entertain two propositions. First, one must presume that the form of government, the constitution, the rules defining membership in the *políteuma* or ruling order (in short, the political regime as such), rather than economic or environmental conditions, is the chief determinant of a political community's character. Second, one must assume that *paideía*, which is to say, education and moral formation in the broadest and most comprehensive sense, is more important than anything else in deciding the character of a particular *políteía*.[11] In one passage of *The Politics,* Aristotle suggests that it is the provision of a common *paideía*—and nothing else—that turns a multitude into a unit and constitutes it as a *pólis;* in another, he indicates that it is the *políteía* which defines the *pólis* as such. Though apparently in contradiction, these two statements are in fact equivalent—for, as the peripatetic recognized, man is an imitative animal, the example we set is far more influential than what we say, and it is the "distribution and disposition of offices and honors [*táxis tôn archôn*]" constituting the *políteuma* of a given polity that is the most effective educator therein.[12] It is not fortuitous that Polybius' celebrated discussion of the Roman *políteía* is, in fact, a discussion of the *paideía* accorded its ruling order. Precisely the same observation can be made regarding Xenophon's account of the Persian *políteía*.[13] Plato, Aristotle, Xenophon, Polybius, and those who came after were all persuaded of one thing: that if certain opinions reign and come to be authoritative within a given political community, it is because their advocates have consolidated dominion there and, in the process, have managed to persuade themselves and their subjects of their right to rule by an appeal to their own preeminence in honoring these same opinions in speech and in deed.[14]

In short, from the perspective of these ancient authors, the modern distinction between materialism and idealism makes little practical, political sense—for what really matters most with regard to political understanding is this: to decide who is to rule or what sorts of human beings are to share in rule and function as a community's *políteuma* is to determine which of the various and competing titles to rule is to be authoritative; in turn, this is to decide what qualities are to be admired and honored in the city, what is to be considered advantageous and just, and how happiness and success [*eudaimonía*] are to be understood and pursued; and this decision—more than any other—determines the *paideía* which constitutes "the one way of life of a whole *pólis*."[15]

This decision may be a matter of chance, to be sure. As even Alexander Hamilton was forced to concede, few, if any, "societies of men" have ever established "good government from reflection and choice"; most, if not all, have been "destined to depend, for their political constitutions, on accident and force."[16] But where circumstance predominates—as, the ancients fully recognized, is usually the case—it is either because the citizens have been overwhelmed by the sheer momentum of events or because they have managed affairs quite ineptly and have allowed things to drift so that fortune comes to function as a lawgiver [*nomothétēs*] in arranging that distribution and disposition of the polity's offices and honors which, more than anything else, determines the *paideía* that makes them a political community. What counts most from the vantage point assumed by Plato, Aristotle, and their successors is the fact that circumstance need not be absolutely predominant. Thus, if ancient political science stresses the limits of human mastery, it nonetheless presupposes the possibility of statesmanship.[17]

My aim here is to resurrect this largely forgotten political science and demonstrate its power. My immediate purpose is to apply its insights to an analysis of ancient Lacedaemon. To this end, in the first chapter, I describe the Spartan way of life, dwelling on the practices and institutions that distinguished the ancient Lacedaemonians from their fellow Hellenes. To this end, in the second, I analyze their form of government—the first in human history known to have embodied an elaborate system of balances and checks—and I attempt to show not only how it cohered with and supported their peculiar way of life, but also how it helped make of the Lacedaemonian *politeía* what the ancients called a *kósmos*: a beautiful, exquisitely well-ordered whole.[18] To this end, in both chapters, I also try to make sense of the claim—first advanced by Tyrtaeus, then restated by Alcman, and later reasserted by Pindar, Herodotus, and Thucydides—that Lacedaemon's peculiar *politeía* gave rise in that city to what the Greeks called *eunomía*: the lawfulness and good order that Homer singled out for praise; that Hesiod personified both as the sister of Peace [*Eirḗnē*] and Justice [*Díkē*] and as the daughter of Zeus and Divinely Sanctioned Custom and Law [*Thémis*]; and that Alcman would later depict as the daughter of Foresight [*Promathéa*] and sister of Persuasion [*Peithṓ*].[19] Finally, in the third and fourth chapters, I explore the genesis of the Spartan regimen and regime, and I trace the Spartans' gradual articulation of an ingenious grand strategy designed to provide for the defense of Lacedaemon and the peculiar way of life fostered by that regimen and regime.

It is only, I believe, when one has seen Sparta whole that one can make sense of her conduct within Hellas in the archaic and classical periods. It is only when one has seen this polity whole that one can begin to understand why Lacedaemon, for all of her defects, nonetheless inspired great admiration and awe and why, even today, she retains a certain allure and elicits from all but her most resolute detractors a profound, if grudging, respect.

*

One remark before we begin: when they alluded to Athens, Corinth, Megara, or Lacedaemon by name as a political community; and, strikingly, even when they spoke of one these *póleıs* as their fatherland [*patrís*], the ancient Greeks employed nouns feminine in gender, personifying the community as a woman to whom they were devoted—which is why I with some frequency use the feminine pronoun to refer to Sparta and other Greek *póleıs* here.

The Spartan Regime

Map 1. Mainland Greece

PROLOGUE
The Spartan Enigma

Patriotism is conducive to good morals, and good morals contribute to patriotism. The less we are able to satisfy our private passions, the more we abandon ourselves to those of a more general nature. Why are monks so fond of their order? Precisely because of those things which make it insupportable. Their rule deprives them of all the things on which the ordinary passions rest: there remains, then, only that passion for the rule which torments them. The more austere the rule, that is, the more it curbs their inclinations, the more force it gives to the one inclination which it leaves them.

—CHARLES-LOUIS DE SECONDAT, BARON DE LA BRÈDE ET DE MONTESQUIEU

T o understand ancient Sparta, the part she played in Greek history, and the role that her image played in the history of the West, one must come to understand the Spartan regime and way of life—which is no mean task.[1] Lacedaemon is now and always has been a great puzzle. She troubled even the ancients. In antiquity, some thought her a democracy; others, an oligarchy. In one passage of Plato's *Laws,* the Athenian stranger describes her constitution as a mixture of monarchy and democracy; a few pages later, the Spartan Megillus admits that even he is at a loss for a name to give the polity: when considering the ephorate as a magistracy, he is tempted to call it a tyranny; when looking at the regime as a whole, he is led to think Sparta the most democratic of all the cities; and it would be altogether strange to deny that she is an aristocracy. But, he adds, there is a kingship in the place, for her two *basileîs* rule for life, and theirs is the oldest of kingships. Aristotle suffered a fate similar to that of Plato's Megillus. When reflecting on the strife between rich and poor that racked most Greek cities, he could describe the Lacedaemonian regime as a mixture of democracy and oligarchy; when thinking of the Spartan way of life, he found it necessary to term the city an aristocracy somehow both democratic and oriented toward the pursuit of virtue.[2]

The confusion persists. In the age stretching from Niccolò Machiavelli to Jean-Jacques Rousseau, Sparta was often considered a model for the constitution of liberty. In the aftermath of the French Revolution, with the spread of liberal democracy, this view seemed discredited; and since the 1930s, scholars have tended to see in Sparta a forerunner of the modern totalitarian state.[3] This recent trend has not entirely stifled debate. But the range of respectable opinion remains narrow and is perhaps best illustrated by remarks made in the mid-1960s by the Wykeham Professor of Ancient History at Oxford and by his counterpart at Cambridge. The former introduced a study of Spartan government with the observation that "Sparta had in some ways a more open constitution than most oligarchies." The latter asked himself whether the Spartans, when assembled for debate on a public policy, were likely to be able to drop the habit of unquestioning obedience he thought instilled in them by their military training. He concluded with the guess that "the Spartan assembly was much closer to the Homeric than to the Athenian in function and psychology." It would not be hyperbole to appropriate for Sparta Winston Churchill's famous description of Russia: Lacedaemon was in antiquity and remains today a riddle wrapped in a mystery inside an enigma.[4]

The quandary in which we find ourselves is partly a function of "the secretiveness" distinguishing the Spartan "regime," which so frustrated Thucydides. Even in the late fifth century, it was difficult to obtain precise information. In consequence, as one scholar recently put it, "many of the problems, and not only those of the remote archaic period, are in a sense insoluble: that is, the evidence is limited and often enigmatic, the range of possible solutions is wide, and there is no criterion but general plausibility to help one judge between them."[5]

Our difficulties are also partly a consequence of the idealization of Sparta already evident in the writings of Critias in the late fifth century. In recent times, scholars have done a great deal of work in attempting to separate out what is trustworthy in the ancient sources from that which is a product of what they have come to call "the Spartan mirage."[6] But even this yeoman service has not sufficed to remove the obstacles entirely. Indeed, the extreme skepticism evident in the recent literature on the subject may even have compounded our difficulties—for it has licensed scholars to reject the ancient evidence where it conflicts with their own conceptions and scholarly predilections.[7] David Hume identified the source of the incredulity that besets us when he remarked, "Ancient policy was violent, and contrary to the more natural and usual course of things. It is well known with what peculiar laws SPARTA was governed, and what a prodigy that republic is justly esteemed by every one, who has considered human nature as it has displayed itself in other nations, and other ages.

Were the testimony of history less positive and circumstantial, such a government would appear a mere philosophical whim or fiction, and impossible ever to be reduced to practice."[8] There is so much in Spartan life that is repugnant to the tastes fostered by the modern regime of liberal democracy that it is, in truth, far harder for us to achieve clarity on this subject than it was for the ancients themselves.

In any case, the establishment of a Spartan empire after the Peloponnesian War made it impossible effectively to maintain the regimen of secrecy. During and after the last years of that epic struggle, outsiders such as Socrates' Athenian students Critias and Xenophon became intimately familiar with Lacedaemonian mores, manners, and laws. The latter is even said to have had his own sons reared and educated in the Spartan *agōgé*.[9] Both of these men went to some lengths in describing the Spartan form of government and way of life. There is no reason to believe that either resorted to fabrication.[10]

In this period, genuine insiders began breaking silence as well. The quarrels occasioned by the dramatic changes attendant on the radical shift that had taken place in the foreign policy of Lacedaemon at the end of the war were severe; and bitterness induced a Spartan king—who was decidedly unfriendly to grand imperial ventures of the sort that his compatriots had embraced at this time, who came to be hostile to the ephorate, and who had been driven into exile in Tegea early in the fourth century—to compose a treatise concerning "the laws of Lycurgus." In it, there is excellent reason to suspect, he addressed the amendment of those laws in later times and the process by which, in crucial regards, they had been altered or abandoned in or long before his own day.[11] We hear a similar tale concerning an experienced Spartan harmost or garrison commander named Thibron, who appears to have belonged to the opposing political camp. This Thibron was temporarily exiled at about the same time, and he is said to have penned a treatise describing and praising with regard to its suitability for war and dominion the *politeía* said to have been established at the outset by Lycurgus at Sparta.[12]

As this evidence suggests, the Spartans were not, as is sometimes supposed, illiterate or very nearly so. In fact, the operations of the Lacedaemonian constitution presupposed something like universal literacy on a relatively high level. Nor were the Lacedaemonians without resources for the study of their own past. There is compelling evidence that, early on, the city established archives in which to preserve for future consultation oracles, treaties, lists of magistrates, laws, and other records of public import.[13]

Later writers from distant parts profited from the surfeit of information that became available during and after the Peloponnesian War. In the universal history he wrote concerning the rise and fall of succeeding hegemonic powers in the period stretching from the Return of the Heraclids to the mid-fourth century, Ephorus of Cumae paid very close attention to Lacedaemon, to her history, her peculiarities, her *politeía,* and way of life.[14] In his dialogues—above all, in his *Republic* and *Laws*—Plato had frequent occasion to display an intimate familiarity with Spartan institutions and practices;[15] and Aristotle, no doubt with the aid of his students, penned a learned treatise on the Lacedaemonian *politeía* and its evolution. In it, if we are to judge by the predilections on display in *The Politics,* which has as its focus the fully developed *politeíai* of his own day,[16] the peripatetic must have devoted close attention not only to the rules defining citizenship and the magistracies and the procedures for decision-making put in place at Sparta, but also to the education and moral formation, the *paideía,* that Lacedaemon gave her young by means of the *agōgé;* to the relations between women and men; to her practices as they pertained to war; and to that polity's property regime and the changes it underwent. Such is certainly the picture conveyed by the surviving excerpts.[17]

   Unlike his detailed study of the Athenian regime, which it must have closely resembled, Aristotle's *Politeía of the Lacedaemonians* is, alas, now lost. In antiquity, however, this seminal work was widely read and frequently quoted, and subsequently it served as a basis for the descriptions and analyses of the Spartan regime articulated by the peripatetic's own pupils Theophrastus of Eresus and Dicaearchus of Messana; by his epitomator Heracleides of Lembus, a third-century adherent of the Lyceum; by the Stoic Sphaerus of Borysthenes; and by later writers, most notably the renowned biographer Plutarch of Chaeronea.[18]

   We need not doubt the overall accuracy of these works. The Lacedaemonians were, in fact, so pleased with the treatise produced by Dicaearchus in or soon after the 330s that—in all likelihood not long after its appearance—they passed a law stipulating that once a year, at the administrative office of the ephors, this particular treatise on the *politeía* of the Lacedaemonians be read aloud in its entirety to those Spartiates then in their prime.[19] If the Spartan *agōgé* survived, as a relic of sorts, the demise of Lacedaemon's ancient political system and the abolition of the dual kingship; if, after a brief hiatus in the second century, it was revived in something like its original form; and if it flourished thereafter for more than half a millennium under Roman dominion so that Cicero and, later, the geographer Pausanias, the biographer Plutarch, and the rhetorician Libanius could observe it in operation—it was at least in part because the works of Critias, Xenophon, Ephorus, Aristotle, Dicaearchus, Heracleides, and Sphaerus, in which it was described in some detail, were available for consultation.[20] When, in an oration, Cicero briefly singled out for praise "the discipline" instilled by the Lacedaemonians and asserted that "they alone, in the earth entire, have lived for more than seven centuries with one set of customs and unchanging laws," he was exaggerating, as was his wont in public discourse. But when, in a philosophical work aimed at a more learned audience, he contended that "the laws of Lycurgus educate the young through toil and distress by forcing them to hunt and run and by making them suffer hunger, thirst, cold, and heat," he is describing rigors that Spartans in the late archaic and classical periods would almost certainly have recognized.[21] In an account of classical Spartan customs and ways, the evidence from the Roman period cannot be accorded as much weight as what we learn from earlier sources of information, and it must be used with caution and care. But it cannot simply be ignored.

Nor need we suppose that, in describing Lacedaemon, the ancient authorities blindly succumbed to adulation. Ephorus was not an admirer of Sparta; and, as classicists are now, finally, beginning to recognize, Xenophon was a writer of great subtlety, capable of intimating what it was imprudent and improper for a beneficiary of Lacedaemonian patronage and a guest-friend of one of Sparta's kings openly to say: that, despite its obvious virtues, the Lacedaemonian regime was fundamentally defective.[22] Plato and Aristotle were far less reticent and reserved. As we shall soon have ample opportunity to observe, in the criticism they directed at Lacedaemon, these two philosophers were unstinting, open, and refreshingly blunt.[23] Apart, perhaps, from Critias—who was, indeed, an out-and-out partisan—none of the figures associated with Socrates can be accused of having been mesmerized by Lacedaemon. There is, moreover, no evidence that Theophrastus, Dicaearchus, Heracleides, Sphaerus, or any of their successors fell into such a trap; and, in the absence of such evidence, it is implausible to suppose that Aristotle's peripatetic followers, whose admiration for their master's judgment knew few bounds, would have done so.[24]

Nor should we assume that in depicting the mores, manners, and political institutions of the Lacedaemonians Plutarch in any way falsified the facts. Of course, in his quest to keep alive the memory of ancient liberty, he did treat Lacedaemon in a manner more sympathetic than had Ephorus, Xenophon,

Plato, and Aristotle.[25] His biography of Lycurgus is, moreover, an encomium of sorts, and his description of the lawgiver owes a great deal to legend and something as well to the imagination, as he readily acknowledges.[26] But with regard to the actual *polıteía* of the Lacedaemonians and its genesis, he displayed his customary discernment and caution; and it was on the Socratics and Aristotle, whom he revered, and on Ephorus, the peripatetics, and their Stoic successors that he principally relied for the details.[27] If not just Plutarch, but, in fact, all of these figures—critics and eulogists alike—found Sparta fascinating and worthy of study, and if, moreover, they had trouble doing full justice to the Lacedaemonian polity in all of its complexity, it is perhaps because the mystery is not itself a mirage.

In the end, the only proper conclusion to reach is that advanced more than two centuries ago by a man who grew up among the Gaelic-speaking Highlanders of Scotland—a people not much less warlike than the ancient Spartans had been. "After all," Adam Ferguson observed, "we are, perhaps, not sufficiently instructed in the nature of the Spartan laws and institutions, to understand in what manner all the ends of this singular state were obtained; but the admiration paid to its people, and the constant reference of contemporary historians to their avowed superiority will not allow us to question the facts."[28] It would, then, be presumptuous to assume without extensive discussion and conclusive evidence that we can somehow dramatically improve upon the efforts of Plato and Aristotle and upon the understanding that they and the most penetrating of their successors articulated. But it should be possible to come closer to understanding the delphic remarks of these learned observers—first, by attending to the Spartan way of life and by carefully sifting what we know and what we can surmise regarding the day-to-day government of classical Lacedaemon; then, by exploring the likely origins of this regimen and regime; and, finally, by tracing the Spartans' gradual, halting articulation of a grand strategy suited to insuring the preservation of the Lacedaemonian way of life. This task has been made easier by the appearance in recent decades of a host of specialized studies aimed at elucidating the working of particular institutions and the importance of particular practices.[29] Even where the hyperskepticism now fashionable among classicists and ancient historians vitiates their conclusions, these studies frequently illuminate the subjects they address. If it is not within our power to dispel entirely the mystery of the Spartan regime, it still may be possible to shed some light on the subject.

CHAPTER 1

PAIDEÍA

> What gives rise to human misery is the contradiction found between our condition and our desires, between our duties and our inclinations, between nature and social institutions, between man and citizen; render a man one and you shall render him as happy as he is able to be. Give him entirely over to the state or leave him entirely to himself—but if you divide his heart, you shall tear it asunder.
>
> —JEAN-JACQUES ROUSSEAU

C LASSICAL Lacedaemon was no ordinary *pólis*. No one thought so in antiquity; no one should think so today.[1] It is by no means fortuitous that Herodotus of Halicarnassus—whose analysis of Spartan mores, manners, and ways is the earliest such surviving account—treats Lacedaemon and no other Greek *pólis* alongside Scythia, Persia, and Egypt as an ethnographic wonder. For that is precisely what she was.[2] The *nómima* of the Lacedaemonians—their customs, manners, and laws—really were incompatible with those of their fellow Hellenes, as Thucydides' Athenians bluntly inform them; and Sparta really was opposed to the other Greek *póleis* in her institutions and practices, as Xenophon repeatedly insists.[3]

The ground of this distinctiveness is clear enough. Of all the ancient Hellenic communities, Sparta came the closest to giving absolute primacy to the common good. She did this—as Plato, Isocrates, and Plutarch recognized—by turning the city into a camp, the *pólis* into an army, and the citizen into a soldier. She did it by taking the institutions and practices embryonic in every *pólis* and developing them to an extreme only imagined elsewhere. Except with the express permission of the magistrates, her citizens were prohibited from traveling abroad and foreigners were forbidden to visit Lacedaemon. As a consequence, she was able to exert an almost absolute control over the circumstances which shaped her citizens' lives. Everything that she did in this virtually self-contained world was aimed at a single end: at nurturing what Lord Macaulay would later refer to as "that intense patriotism which is peculiar to members of societies congregated in a narrow space." This radical fidelity to the principles particular to the *pólis* as a species of political community ex-plains why a city so rarely imitated was so universally admired.[4]

In her inception, Sparta stands in contrast to later republics such as the fledging United States. The citizens of a tiny, warrior community living in a warlike world needed a unity that an extended, bourgeois republic endowed with a dynamic economy and located on a vast and nearly empty continent could afford to dispense with. Pythagoras is said to have compared faction [*stásis*] in the city with disease in the body, ignorance in the soul, division within the household, and a lack of proportion in general. "One must avoid these things," he reportedly observed, "with every means at one's disposal, and one must root them out with fire and sword and with every sort of contriv-ance." The philosopher from Samos was not at all peculiar in holding this opinion. The testimony of Herodotus on the matter is, if anything, more force-ful. The historian from Halicarnassus not only wrote that "*stásis* within the tribe is a greater evil than war waged by men thinking as one"; he added that this was true "to the very degree that war itself is less desirable than peace."[5] For the cities of Hellas, the presence of the enemy without required the sup-pression of dissidence within.

For this reason, the well-known antidote for faction proposed in *The Fed-eralist* by James Madison could never have been applied within the Greek *pólis*. No one in antiquity would have countenanced economic differentiation and a multiplication of religious sects. If the commonwealth was to survive, it was vital for the citizens "to act in unison with each other." As a consequence, the ancient republic sought to solve the problem of *stásis* not "by controlling its effects" in the manner later suggested by the American statesman. It did so, rather, "by removing its causes." As Madison himself had occasion to observe, the Greeks attempted this not by granting free rein to opinion and by encour-aging a proliferation of petty special interests with an eye to balancing them against one another, but rather "by giving to every citizen the same opinions, the same passions, and the same interests." *Homónoia*—unanimity, solidarity, or like-mindedness regarding the advantageous, the just, and the good: this was the goal; and the market economy, though tolerated as a necessity, was perceived as a threat. Where the Greeks distinguished the free and political from the commercial *agorá,* where they excluded the merchant and the crafts-man from political life, and where they simply held the tradesman in disdain, the cause was not some bizarre and irrational prejudice against men of business. Instinctively, the Greeks recognized that the differentiation of interests inevitably fostered by trade and industry was a danger to the hard-won communal solidarity that enabled them to survive.[6]

With the danger of faction in mind, Sparta took great care to insulate the polity from the influence of the marketplace. Fearful that competition for wealth would set the citizens at odds, she coined no money, used flat iron ingots in its place, and, at least at one point, expressly outlawed the private possession of silver and gold. Eager to prevent a differentiation of interests, she barred her citizens from engaging in commerce and prohibited their practice of the mechanical arts. Nowhere were the latter held in less esteem. Lacedaemon even banned visits to the commercial *agorá* by men under the age of thirty. The Spartans were, as Plutarch remarks, "the servants of Ares," not Mammon. They were "the craftsmen of war," not the makers of pots. They had but one purpose in life: to gain a reputation for valor. From childhood on, they trained to secure victory in battle by land.[7]

To eliminate those unfit for this endeavor, the city practiced infanticide, subjecting the newborn to a careful scrutiny and exposing to the elements those who were deformed or otherwise lacking in vigor. Whether, over time, Lacedaemon's eugenic practices had an impact on the physical characteristics typifying members of the Spartiate community, as such practices no doubt did in the case of the horses and dogs the Spartans enthusiastically bred, we simply do not know. But it is clear enough that this was their aim and that the Spartans thought of themselves quite literally as a breed apart.[8]

To enable those who survived this initial test to pursue in due course the chief goal set by the regime, the city authorized a grant to every citizen of a *klêros*—an equal allotment of public land—and servants called helots to work it.[9] The rent determined by the *pólis* and paid in kind by these dependent peasants was sufficient to support in comfort a small household,[10] and the labor of this depressed class made it possible for the Spartans to devote their time and efforts to mastering the martial arts and to gaining that confidence which fortifies civil courage. When asked why they placed their fields in the hands of the helots and did not cultivate the soil themselves, one Spartan is said to have replied that "it was not by caring for the fields but by caring for ourselves that we came to possess those fields." Centuries after the city's decline, Josephus would look back and remark that "these men neither tilled the soil nor toiled at the crafts—but freed from labor and sleek with the palaestra's oil, they exercised their bodies for beauty's sake and passed their time in the *pólis*. To take care of all the needs of life, they employed other men as servants and drew ready nourishment from these. And they were ready to do all and suffer all for this one accomplishment—noble and dear to human kind—that they might prevail over all against whom they marched."[11] While the ordinary Greek city was a community of smallholders and gentleman farmers, Lacedaemon was a legion of men-at-arms.

She was also an aristocracy of masters, a city of seigneurs, a commonwealth of leisured gentlemen—who could be described as both noble and good: *kaloì kagathoí*. The Spartans called themselves *hoi hómoioi*: "the equals, the similars, the peers." In a sense, they were equal. By means of the land grants, the *pólis* abolished among the citizens what James Madison in *The Federalist* would later call the distinction between "those who hold and those who are without property" at all, and she thereby eliminated what he would term "the most common and durable source of factions." Of course, some of the soil did remain in private hands. But although there remained a "various and unequal distribution of property" of the sort that worried Madison in his capacity as a statesman, in late archaic and early classical Sparta the gap between rich and poor was not profound. As men of property, the Spartans had essentially the same interests.[12]

Education

To remove any lingering doubts, the city exercised close control over the education of children and the daily comportment of the citizens. The rich and the poor grew up together, subject to the same regimen; they dressed in a similar fashion and undressed with great regularity to exercise naked in the public gymnasium; and they took their meals together in the common mess [*sussitíon*] thereafter, partaking of the simple fare.[13] The giving of dowries was strictly forbidden. But, thanks to the continued existence of private property, women were able to inherit. In consequence, the magistrates were empowered to fine those who paid more attention to opulence than to virtue in matters of love and marriage. To the same end, there were severe sumptuary laws to deny the great families the public display and use of their riches.[14] An exception was made for the breeding and racing of horses. But even before the Spartans organized for the defense of Laconia a standing force of cavalry, this practice arguably served a military function. No army can do without scouts and messengers. Moreover, the ordinary citizen was allowed the free use of the helots, horses, and hounds of his wealthier fellows-in-arms. As Thucydides, Xenophon, and Aristotle all emphasize, the Spartans shared a common way of life.[15]

Those with scanty resources apart from the civic allotment may still have felt envy—but, if so, it was a jealousy dampened by fear. The helots who tilled the soil were a permanent threat to the city's survival. The "old helots," descended from the ancient Achaean stock ascendant in the Mycenaean age,[16] resided near their masters within Laconia in the southeastern Peloponnesus and gave every appearance of being docile. In time of need, some from among them were even freed and recruited as hoplites into the army of Lacedaemon.[17] Those seized when the Thebans invaded Laconia in 370/369 were so thoroughly broken in spirit that, when their captors asked them to sing the verses of Terpander, Alcman, and Spendon the Laconian, they resolutely refused to do what their Spartiate masters did not allow. And yet—when the opportunity presented itself—many of these Laconian helots nonetheless proved to be fully capable of rebellion. Aristotle rightly speaks of them as a hostile force "continuously lying in wait for misfortune" to strike.[18]

In this regard they were by no means alone: throughout much of the archaic and nearly all of the subsequent classical period, the Spartans controlled not just Laconia, but the neighboring province of Messenia in the southwestern Peloponnesus as well. The latter region was fertile and exceedingly well watered but extremely difficult of access, shut off as it was from Laconia's Eurotas valley by the rugged peaks of Mount Taygetus. There, where the Spartans themselves were few, the helots were numerous, conscious of their identity as a separate people, bitterly hostile to their masters, and prone to revolt.[19] The danger posed by the helots of Laconia and perhaps even that posed by those in Messenia might have been managed with relative ease had Lacedaemon lacked foes abroad, but unfortunately for her that was not the situation: not far from Sparta's northeastern border, her ancient enemy Argos, a large and powerful city, stood poised, watching and waiting to take advantage of any disaster that might strike.[20] Even in the best of times, the helots of the two regions appear to have outnumbered their masters by a margin of four, some say, but quite possibly even seven to one;[21] and in an emergency, the Spartans could never be fully confident that their associates would rally to their cause. The "dwellers-about [períoikoi]," the class of non-Spartiate Lacedaemonians who resided in the subject villages of Laconia and Messenia and retained in privilege a measure of local autonomy, may generally have been loyal—but only, we are told, out of fear. And the city's allies elsewhere within the Peloponnesus were often disaffected and sometimes hostile.[22]

In the early fourth century, one Corinthian leader summed up Sparta's strategic position elegantly by comparing her to a stream. "At their sources," he noted, "rivers are not great and they are easily forded, but the farther on they go, the greater they get—for other rivers empty into them and make the current stronger." So it is with the Spartans, he continued. "There, in the place where they emerge, they are alone; but as they continue and gather cities under their control, they become more numerous and harder to fight." The prudent general, he concluded, will seek battle with the Spartans in or near Lacedaemon where they are few in number and relatively weak. Thanks to demographic decline, the structure of Sparta's defenses was at that time fragile in the extreme. But it had never been more than tenuous, and the Lacedaemonians understood from the beginning what history was eventually to reveal: that it took but a single major defeat in warfare on land to endanger the city's very survival.[23]

As a consequence of the community's strategic situation, fear was the fundamental Spartan passion. It was fear that explained why Lacedaemon was notoriously slow to go to war, and it was fear that accounted for the remarkable caution that she so conspicuously displayed on the field of battle. This omnipresent fear lay behind her flagrant inability in matters of state to distinguish the dictates of interest from the biddings of honor, and it was fear that made the distrust and the deceit that governed her relations with other communities so pronounced and so glaring. Fear, the great equalizer, rendered the Spartan regime conservative, stable, and—despite the presence of a wealthy, landed aristocracy—socially harmonious. The Spartans were well aware of this fact. As Plutarch remarks, they established a temple to *Phóbos,* not to ward off panic in battle, but because they recognized that fear held the polity together.[24] The Spartans had to be friends: as members of a garrison community, they desperately needed each other.

This awareness of need the Spartans magnified by sentiment. Because piety was understood to be the foundation of patriotism, Spartans were from an early age imbued with a fear of the gods so powerful that it distinguished them from their fellow Greeks.[25] Plato had a better understanding of this than anyone since. With the promotion of civic virtue in mind, he wrote, "One of the finest of [Sparta's] *nómoi* is the *nómos* that does not allow any of the young to inquire which of the *nómoi* are finely made and which are not, but that commands all to say in harmony, with one voice from one mouth, that all the [city's] *nómoi* are finely made by gods." Sophocles' Menelaus speaks for Sparta when he asserts,

> Not in a city would the laws ever succeed unless dread was there estab-lished; nor would an army ever show restraint and be ruled unless it had a protective screen of fear and of awe. And even if a man develops great strength, he should be of the view that he can be felled by an evil quite small. For, where there is dread together with shame, know that you have safety. But where it is permitted to be insolent and to do whatever one wishes, be aware that such a city will run before favorable winds and fi-nally into the deep. For me let there be a seasonable dread.

Reverence and dread came easily to a people living in fear. More effectively than any other Greek city, Sparta used superstition to reinforce that total obe-dience to the law which constituted civic virtue and that steadfastness in battle for which the Lacedaemonians were famous. It is by no means fortuitous that the most important unit in the Spartan army was called an *enōmotía*. As the word's etymology suggests, this unit of forty or so men was a "sworn band" united by a solemn oath binding its members to remain in formation if they did not wish to bring down on their own heads the wrath of the gods.[26]

Superstition was by no means the only force employed. The Spartans gave to the citizens the same opinions and fostered in them the same passions by means of the *agōgé*, their much-celebrated system of education and moral formation.[27] When a male child reached the age of seven, he was taken from his mother, classified as a *paîs,* and added to an *agélē*—a herd—of boys his own age. When he returned home thereafter, he did so as a visitor: his true home was to be the community of his contemporaries. In this new home, he would learn to think of himself not as an individual, nor as a member of a particular household, but as a part of the community. Apart from that com-munity, he was nothing.[28]

In the *agélē*, the boys were subjected to a regimen of exercise interspersed with sessions dedicated to learning the communal dances, the poetry, and the songs of Sparta. Because physical stamina and the ability to march to the ca-dence of the flute were required for victory in hoplite warfare, the boys were encouraged to compete in athletics, in mock battles, in dancing, and in musi-cal contests. Because endurance and craft were necessary for success when on campaign, they were inured to pain and hardship and kept on short rations; for additional sustenance, they were forced to steal, and those who were caught were severely punished.[29] There is a famous story told by Plutarch regarding a

Spartan boy who died when a fox stolen by his comrades from the stores of the men's mess, which he was resolutely concealing beneath his tunic, gnawed at his vitals. The tale may well be apocryphal, as most scholars assume. It is certainly dramatic. But, in context, the anecdote was nonetheless apt, for, as stories go, it was far less implausible than we might be inclined to suppose. In antiquity, fresh fox meat was considered a great delicacy, especially in the autumn when eating grapes had made these animals plump.[30]

Music was central to Spartan life. This much is clear from Pindar's brief celebration of Lacedaemon: for the Theban poet praises Sparta not only for the prudence of her leaders and the achievements of her warriors, but also for her prowess in the arts.

> There the Counsels of the Elders
> And the Spears of the Young Men are the Best
> And the Choirs and the Muse and the Splendor.

Pindar was not peculiar in linking these notions. By his day, this depiction of Sparta had come to have a familiar ring. Two centuries earlier, when the festival of the Carneia was reorganized, the poet Terpander of Lesbos had written of Lacedaemon that "there the spears of young men blossom, and music with a clear tone, and justice in the broad streets—ally of noble deeds." Later in the seventh century, Alcman had sounded much the same theme, describing Sparta as a place where "playing the cithara well rivals the wielding of iron swords." By the end of the archaic period, the Lacedaemonian zest for music had become proverbial. "The cicada," wrote Pratinus of Phlius, "is a Laconian: ever ready for a chorus."[31]

This phenomenon deserves respectful attention, for it would be a mistake to underestimate the integrating force of the choral performances, the dancing, and the other public rituals that marked the Hyacinthia, the Gymnopaidiai, the Carneia, and the other great festivals of Sparta. Terpander is himself credited with having brought an end to civil strife in the city, and Plutarch suggests that music in general played a vital role in the prevention of *stásis*. Moreover, when Pindar attributed to the poet indebted to Apollo and inspired by the Muse an ability to "infuse into hearts and minds that good order and lawfulness [*eunomía*] which frees men from [intestine] war," Sparta was the city that he had foremost in mind. Though the Lacedaemonians neglected the technical study of this art, Aristotle tells us, they claimed an expertise in distinguishing songs that were serviceable from those that were not. The standard depiction of the Spartiate way of life as grim and forbidding can scarcely do full justice to the place of honor which the Lacedaemonians accorded sports, music, and the dance. As virtually all who have been comrades-in-arms can easily testify, the army camp does have its own peculiar charms.[32]

To grasp the true nature of Spartan life, one must ponder the connection of music with war. The poetry which the Spartiates taught their young was vital for the overall process of indoctrination through which they sought to achieve that total subordination of the individual to the community which the law commanded.[33]

Poetry

It is not easy for the citizens of modern, liberal republics to imagine, much less assess, the influence which poetry exercised over the Lacedaemonians. For the most part, modern political life is prosaic, and our literature reflects little but private concerns. At best, great literature exists—or at least is generally thought to exist—only on the margins of the larger public world. As a result, we tend to forget that there was a time when this was not the case at all. Without Dante, there would arguably never have been an Italian people. Luther's translation of the Bible shaped not only the German language but the generations of men and women who were to speak it. Much the same could be said of the impact of the King James Bible, Shakespeare, and Milton on English and the English-speaking peoples. To begin to grasp the importance which poetry had at Sparta, we must remember that it was once considered the supreme form of rhetoric—a form with more immediate power and far greater longevity than ordinary writing and speech.

Though utterly foreign to us, this understanding of the dignity of poetry was still very much alive when Goethe remarked to his companion Eckermann,

> If a great dramatic poet is at the same time productive and occupied by a powerful, noble way of thinking, which runs through all his works, he may achieve the result that the soul of his plays becomes the soul of the people. I should think that this would be something well worth the trouble. From Corneille proceeded an influence capable of forming the souls of heroes. This was a matter of no small consequence for Napoleon, who had need of an heroic people; for this reason, he said of Corneille that, if he were still alive, he would make him a prince. A dramatic poet who knows his intended purpose should therefore work without ceasing at its higher devel-

opment in order that his influence on the people may be beneficial and noble.[34]

As the example set by Dante, Luther, and those who composed the King James Bible suggests, Goethe's claim can be applied not just to drama but to poetry in general—and similarly to a prose so elevated in tone that it transcends the form. The Greeks shared Goethe's conviction. That is why they habitually employed the same word—*ιδιότēs*—to point out both the private individual and the writer of ordinary prose. In their world, political life was anything but prosaic; and for them, poetry was public speech par excellence. As the Greeks recognized, the propagation of the works of a particular poet had public consequences of untold importance. The soul of Spartan verse was to become the soul of the Spartan people.

Of the examples of Spartan poetry surviving in his own time, Plutarch remarked, "They were for the most part eulogies of those who had died on Sparta's behalf, celebrating their happiness; censure of those who had fled in battle, depicting their painful and unfortunate lives; and professions and boasts of virtue of a sort proper for the different age-groups." Although he acknowledges that the Spartans were quite familiar with the *Iliad* of Homer and his *Odyssey,* Plato claims that they regarded these works as depicting the Ionian, not the Laconian way of life. Plutarch attributes to Lycurgus the discovery in Crete and propagation elsewhere of the Homeric epics. But there is, in fact, no indication that young Spartans ever followed the normal Greek practice of memorizing extended passages selected from Homer; they seem, instead, to have concentrated on the verses of Tyrtaeus. When on campaign, the Spartans would chant this poet's songs as they marched. In the evening after dinner, they would first raise the paean, and then each, in turn, would sing something by Tyrtaeus—with the polemarch acting as judge and awarding extra meat to the victor.[35]

The poetry of Tyrtaeus did much to reinforce the exaggerated piety that was the foundation of Spartan morale. In one of his poems, the bard praised Lacedaemon as a law-abiding community, well-ordered, possessing *eunomía.* In a passage replete with allusions to oracles, to prophecy, and to men dear to the gods, he justified the Spartans' control over their vast domain by an appeal to divine right, singing,

> The son of Kronos, husband to splendidly crowned Hera,
> Zeus himself gave this city to the sons of Heracles,

> The men with whom we made our journey, when we left
> Windy Erineos for the broad isle of Pelops.

For the Heraclid kings and their Dorian followers, the Eurotas valley was pre-cisely what Israel had been for Moses and the Jews of the Exodus. Laconia was a fertile and well-watered territory ripe for the taking. Like Canaan, as de-scribed in Deuteronomy, it was "a good land, a land of brooks of water, of fountains and depths that spring out of valleys and hills; a land of wheat, and barley, and vines, and fig trees, and pomegranates; a land of oil, olive, and honey."[36] The Eurotas valley was all this and more. For a people reared on Tyrtaeus, Laconia was nothing less than the promised land.

In another passage, almost certainly drawn from the same work, Tyrtaeus attributed Sparta's political order not to human action, but to the intervention of the gods, tracing its origins to advice sought from the oracle of Apollo. Of a trip undertaken to Delphi by Sparta's two kings, the poet wrote,

> Having listened to Phoebus, they carried home from Pytho
> Oracles of the god and words certain of fulfillment:
> "To rule in council is reserved for the god-honored kings,
> To whom the lovely city of Sparta is entrusted as a care.
> It is reserved also for the *gérontas,* men elder in birth.
> Then the commoners, making reply with straightforward decrees,
> Shall speak and accomplish all that is noble and just,
> Not giving to the city a counsel that is crooked.
> So shall victory and power attend the multitude of the *dêmos.*
> For thus has Phoebus spoken of these things to the *pólis.*"[37]

By trusting in the authority of Tyrtaeus, the Spartans could rest assured that they had the same divine sanction for the organization of their community that they possessed for their acquisition of the southeastern Peloponnesus.

Tyrtaeus' poetry was evidently wide ranging. In one of the small handful of surviving fragments, he celebrated Sparta's original conquest of Messenia; in two others, he alluded to the fate suffered by her helots. The members of this servile class were not simply men "distressed with great burdens like asses, carrying to their masters under painful necessity half of all the fruit that the fields bear." They suffered insult in addition to injury, for they were forced "themselves (and their bedfellows likewise) to mourn for their masters" when one such encountered "the sad fate of death."[38] The poet presumably had more to say on the subject. He may even have gone on to describe the manner in which the Spartans ritually reinforced the boundary between master and servant by deliberately humiliating the helots—making them appear in public in a costume suggesting their kinship with animals, whipping them at regular intervals for no apparent reason, getting them disgustingly drunk, and even requiring that they sing degrading songs. The presence of a servile class, the derisive treatment to which its members were forced to submit, and the manner in which they actually comported themselves—these contributed much to the education of the Spartan young. As Tyrtaeus seems to have recognized at the start, the helots were a permanent reminder to the Spartans of their own exalted status and a warning of the fate that might be theirs if they failed to justify their claim to superiority and dominion by victory on the field of battle.[39]

Young Spartans could hardly fail to appreciate the point. While undergoing the *agōgḗ,* they occupied a liminal status intermediate between that of the helots and that of the *hómoioi,* and they sampled both worlds. Much was done to remind them of the distance separating them from the Spartiates and to suggest at least the possibility of their kinship with those already set permanently apart as their fathers' inferiors. The hair of these young Spartans was short-cropped, not long. They slept under the stars rather than in the men's house or with the women at home. Like country bumpkins, they were filthy and rarely bathed, and they wore no tunic, just a cloak, which was replaced but once a year. Like calves and colts, by which names they were known, they were gathered in herds [*agélai*] called *Boúai* at Lacedaemon under the direction of herdsmen [*Bouagoí*]. But like foxes living on the margins of a village or town, with whom they were also deemed comparable, they stole food from the men's mess, as we have seen. If these boys learned the martial dances for which Lacedaemon was famous, this was apparently not all. For, adorned with masks, they are thought to have performed a great variety of less dignified dances— some terrifying, some comic, some obscene, some violent. And if we can trust the scattered testimonia and the evidence provided by the surviving ex-voto terracotta masks, they mimed not just men but animals, satyrs, and grotesque members of the female sex. These Spartan youths were sometimes armed, but only with sickles and weapons of the sort issued to helots on campaign: for the hoplite panoply was reserved for citizen-men. Like the helots of Tyrtaeus, these neophytes were distressed with toil; and like that subject race, they had ample experience of the whip. They suffered flagellation if judged soft or fat. They were flogged if caught stealing food. In one famous ritual, which was solemnly reenacted as an ordeal each year, two groups of boys waged battle about the shrine of Artemis Orthia: one intent on running off with the cheese piled high on the altar, the other wielding whips in defense of the agricultural products prepared for the virgin goddess. If these young Spartans repeatedly endured injuries and insults like those to which the helots were subjected, it was to establish—by a display of endurance and the fact that, in the face of pain, they were utterly unfazed—their worthiness to pass on from the threshold and join the ranks of the only Lacedaemonians who were in the fullest sense of the word free men.[40]

The bulk of Tyrtaeus' poetry dealt neither with just conquest nor with the proper form for organizing rule nor even with the suffering inflicted on the helots. He composed his verse in the middle of the seventh century—much of it during the Second Messenian War, when the Spartans fought doggedly to recover leverage over the rich province they had, in effect, acquired on the western side of Mount Taygetus some two generations before. Tyrtaeus' principal subject was not peace, but war. In one of his hortatory elegies, he drew the attention of his compatriots to the manner in which their well-being depended on the fate of the city itself.

> It is a noble thing for a brave man to die,
> Falling in the front ranks, doing battle for the fatherland.
> But for a man to forsake his city and his rich fields
> And to go begging is of all things the most grievous
> As he wanders with his dear mother and his aged father,
> With his small children and his lawful, wedded wife.
> For he is hated by those among whom he goes as a suppliant
> Yielding to need and loathsome penury;
> He disgraces his lineage; he refutes his splendid appearance,
> And every dishonor and evil follows in his train.
> Now if no heed is paid to a wandering man
> And neither reverence nor regard nor pity is his,
> Let us then fight with spirit for our land and children
> And let us die, not sparing our lives.

In the young men posted in the phalanx' front ranks, the poet sought to instill what he called "a spiritedness great and firm." He encouraged them not to hold life dear as they did battle with the foe; he exhorted them to stand closely bunched; and he warned them never "to make a start of fear and shameful flight." There is something splendid, he argued, about the death in battle of a young man, blessed with the bloom of youth, admired by his fellows and beloved of women. But there is no sight quite as disgraceful and none as horrid as that of a graybeard fallen in the front ranks, "sprawled on the earth before the young men, breathing out his life in the dust, and clasping his hands to a bloodied groin." The Spartan king Leonidas reportedly spoke of Tyrtaeus as "a poet good for stirring up the young [*néoi*]."[41] It is not difficult to see why.

In a similar poem, Tyrtaeus reminded his compatriots that their leaders and others in their ranks were descended from "Heracles the unconquered." There, he urged them to treat "life as something hateful" and to hold "the black ruin of death as dear as the beams of the sun."

> Of those who dare to stand by one another and to march
> Into the van where the fighting is hand to hand,
> Rather few die, and they safeguard the host behind.
> But for the men who are tremblers all virtue is lost.
> No one can describe singly in words nor count the evils
> That come to a man once he has suffered disgrace.
> For in dread war it is alluring to pierce from behind
> The back of a man in headlong flight,
> And disgraceful is the corpse laid out in the dust,
> Thrust through from behind by the point of a spear.

After issuing this admonition, the poet urged each of the hoplites to close with, wound, and take out his foe. "Placing foot next to foot, pressing shield against shield, bringing crest near crest, helm near helm, and chest near chest, let him battle it out with the man [opposite], grasping the handle of his sword or the long spear."[42]

Tyrtaeus' debt to Homer was enormous. This much is obvious from his diction alone. But despite all that he owed his great predecessor, the Spartan poet rejected the Homeric precedent and radically altered the heroic ethic. Tyrtaeus did not glorify that Achilles who had valued his own honor above the interest of the Achaean host; nor did he celebrate the exploits of Odysseus "the man of many ways" who wandered through "the cities of many men and learned their minds." He heaped praise not on the great individual who sought "to be the best and to excel all others," but on the citizen who never traveled abroad except on campaign and who fought gamely alongside his companions in the city's hoplite phalanx.[43]

To make his point in the boldest possible fashion, Tyrtaeus turned to the mythological tradition. To bring home to his listeners the inadequacy of the traditional understanding of human excellence, he provided them with a list of legendary individuals who exhibited qualities and faculties universally admired but who nonetheless performed in a fashion that called into question the esteem conventionally conferred on those very qualities and faculties. As the poet indicated in the priamel of his most famous work, there was only one trait truly worthy of celebration:

> I would not call to mind a man nor relate a tale of him
> Not for the speed of his feet nor for his wrestling skill
> Not if he possessed the stature and force of a Cyclops
> And could outpace Boreas, the North Wind of Thrace
> Not if he were more graceful in form than Tithonos
> And exceeded Midas and Cinyras in wealth
> Not if he were more fully a king than Tantalid Pelops
> And possessed the soft-voiced tongue of Adrastus
> Not if he had reputation for all but prowess in battle.[44]

Quickness, agility, brute strength, physical beauty, the golden touch, regal bearing, and even the eloquence evidenced by the poet himself—though men longed for these, they were of little import when distinguished from and compared with capacity in war.

To support this revolutionary notion, Tyrtaeus introduced a new, fully political standard for measuring the merit of men. No longer would the Spartans assess a man's status by anything other than his contribution to the welfare of the *pólis* as a whole. After dismissing those qualities which were so widely thought to be virtues, the poet went on to explain,

> For no one ever becomes a man good in war
> Unless he has endured the sight of the blood and slaughter,
> Stood near, and lunged for the foe.
> This is virtue, the finest prize achieved among human kind,
> The fairest reward that a young man can carry off.
> This is a common good, shared by the entire city and people,
> When a man stands his ground, remains in the front ranks
> Relentlessly, altogether forgetful of disgraceful flight,
> Nurturing a steadfast, patient spirit and soul,
> And heartening with words the man posted alongside.
> This is a man become good in war:
> With a sudden attack, he turns the rugged phalanx
> Of the enemy host, sustaining with zeal the wave of assault.[45]

Tyrtaeus was the supreme poet of civil courage. The virtue he admired with so passionate an intensity is the particular excellence of the man who subordinates not just his own mundane concerns but even his ambition and his yearning for immortal fame to the larger and enduring needs of the community at large. It would be tempting to conclude that Tyrtaeus simply preferred Hector to Achilles and Odysseus. But it is virtually certain that the Spartan poet would have faulted the Trojan champion for the foolish pride evident in his rejection of Priam's appeal to prudence and in his decision to meet Achilles alone in single combat apart from the forces of Troy.[46]

To reinforce his celebration of bravery in the city's cause, Tyrtaeus added encouragement and an admonition—for, in the end, justice was to be done: the brave would be rewarded and the cowardly, punished. Even death would lose its sting. What made this achievement possible was not the activity of the poet in calling to mind the feats of the heroes. Here, too, Tyrtaeus broke with Homer. If death was to rule no more, it was because of the public memory guaranteed by the continued existence of the *pólis* itself. While ordinary Spartans were buried in a manner both simple and frugal, wrapped in the purple cloak worn in battle and crowned with olive leaves, the city's champions were treated like the demigods honored in her hero cults.[47] As Tyrtaeus puts it,

> And he who falls in the front ranks and gives up his spirit
> So bringing glory to the town, the host, and his father
> With many a wound in his chest where the spear from in front
> Has been thrust through the bossy shield and breastplate:
> This man they will lament with a grievous sense of loss
> The young and the old and the city entire.
> His tomb and his children will be noted among human kind
> And the children of his children and his lineage after them.
> Never will his shining glory perish, and never his name,
> For he will be an immortal though under the earth, the man
> Who excels all others in standing his ground in the fight
> For his children and land, he whom the raging Wargod destroys.[48]

Tyrtaeus then devoted the final ten lines of this remarkable poem to recounting the honors that were customarily showered on those brave men fortunate enough to survive. By the end, it has become evident that courage in battle confers on a man all of the advantages normally attributed to the qualities and faculties conventionally admired.

> But if he eludes the doom of death, which lays bodies out,
> And, conquering, seizes by spearpoint the shining object of prayer
> All will honor him, the young together with the old,
> And he will enter Hades after enjoying many delights
> Having grown old in distinction among the men of the town.
> Nor will any wish him harm, denying him reverence or right.
> And all—the young, those his own age, and those
> Older than he—will yield him place on the seats.
> This virtue a man should attempt with whole heart to attain,
> Straining for the heights and never ceasing from war.[49]

This was a communal poetry fit for the education of citizen-soldiers who would be expected to spend their lives at home in Laconia and to risk them abroad on the city's behalf. The Spartans committed these and similar verses to memory and recited them about the campfire and while on the march for the same reason that they prepared for combat in ritual fashion by combing out their long hair and donning cloaks of royal purple in such a manner as to terrify and discomfit their foe. Like the wine which the Lacedaemonians customarily imbibed before battle, like the strains of the flute played by men occupying an hereditary office, which accompanied their steady march into combat, and like the paean which they chanted as they closely approached the enemy phalanx, the songs of Tyrtaeus were an intoxicant intended to reduce tension, dull pain, and make men—at least momentarily—forget the specter of death. With the city's poets in mind, Plutarch suggests, the Spartan king would sacrifice to the Muses at the onset of battle. His purpose was to remind Lacedaemon's warriors to accomplish feats worthy to be remembered by the city in song.[50]

The World of the *Sussítíon*

In the late archaic and early classical periods, when Lacedaemon was populous and may even have suffered for a time from overpopulation, the young men who survived the *agōgé* and became Spartiates are likely to have been a highly select group.[51] On their long journey to manhood,[52] they had been subjected to a formal magisterial scrutiny [*dokimasía*] at regular intervals: initially, at birth; then, almost certainly, as boys [*hoi paîdes*] at seven; as youths [*hoi paidískoi*] at twelve, thirteen, or fourteen; and finally, at twenty, when, as *eirénes,* they joined the warriors variously called *hoi hēbôntes* and *hoi néoi*.[53] As a *païs* neared adolescence and become a *paidískos* and, again, as he approached *hébē*—the threshold of manhood—his physical training became more and more rigorous and the tests of his strength and courage more and more severe. The final test, the period of concealment [*krupteía*], appears to have taken place after he left the age-category of the *paidískoi,* when he was technically a young man [*néos*] but not yet an *eirén*—in the very year in which he was slated to reach his twentieth birthday. For a full twelve months, the young man withdrew from the community and was thrown back entirely on his own resources. Armed with a dagger, he hid in the wilds during the day, only to emerge at night to secure provisions by theft and to kill any helots found roaming about after curfew. The *krupteía* helped terrorize the helots and head off servile rebellion, and it functioned as a rite of passage marking the boy's completion of the journey from childhood to manhood.[54]

In the late archaic and early classical periods, when Lacedaemon was populous and the city could afford to be discriminating, his performance in this last ordeal may well have determined his fate: he could become a full citizen and join the *hómoioi* if and only if he submitted to the Spartan regimen, successfully completed the *agōgé,* and was accepted into a men's mess [*sussítion*]. It was, it appears, only under these circumstances that he could actually take up possession of the allotment of land reserved for him shortly after his birth and begin to collect the rent intended for his support. Those judged to have fallen short in the *agōgé* were not just denied entrance into a *sussítion* and excluded thereby from the august ranks of "the equals, the similars, the peers." They were deprived of what was called "the ancient portion [*archaîa moîra*]," and they were pointedly singled out and referred to, ever after, as *hupomeíones* or "inferiors."[55]

Composed of about fifteen men of all ages, the *sussítion* was not just an arrangement for meals. It was an elite men's club, a cult organization, and, at the same time, the basic unit in the Spartan army. If a single member found a candidate objectionable and blackballed him, the young man would be denied entrance. If admitted, he would dine for the rest of his life in what Persaeus called "a small polity [*políteuma*] of sorts," eating what his companions ate and drinking only a moderate portion of wine, discreetly discussing public affairs and more private concerns, gently teasing his comrades, and otherwise comporting himself always in the dignified, respectful fashion which the old demand of the young and the young nearly always expect from the old.[56] Until he was forty-five, he was classed as a *néos* or young man. Every ten days, he and the others within this age-category were expected to demonstrate that they were in good shape by presenting themselves naked for inspection by the magistrates; and, except when he was on active service abroad or doing garrison duty and conducting patrols elsewhere in Laconia or Messenia, each of these men would spend his nights in the men's house of his *sussítion* or camped under the stars "with the other *néoi.*"[57]

The rationale behind these arrangements was perfectly evident to the shrewdest of the ancient observers. "In time of peace," Dionysius of Halicarnassus remarked, the *sussítia* "greatly aided the city by leading men towards frugality and moderation [*sophrosúnē*] in their daily lives." This advantage he thought important, but not decisive. The Spartan institution accomplished something of at least equal, if not greater importance. "In time of war," Dionysius explained, "it instilled in every man a sense of reverential shame [*aidós*] and a prudential concern that he not desert the man posted beside him in the city's battle line—for this man was a comrade with whom he had made libations, conducted sacrifices, and shared in common rites."[58] At Lacedaemon, the pressure to perform never let up.

In fact, acceptance into a *sussítion* marked not the end of competition, but its intensification. From among the *hēbôntes* at their acme—Spartiates who had survived the *krupteía,* joined a men's mess, and distinguished themselves in service to the city in peace and war—every year the magistrates chose as *hippagrétai* the three whom they judged the ablest. Each of the three then had the privilege of electing from among their fellow *hēbôntes* a battalion of precisely one hundred men. In every case, he had to specify why a particular individual was chosen and another excluded. The three hundred select men were called the *hippeîs,* and it was their duty and privilege to accompany the king into battle and to fight by his side. After the initial choice was made, each of those within this royal bodyguard had to defend—sometimes with their fists—not just the exalted status of his elite unit, but also his own particular right to membership in it. There was, in short, an unending competition with all among the *hēbôntes* who had been denied the honor of admission.[59]

A further rivalry existed within the ranks of the royal bodyguard itself. When a man reached the age of forty-five, he graduated from the class of *néoi* and was therefore no longer eligible to serve among the *hippeîs.* The five members of the graduating class who had most distinguished themselves during their years of service as *hippeîs* were then singled out, given the honorific title "doers of good deeds [*agathoergoí*]," and made available to the *pólis* and the magistrates for a full year as special agents prepared to take on any mission that might be deemed appropriate.[60] Thereafter, they would permanently rejoin the *sussítion* to which they had been elected so many years before. Only at this stage in life, when a Spartan had joined the ranks of the older men [*hoi presbúteroi*], did he become eligible to take charge of the *agōgé* as *paidonómos* and to hold what Xenophon called "the greatest offices" of the city. Only at this point could he hope to be given permission to journey abroad.[61]

In general, when a boy became a man, his *sussítion* supplanted the herd as his true home. His ties to his parents, his wife, and his children were intended to be weak: he had left his mother's care and had been removed from his father's authority when he was seven; and although he was expected to take a spouse well before he reached the age of forty-five and was subjected to civic disabilities and to rituals of harassment and humiliation if he failed to do so in a timely fashion, he would not as a husband then live with his wife. During the initial period of their marriage, shame and dread governed the comportment of the couple. The *néos* visited his bride's bedroom in secret at night, and all their relations were conducted under the cover of darkness. The Spartan might beget a child. But at least until he had himself joined the *presbúteroi,* he would not live within his own household; and even then, his sons would depart from that household at a tender age.[62]

There seems to have been a shortage of Spartiate women, perhaps as a consequence of female infanticide. In keeping with this presumption, Xenophon reports that the law sanctioned a husband's permitting a friend and fellow citizen to engender legitimate offspring with his lawful, wedded wife. Indeed, if the man was elderly and his bride was young, he was not just allowed, he was expected, to be generous in this fashion. It is in this context that we should consider Polybius' report that it was in accord with ancestral practice at Lacedaemon for brothers to share a spouse. As Plutarch remarked, the institution of marriage existed at Sparta solely for the procreation of children, and the practices associated with it presupposed on the part of the husband "a strong and unadulterated lack of passion [*apatheía*] with respect to his wife." It is easy to see why Josephus described the Spartan regime as unsociable and accused the Lacedaemonians of slighting matrimony.[63]

The tendency evident in these arrangements was exacerbated by the Spartan practice of pederasty. In Lacedaemon, the boys apt to be desired were neither shy nor coy. In fact, when a boy reached the age of twelve, he assumed the role of a beloved [*erómenos*], and he aggressively sought out from among the *néoi* and eagerly took as his lover a figure whom the Greeks called an *erastés* and the Spartans dubbed an *eispnélas* or "breather-in." From this day on, the man with whom he made this connection was to be far more than just his sexual partner. He was to be the boy's patron, his protector, and friend.[64]

At Lacedaemon, this particular species of homoerotic relations was not simply a practice sanctioned by custom. As among some tribes in Australia and Melanesia, it was a political institution. It was not only the case that a boy lacking an *eispnélas* was an object of disdain: a young man of distinguished background could, in fact, be severely punished by the magistrates for refusing to select from among the early adolescent boys what the Greeks called a *paidiká* or for preferring as his *erómenos* a boy endowed with wealth to one virtuous in character. As a surrogate father, the *eispnélas* would be held personally responsible for the conduct of the boy that he chose. It was his task to prepare the boy for his duties as a citizen and soldier, and he was probably expected to ease the admission of his *paidiká* into a *sussítion.* When this was accomplished, the younger of the two would in turn become an *eispnélas* himself and take on a surrogate son, abandoning the passive for the active homoerotic role as the entire process repeated itself in accord with the elaborate rituals and rules of decorum that governed its course. Finally, when the time came for marriage, the young man carried off his bride in a ritual abduction, then left briefly to dine with his mess, and returned to find her waiting in the dark, dressed in the cloak of a man, her hair cut short in the style of a boy.[65] For some, this transvestism no doubt eased what must have been an awkward transition to heterosexuality.

The institution of pederasty did not preclude affection between husband and wife. But, as Plutarch appears to have recognized, it was designed to ensure that the emotional ties to the homosexual be stronger than those to the subsequent heterosexual partner. The ultimate purpose was that a young man's loyalty be fixed neither on the parents he had left, nor on the wife and son he so rarely saw, but rather on his *erastés* and *paidiká.* In normal circumstances, both were apparently members of his *sussítion;* and as a consequence, the two would usually be stationed in his immediate vicinity—though not ordinarily, given the difference in age, on either side of him in the battle formation. It is not fortuitous that the Spartans customarily sacrificed to Eros before drawing up their phalanx. They apparently thought that victory and their safety would depend on the love that united the men about to be posted.[66]

The attempt to loosen familial ties was part of a larger scheme. The household [*oîkos*] was the chief obstacle to the city's complete psychological absorption of the individual. For the ordinary Greek, as the initial sympathy of the chorus and of the people of Thebes for the protagonist in Sophocles' *Antigone* makes clear, the *oîkos* represented a focus of loyalty independent of and potentially opposed to the community in arms.[67] It provided the citizen with an identity separate from his citizenship, and it consoled him, as his death approached, with the prospect of living on through his offspring. Essential though it may have been for the production and early rearing of children and thereby for the survival of the *pólis,* this rival stood in the way of the strategy

for preventing faction, attributed to the ancient city by James Madison, centered on giving "to every citizen the same opinions, the same passions, and the
same interests." As long as men felt the desire to increase their property and
to pass it on to their progeny, they would be at odds.

The social and economic arrangements at Sparta seem to have been aimed
at suppressing the private element in human life, at making the adult male
Spartiate an almost entirely public being by eliminating to the greatest degree
possible the last refuge of privacy—the family. Thomas Jefferson came close to
the truth when he borrowed the baron de Montesquieu's metaphor and called
the Spartan government "the rule of military monks."[68] Like a monastery, the
city herself attempted to fill most of the functions elsewhere conceded to the
household: she granted the citizen landed property and servants; she secured for
him both surrogate father and surrogate son; and she provided him with bed,
board, and lover, integrating him into the larger community by means of an
all-male social unit of a size perfect for engaging and keeping his loyalties and
for promoting small-unit cohesion on the battlefield.[69] He spent his entire life
in the public eye, being judged and praised or blamed by his fellows. For this
reason, it is true to say that Sparta exercised greater control over her citizens
than any regime that has existed anywhere else at any time. She exercised this
control not through terror, but rather through the power of public opinion in
a tiny, close-knit community that never included more than nine or ten thousand male adults: a *pólis* in which everyone knew virtually everything that
there was to know about everyone else. The force of public opinion—powerful
as it is in any small town—was magnified at Sparta by a set of institutional arrangements designed to make it fully dominant. The Spartans foreswore gold
and silver coinage and encouraged homosexuality for the same reason. The
agōgḗ and all that followed it were aimed at forming the completely public-
spirited man—the man who would never leave the formation and who would
depart from every battle in the posture demanded by his mother: with his
shield or on it.[70]

No one understood this better than Herodotus. In *The Inquiries*, he represents the exiled Spartan king Demaratus as having been in attendance at
a review of Xerxes' troops not long before the battle of Thermopylae. When
Xerxes asks whether the Greeks would dare to resist Persia, Demaratus replies
that the Spartans would fight to the end. He concludes by saying: "As for the
Spartans, fighting each alone, they are as good as any, but fighting as a unit,
they are the best of all men. They are free, but not completely free—for the law

is placed over them as a master [*despótēs*], and they fear that law far more than your subjects fear you. And they do whatever it orders—and it orders the same thing always: never to flee in battle, however many the enemy may be, but to remain in the ranks and to conquer or die."[71] The Spartan was to be brave and steadfast even in the face of certain death. That was the goal which the institutions of the Lacedaemonians attempted to achieve.

Privacy's Revenge

There was, of course, a gap between ideal and performance. There always is. It is striking just how many of the Spartan anecdotes collected by Plutarch presuppose close ties between mother and son, and fathers clearly took an interest in the progress of their sons and evidenced pride in their accomplishments.[72] It is, moreover, very revealing that the Spartans were notorious both for their corruption when abroad and for being open to bribery when freed from the purview of their fellows.[73] This gap should not come as a surprise; it is what we would normally expect. Spartan institutions ran against the grain. As even Rousseau was forced to acknowledge, the attempt to suppress altogether the private element in human life requires doing violence to human nature.[74] This is reportedly why the late archaic lyric poet Simonides gave Lacedaemon the epithet "man-subduing [*damasímbrotos*]."[75] It is impossible entirely to expunge the normal preference for one's own flesh and blood and to eliminate the universal desire of human beings to amass wealth as a hedge against hardship and as a legacy for their offspring.

To these propensities, the Spartans were themselves forced to give a grudging recognition. In describing the shortcomings of the Spartan regimen, Dionysius of Halicarnassus acknowledges that "the Lacedaemonians allowed those who were the oldest to strike with their canes citizens who were behaving in a disorderly fashion in any public place." But then he immediately adds that, in one critical respect, they were much more like the Athenians than the Romans: "They made no provision for and took no precaution against what might take place in the home; instead, they regarded the door to each man's house as a boundary stone marking out the sphere where he could conduct his life freely and as he wished."[76] The contradiction between desire and duty, between unaccommodated human nature and the needs of the *pólis,* and between a man's character as an individual and his status as a citizen—ultimately, this contradiction cannot be resolved. Try as one may, it remains as impossible to give a man entirely over to the community as it is to leave him entirely to himself.

The chief effect of the attempt at a suppression of the private element in human life was to make the pursuit of wealth dishonorable. But what the Spartans disdained in public they often longed for when alone. Unlike the heavenly city of Plato's *Republic,* the Spartan regime did not eliminate private property and the family altogether. The Spartiate could distinguish between the children and the estate which belonged to him and the children and the estate which did not. He had a stake in protecting those children and in increasing that estate which brought him into conflict with his peers. This was the very conflict which the absence of coinage, the encouragement of pederasty, the *agōgḗ,* and the *sussitía* were designed to expunge. As Plato had occasion to remark, the Lacedaemonian legislator sought to form a man who loved toil, victory, and honor—toil for the common cause, victory in the struggles of his people, and the honor which only his city and fellow citizens could confer upon him.[77] The lawgiver sought to redirect, transform, and harness the spirit of competition to serve the city. He tried to replace as much as possible the love of one's own property and progeny and the hatred of those outside the family implicit in that attachment with the love of one's own city and citizens and the hatred of foreigners implicit in that commitment.

Xenophon rightly regarded this project as a partial failure. As he intimated in his *Politeía of the Lacedaemonians,* the punitive education given young Spartans produced men equipped with a powerful sense of reverence and shame [*aidós*] who prided themselves on possessing a moderation [*sophrosúnē*] that they, in fact, lacked. When under the gaze of their fellow Spartans, these men could be relied on to conduct themselves with courage and self-restraint in an admirable fashion. But, when alone or abroad, they frequently succumbed to temptation—and the disgraceful desires that were by and large contained, if not entirely suppressed, when their hegemony was confined within the Peloponnesus were later unleashed and proved fatal to their enterprise when, in the wake of the Peloponnesian War, they sought to establish their dominion throughout Hellas.[78]

Plato agreed wholeheartedly with his fellow Socratic. In his judgment, the Spartan regimen produced men torn between their public duties and the private wants engendered by the remnants within their *pólis* of the distinction between mine and thine. "Such men," he observed, "will long for money just as those in oligarchies do; and under the cover of darkness, like savages, they will pay honor to silver and gold." The consequence was a clandestine Spartan disobedience of the law against the possession of gold and silver so widespread and pervasive that there was "not in all of Hellas as much gold and silver as is held privately in Lacedaemon; through many generations, it has been entering that place from every part of Greece and often from the barbarians as well, but to no other place does it ever depart. As in the fable of Aesop, what the fox said to the lion is true: the tracks left by the money going into Lacedaemon are clear, but nowhere can anyone see traces of it going back out." To this result, the custom of treating a man's home as a realm truly private made a profound contribution. The Athenian philosopher speaks of the "magazines for storage and domestic treasuries" of the Spartiates, and he mentions the "walls surrounding their houses" which are "exactly like private nests where they can make great expenditures on women and on whomever else they might wish"—and the evidence bears out his claim that these houses were stocked with valuables.[79]

Aristotle shared Plato's judgment of what the latter, with an eye to its obsession with glory and honor, termed the timocratic regime. He took note of the sumptuary laws limiting the expense and specifying the character of funerals, and he was aware of the regulations governing the comportment of the women and denying them the right to let their hair grow long, to wear jewelry in public, and to otherwise adorn themselves. But he thought these and the other similar *nómoi* grossly inadequate, and he contended that the Spartan legislator had, in fact, mixed "the love of honor" with "the love of money" and had thereby formed "private individuals covetous of wealth." Like the Halicarnassian Dionysius, the peripatetic philosopher attributed this, in part, to the absence of laws regulating the household. In particular, like Plato, he faulted Spartan institutions for their failure to bring under control "the women, who live intemperately in every kind of licence and luxury," observing that "the necessary consequence is that riches are held in honor, especially when the citizens fall under the rule of their women, as tends to happen among peoples devoted to soldiering and war. . . . The arrangements regarding the women not only introduce an air of unseemliness into the regime; they tend to foster avarice as well."[80]

The Spartans may have been grudging when it came to making concessions to the private needs of mankind, but the concessions which they were forced to make nonetheless had an extraordinarily important effect. In fostering public-spiritedness, the Lacedaemonians went further than any other community before or since, but they inevitably fell far short of that at which they aimed. It is not at all surprising that Sparta eventually succumbed. Nor is there anything odd in the fact that she lost her hold on Messenia just over a generation after the ephor Epitadeus, who held office in the wake of the Peloponnesian War, persuaded his compatriots that it was perfectly proper for a citizen to be able to give or bequeath his public allotment of land to whomever he pleased. From the outset, the Spartan *polıteía* was fragile in the extreme, and the oracle which is said to have warned that "the love of money and nothing else will destroy Lacedaemon" was right on the mark.[81]

The Spectacle of Courage

What is truly surprising, then, is not Sparta's ultimate failure but, rather, her long years of success. What was extraordinary was her capacity to produce public-spirited men. When Isocrates wrote that the Spartans "think nothing as capable of inspiring terror as the prospect of being reproached by their fellow citizens," he was not just mouthing a cliché. In 480, when Lacedaemon consulted the Delphic oracle on the eve of Persia's advance, she was told that a king must die if the city was to be saved. The Spartans did not shirk what was demanded, but dispatched Leonidas soon thereafter with the customary royal bodyguard of three hundred, taking care only to preserve the number of citizen households by enrolling as *hippeîs* to accompany the king none but mature men blessed with surviving sons.[82] In sacrificing their lives for the city, Leonidas and his companions did no more than their compatriots expected.

According to the fourth-century Athenian orator Lycurgus, there was a law at Sparta "expressly stipulating that all those unwilling to risk their lives for the fatherland be put to death." The rationale behind the statute was straightforward. "The fear of one's fellow citizens is strong," Lycurgus explained. "It will force men to undertake risks when confronted with the city's enemies. For who, seeing that the traitor is punished with death, would desert the fatherland in its time of peril? And who, knowing that this would be the punishment awaiting him, would value his life contrary to the city's advantage?"[83]

One may justly wonder whether such a law existed or was even required. Xenophon makes it clear that in Lacedaemon cowards were formally expelled from the ranks of the *hómoıoı*, then generally shunned; and Plutarch tells us that they were subject to assault from passersby and that, as a sign of their degraded status, they were required to wear cloaks with colored patches and to go about unbathed with one cheek shaven and the other not. Something of the sort was apparently the fate of the two members of the three hundred who missed dying at Thermopylae. One had been sent to Thessaly as a messenger: on returning to Sparta, he found himself in such disgrace that he hanged himself. The other had a similar excuse, suffered similar reproach, and was expelled from his *sussitíon* and deprived of his political rights. No Spartan would give him a brand to kindle his fire; no one would speak to him; and echoing Tyrtaeus' description of those who sacrificed all virtue by wavering in battle, the Spartiates called him "the trembler." In due course, he, too, chose to commit suicide. Within the field of vision of the entire army at Plataea, this man thrust himself forward alone in front of the Spartan line against the spears of the oncoming Persians.[84]

The battle of Thermopylae was the most dramatic, but not the first such occasion. Well over a half-century before Leonidas' last stand, the Spartans had sent out on a special mission another three hundred picked men (in all likelihood, the *hippeîs* this time as well). Their task was to defend the Lacedaemonian claim to the borderland Cynouria against Argos by defeating a like number of Argive warriors. At the end of this Battle of the Champions, there was but one Spartan alive; and though his survival was the ground for Sparta's continuing claim to the disputed province, that very survival had rendered him suspect of cowardice. The man apparently found insupportable the prospect of living his life in disgrace, and he ultimately chose death instead.[85] At Lacedaemon, a life without honor in the eyes of one's fellow citizens was a life not worth living.

This ethic was still very much alive early in the fourth century when a regiment [*móra*] of Spartans suffered ambush in the Corinthiad near Lechaeum. This much is made strikingly clear by a passing remark in Xenophon's report. Early in the skirmish, a number of Spartans were wounded by javelins hurled by enemy peltasts; the polemarch immediately ordered that these men be carried to safety by the helots who ordinarily bore their shields. The remaining members of the *móra* were less fortunate: roughly two hundred and fifty hoplites lost their lives in the encounter, while only a handful managed to flee, some by plunging into the sea and others by seeking refuge with the cavalry. To the latter, Xenophon gives remarkably short shrift. In speaking of those who had been wounded and then borne to Lechaeum, he observes, "In truth, these were the only members of the *móra* who were saved."[86] It mattered not a whit that the battle had already been lost when the other survivors took to heel. Any Spartan who managed to preserve his life by taking refuge in flight was classed as a trembler. As such, he might as well have been dead.

The enviable reputation that they had earned greatly aided the Spartans in the conduct of war. By the same token, when these men failed to live up to that reputation, the event could have a devastating impact on the morale of the city and of her allies as well. In 425, as we have already had occasion to note, when the Lacedaemonian contingent on the island of Sphacteria surrendered to the Athenians, a shudder ran through Greece. According to Thucydides, "the Hellenes supposed that the Lacedaemonians would never surrender their arms in response to starvation or to any other form of compulsion, but that they would instead hold fast to their weapons, fight to the best of their abilities, and so give up their lives. The Greeks simply could not believe that those who had surrendered were *hómoioi* like those who had died." To bring home to the prisoners the enormity of what they had done, one citizen of a community allied with Athens is said to have posed to one of the men captured on the island a simple question—whether "those of the Lacedaemonians who had died were not the elite—gentlemen both noble and good [*kaloì kagathoí*]." The arrow, he was told in reply, that could pick out the brave men would be worth a great deal.[87]

The presence of tremblers in substantial numbers could pose a serious political problem for the Spartans. The men captured on Sphacteria returned home just a few years later after the Peace of Nicias had been ratified. Though the *pólis* then suffered from an exceedingly severe shortage of manpower, those taken prisoner in 425 were for a time deprived of their citizen rights. Some of the captives had come from families of particular prominence, and the citizens reportedly feared that out of bitterness at suffering disgrace these men would be eager to start a revolution. In due course, therefore, the Spartans reversed their decision,[88] but a certain sense of awkwardness must have remained.

The same problem presented itself again after the battle of Leuctra in 371—but this time in a fashion far more severe. For the Spartan army itself had on this occasion suffered a decisive defeat, and a very large proportion of the surviving adult male citizen population had been guilty of flight. To inflict on so many men the disabilities required by the law would be to risk revolution at a time when the city itself might be in danger of being destroyed. The king Agesilaus provided the solution, proposing simply that the laws be allowed to sleep for a day but that they be enforced thereafter with the same rigor as in the past.[89] Even then, the survivors could expect to be held in disgrace.

Xenophon tells us that the news of the disaster at Leuctra reached Lace-daemon on the last day of the festival of the Gymnopaidiai. Upon being informed, the ephors chose not to suspend the choral performance of the men which was then under way, but they did in due course report to the various families the names of those who had lost their lives. The women were instructed at this time to make no lament and to bear the calamity in silence. Xenophon's description of what followed reads like an eyewitness report, which it may well have been. "On the next day," the Athenian observes, "it was possible to see those whose relatives were among the deceased walking about in the full light of day, their faces bright and beaming. But one saw few of those who had been told that their kin had survived, and these few were making their way with countenances sullen and dejected."[90] After a defeat in battle, the Spartans were more likely to mourn the living than the dead.

The ancients wondered at this spectacle, and so should we. The first and most important step that anyone can take in attempting to understand it is the recognition that Pericles was correct when, in the funeral oration reported by Thucydides, he singled out Sparta, from among all the Greek cities, as the *pólis* that went the furthest in promoting civil courage. By giving "to every citizen the same opinions, the same passions, and the same interests," her social and economic institutions were intended—as Isocrates, Demosthenes, and Polybius point out—to foster that sense of solidarity and like-mindedness which the Greeks called *homónoia* and Sparta's great admirer Jean-Jacques Rousseau dubbed "the general will."[91] As we shall soon see, Lacedaemon's political constitution served precisely the same function.

CHAPTER 2

POLITEÍA

Nothing is better suited for the maintenance of mores than an extreme subordination of the young to the old. They are both restrained—the former by the respect they have for the old; and the latter by the respect they have for themselves.

—CHARLES-LOUIS DE SECONDAT, BARON DE LA BRÈDE ET DE MONTESQUIEU

OVER three-quarters of a century ago, Lewis Namier prefaced his now classic study *The Structure of Politics at the Accession of George III* with a brief discussion of the reasons why he had at least temporarily abandoned an attempt to write a narrative history of British public life in the age of the American Revolution. "Too much in eighteenth-century politics requires explaining," he explained.

> Between them and the politics of the present day there is more resemblance in outer forms and denominations than in underlying realities; so that misconception is very easy. There were no proper party organizations about 1760, though party names and cant were current; the names and the cant have since supplied the materials for an imaginary superstructure. A system of non-Euclidean geometry can be built up by taking a curve for basis instead of the straight line, but it is not easy for our minds to think consistently in unwonted terms; Parliamentary politics not based on parties are to us a non-Euclidean system, and similarly require a fundamental readjustment of ideas and, what is more, of mental habits. A general explanation registering the outstanding differences may be understood but cannot be properly assimilated; one has to steep oneself in the political life of a period before one can safely speak, or be sure of understanding, its language.[1]

With the advantage of hindsight, one may reasonably question whether Namier actually managed in the end to sort out the politics of late eighteenth-century England. His failure no doubt owes much to the contempt he exhibited for what he calls "party names and cant" and to his resulting neglect of the central importance always occupied by opinion in political life. Even if one were seriously to entertain the absurd supposition that public figures rarely mean what they say and say what they mean, it is surely the case that their rhetoric is designed to secure the support of their listeners, and the need to retain that support thereafter inevitably places limits on the speakers' subsequent freedom of action.[2]

This objection should be noted and assimilated, then safely put aside, for much of what Namier had to say nonetheless remains apt, and his strictures against anachronistic reconstructions apply not just to public affairs in Britain's Augustan age, but—with even greater force—to politics within the ancient cities of the Hellenes. To be sure, it would hardly be proper to speak of classical Greek politics as a non-Euclidean system. In fact, there may well be something to the view that the "new science of politics"—pioneered by Thomas Hobbes, James Harrington, and John Locke and further developed by the baron de Montesquieu, David Hume, and the American Founding Fathers—is a creation which bears a striking resemblance to a system of geometry "built up by taking a curve for basis instead of the straight line."[3] But, though true, this begs the point to be made here—for, revolutionary though it once was, their application of this "new science of politics" has decisively shaped subsequent history and thereby our own experience, expectations, and presumptions; and this fact may be the greatest obstacle to our comprehension of earlier times. It really is difficult for our minds to think in unwonted terms, and the attempt to understand the character of ancient political life does, in fact, require of us a fundamental readjustment of ideas and of mental habits as well. One might even say that one has to steep oneself in the political language of a period before one can safely describe or be sure of understanding its political structure.

It would, for example, be an error to apply to the Greek *pólis* the modern distinction between state and society. The ancient Hellenes knew neither these words nor the two things they denote. In antiquity, there was no Greek state.[4] The ancient Hellenic republic was, as James Madison would later observe, "a pure democracy, . . . a society consisting of a small number of citizens, who assemble and administer the government in person." The *pólis* really was, as the Greeks often remarked, the men. In one poem, Alcaeus of Mytilene contended that "warlike men are a city's tower of defense." In another, which survives only as paraphrased by later authors, he played variations on the same theme:

> Neither stone blocks
> Nor ships' timbers

> Nor even the carpenter's art
> Can make a *pólis.*
> But where there are men
> Who know how to preserve themselves
> There one finds walls and a city as well.[5]

Because they shared the poet's conviction, the Hellenes never spoke in an abstract way of the deeds of Athens, Corinth, Megara, and Lacedaemon. These were places, not polities. As the public inscriptions assert, the real actors were the Athenians, the Corinthians, the Megarians, and the Lacedaemonians. The people wielded the power, and they constituted both state and society wrapped up in one. With only trivial exceptions, the Greek cities had no bureaucracies, no magistrates blessed with long tenure, no professional armies. It was futile to try to distinguish the governors from the governed; the *pólis* itself depended on the identity of soldier and civilian; and the farmer had the right to own land solely by virtue of his status as a citizen.[6] The differentiation of roles which the distinction between state and society presupposes simply did not exist. In principle and to a substantial degree in practice, the citizen body was homogeneous and self-governing.[7]

Just as there was no Greek state, so there was no civil society with which it could interact. The city was, as Aristotle argued, a political community [*koinōnía*]: it was a *Gemeinschaft,* not a *Gesellschaft.*[8] The *pólis* was not a conspiracy of self-seeking individuals joined for mutual profit and protection in a temporary legal partnership that would be dissolved when it ceased to suit their interests; it was a moral community of men permanently united as a people by a common way of life. As a human being, the Greek possessed no rights against the commonwealth; as a citizen, he might demand and be granted certain privileges—but these would be more than outweighed by his duties to the community at large. Here, as is often the case, language is the shadow of political reality: it is by no means fortuitous that the English word *idiot* is derivative from the Greek term employed to designate those who preferred private pleasure to public endeavor. Because they were shirkers who took what the city had to offer and gave little or nothing in return, men of this stripe incurred scorn and ill will. In short, the peculiar division between a narrow public and a broad private realm characteristic of bourgeois regimes was utterly alien to the Greek experience. The civic community's claim was, in principle, total: only the *oîkos* proved capable of resisting absorption; and, as we have seen, this was solely because the city depended on the preservation of this one refuge of privacy for the procreation, rearing, and nourishment of its future citizens.[9]

If, then, one desired to understand a particular *pólis* and its operations, the proper procedure for one to follow, at least at the outset, would be to take the ancient witnesses at their word. This is precisely what Adam Ferguson did when he prefaced his observations regarding the Spartan constitution with the remark that "we may easily account for the censures bestowed on the government of Sparta, by those who considered it merely on the side of its forms. It was not calculated to prevent the practice of crimes, by balancing against each other the selfish and partial dispositions of men; but to inspire the virtues of the soul, to procure innocence by the absence of criminal inclinations, and to derive its internal peace from the indifference of its members to the ordinary motives of strife and disorder." This is what Jean-Jacques Rousseau did when he drew attention to the absence of "partial societies" in ancient Sparta.[10]

There were, in fact, no organized political parties in any of the republics of archaic and classical Greece; there was no formed opposition. Indeed, prior to the appearance of Edmund Burke's *Thoughts on the Present Discontents*—which was published on the eve of the American Revolution, in the very period which elicited Namier's interest—partisanship and party government were all but universally held in bad odor. Of course, before that time, when emergencies had presented themselves, would-be statesmen had openly banded together in associations at least putatively aimed at preserving or restoring the traditional rights of the citizens and the ancestral constitution. But these alliances never acknowledged partisan purpose; they always claimed to speak for the whole and to be strictly defensive in character. In principle, they were intended to be temporary, for they were explicitly directed at eliminating the need for party divisions altogether. They would otherwise have had to present themselves as conspiracies—which was a characterization that they reserved for those against whom they had mounted their assault. Prior to 1770 in the modern era, no respectable figure had ever even dared to argue that party government, formed opposition, and a lasting division of the community into political parties could ever be condoned, much less merit esteem.[11]

In this respect, the Greeks were typical. The Greek language actually lacks a word to designate such a formed and lasting opposition. The word *stásis* refers not to a political party in the modern sense, but to a faction, as we have seen. To be precise, it refers to a group of men who "stand together." In the *póleis* of ancient Hellas, men sometimes attached themselves to a recognized leader able to benefit them or committed to the cause they espoused. They did not join permanent associations, and—even when embroiled in conspiracy—they never publicly admitted to partisan design. The ancient authors acknowledge the political importance of the divisions defined by wealth and birth when they refer to "the many" and "the few," to "the commoners" and "the notables," to "the mob" and "the gentlemen both noble and good." But when they wish to identify the politically active groupings, these writers speak of "those about Thucydides," they contrast "the friends of Pericles" with "the friends of Cimon," or they offer remarks in a similar vein. Where such a political grouping was aristocratic in character and had its origins as an exclusive social club, it might also be referred to as a companionship or *hetairía*.[12]

Within this world, Lacedaemon formed something of an exception, and she did so in precisely the fashion which Ferguson and Rousseau indicated. On the whole, the Spartans of the sixth and fifth centuries really do seem to have been indifferent to many of the *ordinary* motives for strife and disorder. The politically disruptive *social* divisions within the citizenry, which so afflicted the other Greek cities, were apparently unknown in Lacedaemon. In any case, we hear little of them. Their absence, however, did nothing to preclude the give and take of political struggle and the fleeting formation of factions around prominent figures. There is no dearth of evidence for political disputation at Sparta. The measures taken "to give to every citizen the same opinions, the same passions, and the same interests" might reduce the bitterness of controversy, but they could not eliminate it altogether. Despite the fundamental consensus regarding ends, the Spartans could always dispute over means; and although the regime sought to channel ambition [*philotimía*], it did nothing to stifle that breeder of quarrels. Indeed, as Aristotle points out, it made the citizens "greedy for honor [*philótimoi*]," and Plutarch is surely right when he contends that this was deliberate. "The Spartan legislator," he observes, "seems to have introduced the spirit of ambition [*to philótimon*] and the fondness for strife into the regime as a fuel for virtue, supposing that there should always be a certain disagreement and contest for superiority among good men and believing that it was not right to call *homónoia* that lazy complaisance which yields without debate and contention."[13]

At least while the Atlantic and Pacific oceans sufficed to isolate and protect it, the liberal republic established by the American Founding Fathers could almost do without men of warlike demeanor. But to defend the city, Sparta was always in need of spirited men—and to maintain solidarity within the ranks, she had to keep their rivalry firmly under control. Among the Greek writers, there was no one who praised the competitive spirit with greater vigor than the Theban poet Pindar. But he, too, could preach moderation, chanting, "The men in the *póleis* who court *philotimía* to an excess—they stir up a visible and palpable grief." Their own warlike character posed a problem for the Spartans, and they dealt with that problem—as other cities also tried to do, albeit with less success[14]—through their *politeía:* by encouraging ambition and at the same time subordinating the pursuit of honor to the needs of the *pólis.* The Lacedaemonian constitution was designed—above all else—to reinforce the fundamental consensus and to regulate the struggle for office, for power, and for glory.

Sparta was neither a monarchy nor a democracy. We hear little of court intrigue and even less of demagoguery. The most subtle of the ancient authors described it as a mixed regime. According to Aristotle, the two kings [*basileîs*] represented the monarchical element; the council of elders [*gerousía*], the oligarchic element; and the ephorate, the democratic element.[15] In order to secure the consent of the governed, Sparta ensured the participation of every element of the citizen population in the administration of the city; in order to prevent the emergence of an overmighty subject, she employed an elaborate system of balances and checks to restrain her magistrates from excess. These safeguards were essential. In general, ancient policy really was violent—and nowhere more so than at Lacedaemon. The fostering of citizen virtue and the enforcement of the Spartan regimen necessitated the establishment and maintenance of a vigorous inquisitorial tribunal. This could not be accomplished without a concentration of extraordinary power in the hands of Sparta's officials.

Basileía

The most dangerous element within the Spartan regime was, without a doubt, the kingship.[16] Even a cursory glance at the privileges and prerogatives associated with that office is adequate to demonstrate the truth of this proposition. Two Spartiates were not among "the equals." Two held office for life; two escaped the *agōgḗ;* two took their meals outside the barracks. Other Spartiates served in the *gerousía,* but only a king or his regent could serve in that venerable body before his sixtieth year. Other Spartiates sacrificed to the gods, but only a king or regent could do so year after year on the city's behalf. Other

Spartiates commanded troops, but only a king or his regent could normally lead out the Spartan army and the forces of the Peloponnesian League. Prior to the fifth century and, apparently, for a few years after its beginning, the two *basileîs* ordinarily shared the command; and when acting in concert, they could reportedly wage war against any territory they wished. It was a sacrilege for a Spartiate to resist their authority to do so. As hereditary generals and priests with life tenure, the Agiad and Eurypontid kings stood out from the ranks.[17]

In the strict sense, the two kings were not Spartiates at all. Envoys sent on missions abroad could claim to represent two entities at the same time: "the Lacedaemonians and the Heraclids from Sparta."[18] Tradition taught that the Spartiates were Lacedaemonians precisely because they were adherents of men who traced their ancestry back to Heracles, the son of Zeus. The Athenians and the Arcadians might think of themselves as autochthonous: "always possessed of the same land," and even "born from the earth."[19] But the Spartans were acutely aware that they were interlopers in the Peloponnesus, that they had invaded and seized Laconia by force, and that their servants—the "old helots" of the province—were descended from the original Achaean stock, which had ruled Lacedaemon in the epoch described by Homer. As Dorians, the Spartans had no legitimate place in what was, in fact, an alien land. The righteousness of their cause and its continued success were founded on the quasi-feudal relationship binding the citizens to their two kings. For the first Dorians to call themselves Spartans had purportedly been among the followers of the male lineal descendants of the old Achaean prince Heracles, whose sons were thought to have inherited from their illustrious father and to have passed on to their offspring the right to rule Argos in particular and the Peloponnesus more generally. As long as their *basileîs* were Heraclids, the Spartans of later times could rest confident in the legitimacy of their tenure in Laconia and in the support of the gods. But if they expelled their charismatic kings or countenanced an illegitimate succession, they could expect to suffer the fate which the gods had reserved for their Dorian neighbors in Messenia. The Spartans justified their conquest of that province and their reduction of its inhabitants to a servile condition on the grounds that the Dorians of Messenia had extinguished their own claim to the land when they drove out their Heraclid king. That province's Spartan conquerors had merely reasserted Heraclid control.[20]

At the start of each generation, the conquest community experienced a rebirth. While a *basileús* lived, he was sacrosanct. And when he died, there were elaborate burial rites—"more majestic," Xenophon pointedly tells us, "than properly accords with the human condition." The market was closed; assembly meetings and elections were temporarily suspended; and the entire community—the Spartans, the *períoikoi,* and even the helots—went into mourning for a period of ten days. "In this fashion," Xenophon observes, "the laws of Lycurgus wish to show that they give the kings of the Lacedaemonians preference in honor not as human beings, but as demigods."[21]

The renaissance came with the choice of a new *basileús*—normally the eldest surviving son of the deceased. When this man assumed the royal office, there was a cancellation of all debts owed his predecessor or the public treasury, and the citizens purportedly celebrated the man's accession with the same choral dances and sacrifices which they had employed in instituting their founders [*archagétai*] as kings of Lacedaemon at the time of the original conquest. At Lacedaemon, history was an eternal return of the same. The king's death brought one cycle to an end; ritual alone could guarantee its repetition. It is not fortuitous that the Spartans sometimes referred to their current kings as *archagétai:* the Heraclid *basileîs* of each new generation refounded the *pólis* by renewing her claim to the land. If the magistrates exhibited an almost obsessive concern to insure a legitimate succession, they had good reason. The same concerns dictated the law barring the Heraclids from having children by any woman from abroad.[22]

In a community in which military concerns predominate and in which there is a popular element in the constitution, generals—even hereditary generals—are men of great power and influence. A soldier's opportunity to distinguish himself on the field of battle and to gain the admiration and support of his comrades depends more often than not on the goodwill of his commander. This was particularly true among the Lacedaemonians. When on campaign, a Spartan king or regent conducted the sacrifices, and he exercised an almost absolute sway: he had the power to appoint his own officers, to issue orders to all and sundry, to send troops wherever he wished, to raise fresh forces, to execute cowards, and even to levy money. No matter what happened, until the army returned home, his word was law.[23] One need only reflect on the political consequences of replacing the consulship at Rome with a dyarchy to start to grasp the importance that the Spartan kings must have had. And after that beginning, one must ponder the same issue anew: for in Rome a man was arguably first a citizen and then a soldier, while in Sparta the priorities were without a doubt reversed.

The two kings possessed other politically important prerogatives as well. One of these privileges was symptomatic of royal preeminence in the making of foreign policy. In antiquity, it was not the practice for a city to maintain resident ambassadors in the polities with which its citizens had frequent dealings. Instead, the Greeks adapted the traditional aristocratic institution of guest-friendship [*xenía*] to serve the needs of the political community as a whole. Ordinarily, the citizens of one community selected from among the citizens of another one or more vice-consuls called *próxenoi* to provide hospitality when they dispatched embassies and, in general, to look after their interests in that particular locality. Here, in typical fashion, Lacedaemonian practice diverged from the norm. The Spartans insisted on regulating and controlling all intercourse with outsiders. They were unwilling to allow foreigners to choose their own representatives from among the citizens of Lacedaemon, and theirs, tellingly, is said to have been the only city in Hellas that was not, in the time of Philip of Macedon, ruined by treachery on the part of her own citizens. There is also evidence suggesting that the two kings selected those who served as Sparta's *próxenoi* abroad, but there is no certainty. What we do know is that they named vice-consuls at Sparta for the various cities that had relations with her, and there is reason to suspect that the pertinent cities were then invited to ratify the choice.[24] Thereby, the kings not only conferred honor on the men selected for the posts; they also secured for themselves, even in time of peace, a formal role in the conduct of foreign affairs.

In similar fashion, the *basileîs* appointed the four officials known as the *Púthioi*—each naming two to keep the records of the oracles for him and to share his mess. When the city herself wished an oracle from Delphi concerning a given matter, she chose her messenger from among these four men. This practice assured royal predominance in religious matters and made the manipulation of religion for political purposes almost the sole prerogative of the two dyarchs.[25] In a community as traditional and as pious as ancient Lacedaemon, this could have extraordinary consequences. A wily king like Cleomenes son of Anaxandridas could use religion to control the city.[26]

In their capacity as generals, the kings were charged with maintaining the elaborate system of public carriage roads that enabled the Spartiates to transport foodstuffs and to patrol and efficiently police their vast domain. With military necessity in mind, the dyarchs may also have superintended the extensive network of cart roads constructed within the Peloponnesus by their allies. For these were designed on the same model as the roads in Laconia and Messenia and for a similar purpose; and on all of these roads, both those within the territory controlled by Lacedaemon and those laid out in other parts by their allies, where the ground was rough, there were deep grooves carved in the stone to accommodate wheeled vehicles, all of them built on precisely the same gauge.[27]

Lacedaemon's kings were also responsible for legalizing the adoption of children and for securing husbands for heiresses left unbetrothed by their fathers.[28] The last two functions were of untold importance: because the Spartiates were barred from commerce and the possession of coinage, the only legal way open to them for the amassing of a fortune was to inherit privately owned land or to marry its owner. The rights of the kings in matters of adoption and with regard to heiresses provided them with substantial patronage. To grasp fully the political leverage which this gave the two *basileîs,* one need only reflect once again on the contradictory nature of the man produced by the Lycurgan regime.

On one occasion, the historian Macaulay paused to consider the licentiousness that prevailed in the arts in England in the wake of the restoration of Charles II. "In justice to the writers of whom we have spoken thus severely," he remarked, it must be acknowledged

> that they were, to a great extent, the creatures of their age. And if it be asked why that age encouraged immorality which no other age would have tolerated, we have no hesitation in answering that this great depravation of the national taste was the effect of the prevalence of Puritanism under the Commonwealth. To punish public outrages on morals and religion is unquestionably within the competence of rulers. But when a government, not content with requiring decency, requires sanctity, it oversteps the bounds which mark its proper functions. And it may be laid down as a universal rule that a government which attempts more than it ought will perform less. . . . And so a government which, not content with repressing scandalous excesses, demands from its subjects fervent and austere piety, will soon discover that, while attempting to render an impossible service to the cause of virtue, it has in truth only promoted vice.[29]

Something of the sort could be said of ancient Sparta. But there the dividing line between excessive discipline and reactive license was marked out in space and not in time. One Athenian wag summed up the situation nicely: in public, he observed, the Lacedaemonians were clearly the better men; in private, however, the Athenians surpassed them.[30]

The Spartiates resembled their houses.[31] They were austere without, but not so within. These were men torn between their public responsibilities and their private inclinations. They openly pursued honor and fame. But in secret, as we have seen, they coveted wealth. Plato's description merits repetition: under the cover of darkness, like savages, the Spartans paid honor to silver and gold. It should not be surprising that these men were susceptible to bribes, and bribes were precisely what the two kings were in a position to bestow. Through their exercise of oversight with regard to adoptions and through their tutelage over unbetrothed heiresses, Sparta's dyarchs were able in the most important of ways to help their friends and deny their enemies aid.

The royal power to shower with property those who were cooperative and to punish those who were not was undoubtedly of great import in the archaic period and in the fifth century. Thereafter, it may even have increased—at least for a time. By the mid-fourth century, however, when Aristotle penned *The Politics,* the two kings had apparently been deprived of the right to dispose of unbetrothed heiresses.[32] Precisely when the girl's father was given the right to appoint a tutor to handle this task remains unclear. But it is reasonable to suspect that this reform followed in the wake of the general liberalization of property law at Sparta that took place shortly after the Peloponnesian War. It was at this time, we are told, that Epitadeus—who was apparently unfriendly to his own son—managed to secure the passage of legislation granting the holder of a *klêros* the right to leave that piece of property to whomever he pleased or even give it away. The consequences were startling. The law at Lacedaemon specified that no Spartiate who failed to make the required contribution to his *sussition* could retain his rights as a citizen; and as time passed, property came to be concentrated in the hands of the few—many of them women. To explain this development, Aristotle alluded to the greed of the Spartan notables, to the size of the dowries that came to be given under the new dispensation, and to the great "multitude of heiresses," observing that, in his own time, in and after the middle of the fourth century, "nearly two-fifths of the entire country" was "owned by women."

Corruption evidently contributed much to the concentration of property, but the wars of the fourth century were presumably important as well. The measure carried by Epitadeus, in effect, legalized the giving of dowries, and it also made possible a disguised sale of the civic allotment. This enabled citizens too foolish to foresee the consequences or too eager for private enjoyment of the pleasures that money can buy to trade the patrimony of their sons for the means of their own delight.[33] At the same time, the disasters which struck Sparta in the wars of the period eliminated a good many men and left the land in the hands of their wives, sisters, and daughters. These women, inured to "every kind of licence and luxury," were hardly likely to be eager to confer their estates on the impoverished sons of the prolific. They were no doubt much sought after by the surviving Spartiates, both the landless men intent on securing the property needed if they were to make the required contributions to a *sussitíon* and those possessed of an estate but caught in the grips of an unquenchable thirst for additional wealth. Prosperous Spartiates with only daughters for heirs would naturally try to find the best possible match, and money no doubt tended to marry money. But if a girl's father died before she was betrothed, her fate may still—prior to the fourth century—have become the responsibility of the two kings. We do not know whether Sparta's dyarchs disposed also of widows, but—while it lasted—the power they possessed to oversee adoptions and to marry off unbetrothed heiresses was power enough.

These two functions contributed greatly to the influence which the two kings exercised over the allocation of property, but they by no means exhausted that influence. The two *basileîs* had other resources from which to benefit their political allies. Of all the Spartans, the wealthiest were the two kings. They owned choice land in many of the towns of the *períoikoi*. In addition, they received anywhere from one-tenth to one-third of the booty captured in battle; they claimed the hides and chines of whatever animals were sacrificed; and they took a piglet from every litter raised in Lacedaemon. At the same time, they benefited from a special tax levied on the citizens and the *períoikoi;* and of course, because of the power they exercised in the conduct of foreign affairs, they gained more from the gold and silver that flowed into Sparta from abroad than any other citizens.[34] No one was in a better position to bestow gifts.

From the coincidence of what the Spartiates desired and what the kings could provide, it would be easy to suppose, but wrong to conclude, that the two *basileîs* were virtual tyrants within Lacedaemon. To be sure, the dyarchs were capable of working great harm. Aristotle stresses this fact himself.[35] But caution is required regarding this matter, for things would have been much worse had there not been two circumstances working to prevent tyranny—the power of the ephors and the rivalry between the two kings.

The Overseers

The Spartan ephors were magistrates of no mean importance.[36] On two different occasions, Cicero compared them with the tribunes of the Roman plebs, suggesting that they were a check on the kings in much the same sense that the tribunes were a check on the consuls at Rome. Rousseau fleshed out the Roman's description when he denied that the ephorate existed solely to protect the sovereign people against the government and went on to suggest that, while the office was a regulator of and restraint on the executive power, it served also to safeguard the laws and "to maintain the equilibrium" between the government and the populace.[37] The tribunes represented the plebs only; the ephors were chosen from the political community as a whole.

No one is known to have been ephor more than once, which suggests that iteration in office was prohibited; and the board of five held office for only a year. During that year, however, the ephors exercised by majority vote arbitrary, almost unchecked power. It was only at the end of their period in office that they were called to account for their deeds and subjected by their successors to a formal, judicial examination [*eúthuna*] of the sort employed in other Greek cities to guarantee that magistrates remained responsible to the political community.[38]

In the period before that day of reckoning, the ephors played a predominant role in the making and implementing of public policy. They were empowered to summon "the little assembly"—which appears to have been constituted by the board of ephors and the city's *gerousía*—as well as the "common assembly" of the Spartiates.[39] They could introduce laws, decrees, and declarations of war and peace to the latter through the *gerousía;* and when the "common assembly" met—whether on an extraordinary occasion or at the regular monthly time—they decided who would present a particular proposal. One of their number then presided, put the question, and determined whether those shouting for the measure outnumbered those shouting against. It is an indication of their central importance that Xenophon—the ancient writer most intimately familiar with Spartan practice and parlance—thrice ascribes important decisions to "the ephors and assembly." It would not be an exaggeration to say that the ephors administered the government at Sparta with the advice and consent of the *gerousía* and the assembly. Aristotle rightly observes that a magistracy empowered to convene a city's assembly, set its agenda, and preside over it is virtually "authoritative [*kúrios*] within the regime."[40]

The ephors were particularly influential in the sphere of foreign relations. It was within their prerogative to determine when and for how long a foreigner might visit Sparta and a Spartan might go abroad. They ordinarily received embassies, conducted negotiations with foreign powers, and decided when to place matters before the *gerousía* and assembly. They had influence, if not control, over the appointment of the harmosts who administered communities under Sparta's dominion, and they were competent to issue these officials directives. In time of war or civic emergency, the ephors called up the army, and they determined which age groups were to march.[41] In foreign affairs, there were few functions that these magistrates did not perform—other than serve as Sparta's commanders in the field.

At home, the ephors' chief task—as the title of their office suggests—was oversight. They enforced the sumptuary laws and determined which pieces of music and poetry would be tolerated within the community. They kept tabs on the *néoi,* checking each day to see that the "young men" in the *sussitía* observed the regulations regarding clothing and bedding and subjecting them every tenth day to a physical examination. Ultimately, they appointed three outstanding members of this age-category who had reached their prime to select from among their fellow *néoi* and command the three hundred *hippeîs* that formed the royal bodyguard. Likewise, the ephors controlled the treasury, disbursing necessary funds, overseeing the collection of taxes, and receiving the proceeds from the sale of prisoners and other booty captured in war. They also manipulated the calendar, intercalating months when this was deemed necessary.[42] At Sparta, the ephors controlled virtually every aspect of daily life.

Each year, when they took office, the ephors declared war on the helots, employing the young men of the *krupteía* to eliminate the obstreperous and those menacingly robust. At the same time, Aristotle tells us, they reissued the famous decree calling on each Spartiate to obey the law, to comply with the customs of the land, and to observe the ancient practice of shaving his upper lip. According to Plutarch, this last injunction was intended as a reminder to the *néoi* that they were to obey the city even in the most trivial of matters.[43]

In overseeing the many aspects of Spartan life and public policy for which they were responsible, the ephors exercised broad judicial powers. At the time they took office, they apparently subjected all of the retiring magistrates to the *eúthuna*. Thereafter, they had the authority to suspend their fellow officials at any time. Individually, the ephors judged civil suits. As a board, they functioned as moral censors and criminal justices empowered to impose fines on malefactors; and, in capital cases, they could hold preliminary fact-finding hearings before joining the thirty members of the *gerousía* to form a jury competent to banish or execute the accused.[44]

The importance of the ephors is perhaps most obvious from their relationship with the two kings. Here, they had clearly defined prerogatives designed to make manifest and to enforce the sovereignty of the political community as a whole. They alone remained seated in the presence of a king; they alone had the power to summon the kings, to jail them, and even to fine them for misconduct; and in and after the fifth century, if not before, when one of the kings led out the army, two of their number ordinarily accompanied him to observe his every action and to give advice when asked.[45]

One Eurypontid king is said to have remarked that "the magistrate rules truly and rightly only when he is ruled by the *nómoi* and ephors." His coupling of the rule of custom and law with the rule of the ephors is not an accident. At the time of his institution, the Spartan *basileús* made a compact with the *pólis* in which he swore to maintain her *nómoi*. Each month thereafter, the ephors exchanged oaths with the kings, the latter swearing to reign in accord with "the established *nómoi* of the city," the former pledging to "keep the kingship unshaken" as long as the latter abided by their "oath to the city." There was a threat implicit in the ephors' part of the bargain, and they had the power to make good on it. Every ninth year, the five chose a clear and moonless night and remained awake to watch the sky. If they saw a shooting star, they judged that one or both kings had acted against the law and suspended the man or men from office. Only the intervention of Delphi or Olympia could effect a restoration.[46]

Similarly, if the ephors judged that a king or regent had acted against the interests of the city, they could arrest him and bring him to trial on a capital charge just like any other Spartan citizen. In the course of the turbulent fifth century, they were to exercise this prerogative time and time again: Cleomenes and his colleague Leotychidas, Pausanias the regent and his royal son Pleistoanax, Agis and his younger contemporary Pausanias the king—all of these were brought to trial (some repeatedly) and all but Agis were eventually convicted and banished or immured and starved to death.[47] Of the fifth-century kings, only three—Leonidas, his son Pleistarchus, and Archidamus—are not known ever to have been tried for a capital crime, and even this statistic may be misleading. Leonidas and Pleistarchus bore the full weight of royal responsibility for periods so brief that their escape could not be deemed significant. And neither of their reigns nor that of Archidamus is sufficiently well attested to justify our being certain from the silence of the sources that none of them was ever in danger.[48] The only reasonably safe conclusion is that none of them was ever convicted of a capital crime.

The fact that Sparta's kings were so often tried and so often convicted should not be taken as evidence of congenital criminality. Sometimes, of course, there was wrongdoing, but even here the motive for prosecution was more often than not political. Theophrastus stresses that even at Sparta "the lust for victory [*philonikía*]" played a substantial role in trials,[49] and this is precisely what we would expect when the kings were involved. There is no evidence that the Spartans distinguished between the judicial and the political functions of their magistrates, and the removal of a king was a matter of enormous political consequence.

It is a measure of the ephors' importance that the kings had to court them. It would no doubt be an exaggeration to say that the Spartan kings lived in terror of the ephors, but they cannot have been unaware of their vulnerability. Polybius claims that the kings obeyed the ephors as children, their parents. This may be hyperbole—but Xenophon, Plato, and Aristotle are surely not far from the truth when they compare the powers of the ephors to those of tyrants.[50]

It might seem that the kings were virtual prisoners of the ephors. Two sets of circumstances precluded this. In the first place, the kings were kings for life, while the ephors held office but for a year and apparently could never again serve. Equally important, the kingships were hereditary, while the ephorate—which was a democratic office for which every Spartiate who was a *presbúteros* over the age of forty-five was eligible—came, Plato tell us, "near to being an allotted power" and seems to have been filled either by lot from a large elected pool or by some other similar procedure, in which election played a part, that was no less subject to the vagaries of chance. Given the extraordinary power concentrated in the office, if the ephors had been directly elected—as many scholars think they were—there would have been intense competition and canvassing; chance would have played next to no role in determining the outcome; and the electoral process would frequently have turned into a plebiscite on policy. But of this there is not a hint in our sources for the archaic and classical periods.[51]

Thus, as board after board of ephors served, then retired, and as the *gérontes* slowly died off, a strong king endured, exercised his prerogatives, and worked the political and social system to benefit his friends and to impose a burden of gratitude on those judged to be politically prominent. Nearly always, Aristotle tells us, the ephors were nonentities utterly undistinguished; and, at least in his day, when the public allotments had been privatized, they tended to be poor men who were easily bribed. In a given year, a particular king might find himself in difficulties and might deem it prudent to remain quiet, but he knew that the annual game of chance by which the ephors were chosen always offered the hope for a board more favorable to his cause or more easily corrupted. The institution of the ephorate would not alone have staved off tyranny. The fact that the kingship was dual was essential for accomplishing that feat. When the two kings were united, the ephors may not have had the authority to withstand them.[52]

In his account of the foundation of the Roman republic, Dionysius of Halicarnassus depicts the great Brutus as a somewhat scholarly advocate of dividing the royal office between two consuls. The Lacedaemonians have done so "for many generations," he explains.

> And because of this arrangement of their *políteuma,* they have maintained the best order [*eunomeîsthai*] and they have been the most successful and happy [*eudaimoneîn*] of all the Hellenes. If the power is divided in two and each has the same strength, those who hold sway will be less insolent and less oppressive. From this equal sharing of honor and lordship [*isotímou dunasteías*], the most likely result would be that each will feel a sense of reverence and shame [*aidós*] before the other, that each will be able to prevent the other from conducting his life in accord with the dictates of pleasure, and that each will compete with the other in seeking a reputation for virtue.

Centuries after the decline of Lacedaemon, this was the historian's analysis of the kingship at Sparta.[53]

It was almost inevitable that there be rivalry between the two *basileîs.* As Dionysius' testimony suggests, the aristocratic ethos virtually dictated the conflict between the two houses which came to be the norm. It is symptomatic of the situation that, in the fourth century, each Spartan house appears to have had clients of differing political persuasion in cities of the Peloponnesus such as Phlius, Mantineia, and Elis. If the leading men in those cities looked to the two kings for aid and comfort in their struggles against each other, the same is likely to have been true for the Spartiates. The two thrones were natural foci of power and influence. The character of the political and social organization of Lacedaemon strongly encouraged the political class to group itself into two factions around the two thrones.[54]

A division along these lines did not always come to pass. As we will soon learn, Theopompus and Polydorus were allies, not rivals, in the early seventh century and succeeded in carrying out a thorough reform against bitter aristocratic opposition. And where there was no such division, it did not by any means guarantee consensus. As I point out elsewhere, Cleomenes' success in eliminating the hostile occupant of the rival throne and in replacing him with a dependent of his own did not end all opposition to his schemes in the late sixth and early fifth centuries.[55] Moreover, Sthenelaidas the ephor managed to push Sparta into war in 432 despite the firm opposition of the Eurypontid monarch Archidamus and almost certainly without the support of the rival house.[56] Sparta's *basileîs* were important, not all-important. In general, they were at the center of conflict—and where the two kings are not known to have been friends and allies or proponents of the same policy, it is reasonable to suspect that they were at odds.

The Elders

The *gerousía* was the least dangerous branch of the Spartan government, but not the least important. In fact, Plutarch came very close to the mark when he described the Spartan regime as a mixture "of democracy and kingship, with an aristocracy to preside over it and adjudicate in the greatest affairs." In normal circumstances, when the ephors were nonentities and the two kings were rivals of no particular talent, the *gérontes* were in a position to exercise great influence, though not to initiate policy. One measure of their authority is the fact that Demosthenes speaks of this body of men as "the master [*despótēs*] of the many." Dionysius of Halicarnassus advances a similar claim, contending that, while Sparta retained her independence, "the kings of the Lacedaemonians were not autocrats able to do whatever they wished, for the *gerousía* possessed full power over public affairs."[57]

Even if we were to discount these assertions and to suppose them hyperbolic, as we probably should, we would still have to acknowledge that the *gerousía* was a formidable instrument of government. Even if it had been effectively divorced from the exercise of power, the prestige of its members would have been sufficient to guarantee that its recommendations were generally honored. Demosthenes and Aristotle both speak of election to membership in the *gerousía* as "the prize allotted to virtue," and Plutarch makes it clear that being selected was the highest honor which could be conferred by the *pólis* on a citizen. Elsewhere, by means of an anecdote, he makes manifest the political import of being in this fashion esteemed. On one occasion, when a certain Demosthenes, a Lacedaemonian notorious for his lack of self-discipline, brought a sensible measure before the Spartan people, they voted its defeat. Fearful lest the opportunity pass, the ephors acted quickly, selecting by lot one of the *gérontes* to present the proposal once again. "So great," the biographer concludes, "is the influence that can be attributed in a republican regime [*politeía*] to confidence in a man's character and to its opposite."[58]

As the Spartan name suggests, the *gerousía* was a council of the aged. Twenty-eight of its thirty members—all but the two kings—were always men of experience and proven worth over the age of sixty. Drawn exclusively from the priestly caste that seems to have constituted the city's ancient aristocracy, directly elected by popular acclamation, and guaranteed the office for life, the *gérontes* performed three functions: the first, probouleutic; the second, judicial; and the third, sacerdotal. With the ephors presiding, the "old men" met to set the agenda for the assembly, and thereafter they could annul any action on its part that exceeded the authority which they thereby conferred. In capital cases, the *gérontes* joined the ephors in forming a jury; and in circumstances left unclear, they apparently functioned as augurs.[59] No legislation could be enacted and no war declared without their permission, and it was prudent for magistrates to consult the *gérontes* on all matters of administration entrusted to their care.

The kings and the ephors had particularly strong reasons for heeding the advice of these old men. Whether a king or former official was eventually indicted for malfeasance of office, because it was left to a board of ephors annually and more or less arbitrarily chosen, was largely a matter of chance. But whether the defendant would then be convicted, because the matter was entrusted to a tribunal dominated by *gérontes* elected for life, was a subject for calculation—even if, in capital cases, as one scholar argues, the verdict and sentence had to be confirmed by the public assembly.[60]

It is no wonder that we are expressly told with regard to the *gerousía* what is not said at all with respect to the ephorate—that those eligible for election actively sought the office and openly canvassed—and scholars rightly suspect that the factions that tended to grow up around the two royal houses played a crucial role in promoting the selection of their adherents. There were, to be sure, limits to what the *gérontes* could accomplish: except perhaps in a period of general disarray, the "old men" could not have pushed legislation through the assembly releasing their fellow aristocrats from the egalitarian restrictions that so limited their wealth and its use. But, much of the time, albeit within clear confines, the *gerousía* was in a position to be the arbiter of events. If great seriousness was attached to the selection of the *gérontes,* Isocrates tells us, it was because this handful of elderly men "presided over the disposition of all public affairs."[61]

Like the Nocturnal Council described in Plato's *Laws,* the *gerousía* was the guardian of the constitution. It served a function comparable to that which Alexander Hamilton would later attribute to Britain's House of Lords. The *gérontes* had a greater stake in stability than any other group at Sparta. As wealthy aristocrats, they had no pressing need to tamper with the system of land allotments; as recipients of the city's highest honor, they should generally have been satisfied with existing political arrangements; and as old men on the threshold of death, they had little for which to hope from revolution or re-form. In short, like England's peers, they had "nothing to hope for by a change, and a sufficient interest by means of their property, in being faithful to the National interest." In consequence, they formed "a permanent barrier ag[ain]st every pernicious innovation" and endowed the government with "a permanent will." Their very "duration" in office was "the earnest of wisdom and stability."[62] Though the turnover must sometimes have been rapid as death took its toll, the fundamental character and bias of the *gerousía* must have been always the same. So, at least, one would judge after reading the *Rhetoric* of Aristotle.

In that great but neglected work, the peripatetic makes much of the fact that an orator, called upon to address a particular group and eager to achieve a particular end, must pay careful attention to the character of his listeners and couch his rhetoric in a fashion that will move them in the way he intends. There are many differences which distinguish types of men—even within a particular political regime—and the statesman must pay attention to them all. Among these differences, Aristotle singles out age. His awareness of its impor-tance causes the philosopher to dedicate an extended digression to a discus-sion of the qualities which separate young men in the cities of Greece from those, like the *gérontes* of Sparta, who have lived for a long time, observed many events, learned much from experience, and then finally entered their twilight years. The result is a psychological portrait of considerable subtlety which may throw a great deal of light on the nature of the Spartan regime.

"In character," Aristotle observes, "the young are guided by desire and prepared to act in accord with its dictates." They are particularly vulnerable to sexual license because they lack full self-control. At the same time, "they are quick to change and fickle in their desires"; and because "their impulses are keen but not grand," they tend to oscillate between violent passion and sudden disinterest. In addition, "young men are spirited, sharp-tempered, and apt to give way to anger." They are unable entirely to restrain the spirited part of their souls; and "owing to *philotımía,* they cannot endure being slighted and become indignant when they suppose that they have been wronged." But although the young love honor, "they love victory even more" because they desire the "superiority" which only victory can bring. Accordingly, they attach little value to money "because they have never experienced the trials arising from want." This dearth of unpleasant experience has other consequences as well. In particular, the young are good-natured, quick to trust, and full of hope. In addition, "they are hot-blooded—like men drunk on wine." They have themselves had little opportunity to blunder; and because the future before them seems open, they are guided by hope. "In the first days of one's life," Aristotle observes, "one has nothing to remember and everything to look forward to."

Both because the young are hot-blooded and because they so easily give way to hope, they tend to be courageous. "An angry man is not likely to know fear," Aristotle explains, "and hope is good for generating confidence." This courage is balanced by a certain vulnerability to shame, a certain natural bashfulness; and since the young "have been educated in accord with convention and have not yet conceived of other things as honorable," they can easily be kept under control. Furthermore, because they have "not been laid low by life and are as yet untried by harsh necessity," young men tend to be high-minded and magnanimous—to be what the Greeks called "men of great soul [*megalóp-suchoı*]"—and to think themselves "worthy of great things." As a consequence, the young choose "to perform deeds of nobility rather than works of advantage and to govern their conduct in accord with the dictates of good character rather than in accord with those of calculation." This distinction is important because "calculation aims at the advantageous while virtue seeks the noble." Furthermore, men are more likely when young to "hold friends and companions dear." In their early years, "they take delight in living together and do not yet judge anything with an eye to advantage [not even their friends]."

The blunders characteristic of young men are linked with vehemence and excess. "They do everything in excess," the peripatetic observes. "They love too much, and they hate too much, and they do all things in a similar fashion." This quality he attributes to the passionate attachment which the young exhibit for their own opinions. They think they know everything. Accordingly, when young men "treat others unjustly, they do so out of arrogance [húbris], not wickedness." In similar fashion, the young like to laugh, and they are particularly fond of jesting, which Aristotle calls "the húbris of the educated man." This arrogance would be intolerable were it not balanced by pity. According to Aristotle, the young measure those about them by their own lack of malice, and they quite naturally assume that men unjustly suffer all that they have to endure.[63]

Aristotle structures his description of elderly Greek men in much the same fashion, contrasting their tendencies with those of the young. "Because the old have lived through many years," he observes, "they have often been deceived and have made many more blunders than the young." Most matters involving mankind turn out badly, so that their experience of the world causes the aged to be hesitant.

> They "suppose" only; nothing do they "know." And being of two minds, they always add a "possibly" or a "perhaps." They speak of everything in this fashion and say nothing without reservations. The old are, in addition, ill-disposed—for this trait is grounded in the assumption that all things tend to get worse. They are suspicious because of mistrust and mistrustful because of experience. And because of these things, they neither love nor hate with any vehemence, but . . . they are always loving in the expectation of hating and hating in the expectation of someday loving again. They are, in fact, pusillanimous [mikrópsuchoi]. Life has laid them low, and they desire nothing great or out of the ordinary but, rather, only those things which support staying alive. As a consequence, the old are anything but liberal with their substance: property is a necessity and experience has taught them that wealth is difficult to get and easy to lose. They are also cowardly and foresee danger from everything—for they are in temperament opposed to the young. Where the latter are hot-blooded, the former are cold-blooded—so that old age has paved the way for their becoming cowards (cowardice being a certain coldness of blood).

This cowardice has deep roots. Sensing that they are near death, "old men hold life dear," and they tend also "to be fonder of themselves than is proper." Because they are selfish in this fashion, "the old live for advantage and not for the noble," and they prefer what is good for themselves to what is good in and of itself. They are not bashful like the young, but shameless; and "in concerning themselves less with the noble than with the useful, they exhibit a contempt for reputation."

Aristotle contends that their position in life affects even the time orientation of the elderly. Where the young thrive on hope, the old look to memory; where the young live in the future, the old live in the past. They tell stories because "they love to remember." Aristotle emphasizes also that, while old men "are sharp in temper, they are weak in their anger." In fact, their desires are in general weak, and their "actions owe less to passion than to profit." For this reason, the philosopher can remark that "such men only seem to be moderate [sōphronikoí]—for their desires have waned and they are enslaved to gain." Accordingly, the old are strikingly different from the young.

> They live more by calculation than in accord with the dictates of moral character—for calculation aims at the advantageous and character aims at virtue. And they treat others unjustly out of wickedness, not out of insolence [húbris]. The old may be prone to pity but not for the same reasons as the young. The latter feel pity out of a sense of fellow-feeling [philanthrōpía]; the former out of weakness—for the old think that they, too, may suffer everything and this inspires pity—whence they are disposed to complain and are neither jesters nor lovers of laughter. For querulousness is the opposite of the love of laughter.[64]

As should be evident, the young and the old are opposed in virtually every respect—and the young are not only far better suited to war because of their physical strength; they are better suited to such pursuits by temperament as well.

But the very qualities which make it proper that young men serve in the front lines in time of battle render them unfit for rule, particularly in a regime like that of Lacedaemon. Fighting and the actual conduct of war may favor the passionate and the bold, but diplomacy and statecraft generally require caution and precise calculation. The qualities which render old men less generous and more selfish than the young render them also shrewder, less trustful of foreigners, and far less apt to embark on grand but foolish ventures. In foreign affairs, where interest presides, pusillanimity is certainly not a virtue, but then neither is the excessive high-mindedness of the young. Statesmen should not be bashful. They must, in fact, be prepared to be shameless on occasion. In particular, they must be ready to sacrifice the noble for the sake of advantage, for they must care more for the city's survival than for its reputation. Furthermore, in making peace and in preparing for war, the rulers of a community must neither love nor hate with any real vehemence. Instead, they must cherish the city's friends and allies in the full expectation that someday enmity will be required, and they must be hostile to her foes in the full knowledge that these may well become friends and allies at some point in the not too far distant future.

Similarly, the young are hardly fit for rule in any regime aimed at fostering *homónoia* and at achieving stability. Young men are in all places an unsettling element. Even where reared in accord with the spirit of the laws and encouraged to deem honorable precisely what convention prescribes, they rarely display that reverence for the past and that veneration for tradition which is the foundation of communal solidarity. In contrast, because the old are backward-looking and enslaved to memory, they tend naturally to assume that precedent should govern in all cases and that what has been done from time immemorial has an authority and a sanction almost religious in character.

It is not fortuitous that the Spartans rarely conferred political responsibilities on anyone young. Within any community, Aristotle observes, there are two functions—the martial and the deliberative—and both justice and good sense dictate that they be distributed to the young and to the old, respectively: for the young are generally strong, and the old are often prudent. Nor is it an accident that the Spartans were famous throughout ancient times for the exaggerated respect which they paid to age.[65]

Where they received such attention, the old were in a position to do great service. Because they were at leisure, they could act as censors willing to oversee not just public affairs, but private matters as well. Plutarch emphasizes that the old men of Sparta kept watch over the young, attending their workouts in the gymnasium and their games and taking note of their general comportment throughout the day. Simply by their presence, they inspired fear in those likely to transgress and reinforced the shame and the yearning for excellence which guide those inclined to be virtuous. In these circumstances, he notes, "the young tend to cultivate and follow the lead of the old, and the latter, in turn, manage to strengthen and encourage the innate orderliness and nobility of their disciples without incurring envy thereby." The Spartans were fully aware of the character and import of this relationship: an older man who witnessed wrongdoing on the part of a young man and failed to administer the proper reproof was subject to punishment himself.[66]

The depiction in Aristotle's *Rhetoric* of the differences between the young

Greeks and the old is perhaps overdrawn; it may introduce more clarity into the matter than actually exists. But his discussion is, nonetheless, strikingly reminiscent of the one description we have of a member of the *gerousía* addressing the Spartan assembly. In that account, the Heraclid Hetoimaridas is represented as having gone to great lengths in attempting to persuade his compatriots and, in particular, the bold and impetuous young that it is imprudent for a land power like Sparta to go to war against a maritime power like Athens for the hegemony of the sea.[67] In truth, most of the time, the *gérontes* must have been a force for that caution for which Sparta was so notorious. Most of the time, the *gerousía* must have been a bastion of tradition. Precisely because the *gérontes* were not in a position to initiate positive action, they could exercise extraordinary influence and even power without becoming themselves a threat to the regime; and in the end, their oversight was the best guarantee against any disruption of that set of social and economic arrangements that fostered Spartan *homónoia*.

A Mixed Constitution

There is little purpose in disputing whether the Spartan regime was aristocratic or egalitarian and whether its constitution was democratic, monarchical, or oligarchic. As Plato, Aristotle, and the other ancient writers understood, the truth was more complex. In a "well-mixed" regime such as Lacedaemon, the peripatetic tells us, "each of the extremes is revealed in the mean." For those within the Lacedaemonian citizen body, the social and economic arrangements were far more egalitarian than any known elsewhere in Greece. But— at least in the late archaic and early classical periods, when Sparta was still populous—that citizen body was itself recruited by a weeding-out process in which prowess and courage, cunning and hardiness, and physical beauty and charm all played a great part. As a *pólis* that placed greater emphasis on fostering civic virtue than did any other community in Hellas, Sparta was—even by Greek standards—extremely aristocratic. At the same time, however, Lacedaemon was a republic. Ultimately, she referred all fundamental decisions to a popular assembly, and she selected her most powerful magistrates from the entire citizen body by a procedure akin to the lot. In this respect, she was—by those same Greek standards—extraordinarily democratic.[68] Nonetheless, the presence of hereditary *basileîs* claiming descent from Zeus points to divine-right kingship, and that of a small, elective council drawn from a narrowly defined pool and endowed with broad probouleutic and judicial powers suggests oligarchy or even aristocracy. It is no wonder that the ancient writers were perplexed and found it necessary to jettison the familiar terminology. To speak of Sparta as a kingdom, an aristocracy, an oligarchy, or even a democracy would be to take the part for the whole.

Lacedaemon was, in fact, all and none of the above. Hers was, as the ancient writers ultimately concluded, a mixed regime—an uneasy compromise, hard to sustain, between competing principles that managed to prevent or at least retard the emergence of partial societies by somehow admitting and somehow denying the claims of every constituent group. As a mixed regime, the polity attempted (with considerable success for an extended period) to protect each element within the community against the others and to elicit loyalty and devotion from all. The prerogatives conferred on the *basileús* and the influence that went with those prerogatives bolstered kingship and satisfied in some measure the ancient Heraclid claim to rule; the sharing of those prerogatives and that influence between two rival houses and the subjection of both kings to the oversight of the ephors prevented one-man domination. By its very existence, the *gerousía* guaranteed that noble birth would be honored, and the responsibilities reserved for that council prevented not just the wholesale redistribution of the land inherited by the traditional aristocracy but the public discussion of any such measure as well. At the same time, the ephorate and assembly safeguarded the property, the political rights, and the other privileges of the common people. While it all lasted, each element had its rights and dignity reinforced, and that fact goes a long way toward explaining the stability of the constitution and its capacity safely to concentrate in the hands of the magistrates the extraordinary power that was required for the enforcement of the Spartan regimen.

Eventually, of course, that regimen—and, with it, the Spartan constitution—collapsed. Tacitus came reasonably close to the truth when he claimed that "all nations and cities are ruled either by the people, or by the leading men, or by individuals" and then added with regard to the mixed regime: "The form of commonwealth that is selected and composed from these [three] types, it is easier to praise than to achieve, and, if achieved, it will hardly last for long." But, here again, Lacedaemon's real failure is less striking than her remarkable success, and Rome's greatest historian admitted as much when he conferred on Sparta a distinction he resolutely denied the Roman republic: inclusion among what he termed "well-constituted civic communities [*civitates*]."[69]

One would be hard put to charge John Stuart Mill with being a partisan of Sparta. Lacedaemon was, in his view, "memorable for the peculiar pettiness of its political conduct." Furthermore, Mill gave great emphasis to the fact that, when temporarily liberated from supervision by his fellow citizens, a Spartan "was not only the most domineering and arrogant, but in spite of, or rather by a natural reaction from his ascetic training, the most rapacious and corrupt of all Greeks." And yet, despite the distaste that he consistently displayed, the great nineteenth-century liberal could not help being moved by "the steadiness of the Spartan polity, and the constancy of Spartan maxims." He was even prepared to acknowledge that the "habitual abnegation of ordinary personal interests, and merging of self with an idea"—so evident at Lacedaemon—"were not compatible with pettiness of mind. Most of the anecdotes and recorded sayings of individual Lacedaemonians breathe a certain magnanimity of spirit." To these concessions, Mill ultimately added another of equal or even greater importance: "There is indeed no such instance of the wonderful pliability, and amenability to artificial discipline, of the human mind, as is afforded by the complete success of the Lacedaemonian legislator, for many generations, in making the whole body of Spartan citizens *at Sparta* exactly what he had intended to make them."[70]

Aristotle shared Mill's misgivings. Like Xenophon, who conveyed his criticism by indirection, and like Plato, who was forthright, the peripatetic thought it morally obtuse and politically imprudent that the Spartan lawgiver had designed the Lacedaemonian regime for the cultivation of martial virtue almost to the exclusion of all other forms of excellence. The Spartans he bluntly accused of having turned their children into wild animals, and their polity's dramatic decline in his own time he traced to the fact that the Spartiates had not been properly instructed in the refined use of leisure and in pursuits suited to times of peace.[71] But, like Xenophon, Plato, and Mill, Aristotle nonetheless admired the achievements of early Lacedaemon. Although, as we shall see, he was not among those who believed that everything attributed by tradition to Lycurgus was actually his work, he was nonetheless prepared at times to speak as if this were so. This composite, quasi-fictional figure he ranked as one of "the best lawgivers," alongside Solon and Charondas. He drew attention to the fact that Lycurgus had transformed a tyranny into an aristocracy, and he praised him for having been almost alone in making provision for the *paideía* and moral formation of the citizens of the political community within which he lived. In his treatise on the *politeía* of the Lacedaemonians, Aristotle appears to have argued that the honors that Lycurgus received at Sparta, where he was revered, were nonetheless inferior to those that Lacedaemon's lawgiver deserved. In his *Rhetoric,* the peripatetic singled out as an exemplary rhetorical theme Alcidamas' claim that "the Lacedaemonians flourished [*eudaımónēsan*] as long as they employed the laws of Lycurgus."[72]

To understand fully the logic underpinning the remarkable regime that Lycurgus is said to have founded and to grasp the implications of that logic for the articulation of a grand strategy for Sparta, we will have to consider the genesis of Lacedaemon. Then, we will have to examine her evolution early on as a political community.

CHAPTER 3

Conquest

The immense literature about Roman law has been produced by excogitation from a relatively small amount of evidence, of which a substantial part is suspect because of interpolations. [John] Ducane had often wondered whether his passion for the subject were not a kind of perversion. There are certain areas of scholarship, early Greek history is one and Roman law is another, where the scantiness of evidence sets a special challenge to the disciplined mind. It is a game with very few pieces, where the skill of the player lies in complicating the rules. The isolated and uneloquent fact must be exhibited within a tissue of hypothesis subtle enough to make it speak, and it was the weaving of this tissue which fascinated Ducane.

—IRIS MURDOCH

WHAT the novelist Iris Murdoch says, in passing, about Roman law and early Greek history is especially true of early Sparta.[1] The evidence for the origins of Lacedaemon, her constitution, way of life, and grand strategy is not just scanty. Not seldom, it reflects a bias; and, more often than not, the modern researcher is ill placed to discern the nature of that bias and to fathom its depths. In effect, scholars find themselves in the position of children eager to reconstruct a vast jigsaw puzzle—who are aware that the great majority of the pieces are missing and that many of those which have survived are broken, and who then discover, to their great dismay, that their situation is complicated by yet another, perhaps even graver deficiency: for they have not the vaguest notion what the puzzle would look like if they actually managed to piece it together.

Some scholars argue that the surviving ancient literature touching on early Greece in general and on Sparta in particular is worthless as evidence. It reflects legends and traditions, and these, they say, are largely invented out of whole cloth to serve the interests of those on whose behalf the stories are told.[2] This claim one must, I think, qualify. For what we know of traditions in other places and times suggests that most of the time only a part of what is contained therein is pure invention. If the interests of those responsible for passing on such lore play a role, as on occasion they surely must, it is chiefly in helping to guide the process by which what is known is filtered. Some events, supportive of the pretensions of those who welcome their retelling, will be remembered, retold, and even reenacted in ritual,[3] while others, to which they are indifferent or which they find embarrassing, may be relegated to oblivion—especially if they are not entertaining. What survives from the past even in modern times is never more than part of the story. This is doubly true with regard to pre-literate or semi-literate cultures. The stories told will almost certainly be dramatic, and they may well be confused, conflated, and in some measure partisan as well. But they are most unlikely to be wholly and simply false.[4]

One might, of course, argue, as anthropologists of a postmodern bent are now wont to do, that ethnic identity of the sort asserted by the Spartans, Messenians, and Athenians at the micro level and by the Dorians and the Ionians at the macro level is an artifact "socially constructed and subjectively perceived," which is "perpetually renewed and renegotiated through discourse and social praxis"; and this assertion, though phrased in the pompous academic jargon fashionable among social scientists, is no doubt true. Herodotus was on the mark when he drew a sharp distinction between nature [*phúsis*] and *nómos*—mores, manners, custom, convention, law—and then seized on and trumpeted Pindar's claim that *nómos* is "king of all." His *Inquiries* are designed in part to substantiate this distinction and the attendant assertion and to explore their implications. *Phúsis* may divide the animal kingdom into species, but it is *nómos,* rooted in thinking [*nomízein*] and crafted by men in response to the circumstances in which they find themselves, that sorts human beings into tribes, peoples, and nations. But the fact that all such human communities have their foundation in the imagination does not, in and of itself, render fictive the kinship their members assert.[5]

Ethnic connections may be recognized and celebrated, and they may be largely ignored and even abandoned or repudiated. In principle, ethnicity can even be invented *ex nihilo*. In practice, however, this never or almost never happens. The human imagination generally has to have something on which to work, and ethnogenesis rarely, if ever, takes place in a vacuum. The formation of a self-conscious kinship community nearly always presupposes some sort of prior connection—a shared language or religion; shared mores, manners, and ways; a common origin and history; a likeness in looks, if not, in fact, all of the above. When human beings huddle together for offense or defense, claiming to be kin and excluding putative outsiders, far more often than not a substantial proportion of them are, in fact, at least distantly related by blood. Time and time again, in recent years, DNA studies have shown that particular peoples who claim a common ancestry are, in fact, for the most part of common descent.[6] It is, moreover, as this suggests, a mistake to suppose that oral traditions having to do with the foundation of communities and the great crises they weather are apt to die out quickly.[7]

More can be said of particular pertinence to Hellas. For the Greeks were peculiar. Among them, as the Homeric epics both testify and preach, remembrance loomed large. In Mycenaean and post-Mycenaean Greece, manners and mores were aristocratic; and, in and before the classical period, Greeks of rank—the Spartans above all others—were obsessed both with genealogy and with the tales told concerning the foundation of the communities in which they and others lived. Like Arabs of similar stature today, the well-born in ancient Hellas regarded knowing who they and their neighbors were and whence they all came as a matter of the highest importance.[8]

Rarely, moreover, did the stewards of memory have anything like a fully free hand. In ancient Hellas, there were constraints on the formation of tradition, and these were favorable to its veracity. In the archaic and classical periods, Greece was divided into something on the order of one thousand independent, jealous, quarreling, often mutually hostile political communities—each with its own ruling order, its own peculiar interests, its own civic religion, its own agenda, and its own traditions.[9] Where Hellenic traditions are utterly incompatible with one another, as is sometimes the case, we may be at a loss—as Herodotus, the first to confront this problem, readily acknowledges he sometimes was.[10] But where they coincide or overlap, where the ancestral lore of one Greek community dovetails with that of one or more others, as is commonly the case, we would be ill-advised to dismiss its testimony out of hand—for, most of the time, the only plausible reason for such a consensus is that, in its rough outlines, the tradition happens to be true.

There is one more indication that Greek tradition deserves attention and respect. Time and again, the hyperskepticism to which classical scholarship is periodically prone has been belied by new discoveries. Heinrich Schliemann may have lacked the intellectual sophistication possessed by those who dismissed his enterprise as a crackpot endeavor, but when he uncovered the ruins of ancient Troy in Anatolia, of Mycenae and Tiryns in the Peloponnesus, and of Orchomenos in Boeotia, he demonstrated that, with regard to the Greek legends, naive credulity is more apt to bring one close to the truth than is a proud and systematic refusal of trust. Denys Page was less well-schooled in social and anthropological theory than Moses Finley, but the work of Hittitologists has proven the plausibility of his suspicion that there really must have been a Trojan War and that it somehow must have involved the Hittites as well as the Trojans and their Mycenaean attackers.[11] Even tales that fly in the face of common sense, such as the account of Theseus and the Minotaur, may contain a kernel of truth, as was shown by the excavations at Knossos on Crete undertaken by Sir Arthur Evans and the frescoes on the walls of the palace he uncovered.

The Dorian Invasion

The legend that told of Lacedaemon's founding was self-serving. Of that there can be no doubt. But the manner in which it bolstered the interests of the ruling order betrayed an uncomfortable truth: the Spartans were interlopers in Laconia. They had no business being there, and they knew it. This fact they evidently found a source of embarrassment, for the legend that they embraced was a tacit acknowledgment that might cannot make right and an apology for conduct that otherwise, we can see, would have been hard to defend. The means by which the Spartans justified their intrusion into a land not originally theirs revealed the tenuous character of their claim that their seizure of this land and their subjugation of a great many of its previous inhabitants were defensible and just.

According to the calculations of Greeks living in the historical period who attempted to make chronological sense of the ancient legends on the basis of the genealogical lore preserved by the old Greek families, the Achaeans, Argives, and Danaans who fought the Trojan War brought that struggle to a conclusion in 1184/3 and then sought to make their way home. A generation before that war, tradition held, a son of the hero Heracles, intent on reclaiming what he represented as his birthright, made an abortive attempt at the isthmus of Corinth to force an entry into the Peloponnesus by land; and, subsequently, one of the hero's great-grandsons is said to have failed in another attempt. Two generations after the Trojan War, tradition reported, great-great-grandsons of the hero finally managed to achieve the same end by less conventional means, taking to the sea and bringing with them into their promised land a Dorian host, riding on rafts across the narrowest part of the Corinthian Gulf. From the heirs of those putatively left in charge by Heracles, they then wrested the

Argolid in the northeastern Peloponnesus, Laconia in the southeast, and Messenia in the southwest as well.[12]

The Lacedaemonians were by no means alone in this conviction. Their tradition in this regard coincides in all of its crucial details with those of the Argives and the Messenians. It dovetails with the legends told by the Arcadians and the inhabitants of Achaea on the southern shore of the Corinthian Gulf, who claimed to be among the few indigenous peoples left in the Peloponnesus.[13] It fits the ancient lore of the Athenians, and, in other regards, it actually makes rough sense.

There is, for example, archaeological evidence confirming that the great Mycenaean kingdoms within the Peloponnesus built a wall at the isthmus of Corinth, presumably to stave off an invasion, precisely as tradition asserts; and there is similar evidence suggesting that, throughout Hellas, the Mycenaean kingdoms subsequently fell to invasion from abroad over the course of two or three decades at about the time stipulated in the legend.[14] Moreover, in the classical period the Argives, the Spartans, and the Messenians are found to be speaking a dialect of Greek unknown, as far as we can tell, in Bronze Age Argos, Sparta, and Messenia; and, in the districts within the Peloponnesus that came to be occupied by Dorian peoples, there are nearly always the remains of another population, said by tradition to be old Achaean in origin, who serve as their subjects.[15]

Within the Peloponnesus, the regions of Arcadia and Achaea are, moreover, exceptions that prove the rule. Their inhabitants in the classical age bear a certain similarity to the Basques, the Welsh, and the Bretons of modern times. They live in mountainous backlands less friendly to human habitation than the well-watered plains nearby; they think of themselves, in contrast with their neighbors, as a people indigenous to the land; and in the case of the Arcadians, they speak a tongue directly descended from that reflected in the syllabic script employed by the peoples known to have been dominant in an earlier epoch in the fertile lowlands nearby. That, as their own traditions intimate, the Arcadians of this later age included within their ranks a substantial remnant descended from Mycenaean stock and driven as refugees from friendlier lands—this one need not doubt; and, though the linguistic evidence suggests that the history of Achaea was, from an ethnic perspective, more complex than that of the Arcadia and that, as a consequence, a northwest Greek dialect came to be there predominant, something of the sort may well be true for the residents of that region as well.

In short, there is no explanation for what we can surmise from the available evidence more economic than the one offered by the legend concerning the Return of the Heraclids.[16] If Ockham's razor is to be applied, as it must be if we are not to allow our imaginations to run riot, we must assume that the Spartans of the classical period were descended from Dorian adventurers recruited by chieftains of Mycenaean ancestry who led them from northern Greece—from Hestiaiotis, from the highlands of Mount Pindus, or from Erineos in the upper reaches of the Cephisus river valley in Doris—down to Naupactus on the northern shore of the Corinthian Gulf, then across that body of water into the Peloponnesus in a quest to recover what they represented as a land given their forefather by all-mighty Zeus.

An Unsettled Age

According to this legend, after the conquest, the Argolid was allotted to the Heraclid Temenos, Messenia to his brother Kresphontes, and Laconia to their brother Aristodemos—or, if one prefers to believe the version that circulated outside Sparta, to Eurysthenes and Prokles, the twin sons who survived Aristodemos. It was from the last two that the Agiad and Eurypontid kings of later times respectively claimed descent.

The truth is without a doubt considerably messier. In his *Inquiries,* Herodotus traces the genealogy of the Agiad king Leonidas and that of his Eurypontid colleague Leotychidas back to Heracles; and, in his *Guide to Greece,* Pausanias the cultural geographer traces what he represents as the succession in both royal houses from Heracles down to the time when the dual monarchy was abolished.[17] Where they overlap in time, the two Agiad lists are identical and the two Eurypontid lists for the most part coincide; and, where the latter two lists are at odds, the discrepancies can for the most part easily be explained and the lists reconciled. One need only acknowledge the obvious: that the genealogy of a given Spartan king is something other than a list of the kings in his line preceding him. For, within the two royal families, the throne did not always in any extended period pass directly from father to son.

Other sources of confusion are, however, less easy to work one's way around. In and after the sixth century, we know of childless kings and of cases of disputed paternity, where a putative son was not allowed to succeed his supposed father. Given that what we have appear to be genealogies, for a scholarly reconstruction of these lists as lists of kings to be wholly accurate,

Table 1

The Early Agiad and Eurypontid Kings of Lacedaemon

A Partial Reconstruction

The Agiads   **The Eurypontids**

Agis I, late tenth century   Eurypon, early ninth century
Echestratos, early ninth century   Prytanis, mid-ninth century
Leobatas, mid-ninth century   Polydektes, late ninth century
Dorussos, late ninth century   Eunomos, early eighth century
Agesilaos I, transition from ninth   Charillos, ca. 776–48
   to eighth century
Archelaos, ca. 786–59   Nikandros, ca. 748–18
Teleklos, ca. 759–39   Theopompus, ca. 718–668
Alcamenes, ca. 739–698   Anaxandridas I, ca. 668–59
Polydorus, ca. 698–64   Archidamus I, ca. 659–44
Eurykrates, ca. 664–39   Anaxilas, ca. 644–24
Anaxandros, ca. 639–14   Leotychidas I, ca. 624–599
Eurykratidas, ca. 614–589   Hippokratidas, ca. 599–74
Leon, ca. 589–59   Hegesicles, ca. 574–49
Anaxandridas II, ca. 559–24   Ariston, ca. 549–14
Cleomenes I, ca. 524–490   Demaratus, ca. 514–491
Leonidas I, 490–80   Leotychidas II, 491–69
Pleistarchus, 480–59   Archidamus II, 469–27

it would have had to be the case that there were no childless kings and no
cases of disputed paternity in the tenth, ninth, eighth, and seventh centuries—
which is, in the circumstances, most unlikely. The lists printed here can at best
be only a rough and ready guide.

   That is one difficulty. There is another. Although the Agiad and Eurypontid genealogies provided by Herodotus and Pausanias are exceedingly long,
they are not long enough to justify the assertion that the eponyms at the head
of the two lists lived before the tenth century, as the legends presume. To do
this, one would have to posit, as in desperation the ancient chronographers
sometimes did, that on average, in post-Mycenaean Greece, a generation lasted
forty years—which is to say, that the average father on such a list was forty

years old when the son mentioned on it was born. In ordinary times, such a presumption would be implausible. In a time of endemic warfare—the early reaches of it a period of profound disorder—it is inconceivable. In the tale we are told, there is evidently an important chronological gap.[18]

Moreover, tradition held that in Laconia the town of Amyclae managed to avoid destruction at the time of the original invasion. The early fifth-century Theban poet Pindar appears to have regarded it as pre-Dorian, and there is later literary evidence suggesting that it may at some point in this period have had its own king. The archaeological record is consistent with the assumption that what scholars call a sub-Mycenaean community survived the collapse of Mycenaean civilization for some time in the vicinity of Amyclae, and it suggests that, in the immediate aftermath of the Bronze Age, the population of Laconia was elsewhere—except, for a time, at the coastal refuge Epidauros Limera—exceedingly sparse.[19]

Not until the second half of the tenth century are there any material remains suggesting the presence of a settlement in the vicinity of the hill, modest in height, that later served as the Spartan acropolis. In that very period there is, for the first time, evidence near Amyclae and elsewhere for a sharp change in material culture—with the sudden appearance of painted pottery in a style, reflecting the invention of new techniques of production, radically distinct from the style dominant at the end of the Mycenaean age. Tellingly, this particular style of Proto-Geometric pottery closely resembles the ceramic ware in use at this time in Aetolia and elsewhere in northwestern Greece where the Dorians are said to have made their homes before they were induced to cross the Corinthian Gulf.

From this, one might conclude that Laconia was subject to two invasions —a violent assault by an unknown foe roughly two generations after the Trojan War, and an infiltration of Dorians nearly two centuries thereafter—and that in the legends these two incursions were telescoped and conflated, as often happens with oral traditions. It is also possible, however, that there was only one invasion and that some of the original invaders stayed on, not settling down right away in any one place for the practice of agriculture, but tending herds of cattle or flocks of sheep and goats like the transhumant Vlachs of a much later age; moving back and forth seasonally between summer pastures in northern Greece and the warmer climate of the southern Peloponnesus, as the latter would do; and, like them, leaving nary a trace.[20]

Students of ancient history should take Thucydides' warning to heart.

Were it not for his cautionary words, we would be inclined to judge on the basis of the physical remains that Athens was a much greater power than it actually was and that ancient Lacedaemon was politically inconsequential.[21] An absence of evidence—archaeological or literary—need not be evidence of absence.

The supposition that the first Dorians in Laconia may initially have practiced transhumance has this virtue. It helps explain the cultural presumptions that occasioned the Spartans' describing in pastoral terms the institutions and practices constituting their *agōgḗ*. It makes sense in similar fashion of the nomadic, pastoral features evident in the cultic reenactment of the Dorian invasion that took place every year during the festival of Apollo Carneios, and it is consistent with the fact that, in our literary sources for early Sparta, cattle-raiding looms large.[22]

The Emergence of Lacedaemon

On one question, the archaeological evidence is dispositive. Dorian Lacedaemon began to take shape in the decades following 950. At first, if the geographer Pausanias is to be trusted, the town of Sparta, insofar as there was one, was constituted by the four villages—Pitana, Mesoa, Limnai, and Konosoura—grouped about the Spartan acropolis which are mentioned in inscriptions of the Roman period. The Agiad kings, recognized as the senior branch, were buried in Pitana—where, as it happens, we have the earliest archaeological evidence for settlement. Their Eurypontid colleagues appear to have had graves and homes in Limnai—a once marshy area near the Eurotas, which appears to have been settled some decades thereafter.[23]

To this amalgam of four villages, a fifth was added quite early in the history of Lacedaemon. Of this, there can be little doubt—for, in his *Politeía of the Lacedaemonians,* Aristotle specifies that, at a certain point, the Spartan army consisted of five regiments or *lóchoi,* which was no longer the case in and after the late fifth century; and a passing comment in Herodotus makes it clear that, at the time of the Persian Wars, each of these *lóchoi* was drawn from one of the constituent villages of Lacedaemon.[24]

The fifth village can hardly have been any place other than Amyclae, a sizable settlement of great historical importance which was located on the Spartan plain to the west of the Eurotas a few miles to the south of the Lacedaemonian acropolis. No one, not even the most skeptical of scholars, doubts that the Amyclaeans were at some point admitted to Lacedaemon's Spartiate ruling order. On this question, the epigraphical evidence from the Roman period is dispositive. The only issue in dispute is whether the Amyclaeans were made "new citizens [*neopólitai*]," as they are called in the pertinent inscription, early on or quite late; and there is good reason to think the former possibility far more likely than the latter.[25]

To begin with, such a supposition makes geopolitical sense. Amyclae was too close to the administrative center of Lacedaemon and too well-situated on fertile land in the Eurotas valley to have been left for long to its own devices. Moreover, it would have been easy for the Spartans to incorporate such a community within the Lacedaemonian ruling order at or near the time of that order's inception when the situation was fluid and the grounds for inclusion and exclusion had not yet been clearly defined. Later on, pride on the part of the members of that august ruling order would have been an almost insuperable obstacle. Furthermore, if, in the archaic and classical periods, the Amyclaeans had been classed as *períoikoi* and not *Spartíatai,* it would also be hard to explain why we hear so much about their history and customary conduct from figures such as Pindar, Xenophon, and Aristotle. None of the communities known to be composed of *períoikoi* receives any attention of this sort on any scale, whereas Amyclae is actually mentioned more often by fifth- and fourth-century writers than any of the Spartiate villages located about the Lacedaemonian acropolis apart from Pitana. Indeed, the three other villages in that locale listed by the geographer Pausanias and visible in the inscriptions of the Roman period are not mentioned by any classical or Hellenistic source. Moreover, when Athens and Sparta ratified the ill-fated Peace of Nicias in 421, it was not on their acropolis that the Lacedaemonians chose to have the inscription set up recording its terms. It was at Amyclae.[26]

Regarding the evidence for early Sparta, there is yet another complication requiring attention. Herodotus' lists of the ancestors of the Agiad Leonidas and of his Eurypontid colleague the younger Leotychidas are suspiciously equal in length. We are evidently meant to believe the impossible: that the number of generations separating each from Heracles was precisely the same. Moreover, two of the names near the beginning of Herodotus' list of the Eurypontids—Prytanis ("Presiding Officer") and Eunomos ("Well-Ordered by Law")—have an abstract quality, which has led scholars to wonder whether they might not be interpolations meant to sustain the presumption that, from the outset, Sparta was a single community with two kings. It is, they suggest, more likely that, as a polity, Lacedaemon was the product of an amalgamation of two small neighboring communities hitherto at odds—each led by a chieftain claiming descent from Heracles. Such an hypothesis would make sense of the story that we are told of a struggle early on between Pitana and Mesoa, on the one hand, and Limnai and Konosoura, on the other, for control of a religious sanctuary that these four villages subsequently shared.[27]

One thing, however, is clear. Amyclae to the south was at the outset an independent community. Such is the tale told by Pindar in the early to mid-fifth century and by later authors; and this helps make sense of the fact that Amyclae had a religious cult, that of Apollo Hyakinthos, particular to itself, while the four villages near the Spartan acropolis celebrated at the sanctuary once in dispute an important festival—that of Artemis Orthia—in which the Amyclaeans had no part.[28]

If, in this case, the traditional stories—collected, assessed, and retold by Pausanias the travel writer a thousand years later in the era of the emperor Hadrian—are worthy of trust, as, given his considerable acumen and, above all, his attentiveness to local lore, they generally are, it was not until the middle of the eighth century that the Spartans consolidated their hold on the valley formed by the Eurotas River. First, we are told, after securing support from Delphi, the Agiad Archelaos and his Eurypontid colleague Charillos turned to the north and destroyed Aigys. In the process, they took control of the region containing the headwaters of the Eurotas; and, at this time, they may also have seized the Belminatis to the northwest. Soon thereafter they are said to have invaded Cynouria—northeast of Mount Parnon and south of the Argolid.[29]

Archelaos' successor Teleklos reportedly then turned south, conquered Pharis and Geronthrae, colonized them both, and absorbed Amyclae into the Spartan confederacy. Teleklos is also said to have crossed Mount Taygetus, to have established three Spartan colonies along the river Nedon east and up-stream from the ancient city of Pherae on the Messenian Gulf, and to have taken or colonized Pherae itself. Further south, we are told, at the sanctuary of Artemis Limnatis on the western slopes of the great mountain at the top of the Choireios gorge near the southeastern border of Messenia, this Agiad king met a violent end at the hands of Messenians from the great valley below and to the northwest.[30]

It was during his reign that Sparta must have begun working out the terms of her relations with the various subordinate communities on both sides of Taygetus made up of those who came to be called *períoikoi*. Some of these

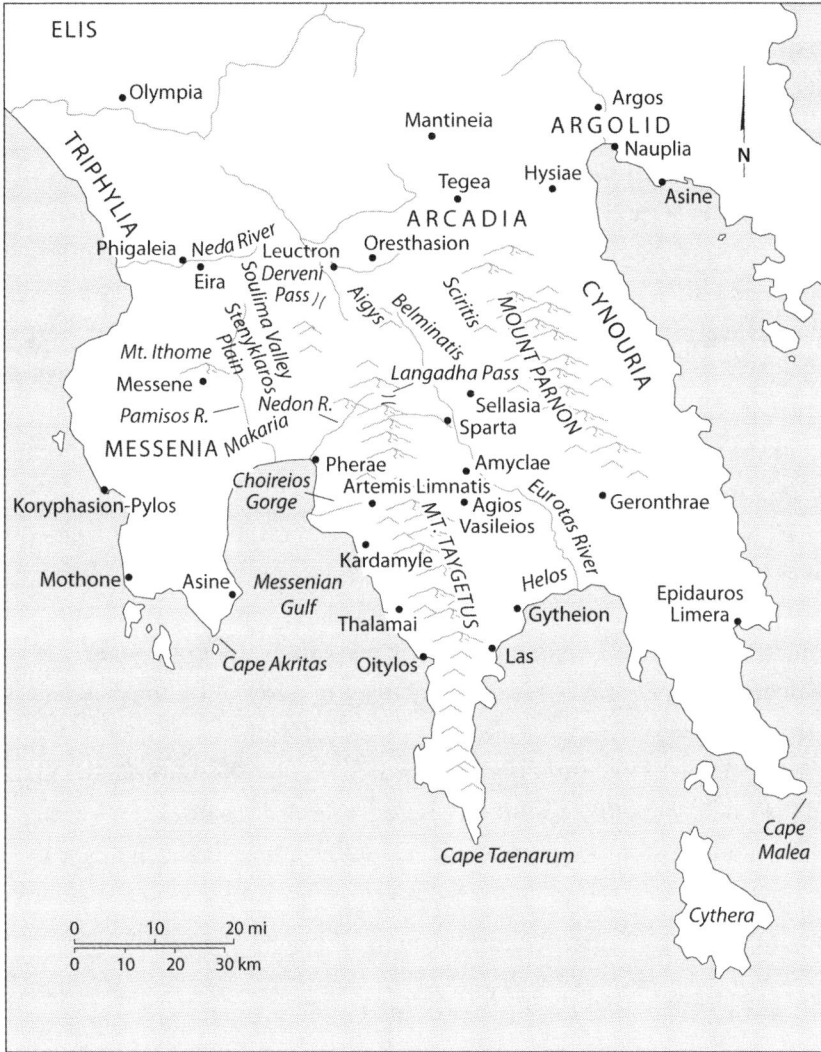

Map 2. Laconia and Messenia

communities were purportedly founded by Sparta as colonies; others, which are attested archaeologically as early as Sparta itself, seem to have been conquered or cowed and neither fully absorbed nor destroyed.[31]

Teleklos' successor Alcamenes is supposed, thereafter, to have taken Gytheion in southwest Laconia, to have conquered Helos in the southeast, and to have reduced the old Achaean population farming the rich plain near the latter town to the status of helots—"captives," some say, or "bondsmen"—condemned to work their own land for the benefit of their Spartan overlords.[32] It is perhaps to this Alcamenes that we should credit the pacification of the peninsula, now called the Mani, stretching south from Gytheion to Cape Taenarum and then north from there along the Messenian Gulf to Pherae, which was located where Kalamata sits today.[33]

It was purportedly in the wake of his consolidation of Lacedaemon's hegemony within southern Laconia that Alcamenes and his Eurypontid colleague Nikandros took the momentous step of launching the First Messenian War, aimed at securing for Lacedaemon the Stenyklaros plain in the upper part of the great and fertile valley created on the western side of Mount Taygetus by the Pamisos River. Tyrtaeus, who lived in the seventh century, tells us that this struggle lasted twenty years and that Nikandros' successor Theopompus was responsible for bringing it to an end.[34]

We do not know the precise dates for this war, but there is suggestive evidence. The Olympic Games were founded, we are told, in 776. If we are to judge by the dedications at Olympia datable to the tenth, ninth, and eighth centuries and by the list of those said to have won the foot race there, the cult site dedicated to Zeus was at first a sanctuary of purely local interest, and the games that grew up in its shadow were initially dominated, as is only natural, by those who lived nearby in the western Peloponnesus—above all, the Eleans and their neighbors to the south in Messenia. The fact that the last Messenian to have won the foot race purportedly did so in 736, while the first Spartan to achieve this honor reportedly did so in 716, may then be telling. At the very least, it suggests that when Pausanias, following the Hellenistic chronographers, dated the beginning of the twenty-year war later mentioned by Tyrtaeus to 743 and its end to 724, he was not far off the mark.[35]

None of this is certain, to say the least. Some would even assert that Pausanias' chronology—rooted, as it is, in a chronographic system founded on the list of Olympic victors—is worthless.[36] But I wonder. If the list really is a fabrication, why is it dominated in its early years by *póleis* in the vicinity of Olympia? Moreover, as a reconstruction of the past, the chronology based on this list has three considerable virtues. It is consistent with tradition; it fits with the smattering of archaeological evidence that we possess; and it makes sense in the context of what we can surmise regarding what was then happening elsewhere in Greece. The epoch assigned by tradition to Sparta's consolidation of her hold on Laconia and to her initial incursion into Messenia coincides with a time when other Greek cities were expanding into their hinterlands or sending colonies abroad, and everything that we know of the period suggests that it was a time when the population of Hellas appears to have grown by leaps and bounds and to have threatened in many places to exceed the carrying capacity of the land.[37]

Throughout Greece, the situation following the Trojan War and the violent collapse of the great Mycenaean kingdoms appears to have been exceedingly fluid. Wherever we look, we find evidence for immigration on the part of families and clans of quite disparate origins. In Laconia, there is reason to suppose that some, at least, of ancient Achaean stock found their way into the Spartan ranks—for the dialect spoken at Lacedaemon preserves certain pre-Dorian elements suggesting an affinity with Arcadian, and at Amyclae in particular there is clear evidence for a measure of religious continuity between Mycenaean and Dorian Sparta.

Three stories illustrate the degree to which matters in Laconia were in flux. The first of these—told in brief by Pindar and Pausanias and in much greater detail by Herodotus—concerns the Minyans, a people purportedly descended from the crew of the Argo. According to the legend, they sought refuge in Lacedaemon after being driven from Lemnos by that island's pre-Greek Pelasgian population. Because Castor and Pollux, the sons of Tyndareus and brothers of Helen and Clytemnestra, were thought to have been among those who sailed with Jason as Argonauts, the Minyans were, we are told, invited to join the Spartans. And when they agreed to do so, they were not only given land allotments and a share in governance; they were also distributed into the three tribes found in all the Dorian lands—the Hylleis, the Dymaneis, and the Pamphyloi. But when these newcomers displayed insolence, demanded a share in the kingship, and engaged in putatively impious acts, the Spartans turned on them and saw to their removal from Lacedaemon. Most found refuge within the Peloponnesus—in Triphylia along its west coast to the north of Messenia and to the south of Elis. But one contingent is said to have joined an expedition already being organized with official sanction by a Spartan of Theban origin purportedly descended from Cadmus through Oedipus and Polyneices. This notable was, we are told, intent on joining the Phoenicians said to have been left on the island of Thera by Cadmus some eight generations before and on founding a colony in that location with their assistance.[38]

The second story is similar and may be a variant of the first. It is told in two versions set in two different epochs. According to both versions, refugees

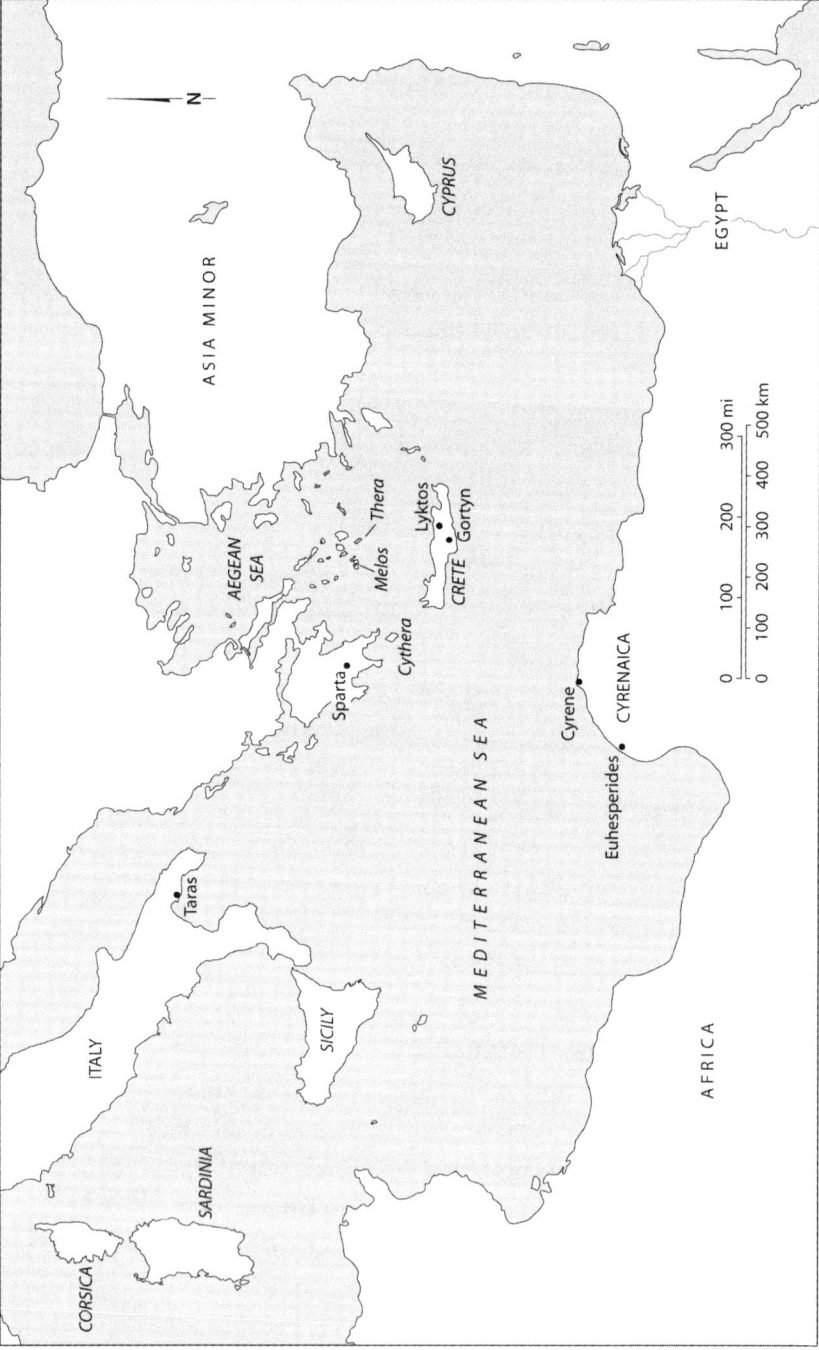

Map 3. Sparta in the Mediterranean

arrive from Lemnos and Imbros, are allowed to settle at Amyclae, and subsequently revolt; then, they are made to join a Spartan colony destined for Crete and led by Lacedaemonians named Pollis and Delphos; and, en route, this expedition pauses to found a settlement on the island of Melos. Conon puts their arrival in Laconia shortly after the Return of the Heraclids, emphasizes the exclusion of these immigrants from the magistracies and the council, and has them end up on Crete at Lyktos. Plutarch has them arrive at a time of Spartan-Messenian conflict, marry Spartan wives, stir up trouble with the helots, and end up also on Crete but at Gortyn.[39]

The third story, told in variant forms by Aristotle, Antiochus of Syracuse, Ephorus of Cumae, Diodorus the Sicilian, Pausanias, and Polyaenus, concerns the *Partheníai*—the so-called "sons of the virgins"—who were somehow conceived, so we are told, during the first Messenian war when most of the Spartans were away on campaign. When they came of age after that long struggle, they were denied land allotments in the newly conquered territory; and when, in response, they caused a disturbance, they were dispatched in 706 to found a colony at Taras on the boot of Italy.[40]

Not one of these stories, as told, makes full sense. But it does seem clear that there was considerable turmoil in early Lacedaemon, as Thucydides contends; and it is reasonable to suppose that these disturbances had something to do with the city's absorption of Amyclae, with her assimilation of a part of Laconia's pre-Dorian population and of refugees from elsewhere in Mycenaean Greece, and with her subjugation of the remainder of Laconia and of the Stenyklaros plain in Messenia. Thera, Melos, Lyktos, Gortyn, and Taras all had institutions similar to those of the Spartans, and they all traced their origins to Lacedaemon. Their foundation legends are in large part plausible, and the archaeological record suggests a timing for events. As the ancient reports assert, there may well have been a settlement on Thera prior to the putative arrival of the colonists from Sparta near the middle of the eighth century. Melos, Lyktos, and Gortyn appear to have been established some time not long before this expedition; and Taras in Italy, at that century's end.[41]

The differences in the three stories are also telling. Before they began acquiring territory—under the very early kings, as Ephorus and Aristotle report—the Spartans were generous in incorporating strangers into their community.[42] Later, however, when their domain had increased, they were inclined to guard their privileges as Spartiates jealously; and after they had seized the Stenyklaros plain in Messenia, they were prepared to exclude even the native-born.

A Military Revolution

Inclusion by way of exclusion—this is what defines a political community, and by the end of the eighth century, as the story of the *Parthenía* makes clear, Lacedaemon had achieved definition. In the course of conquering Laconia and of seizing Cynouria and the upper reaches of the Pamisos valley, the Agiad and Eurypontid kings and their Dorian followers were forced to pose to themselves a question: who is to share in the spoils, and who is to be left out? And this in turn required that they ask another question: who is to decide?

In the beginning, these questions were no doubt easily answered, and though the Heraclid kings, like warrior chieftains in other places and times, must have had considerable latitude in the disposing of loot, they were presumably constrained in one particular. As the dispute that arose between Agamemnon and Achilles in the first book of Homer's *Iliad* reminds us, captains of this sort have to satisfy those who do the fighting, and particular attention has to be paid to those warriors who prove to be indispensable.[43]

This task must have become more complicated, however, as time passed—for, in the first half of the seventh century, a military revolution took place in Hellas that altered the political playing field. We do not know with any certainty how fighting was conducted in the century preceding this revolution. But the odds are good that, for the most part, it looked something like the fighting said in the *Iliad* to have taken place in the open plain before the city of Troy.

Of course, Homer's account of open-field combat leaves something to be desired. He is evidently aware that, in Bronze Age Greece and Asia, chariots were deployed. But he has almost no clue as to the manner in which (in Asia, if not also in the Balkans) they were then employed in combat—by the Achaeans and, of course, by the Egyptians, Assyrians, Babylonians, and Hittites—as platforms from which to confront chariots from the opposing side and to fire arrows, throw javelins, and bear down on an infantry line in disarray. And so he depicts the Achaean, Argive, and Danaan warriors at Troy as having used them almost solely, in the manner of limousines, as prestige vehicles for getting to and from the field of battle.[44]

Once they have arrived at the scene of conflict, Homer's heroes almost invariably dismount and fight on foot. There are indications in his text suggesting an awareness on their part of the advantages associated with marshaling one's forces. Moreover, when cornered at the trench and palisade protecting the ships they had drawn up along the beach, the Achaeans are forced to crowd together, and they do briefly fight shoulder to shoulder to good effect in close array. This they do again when they struggle to prevent the Trojans from dragging off Patrocles' corpse. In open-field combat, however, Homer's heroes operate as aristocratic "forefighters [*prómachoi*]," strutting about before a multitude constituted by their own retainers, then surging forward to hurl javelins and wield thrusting spears and swords in hit-and-run attacks.[45]

It is possible that, in these passages, Homer is repeating an account of infantry battle that was passed down from bard to bard from quite distant times. But the discrepancy between his account of the use of chariots and what we know concerning actual chariot warfare in late Bronze Age Egypt and western Asia suggests that something has been lost in transmission, that he is for the most part depicting the infantry tactics of much more recent times, and that, in describing chariots and their use, he is giving us an adaptation of what he knows regarding the manner in which aristocrats in his time made their way by chariot or on horseback to sites of conflict and, perhaps after skirmishing, dismounted to hurl javelins at one another and close with thrusting spear and sword.[46]

It is, of course, conceivable that Homer's treatment of open-field combat chiefly as a struggle between individual grandees operating as *prómachoi* is a distortion of the reality of combat, reflective of the demands of the epic genre within which he is writing. After all, mass combat, which was known as early as the third millennium in Mesopotamia, lends itself less readily to dramatic personal confrontations than face-offs between individual heroes. Here, however, we should not underestimate the degree to which, within an aristocratic society, prowess of the very sort described in the *Iliad* was, in practice, demanded of men born to high rank who were intent on asserting and retaining their prerogatives. There may well be evidence in Homer allowing us to infer an occasional resort to mass combat, but there is no indication that forming up in a disciplined phalanx was central to the Homeric way of war.

The moral horizon of the poem is also telling. In the *Iliad,* Homer's Sarpedon wonders out loud why, in Lycia whence they have come to help defend Troy, he and his friend Glaukos son of Hippolochos "are honored before others with pride of place, meats, and beakers of wine filled to the brim"; and he asks why "all men look on us as if we were gods" and why "we are awarded a great estate by the banks of Xanthos, with land well-suited to orchards and vines, and ploughland fit for bearing wheat." To the questions posed, he has a ready answer. "It is incumbent on us," he tells Glaukos, "to take our stand among the Lycians out in front and do our part in the heat of battle, so that a man of the Lycians, thick-laid with armor, may say of us, 'Indeed, not without glory and renown are those who hold sway in Lycia, these kings of ours who feast upon fat sheep and drink choice sweet wine, since indeed in them there is strength of courage, for they fight among the Lycians out front.'" Sarpedon's analysis of the role he and Glaukos must play as *prómachoi* should give us pause, for it not only captures perfectly the imperatives driving aristocratic societies of a martial cast. It also instructs succeeding generations in that ethos. For in societies where books possess great moral authority, as Homer's *Iliad* undoubtedly did, life is as apt to imitate literature as literature, life. In antiquity, the conduct of war was powerfully influenced—if not, in fact, governed—by the elaborate code of honor reflected in the *Iliad* and inculcated by it.[47]

Homer's *prómachoi* may in some measure be creatures of fantasy, literally and figuratively larger than life. But they continued in later years to loom large in the Hellenic imagination. Greek vase painters found it impossible to depict with any accuracy a formation of infantrymen in serried ranks, bunched shoulder to shoulder in close array within each file; and rarely did they even try to do so. Instead—no doubt to the delight of those of their well-heeled, well-born patrons, who had been reared on epic tales of derring-do—they devoted themselves to representing warriors in individual combat. Well before the Persian wars, however, the world of the *prómachos* and of individual combat more generally had, in practice, all but disappeared. There may have been a bit of skirmishing for old times' sake between the lines just before a battle began, and there could well be considerable fighting of this sort in its wake. But by the early fifth century we know that except in unusual circumstances—when they had to engage in combat on rough, uneven ground unsuited to heavy infantry—the Greeks brought matters to a decision not by squaring off as individual champions but by engaging in combat arrayed in a phalanx. Generally, they lined up in files eight men deep—deployed in such a manner that combat avoidance was well-nigh impossible—with the individual soldiers, who came to be called hoplites, brandishing thrusting spears eight feet in length and bearing round, interlocking shields in such a fashion as to form something resembling a wall.[48]

Figure 1. Clash of phalanxes represented on the Protocorinthian olpe known as the Chigi Vase, ca. 640 (at Museo Nazionale Etrusco di Villa Giulia 22679; from Ernest Pfuhl, *Malerei und Zeichnung der Griechen* [Munich: Bruckmann, 1923], pl. 59).

We do not know precisely when hoplite protocols of this sort were first introduced; and, given the never-ending fluidity of war, there is every reason to suppose that the tactics and the equipment associated with this species of warfare were gradually refined over time. But we do know that something looking very much like an attempt to depict the fully developed phalanx, complete with a flute player piping to help the soldiers march in unison, is to be found on the so-called Chigi vase, which can be dated on stylistic grounds to around 650; and, as it happens, the second half of the seventh century is the period when the Lacedaemonians begin dedicating lead figurines of hoplites in large numbers at the sanctuary of Artemis Orthia and the Menelaion in Laconia, and it was then also that the Hellenes more generally begin dedicating hoplite armor at Olympia. No less telling is the fact that large emblazoned round shields outwardly resembling the shield characteristic of phalanx warfare begin to be depicted by vase painters late in the eighth century. Moreover, at some point between 690 and 680, a vase painter depicted on the back of such a shield the telltale midshield armband and rim grip employed by the hoplite; and, around 675, another vase painter juxtaposed with two pairs of warriors fighting one another a flute player, whose only known function in war was to mark time so that each of the hoplites in a phalanx could keep pace while marching into battle alongside his comrades. In short it is a reasonable supposition that the shield wall first made its presence felt in the Peloponnesus at some point in the second half of the eighth century.[49]

As a warrior, the hoplite was distinguished not by the helmet on his head, nor by the greaves, cuirass, or corslet he may have worn—though these all formed part of the standard hoplite panoply. He was set apart, instead, solely by the peculiar shield that he bore. The long thrusting spears that hoplites carried and the short swords to which they resorted when these spears were broken or lost did little to distinguish them from infantrymen of other sorts. Their hallmark was the *aspís;* and, tellingly, the Greeks sometimes thought it sufficient to refer to this shield as the *hóplon,* using for this particular item the generic term for hoplite equipment. It was, after all, the *aspís* that made the hoplite a hoplite. This shield was designed for phalanx warfare, and it was very nearly "useless" for anything else. So, at least, we are bluntly told by Aristotle, who had this advantage over modern military historians: he had actually seen Greek infantrymen equipped with the hoplite panoply. He may also have witnessed hoplite armies practicing maneuvers, and he certainly had ample opportunity to converse with those who had borne the *aspís* in battle. When he spoke on such a question, he spoke with a discernment and an authority that we cannot ever hope to duplicate.[50]

It is easy to see why the *aspís* would be of little use and perhaps even burdensome to an infantryman fighting in the manner of a *prómachos.* This shield was round and, as the Greeks put it, "hollow" (which is to say, from the perspective of the man bearing it, the *aspís* was concave). It was also roughly three feet in diameter; and, depending largely on whether its core, usually constructed of poplar or willow, was faced with bronze, it could weigh up to twenty pounds. For an isolated individual, a fifteen-pound shield (which was evidently the norm)—borne on his left arm and, when possible, supported at the lip on his left shoulder—was an encumbrance more unwieldy and awkward than we are apt to imagine. In ancient times, as we must with some frequency remind ourselves, human beings were considerably smaller in stature than they are today.

The *aspís* borne by the hoplite had a bronze armband in the center, called a *pórpax,* through which the warrior slipped his left arm, and a leather cord or handle on or near the shield's right rim, called an *antilabé,* for him to lay hold of with his left hand. This shield might provide adequate cover for a warrior temporarily stretched out sideways in the manner of a fencer with his left foot forward as he prepared to hurl a javelin or to put his weight behind a spear thrust. But this pose could not long be sustained, for it left him exceedingly vulnerable to being shoved to the right or the left and knocked off his feet. Moreover, the minute he pulled his left foot back for any reason or brought his

Figure 2. Fallen hoplite with hollow shield and *pórpax* (Trojan warrior), probably Laomedon, situated on the east pediment of the Aphaia temple at Aegina, ca. 505–500 (now in the Staatliche Antikensammlungen und Glyptothek in Munich; Photograph: Daderot, Wikimedia Commons, Published September 2016 under the following license: Creative Commons CC0 1.0 Universal Public Domain Dedication).

right foot forward while actually hurling the javelin or driving the thrusting spear home, he would have turned willy-nilly to face the enemy; and, when he was in this posture, the *aspís* left the right half of his body unprotected and exposed, and it extended beyond him to the left in a fashion of no use to him as a solo performer. Even if the hoplite ordinarily stood, as one scholar has recently suggested, in an oblique position, braced with his legs wide apart and his left foot a bit in advance of his right so that he could rest his shield on his left soldier, his right side will have been in some measure exposed. As this analysis should suggest, when infantrymen equipped in this fashion were operating on their own, cavalry, light-armed troops, and enemy hoplites in formation could easily make mincemeat of them; and the same was apt to happen when agile light-armed troops equipped with javelins caught hoplites in a situation unsuited to seeking a decision by way of phalanx warfare. The hoplite

Figure 3. Hoplite poised for assault, figurine, formerly part of a bronze vessel, ca. 510–500, found at Dodona (Photograph: bkp Berlin/ Staatliche Museen zu Berlin—Preußischer Kulturbesitz/Johannes Laurentius/Art Resource, NY).

was, as Euripides contended, "a slave to the military equipment that he bore [*doûlos . . . tōn hóplōn*]."[51]

When, however, men equipped with the *aspís* were deployed in close order in ranks and files on suitable ground, this peculiar shield made each hoplite warrior a defender of the hoplite to his left—for, as Thucydides explains, it covered that man's right side. It is this fact that explains the logic underpinning a statement attributed to the Spartan king Demaratus to the effect that "men don helmets and breastplates for their own sake, but the *aspís* they take up for the sake of the formation which they and their fellows share."[52] Were it not for the particular advantages that the *aspís* equipped with a *pórpax* and an *antílabé* afforded an infantryman deployed in a closed formation, the Greeks would never have adopted it in the first place. Instead, they would have stuck with the round shield equipped with a single grip in the center that, as the Assyrians had demonstrated, could be used to good effect in almost any circumstance—which, in fact, we know, some of the Greeks in and for a time after the seventh century continued to employ. Given the relative uselessness of the center-armband-and-rim-grip shield in the absence of the phalanx, however, the sudden appearance of the *aspís* on vase paintings in the late eighth and early seventh centuries powerfully suggests—and arguably proves—the presence of the phalanx, and this in turn implies the employment, at least in certain circumstances, of the hoplite tactics for which this shield was so obviously designed.[53]

A Moral Revolution

Initially, having those heavily armed form up in a phalanx was but one tool in the infantry commander's kit. The old ways lived on. The vase painters of the seventh century frequently depict soldiers in the hoplite panoply carrying two spears of different length—a javelin for hurling and a thrusting spear. The Mytilenian poet Alcaeus notes the usefulness of greaves as a protection against such missiles, and his fellow lyricists Callinus of Ephesus and Archilochus the mercenary allude to the characteristic thud heard when such missiles landed nearby. The vase painters also depict archers sheltering behind the shields of those more heavily armed, just as bowmen did in Homer's *Iliad;* and tellingly, in one battle description, Tyrtaeus describes light-armed troops, armed with javelins and stones, doing the same. It is also conceivable that, at first, the phalanx consisted of a single rank of hoplites seconded by a host of archers and other light-armed troops. This is, in fact, what one should expect—for human beings are creatures of habit; and in warfare it is rare that new tactics immediately and comprehensively displace the old. The eighth and seventh centuries constituted a time of transition and experimentation. None of this alters, however, the essential fact—that, where the shield wall was employed, battles were no longer decided by *prómachoi* hurling javelins and light-armed troops sheltering behind their shields.[54]

The military revolution under way late in the eighth and early in the seventh century had profound moral implications. Nowhere are they more starkly visible than in the critique, which we have already reviewed, that the Spartan poet Tyrtaeus directs at the broad understanding of human excellence evident in Homer and in the mythological tradition. For in dismissing—as qualities of no great significance—speed, agility, physical strength, comeliness of body, wealth, regal bearing, and persuasiveness in speech, he makes of stamina, grit, endurance, and courage of the sort displayed in hoplite warfare the virtue supreme. It is with this in mind, as we have seen, that he writes, "Each man should treat life as something hateful and hold the black ruin of death as dear as the beams of the sun"; and in this context, with an eye to the soldiers protecting one another by "forming" what he elsewhere calls "a fence of hollow shields," he emphasizes the need for Sparta's infantrymen "to stand by one another and to march into the van where the fighting is hand to hand." When they do so, he tells us, "Rather few die, and they safeguard the host behind." It is also with the phalanx in mind that he limns this portrait of the hoplite warrior:

> Let him take a wide stance and stand up strongly against them,
>   digging both heels in the ground, biting his lip with his teeth,
>   covering thighs and legs beneath, his chest and his shoulders
>   under the hollowed-out protection of his broad shield,
>   while in his right hand he brandishes the powerful war-spear,
>   and shakes terribly the crest high above his helm.
> Our man should be disciplined in the work of the heavy fighter,
>   and not stand out from the missiles when he carries a shield,
>   but go right up and fight at close quarters and, with his long spear
>   or short sword, thrust home and strike his enemy down.

"Placing foot next to foot," Tyrtaeus concludes, "pressing shield against shield, bringing crest near crest, helm near helm, and chest near chest, let him battle it out with the man [opposite], grasping the handle of his sword or the long spear."[55]

The shift in tactics that produced the species of warfare described in these passages had profound political implications as well. As we have already seen, when a Spartan king marched off to battle, he was accompanied by an elite bodyguard of three hundred warriors. It is revealing that—although, by the time that we learn of its existence, this bodyguard was made up entirely of hoplites—its members were nonetheless called *hippeîs* or "horsemen." Aristotle informs us that, in earlier times, the cities of Greece were governed by aristocracies. Their power he traces to the military predominance of men on horseback, and he cites as examples Chalcis and Eretria, which were located at opposite ends of the Lelantine plain on the island of Euboea. In these cities, he reports, there had existed in the archaic period equestrian ruling orders composed of men who were respectively called *Hıppobótaı* or "Horse-Breeders" and *Hıppeîs.*[56]

These Euboean cities were by no means peculiar. There is evidence suggesting that, early on, Thebes as well was governed by those who bred horses. In his *Antigone,* which is set in the distant past, Sophocles describes her tellingly as a city "rejoicing in her many chariots," which was renowned for their beauty. Thebes' heritage in this particular long remained a source of communal pride. In the late fifth century, the city fielded an elite hoplite unit strikingly similar to Lacedaemon's *hıppeîs,* which bore an anachronistic, telltale title: "the charioteers and footmen." Situated in Boeotia on a broad plain suited to cavalry and even perhaps to chariot warfare, Thebes was governed, as late as 479, by an exceedingly narrow aristocracy whose equestrian character can hardly be in doubt.[57]

Aristotle's testimony suggests that, when the royal bodyguard was first formed, Sparta's army was made up of aristocratic champions who ordinarily went off to war mounted on chariots or on steeds and then, like the chariot-borne warriors depicted so vividly in the *Iliad,* dismounted to fight, not primarily with thrusting spears but with javelins and swords.[58] It was, we must suppose, with an army of this sort that Archelaos and Charillos, Teleklos, Nikandros and Alcamenes, Theopompus,, and their colleagues first established Sparta's hegemony throughout Laconia and over the Stenyklaros plain in Messenia.

Homer, in fact, provides a template by which we can understand the practices customary in early Greece by dint of which raiders from one community could extract from another such community one-half of the harvest gathered by its citizens, as the aristocrats of Lacedaemon reportedly did from Messene each year. Whether this took place at harvest time; in the fall, after the ephors, upon taking office, had in ritual fashion legitimized a raid by declaring war; or in a less orderly way we cannot say.[59] It is, however, we must suspect, their preeminence on the field of the sword in these early days that explains the existence at Sparta in later times of an equestrian aristocracy, possessing private property in abundance, which was accorded privileged access to high office as members of the *gerousía.*

A small army of horse-borne raiders would not, however, have been adequate to Sparta's needs in the second quarter of the seventh century. We do not know at what moment the hoplite phalanx was introduced and by whom, but there is suggestive evidence. The *aspís* had another name. It was also called the Argive shield,[60] and it was at Argos in about 720 or even before that we have the earliest evidence that warriors were being buried with the full hoplite panoply.[61] This suggests that, in Hellas, the Argives may have pioneered the use of the *aspís,* and this in turn may explain Argos' reported rise to preeminence within the Peloponnesus in the first half of the seventh century.

An Empire Under Siege

Argos' accomplishments in this regard had implications for Lacedaemon. Sparta and Argos were sworn enemies. Tradition reports that the Argives—and the Arcadians—gave aid and comfort to the Messenians during the First Messenian War. We are also told that Argos and Lacedaemon were at odds over Cynouria, a district situated on the Aegean coast of the Peloponnesus southwest of the Argolid and northeast of Laconia. It was presumably with this fertile territory in mind that, at some point early in the second half of the eighth century, the Eurypontid king Nikandros marched north and ravaged the Argolid with the help of the citizens of Asine living on its coast, and the same aim can surely be ascribed to the Spartans who marched north toward the Argolid from Cynouria in 669 and were laid low by the Argives at Hysiae on the northern edge of the Thyreatis plain. It was perhaps at this time that Pheidon, the Heraclid king of Argos, restored the fortunes of his house and reestablished Argive hegemony within the Peloponnesus. It was perhaps at this time that a diminutive Greek *pólis* elicited an oracle from Apollo at Delphi in which the Pythia initially singled out as "best" the soil of Pelasgian Argos, the steeds of Thessaly, the women of Lacedaemon, and the men of Chalcis, victors in the late eighth-century Lelantine War—and then added as an afterthought: "Better even than these are those who reside between Tiryns and Arcadia, rich in flocks: the linen-corslet-bearing Argives, the sharp goads of war."[62]

We do not know whether the Argives deployed a hoplite army at Hysiae, but that they did so does seem likely given the battle's timing, its location, and the ethnic name given the hoplite shield. We do not know whether the Spartans were caught flat-footed on this occasion, fighting with equipment and tactics sadly out of date. But if they were not, their loss can perhaps be chalked up to an inadequate command of the tactics that had all too recently become requisite or to a failure to deploy an army sufficient in numbers.

This last possibility deserves attention. Greek mercenaries, operating in Assyria and Egypt, may well have adapted the round shields of the neo-Assyrians for use in a phalanx by increasing their size and substituting for the single grip in the shield's center the *pórpax* and the *antilabé*. But phalanx warfare, which required ready cooperation and a spirit of solidarity not always to be found among soldiers of fortune, suited far better the moral dispositions of neighbors united by familiarity and a determination to defend hearth and home. Aristocrats are quite likely to have pioneered this species of combat in Hellas proper—for, in the beginning, they were almost certainly in charge. But fighting in phalanx was not, in principle, an aristocratic endeavor. It privileged not prowess but endurance, and it left little, if any, room for individual distinction.[63] The strength of this formation was determined by the weakest link in the chain of men composing it. Moreover, success with such an instrument required the recruitment of a great many more men than could be found within the narrow class of exceedingly wealthy warriors who had in the past fought from chariots or on horseback or who had ridden off to battle each on a chariot or the back of a horse.

The requisite expansion in the size of the warrior class had consequences. It is by no means fortuitous that almost all of the tyrants who emerged within early Greece in its wake were associated with war; that they were at odds with the traditional aristocracy; and that they are said to have been favorable to the *dêmos*. No one understood the political sociology that occasioned this development better than Aristotle. In judging these matters, as in commenting on the *aspís,* he had advantages that no modern scholar (no matter how well informed) can ever hope to equal. He spoke classical Greek as his native language, and he lived in a *pólis*. He understood instinctively what we can only with difficulty and a supreme effort of the imagination ascertain; and, as we can see in his *Politeía of the Athenians,* he devoted a great deal of effort to learning about the developments early on in the various Greek cities that had in time given rise to the mature *pólis* and its characteristic institutions and practices. To this end, almost certainly with the assistance of those who flocked to the Lyceum to study with him, he had collected material on the political development of one hundred fifty-eight different *póleis,* and he or one of his associates had penned a brief treatise on each akin to the one that survives. When, in passing, he tells us that the introduction of the hoplite phalanx gave rise to a modicum of democratization in the conduct of war, we should believe him; and we should do the same both when considering his observation that, in a Greek setting, warfare's democratization could hardly be sustained for long if men of middling wealth were excluded from political influence and when pondering his report that the early tyrants were nearly all populists who owed their stature to their experience in the conduct of war.[64]

As Sarpedon's speech in the *Iliad* implies, deference has to be earned over and over and over again, and one cannot expect that a smallholder or even a gentleman farmer trained and accustomed to put his life at risk in precisely the same manner as the aristocrat alongside him in the phalanx will be behindhand in demanding an equal share. In a world where men like Sarpedon and Glaukos stand out and really earn their keep as a consequence of their prowess as *prómachoi* on the field of the sword, no one will mount a serious challenge to their authority. In such circumstances, men like Hesiod in Boeotia, even when justifiably discontent, will be profoundly reluctant to defy the well-born. In such circumstances, no one will listen to the complaints of a Thersites or defend him from abuse at the hands of an Odysseus.[65] But, in a world in which well-born equestrians are outstanding only in the pretensions and arrogance they display and not at all in the services they perform, deference will not survive serious dissatisfaction; the legitimate complaints of a Thersites will be given a hearing; and some ambitious individual from among the well-born will emerge to take advantage of the discontent.

Plato, who was thoroughly familiar with the ethos of hoplite warfare and who witnessed a great deal of social conflict, knew what he was talking about when he invited his readers to consider the thoughts that "a wiry man, bereft of wealth and burnt by the sun," is likely to entertain when he is "ranged in battle next to a rich man, reared in the shade and possessed of a great deal of superfluous flesh, and then observes the latter out of breath and completely at a loss." In such circumstances, he tells us, the impecunious are likely to mutter to one another in private regarding the oligarchs who lord it over them. "These men are ours," they will say. "For they are nothing." Soldiers who are not retainers and who actually own the land they till may be obedient on the day of battle. But almost never are they servile. The spiritedness required of them in battle rules out submissiveness on their part in times of peace.[66]

Hoplite warfare was a brute fact that the Spartans had to confront. They could not ignore the implications of the new military technology. No political community has ever been able to do the like—not if its members were to have any hope of being able to defend themselves in the future. In history, there is but one iron law. Changes in military technology and tactics that give to those who introduce them a decisive advantage over their adversaries will soon be adopted elsewhere.[67]

Nor could the Spartiates evade the political consequences of this military revolution. If they were to field hoplite armies, they had to make arrangements to satisfy the needs and desires of the great body of men who served in the phalanx. In antiquity, Laconia was sometimes described as "an acropolis and guard-post for the entire Peloponnesus"—for it was, as Euripides tells us, "ringed round by mountains, rough, and difficult for foes to enter."[68] Had the Spartans limited their sphere of control to that region—cut off as it was by Mount Parnon to the east, Mount Taygetus to the west, and rugged hill country to the north—they might have been able to make do for a time with the aristocratic way of war that they had inherited.

But this they did not do, and their decision in this particular had profound consequences. Cynouria was easier to reach from Argos than from Sparta. To assert their control over the coastal strip northeast of Mount Parnon, the Spartans had to defy one geopolitical imperative. To maintain their leverage over Messenia, to the west of Mount Taygetus, they had to defy another. There was nothing natural about the little empire, amounting to nearly 3,300 square miles and constituting two-fifths of the Peloponnesus, that they had carved out for themselves in the southernmost reaches of that great peninsula.[69] Sustaining it required a single-minded devotion to the common good and artifice, skill, and discipline of the highest order.

We do not know precisely when the Spartans faced up to the implications of the changes that had taken place. They may have begun doing so before the battle of Hysiae. The festival of Apollo Carneios was reorganized seven years before, in 676. We hear of a poet from Lesbos named Terpander visiting Sparta on this occasion and of his performance at the Carneia of a poem tellingly entitled *Díkē*—"Justice"—and it is easy to imagine that the reorganization of such a festival as a celebration of justice might be occasioned by a populist political and military reform that had just taken place.[70]

But if, perchance, the Spartans had not yet come to grips with the consequences inherent in their new situation, their loss to the Argives at Hysiae seven years later will certainly have given them food for thought. It is likely that the establishment in 668 of the festival of the Gymnopaidiai—in which the poet Thaletas of Gortyn, who had been present with Terpander at the

Carneia eight years before, is thought to have played an especially prominent role—was occasioned by Sparta's defeat,[71] and it is easy to see how such a pioneering effort, resulting in a festival unique to Lacedaemon, might be connected with other innovations of a political, social, and military nature, similarly peculiar to Sparta, which were meant to have practical consequences.

But if Hysiae did not do the trick, there was one other event that occurred in this period that would have shaken from dogmatic slumber any people similarly situated. Two generations after Theopompus had brought the First Messenian War to a successful conclusion, the Messenians threw off their tributary status and staged a revolt, the Second Messenian War began, and the Argives, the Arcadians, and others within the Peloponnesus once again jumped in with glee to lend the rebels help.[72]

We do not know what occasioned this revolt. But, given its timing, it is easy to guess. When Tyrtaeus, who was a contemporary, spoke of a war fought by "the fathers of our fathers," he is likely to have said precisely what he meant—that the grandsons of the young men finally victorious in the First Messenian War had to confront the revolt that took place in his own day. This would suggest that Pausanias may have been in error when he dated its outbreak to 685, just thirty-nine years after the date he gave for the end of Sparta's original war of conquest.[73]

Elsewhere, Pausanias tells a tale suggesting a slightly later date for the Second Messenian War. The revolt purportedly centered on Andania at the entrance to the Soulima valley. Its initial stage lasted three years and came to an abrupt end when the Spartans bribed the Arcadian general Aristocrates, king of Orchomenos, and his treachery occasioned the Messenians' defeat at the Battle of the Great Trench. So the geographer reports. Kallisthenes, Polybius, and Plutarch agree, and Tyrtaeus, who described the battle, is quite likely to have been their chief source. In the aftermath, Pausanias adds, Aristomenes, the Messenian leader, retreated with his men to Mount Eira near the Neda River on the Arcadian borders. From there, he and his adherents conducted a guerrilla war for another eleven years, and the last holdouts fled from Messenia 287 years before Epaminondas' liberation of the region in 370.[74] This would mean that this particular struggle went on for fourteen years from 671 to 657.

Chronologically, the latter set of dates dovetails with another story told by Pausanias, which may well deserve credit, for it seems to have had its origins in the family lore of a well-known aristocratic clan located far afield. According to it, Aristomenes, the figure who had led the Messenian revolt, managed to escape to Arcadia after its collapse. Not long thereafter, his third daughter married Damagetus, king of Ialysos in Rhodes, and from these two the Diagoridae, renowned in subsequent centuries for their victories in the games at Olympia, Nemea, Isthmia, and Delphi, traced their descent. After conducting his daughter to Rhodes and overseeing her wedding, Aristomenes is said to have died and to have been buried there—before he could undertake a trip he intended to make to Sardis for the sake of securing support for the Messenian cause from the Lydian monarch Ardys son of Gyges, who did not succeed to the throne until 652.[75]

Of course, there is no reason to attribute to Pausanias and the sources that he drew on any great chronological precision, and the fanciful character of much of the story he relates concerning the feats of Aristomenes demonstrates that, over the generations, the tale told within the Messenian diaspora concerning their hero grew dramatically in the telling. But it does not prove the story false in its basic outlines—for there are various ways in which the saga is likely to have been conveyed to posterity.[76]

In the course of his narrative, Pausanias adds a number of details pertinent to this question. First, he reports that Hagnagora, the sister of Aristomenes, was married to Tharyx, a notable from Phigaleia, which occupies a tongue of land in southwest Arcadia wedged between Triphylia and Messenia and is situated just north of the river Neda quite close to Aristomenes' base at Mount Eira. Then, he tells us that in 659—presumably in connection with their war against Aristomenes—the Lacedaemonians seized Tharyx' hometown; that, a short time thereafter, with the help of a contingent from Oresthasion to the east, the citizens of Phigaleia recovered their *pólis;* and that, in the agora, the latter built a memorial to those from Oresthasion who had rallied to their support. This is of significance because there is excellent reason to suppose that the descendants of Tharyx were still prominent in the mid-fourth century when the Messenians recovered their liberty, and it is perfectly plausible to suppose that they and their compatriots kept alive a memory of the travails of Phigaleia, the aid lent their community by the citizens of Oresthasion, and the exploits of their kinsman Aristomenes.[77]

The story was no doubt cherished elsewhere as well. The Messenians who found refuge abroad retained a powerful sense of themselves as a nation in exile, and this they accomplished by keeping the memory of their fatherland and that of the resistance to its subjugation green. There is, moreover, reason to suppose that the Messenians who remained in their ancestral homeland as helots regarded themselves as a nation in bondage. They had families, we know; and, to judge by the results of a systematic field survey recently carried out in the vicinity of Pylos by archaeologists, these families resided not in isolation on homesteads but in villages and towns where they will have had constant contact and interaction with their brethren.[78] Furthermore, these Messenian helots worked land their ancestors had owned, and they shared common cults. They surely knew who they were, and they are apt to have kept alive a memory of the more dramatic events in their past. To dismiss in its entirety their tradition is to underestimate the capacity of the oppressed to treasure that in their own heritage which sustains the hope that they, as a people, might someday once again be free.[79]

It is, we must conclude, certain that there was a Messenian revolt in the time of Tyrtaeus, and it is plausible to suppose that it erupted at about the time suggested by the reports reviewed above and that it lasted, as Messenian tradition asserts, a decade or more. If so, two possibilities present themselves. Both turn on the revolt's proximity in time to Sparta's defeat at the battle of Hysiae in 669.

One could imagine that the Messenians rose up in revolt three or more years before that event and that the Spartans, after bribing the king of Arcadian Orchomenos and defeating the rebels at the Battle of the Great Trench, turned to the northeast to deal with the rebels' Argive allies. It is no less reasonable a guess that the Messenians rose up in revolt soon after the disaster at Hysiae. The Argives' victory over Lacedaemon in 669 could easily have provided the necessary impetus. Subjugated populations are keenly sensitive to the least hint of weakness on the part of their masters; and if offered what they take to be an opportunity, they will be quick to seize it. More, in current circumstances, we cannot know. We can only hope that the papyrologists working patiently to separate, transcribe, and make sense of the remnants of scrolls found at Oxyrhynchus in Egypt, at Herculaneum in Italy, and elsewhere come up with new evidence. If we had the poetry of Tyrtaeus in its entirety, we would certainly know more.

As things stand, however, more needs to be said. For, if we wish to understand what it was that induced the Spartans to adopt the way of life they later led; that encouraged them to establish the remarkable set of institutions which allowed them to conduct their affairs in so orderly, restrained, and sane a fashion for so many years; and that made of them men of the sort who would in obedience to the authorities in Lacedaemon lay down their lives as they did at Thermopylae, we would be well advised to consider how they came to grips with the two events we have just discussed: the military revolution of the early seventh century, and the great helot revolt that took place in its wake.

CHAPTER 4

POLITICS AND GEOPOLITICS

Rich in lovely fruit,
Irrigated by a myriad of streams and springs,
And well furnished with good pasture for cattle and sheep,
Neither bitter and stormy in the windy blasts of winter
Nor, on the contrary, rendered excessively hot by the four-horsed chariot of the sun . . .
Possessed of an excellence greater than can be expressed in words: Messenia.

—EURIPIDES

WHEN asked about the origins of their political regime and of the way of life associated with it, Spartans in and after the fifth century had a ready answer. It was all, they said, the work of a lawgiver named Lycurgus. When asked who this eminent personage was and when he lived, however, they were unsure. Someone at Lacedaemon told Herodotus that this sage lived in the time of the Agiad king Leobatas, for this is what he reports. Earlier, the poet Simonides had claimed that Lycurgus was the uncle of the Eurypontid king Charillos, who appears to have lived two or three generations after Leobatas in the middle of the eighth century; and, in due course, Aristotle—who is known to have penned (or at least commissioned) something like one hundred fifty-eight treatises charting the history and the character, when fully developed, of the various political regimes in Hellas—seconded Simonides' assertion. Hieronymus of Rhodes and others alluded to but not named by Aristotle and Plutarch made the lawgiver a contemporary of Terpander of Lesbos and Thaletas of Gortyn, the inspirational poets who twice visited Sparta—for the Carneia in 676 and to help found the Gymnopaidiai in 668.[1]

This is one source of confusion. There is another. Much of what Lycurgus is said to have done the Spartans attributed to others as well. Lycurgus and the Eurypontid king Theopompus are both credited with having established the ephorate.[2] Lycurgus and the Agiad king Polydorus are both said to have been responsible for the system of public land allotments.[3] The Great Rhetra, which appears to have governed the operations of the Spartan assembly and which is sometimes represented as an oracle from Delphi, is attributed to Lycurgus by some and to Theopompus and Polydorus by others.[4]

In what remains of his *Politeía of the Lacedaemonians,* Aristotle indicates his sensitivity to the fact that something was amiss with the oral traditions concerning the origins of the Spartan regime; and, with a measure of circumspection, he may have addressed this puzzle in that largely lost work. In the fragments of the treatise that we do possess and in his *Politics,* the peripatetic is more often than not strikingly noncommittal concerning the actual achievements of Lacedaemon's celebrated lawgiver. Sometimes, to be sure, in the latter work—where his principal aim is an analysis of the Spartan regime in its maturity, as it existed in his own time—he resorts to a species of shorthand consistent with the oral tradition, and he attributes to Lycurgus responsibility for the Lacedaemonian *politeía* as a whole. Occasionally, therein, he is quite specific and he celebrates achievements that, he evidently suspects, really were the work of an historical figure who lived long before and bore that celebrated name. More frequently, however, in what we have of both works, Aristotle prudently dodges the question of attribution, and he speaks in guarded tones either of what "they say" Lycurgus did or of what "is said" to have been done by Lycurgus; and sometimes, in *The Politics,* he pointedly evades the question of attribution altogether and describes institutions and practices for which the unnamed, generic "lawgiver" of Lacedaemon can be held responsible.[5]

Aristotle was not alone in exhibiting caution. The confusion to which the oral tradition gave rise was so great that, in fury and frustration, the fourth-century historian Timaeus of Tauromenium was driven to suggest that Spartan institutions might have been the work of two lawgivers working at different times—each named Lycurgus.[6]

For Timaeus' suggestion, there is this to be said. It is hard to imagine that the elaborate system of balances and checks fundamental to the operations of Sparta's government was the work of a single moment and man. Like the constitution of England, so much admired by Montesquieu, it was almost certainly the product of a series of compromises and adjustments; and, just as the English in early modern times were apt to defend change as a salutary return to practices employed time out of mind, so the Spartans were accustomed to attribute the accretions of the ages to the genius of a single legislator.[7]

A Tale of Two Revolutions

There is no way that we can bring full order to the confusion that this propensity introduced. Such a task was beyond the capacities of Aristotle, who knew much that has not been vouchsafed to us. We can, however, attempt to follow in the footsteps of the peripatetic and perhaps progress a few steps beyond the place where he stopped, for there is also evidence available to us that may not have been available to him, and it should enable us in some particulars to sort out fiction from fact.

It is, for example, highly unlikely that any great reform was carried out in the age of Leobatas. We first hear of Sparta acting as a political community and acquiring territory in the time of his great-grandson Archelaus,[8] whose reign overlapped with that of the Charillos whom Simonides and Aristotle identify as the nephew of Lycurgus. Moreover, what we know of the archaeology of Laconia would suggest that it was not until about this time that conditions were ripe for a warrior chieftainship based on custom, force of personality, and prowess to give way to a political community grounded in law.

We also possess one important clue. In antiquity, it was the practice both at Sparta and elsewhere to specify years by the name of one of the magistrates annually selected; and in later times, at least, there was a list of ephors eponymous comparable to the list of the archons eponymous that existed at Athens. This list reportedly went back to the year 754—when Charillos, grandfather of the Theopompus who brought the First Messenian War to a successful conclusion some decades thereafter, is likely to have been near the end of his reign. Whether the early entries on such lists are reliable is, of course, an open question. Some scholars even dismiss the Spartan list itself as a late invention. But there is other evidence strongly suggesting that the ephorate existed in eighth-century Lacedaemon, for there are inscriptions showing that the institution later existed at two colonies—Thera in the Aegean and Taras on the boot in Italy—that, as we have already had occasion to note, Sparta is said to have sent out in this period. It is, of course, conceivable that these disparate, distant, and fiercely independent communities slavishly adopted Spartan institutions long after their foundations, as some scholars hypothesize.[9] But for this unlikely possibility, there is not a single shred of evidence.

That the ephorate was established in the mid-eighth century is, moreover, perfectly plausible. In the pertinent decades, Greece appears to have undergone a political transformation. If tradition is to be believed, it was in the 750s that an elected archonship replaced at Athens hereditary kingship and lifelong rule by a member of the royal family, and it is clear that in the aftermath this city was governed by an hereditary aristocracy of men who called themselves the Eupatrids. It was at about the same time that Corinth is said to have replaced the Bacchiad kingship in that city with an annual magistrate chosen from within the sizable Bacchiad clan, and we are told that, at some point before the reign of Pheidon, who turned his kingship at Argos into a tyranny, the Heraclid monarchy of that city had had its prerogatives sharply reduced.[10]

The story told in brief by Ephorus and Aristotle and more fully elaborated by Plutarch suggests that Sparta's trajectory was a variation on this trend. Lycurgus was, they tell us, the uncle of Charillos, the rightful king, and while his nephew was under age, he had served as regent on the young man's behalf. When Charillos came to maturity, Lycurgus dutifully turned over the reins of authority, took leave of Sparta, and sailed off to Crete, where he sojourned for a time at Lyktos, the earliest known Spartan colony. At the time of its foundation, this new establishment had purportedly adopted laws of local origin, which were attributed to the island's legendary ruler Minos. When, in due course, Lycurgus returned to Sparta, he found that Charillos had come to exercise tyrannical power; and, with the help of twenty-eight Spartans from leading families, he effected an aristocratic reform inspired by, if not modeled on, the mode of governance that he had witnessed at Lyktos on Crete.[11]

This story is no doubt a simplification of the truth, and the attribution to Lycurgus of twenty-eight well-born allies makes it read as if it were an aetiological tale told to explain the origins of the aristocratic board of elders at Sparta known as the *gerousía*. There is this, however, to be said in its favor. To begin with, although Lacedaemon is the city first described in our surviving sources as being in possession of a *politeía*—a constitution, a regime, and formalities distinguishing citizens from outsiders—the evidence available strongly suggests that it was on Crete that constitutional government, the rule of law, and citizenship first emerged in Greece. Second, there was at Thera, which appears to have been settled from Lacedaemon in the middle of the eighth century during Charillos' reign, not only a king descended from its founder, as there appears to have been early on also at Taras. There was also, as we have seen, a board of ephors; and, tellingly, there is reason to believe that there was a *gerousía* as well—for that institution is known to have existed at Cyrene, which was founded by Thera in about 630, and at Euhesperides, which was founded, in all likelihood not long thereafter, by Cyrene. Moreover, officeholding on the island of Thera was restricted, as it may well have been in very early Sparta, to a narrow aristocracy—in this case, one made up of the descendants of the original settlers—and, early on, these settlers may have lorded it over a servile population, indigenous to the island, whom they called "helots."[12]

There is this to be said as well for Aristotle's dating of the reform actually carried out by Lycurgus. Those who hold an office are nearly always inclined to promote an increase in its power. Rarely, if ever, do they attempt to restrict the prerogatives that they themselves wield. It is therefore hard to imagine that a king such as Theopompus would establish a magistracy for the purpose of restricting royal power; and yet, as we have seen, this is precisely what the ephorate found at Sparta in later times was designed to do. In short, like the *gerousía,* the ephorate appears to have been instituted at a time when a concerted effort was made to rein in the two kings. The year 754 may have been a turning point in Spartan history.

To this argument, there is one obvious objection. The ephorate at Lacedaemon described by the ancient sources was a democratic office. One could apparently hold that office only once in one's lifetime; and, as we have seen, it was filled by a mysterious process—akin in its results, Plato tells us, to a lottery. This resulted in considerable power being lodged in the hands of men distinguished as nonentities by their ordinariness, whom Aristotle aptly described as *hoi túchontes:* "those who just happened along."[13] It is hard to believe that an aristocratic clique intent on restricting the prerogatives of a dual monarchy would fashion such an office.

Here again, however, the epigraphical evidence may be of use. For it shows that the boards of ephors established in Sparta's colonies on Thera and at Taras were made up of three ephors, not five; that the same was true for the two communities of *períoikoi*—Geronthrae and Taenarum—where we know with certainty the size of the board; and that this was probably the case at Kardamyle as well. It can hardly be an accident that the number of ephors in these communities corresponds with the number of Dorian tribes, and this in turn suggests that the institution responsible for oversight, which Sparta's colonists brought with them in the eighth century and that the towns of *períoikoi* adopted early on, was at that time in their common metropolis tribally based—just as, we know, Lacedaemon's army was.[14]

In later years, however, as we have seen, there were five ephors at Sparta, just as there were five *lóchoi* in the Spartan army and five *agathoergoí.* More-

over, in the early sixth century, when called upon to arbitrate a dispute between Athens and Megara over Salamis, the Lacedaemonians appointed five
commissioners; later in that century, when a colony was dispatched from
Lacedaemon, it was given five co-founders; and in the late fifth century, when
they decided to stage a trial of sorts at Plataea, the Spartans appointed a panel
of five judges. In short, in these latter days, there were as many ephors, *lóchoi,*
and *agathoergoí* at Lacedaemon as there were villages of Spartiates, and, at
least on the occasions mentioned, there were precisely as many arbitrators,
colonial co-founders, and judges.[15]

Because it is repeated over and over again, this numerical correspondence
is highly suggestive. Elsewhere—in Corinth, on Samos, at Eretria on the island of Euboea, in Athens, at Cyrene in Libya, and, on the outskirts of Magna
Graecia, in early Rome—we find evidence of there having been in the archaic
period what we would now call "tribal reforms," in which a citizen's political
identity ceased to be rooted in his membership in ancient kinship corpora-
tions of an aristocratic cast, such as the traditional Dorian tribes, and came
to be based on the accident of his residence in a particular locale; and the
magisterial boards and, at least in some cases, the army were recast to fit the
new political reality. Where such reforms took place, they appear to have been
aimed at reducing deference to the well-born and at promoting a measure of
political equality.[16]

If some such shift took place at Sparta and if it also involved the transformation of an aristocratic magistracy, created as a restraint on the city's two
kings, into a democratic magistracy, it is most likely to have taken place in the
wake of the introduction of hoplite warfare—for elsewhere, as we have seen,
this development appears to have given rise to tyrannies based on popular
resentment of a privileged aristocratic order that had outlived its raison d'être
as an instrument for community defense. There is, moreover, as we have also
seen, reason to suppose that some sort of political and social reform occurred
at Lacedaemon in connection with that city's hoplite reform and that this
transformation coincided with the reorganization of the Carneia and the establishment of the Gymnopaidiai that took place on the occasion of the visits
to Sparta of the poets Terpander of Lesbos and Thaletas of Gortyn.

The Eurypontid king Theopompus, who is said to have been succeeded by
his grandson, appears to have lived an exceedingly long life—marked, at its
end, we must suspect, by the emergence of the hoplite phalanx. We have it on
good authority that he was already king at the end of the First Messenian War

late in the eighth century; and we are told that he was still alive but incapacitated by old age, pain, and sorrow in 669 when his Agiad colleague Polydorus
was defeated in battle by the Argives at Hysiae. As we have already seen, tradition attributed to Theopompus the institution of the ephorate, to Polydorus
the establishment of a system of public land allotments, and to the two together a journey to Delphi for the purpose of securing divine sanction for the
Great Rhetra, which specified the rules governing the operations of the Spartan assembly and sanctioned the articulation of the citizen body in terms of
both the old order of tribes and the new order of villages. It is, moreover, telling
that, after its reorganization, the Carneia was structured in much the same
manner: under the presidency of three groups of five as yet unmarried *néoi*.[17]

All of this would make sense if Theopompus took the lead in effecting
a functional equivalent of the tribal reforms known to have taken place elsewhere, converting the ephorate from an aristocratic office associated with the
Dorian tribes into a democratic office representing the citizens resident in
Sparta's five villages; if the two kings joined together to carry out a reform
establishing the sovereignty at Lacedaemon of an army assembly articulated
into units defined first and foremost by place of residence and only second-
arily by tribe; and if the reorganization of the Carneia and the establishment
of the Gymnopaidiai were connected with this transformation. It would make
even better sense if after the revolt in Messenia—when there was, Tyrtaeus
testifies, social discontent, a shortage of food, and pressure for a redistribution
of land at Sparta[18]—Polydorus rallied support for a reconquest of that rich
province by promising, to the fury and dismay of aristocrats who had once
exclusively profited from the labor of those who farmed the Stenyklaros plain,
that everyone serving in Sparta's new hoplite army would be awarded by token
of his contributions as a Spartan warrior a lifetime interest in an allotment of
land farmed by Messenian helots in the territory reclaimed.

None of this should be regarded as certain.[19] But we are told that Polydorus was assassinated by an enraged aristocrat; and it is revealing that, in
later years, the ephors honored this putative champion of the common people
by having his image carved on their seal of office.[20] Moreover, the hypothesis
suggested here has the virtue of explanatory parsimony. The supposition that
Sparta's constitution contains elements frozen in place, reflecting three distinct stages—monarchical, aristocratic, and democratic—in the city's political
development, would account for the complex and seemingly contradictory
character of that city's institutions. The presumption that there were two

moments of political reform at Lacedaemon—one aristocratic, and the other democratic—would help explain why the ancient writers locate Lycurgus, variously, in the time of Charillos in the middle of the eighth century, and in that of Terpander and Thaletas three-quarters of a century thereafter. It would also help explain why the reforms that took place were attributed by some to him and by others to Theopompus, Polydorus, or the two in tandem.

Even more to the point, such an hypothesis would help make sense of the regimen that the Spartans imposed on themselves. For the *agōgḗ* with its elaborate system of age classes resembles institutions found elsewhere among tribal peoples devoted, like the early Dorians, to hunting and war; and the same can be said regarding the institution of pederasty, the rite of passage called the *krupteía,* and the practice of taking meals and sleeping with one's comrades in the *sussítion.* The survival or revival of these institutions within a fully elaborated political community is likely to have been dictated by peculiar circumstances, such as the need to reconquer, pacify, and hold Messenia while fending off the Argives and the Arcadians; and the same rationale explains the enforcement of a measure of socioeconomic equality within the master class, the practice of exercising naked at the gymnasium, the intense piety exhibited by the Spartans, and their embrace of complex political institutions apt to promote consensus and foster civic solidarity. All of the mores, manners, and ways attributed to the Lacedaemonians make sense as components within a comprehensive grand strategy aimed at protecting, preserving, and upholding the distinctive Spartan way of life. All seem quite logical when one views them from the perspective of the daunting mission that the Spartiates of Polydorus' day chose for themselves when they set out to recover Messenia; and, although some scholars now suspect that at least some of these institutions and practices may have been introduced in the sixth century, in the fifth century, or well thereafter,[21] it seems more reasonable to suppose that they were all instituted early on—as the ancient writers, who knew far more than we can ever hope to know, all presumed. It seems more reasonable to conclude that the various elements in this kaleidoscope fell into place and came to form a *kósmos* well before the late archaic lyric poet Simonides tellingly described Lacedaemon as "man-subduing [*damasímbrotos*]" in and soon after the age when Tyrtaeus first celebrated the achievement of *eunomía* at Lacedaemon.[22] It seems reasonable, in fact, to connect these practices with the fateful decision made in the time of Polydorus—when the Spartans imposed on themselves a species of necessity and chose to make a virtue of it.[23] It is similarly, in light of the renewed sense of civic purpose implicit in the audacious project that the Lacedaemonians then undertook, that one must consider the geopolitical and diplomatic dimension of the grand strategy they worked out in the wake of their suppression of the seventh-century Messenian revolt.

Messenia

In 499, a Milesian notable made his way to Sparta, intent on persuading the Lacedaemonians to support an uprising in Ionia that he had instigated against a power then dominant in Anatolia and elsewhere in western Asia. In pursuing this end, Herodotus reports, this figure tried to persuade the Agiad king Cleomenes son of Anaxandridas that an invasion of Asia would secure for Lacedaemon wealth on a scale almost unimaginable. "It is requisite," he asserted, "that you put aside your battles with the Messenians (with whom you are equally matched) over territory narrowly confined, which is neither especially extensive nor serviceable; and you must also put aside your battles with the Arcadians and the Argives, who possess none of the gold and silver for which men with eagerness fight to the death."[24]

We do not know whether Herodotus accurately described the interchange between the two men. It is conceivable that, many years later, he managed to interview Cleomenes' daughter Gorgo, who, as a youngster, figures prominently in the tale. It is also conceivable (but not at all likely) that he invented the dialogue himself. Either way, however, the story is telling. For, at the very least, it indicates what Greeks in the mid-to-late fifth century thought they knew about the focus of Spartan policy in and before the sixth century—and what they thought they knew is, of course, quite likely to be true.

When one ponders the implications of Sparta's involvement in Messenia, it is with the geographical challenge that one must begin.[25] It cannot have been easy to get a hoplite army from Sparta to Messenia. Mount Taygetus, which lies between the two, was then and is now a formidable obstacle. Today, of course, there is a modern road that runs from Sparta to Kalamata on the Messenian Gulf by way of the Langadha pass. In antiquity, there was a steep road, which the Spartans had rendered fit for carts, that took this route. An individual or small group might with effort have passed this way or by the path that lies a short way to the south, and either may have been the route that Homer charted for Odysseus' son Telemachus when he sent him in the company of Nestor's son Peisistratus from Pylos via Pherae by chariot to Menelaus at Lace-

Map 4. Mount Taygetus and Messenia

daemon.[26] In the eighth century, the Agiad king Teleklos is also likely to have
followed one of these paths—when he conducted Sparta's colonists to the
Nedon valley upstream from ancient Pherae on the mountain's western slopes,
when he seized or colonized Pherae itself, and when he journeyed to the sanctuary of Artemis Limnatis—for the Dentheliatis region, wherein the Nedon
valley is to be found, and the sanctuary near the head of the Choireios gorge
can both easily be reached from the more southerly of these two tracks. The
journey there cannot, however, have been easy.

Sixteen miles directly south of Sparta, there is another pass over Taygetus
—over which a road, made to accommodate carts, ran from the modern village of Xirokambi—where, at Agios Vasileios, a Mycenaean palace, fragments
of frescoes, and Linear B tablets have recently been discovered[27]—across the
mountain to Kardamyle well south of Pherae on the Messenian Gulf. But it is
a trek more demanding yet. Neither pass was well-suited to an army made up
of heavily armed infantrymen, for at times they would have had to march in
something approaching single file, and they would have been highly vulnerable to ambush by light-armed troops experienced in a species of combat better suited to the terrain. Something of the sort was true as well for the path
leading from the modern village of Georgitsi, on the eastern slope of Taygetus
some eighteen miles to the northwest of Sparta, over a high mountain pass
to its counterparts Neochori and Dyrrhachi on the western slope, then down
from there. For, although less daunting, this path was also ill-suited to soldiers
loaded down with the hoplite panoply and with other gear.

Further south, there is today another modern road linking the ancient
Lacedaemonian port of Gytheion on the Laconian Gulf with the modern village of Areopolis on the Messenian Gulf. But if this route was perfectly man-
ageable for travelers, it was far from ideal for an army, for the trek that one
would have had to make was laborious and long. Southwest one would have
marched from Gytheion to Las, then across the peninsula to ancient Oitylos,
and north along the Messenian Gulf past Thalamai, Pephnus, Leuctron, and
Kardamyle. From there, one would have had to round the spur of Taygetus
called Kalathion and make one's way up along the coast, inland around the
Choireios gorge, then westward back to the coast, and northward again along
the Messenian Gulf below Kalamai to Pherae at the bottom of the great plain
called Makaria in the lower Pamisos valley.

In an emergency, Spartans intent on reaching the Pamisos valley in a
hurry will almost certainly have taken the Langadha Pass or the path just to

the south—for the colonies planted along the Nedon River will have afforded them protection on their descent into the heartland of Messenia. That Telekos had in mind something of the sort when he established these colonies in the first place cannot be ruled out. The Messenians said to have murdered him at the sanctuary of Artemis Limnatis may have understood what was at stake. Rarely were the Spartans oblivious to the geostrategic implications of what they did.

For soldiers in no great hurry, there was a much easier road, leading from central Laconia to the Stenyklaros plain on the upper reaches of the Pamisos River. This thoroughfare runs north by northwest from Sparta up the Eurotas River, into the southern reaches of Arcadia via the Belminatis, around the northernmost spur of Mount Taygetus near the settlement of Leuctron (modern Leontari), then westward across the southern reaches of a high plateau, and finally southwest down into Messenia via the Derveni Pass followed by the modern highway. Though long, this road was in no way arduous. Indeed, for heavy infantry loaded with gear and for carts carrying additional provisions, it must have seemed ideal.[28]

We do not know when the Spartans began using the last of these paths as their main route into Messenia. The odds are good, however, that they were unable to do so early on, during the First Messenian War and the seventh-century Messenian revolt, for the Arcadians—through whose territory they would have had to march—were then allied with the Messenians; and the people of the Arcadian town of Oresthasion, which lay not far from that route in what would later be called the Megalopolitan plain, were at this time particularly hostile to the Lacedaemonians, as we have already had occasion to note. It is, moreover, telling that the Agiad king Alcamenes' first reported act when he launched the first of these two wars in the 740s or 730s was to seize Ampheia in northeast Messenia. For this town was located, scholars suspect, on the western slope of Mount Taygetus above the Stenyklaros plain in the vicinity of the Gardiki fortress, which was built in later times near the end of the trail that now leads over the mountain from Georgitsi to Neochori and Dyrrachi and then by way of Akobos to Tourkoleka.[29]

That the carriage road through southwest Arcadia was vital in later times to Sparta's retention of Messenia, however, we need not doubt. For this there can be no better testimony than that offered in deed shortly after Lacedaemon's decisive defeat at the battle of Leuctra by the canny Theban statesman Epaminondas. When he liberated the Messenians from Spartan rule in 369 and had the city of Messene built on the slopes of Mount Ithome, Lacedaemon's greatest enemy also encouraged the Arcadians to construct the city of Megalopolis a few miles north of this strategic road. In so doing, he placed this new *pólis* almost squarely in the way of any invading force that the Spartans might send through Arcadia against Messenia, situating it northwest of the northernmost spur of Taygetus in the center of the great upland plateau through the southern reaches of which runs the road from Laconia to the Derveni Pass and into Messenia.[30]

That Epaminondas was a visionary cannot be doubted, and reflection on this should give us pause. For it highlights the importance for Sparta of the Arcadians and the significance in the eighth century, as in the fourth, of the alliance that this highland people formed both with the Messenians and with the Argives, Sparta's traditional enemy to the northeast. As Aristotle makes clear, when Herodotus had the Milesian adventurer who visited Cleomenes in Lacedaemon stress the importance of Sparta's relations with the Messenians, the Arcadians, and the Argives, he knew whereof he spoke.[31]

The Argives appear to have been a thorn in Sparta's side from the start. Early on, they were the dominant power in the Peloponnesus, and communities such as Sicyon, Aegina, and Epidaurus recognized their hegemony. Herodotus reports that, at this time, Argos controlled the eastern coastline of the Peloponnesus, including Cynouria, all the way down to Cape Malea—as well as the island of Cythera, just off Laconia's southern coast. This claim is consistent with the report of Pausanias the geographer that the Argives helped the people of Helos in the southernmost reaches of the Eurotas valley resist Alcamenes' attack—for, had they not controlled a stronghold nearby, at Epidauros Limera or on Cythera, they would not have been in a position to come to Helos' aid.[32]

There is another report suggesting the importance of Lacedaemon's rivalry with Argos at this time. We are told that, with the help of the people of Asine on the coast to the southeast of Argos, Alcamenes' Eurypontid colleague Nikandros ravaged the Argolid. This report is almost certainly true, for the archaeological record is consistent with Pausanias' further claim that Argos eventually took revenge by destroying Asine at some point in the course of the First Messenian War and that, in the war's aftermath, the Spartans relocated the people of this Dryopian city to a like-named community at a strategic location on the east coast of Cape Akritas in southern Messenia.[33]

Concerning the Arcadians prior to the Persian Wars, we are less well-informed. Pausanias has much to say, to be sure. But it is clear that his exceptionally detailed narrative has been contaminated by the propaganda associated with the liberation of Messenia from Spartan control effected by the Thebans and by the propaganda generated in the same period when the Arcadian League was established. It would, nonetheless, be a mistake to reject his narrative in its entirety, for Pausanias had available to him a literary treasure that we in large measure lack—the poetry of Tyrtaeus in its entirety—and, as we have seen, it is highly unlikely that the stories told by the Messenians and the Arcadians in the fourth century were invented out of whole cloth. There was, after all, an eighth-century war of conquest, and there must have been considerable resistance on the part of the conquered or it would not have lasted twenty years. Moreover, we need not doubt that there was a seventh-century rebellion followed by a long war that severely tested Sparta's mettle, and Tyrtaeus testifies to the involvement of the Arcadians and the Argives in the latter.[34] Events of such a magnitude rarely pass into oblivion.

We should probably not think of early eighth-century Messenia as a single entity. The archaeological record suggests that, in the Mycenaean period, the large, exceedingly fertile region governed from Pylos on Messenia's western shore was more densely settled and more fully integrated than any other district in Greece. Messenia's fate in the aftermath of the Mycenaean collapse appears, however, to have been quite similar to that of Laconia. The region has been surveyed with some care, and there is not much evidence for the presence of a settled population prior to the ninth and eighth centuries. Moreover, if there was a major settlement of the sort that emerged in the vicinity of what would later be the Spartan acropolis in Laconia, it has not yet been found.

Here, however, caution is in order. In the upper Pamisos valley and in the Soulima valley nearby, very little systematic digging has been done; and in such circumstances, as recent discoveries at Troy in Asia Minor should serve to remind us, it is a mistake to base firm conclusions on the presumption that what has not yet turned up does not exist. The literary evidence—and here what we have of Tyrtaeus is helpful—suggests that, in the First Messenian War, the struggle centered on the Stenyklaros plain below Ampheia and that it culminated in a battle near Mount Ithome, where, at the foot of the mountain, soundings on the part of archaeologists leave little doubt as to the presence in this period of an archaic-period settlement of some size in need of further exploration.[35]

It is also pertinent that Sparta's original war of conquest lasted for twenty

years—for, even if the peoples living on or near the Stenyklaros plain initially
had little, if any sense of common ethnic identity before the struggle began, as
some scholars of a postmodern bent are now inclined to imagine, two decades
of intermittent warfare in which they managed to join together and fend off
for a time the Spartan juggernaut will surely have forged one for them, and a
similar argument can be made regarding the seventh-century Messenian revolt, which lasted for a considerable stretch of time as well.[36] There is, moreover, no reason to discount the reports that the Argives and the Arcadians
backed the residents of the Stenyklaros plain in resisting Spartan attacks
during the First Messenian War, for we know that they lent support to the
Messenians two generations later at the time of their revolt. That the Messenian helots of the sixth, fifth, and fourth centuries had an heroic past on which
to look back we need not doubt.

How the Spartans managed, in either of these two struggles, to overcome
the obstacle posed by Arcadia and Argos we do not know with certitude. It
must, however, have been quite a feat, and in the aftermath, the Spartans must
have given considerable thought to permanently solving the problem posed by
the Arcadians. As I have already remarked, we have it on very good authority—
that of Tyrtaeus—that the Argives and the Arcadians were once again involved
in the fighting occasioned by the Messenian revolt. Pausanias the geographer,
our principal source, clearly drew heavily on Tyrtaeus when he composed his
narrative. We should not be quick to dismiss his claim that Sparta's ultimate
defeat of the Messenians at the Battle of the Great Trench was made possible
by the absence of the Argives on this occasion and by the treachery of Aristocrates, king of Arcadian Orchomenos. Moreover, Pausanias' account of Sparta's
conquest of Phigaleia on the Neda River in southwestern Arcadia around 659
and of the role played by the citizens of Oresthasion in bringing about her
subsequent loss of the town makes perfect political and geopolitical sense in
this context. As we have seen, Aristomenes' sister is said to have married a
notable from Phigaleia, and Pausanias reports that—while, initially, the focus
of the revolt in Messenia was Andania in the north of that land near the entrance to the Soulima valley—after the Battle of the Great Trench the Messenian leader and his compatriots continued the struggle for many long years,
fighting a guerrilla war from a base at Eira near the Neda River on the border
between Messenia and Arcadia at a location quite close to Phigaleia.

Pausanias' narrative suggests that Sparta's pacification of Messenia took
place in stages over a great many years. We even hear of fighting near Pylos on

the west coast in the latter part of the century in the time of Polydorus' grandson Anaxandros, and there was apparently fighting toward the end of the century in the time of the elder Leotychidas, a descendant of Theopompus. This, too, makes sense. Given the size of Messenia, the magnitude of the task, and the apparent diversity of its population, half measures were inevitable, but experience would eventually reveal that they could not suffice. A conquest said to have begun—as we would expect, given the military technology of the time—with raids in the Stenyklaros plain could not be fully consolidated if the peripheral districts were left to their own devices. Coming to grips with the consequences of this unfortunate strategic fact may well have occupied the Spartans throughout the seventh century. This would explain the second of the two claims made regarding Epaminondas' liberation of Messenia in 370: that it was accomplished 230 years after that province fell under the Lacedaemonian yoke.[37]

We know next to nothing about Sparta's ultimate organization of her domain in Messenia. There were communities of *períoikoi* south of the Steynklaros plain—at Thouria overlooking the Makaria plain, at Kardamyle and Pherae on the Messenian Gulf, at various sites along the Nedon River on the flanks of Mount Taygetus, at Kalamai inland from the Messenian Gulf, at Korone and Asine on the peninsula ending at Cape Akritas, and at Mothone on the coast in the far southwest, where, we are told, the Spartans settled a population driven from Nauplia by the Argives. Communities of this sort existed as well along the western coast at Koryphasion near Pylos, at Kyparissia to the north, and at Aulon south of the Neda River; and Ampheia, to the northeast on the lower slopes of Mount Taygetus, may have been a community of *períoikoi* as well. That there were others located in the marginal areas within both Laconia and Messenia is certain, and there may well have been as many such communities in the Spartan domain as the one hundred claimed by Androtion.[38]

The field surveys that have been taken suggest that, on the periphery, where the *períoikoi* lived, nucleated settlements were in Messenia, as in Laconia, the norm. In the Soulima valley and to the west of it, however, there are two sites with the remains of extensive buildings at Vasilikò and Kopanaki, and this has sparked speculation that, in Messenia, the helots were set to work on great plantations under the direction of overseers—for in the areas of that province thought to have been worked by servile labor, there is, to date, evidence from the period of Spartan domination for villages and even towns but none for isolated farmsteads of the sort found in large numbers elsewhere in Greece.[39] Regarding such questions, we are, at least for the time being, left to guess.

Five things can, nonetheless, be assumed. First, in the period between the original Spartan conquest and their seventh-century revolt, the Messenians were a tributary people—from whom the Lacedaemonian aristocrats, operating as raiders, extracted one-half of their harvest every year. Second, after the Second Messenian War, ritualized aristocratic raiding gave way to direct rule and systematic exploitation, and equal allotments of land were assigned individual Spartan hoplites. Third, by the time that the seventh-century revolt was fully over, these allotments were farmed largely by Messenians reduced to the status of helots, and a quantum had replaced the earlier quota—with a rent in kind, specified by Spartan law, owed each allotment's proprietor.[40] Fourth, there were overseers—drawn, at least in part, from the Spartan population—who made sure that the work got done and that the produce was delivered;[41] and fifth, west of Mount Taygetus there were substantial Spartan garrisons.

This last point needs emphasis. Lacedaemon could not have retained her hold over so large a population situated in nucleated settlements on so vast a territory had she not continually and forcefully made her presence felt. Moreover, in the mountainous areas within Messenia and on its borders, which were sizable, there was ample territory in which runaways could hide and form gangs of bandits capable, if the lowlands were left unpoliced, of fomenting unrest. Pausanias' reports, suggesting the importance of guerrilla warfare, should not be rejected out of hand. Given the nature of the terrain, it would be surprising were this not so. Here again, an absence of evidence should not be interpreted as evidence of absence. If we know next to nothing concerning the administrative apparatus that Lacedaemon deployed for the purpose of retaining her hold on this rich province, it is because of the policy of secrecy identified by Thucydides.[42]

The Spartan Alliance

As was only natural, when the Spartans had finally arranged matters in Messenia to their own satisfaction, they turned to Arcadia, their neighbor to the north. Initially, however, they did not enjoy good fortune. Theopompus of Chios tells of their loss of a battle off in the direction of Arcadian Orchomenos,[43] and they had even worse luck when they tried to subjugate Tegea.

When the Lacedaemonians—eager for the conquest of Arcadia and intent on dividing its farmland into allotments and on reducing its population to the status of helots—approached, as was their wont, the Delphic oracle for support, their search for assurance was frustrated. Arcadia by Apollo they were denied. But Tegea, within the confines of that region, they were not begrudged—or so it seemed. There the Pythia offered them a dance floor to tread upon and a lovely plain to measure with a line. What they did not know—and learned only when they showed up for battle with fetters for the purposing of enslaving the Tegeans—was that they were destined to lose that battle and that some of them would subsequently wear those fetters while laboring on that beautiful plain themselves.[44]

Thereafter, Herodotus and Pausanias tell us, the Spartans consulted the oracle at Delphi a second time to ask what god they needed to propitiate before they could defeat the Tegeans. On this occasion, they were instructed to bring the bones of Orestes son of Agamemnon back to Sparta; and, when they asked where these were to be found, they were given an enigmatic oracle, directing them to Tegea—where, they were told, that city's heroic guardian was lodged. It was, Herodotus adds, Lichas, one of the *agathoergoí,* who found and retrieved the bones. From then on, in their battles with Tegea, the Spartans are said to have been victorious, and much of the Peloponnesus soon came under their sway.[45]

We do not know precisely when the Spartans suffered defeat in the Battle of the Fetters. Herodotus reports, however, that, in the reign of Leon and Hegesicles early in the sixth century, the Lacedaemonians were successful in all of their endeavors except in those against the Tegeans; and he then goes on to tell us that it was during the reign of Anaxandridas and Ariston in and before the mid-540s, when Croesus neared the end of his reign in Lydia, that they secured their hegemony within the Peloponnesus.[46]

Sparta could not have accomplished this had she not altered her policy. The initial spadework seems, however, to have been done not in Sparta but in Argos. The Argive king Meltas, who lived in the late seventh and early sixth centuries, seems to have been involved in the contests between Sparta and Tegea, for he is credited with having fought a difficult war against Lacedaemon alongside Argos' Arcadian allies, for whom he regained some territory hitherto lost. Although this won him gratitude in Arcadia, the losses that they suffered did not please the Argives, who drove him from Argos—whence, in telling fashion, he fled for protection to his beneficiaries in Tegea.[47]

This seems to have provided Sparta with an opening, and Lichas' purported recovery of the bones of Orestes must be read as part of a diplomatic offensive on Sparta's part—especially since it appears that, at about the same time, the Spartans claimed to have recovered from Achaea on the north coast of the Peloponnesus the bones of Orestes' son Teisamenos.[48] In this fashion, the Spartans were asserting that their Heraclid kings—who were supposed to be Achaeans on the Homeric model, we must remember, and not Dorians at all—were the rightful heirs of Tyndareus, Atreus, Agamemnon and Menelaus, Orestes, and Teisamenos and that, as such, they were the natural leaders of those within the Peloponnesus who regarded themselves as the remnants of Homer's Achaeans, Danaans, and Argives.[49]

In the process, the Spartans eventually had to renounce their quest to enslave the Tegeans and to offer to defend them against the Argives, who had in a dramatic manner driven out their own Heraclid king and repudiated their traditional alliance with the Arcadians. In turn, the Tegeans had to agree not only to cease making citizens of the Messenians who crossed the border in search of asylum, as had been their custom, but also to expel these refugees from their territory.[50]

The treaty recording this pledge was inscribed on a stone slab set up on the banks of the Alpheios River. We are not, however, informed whether this monument was placed, as some scholars suppose, on the Spartan-Tegean frontier where a river of that name ran east of Caryae or located, as others suspect, considerably further west on the Alpheios where it ran between Oresthasion and Leuctron through the plain immediately to the north of Messenia; and we do not know whether this strategically vital district in southwestern Arcadia had come under the control of Tegea in the years following the Second Messenian War—though the concessions extracted at this time from the citizens of that *pólis* might be taken to imply as much.[51] Nor are we told whether, at this time, the Tegeans made a formal commitment to come to Lacedaemon's aid should there be a helot revolt. But, in the circumstances, this seems highly likely. Never for a moment did the Spartans lose sight of the helot threat.[52]

Reaching a settlement with Tegea was one dimension of Sparta's new policy. There seems to have been another dimension as well. For at about the same time—if not, in fact, a decade or two earlier—the Lacedaemonians began presenting themselves to their neighbors as the stalwart friends of liberty and as enemies to tyranny. We do not know precisely when the Spartans adopted this posture and began their policy of ousting tyrants and sponsoring oligarchies in the cities of Greece. By 504, however, they were so renowned for this policy that a Corinthian could not only take them to task for proposing to depart from it. By doing so before an assembly of their Peloponnesian allies, he could also actually hold them to this standard and even force them to abandon their plans for a change of course. It was, he implied, unthinkable that they should jettison the policy that had given them within Hellas the extraordinary moral authority that they then possessed. "The sky will be found beneath the earth and the earth above the sky," he is said to have proclaimed, "and human beings will have their dwelling-place in the sea and the fish, theirs where men were formerly—when you, Lacedaemonians, overturn the equal sharing of power [*ısokratía*] and prepare to bring back tyrannies in the cities."[53]

Plutarch mentions a number of tyrants whom the Lacedaemonians ousted. The earliest among these were the Cypselids of Corinth and Ambracia and Aeschines of Sicyon, the last of the Orthagorids. We also possess in fragmentary form a papyrus mentioning the Agiad king Anaxandridas and a Spartiate named Chilon, who is elsewhere said to have held office as ephor in or soon after 556/55 and to have been elected to the *gerousía* after he reached the age of eligibility. The document expressly links the latter with Aeschines' expulsion from power.[54]

This Chilon, who became ephor at a time when he was already advanced in age, was a consequential man. He was celebrated as one of the Seven Sages of Greece, and Aristotle attributes to him the Greek moral precept *Mēdèn ágan*—"Nothing too much!" At Sparta, he is said to have made the ephorate as important as the kingship. He clearly made a difference, and we can easily guess how, for there is evidence suggesting that he may have been the architect of Sparta's bid for hegemony within the Peloponnesus.[55]

By Herodotus we are told a remarkable story concerning Anaxandridas. This Agiad king is said to have married his sister's daughter and—despite the homoerotic ethos of ancient Lacedaemon and the practice of wife-sharing— to have become exceptionally fond of the dame. Because, however, his wife had borne him no son and heir, the ephors urged him to divorce her and marry another woman. When he refused, the ephors consulted with the *gérontes* and presented him with another suggestion, intimating that, if he did not take it, there would be dire consequences. He was on this occasion asked to marry a second wife, and this—no doubt reluctantly—he in obedience did. We do not know whether Chilon was a member of the board of ephors that made Anaxandridas an offer he could not refuse, but we can reasonably presume that he had something to do with the outcome, for the woman that the king ended up marrying was none other than Chilon's niece or second cousin.[56]

Anaxandridas' son by this second wife was his successor Cleomenes; and later, when the latter in turn was king, he involved himself in an effort to duplicate at Athens Chilon's feat in suppressing tyranny at Sicyon. Moreover, when a priest tried to bar him on ethnic grounds from entering a temple on the Athenian acropolis, Cleomenes forced his way in, asserting that he was not himself a Dorian, but an Achaean.[57]

There is additional evidence pertinent to the shift in Spartan policy. After the birth of this Cleomenes, Anaxandridas' hitherto barren first wife unexpectedly bore him first one son and then two others. The Agiad king seized upon the arrival of the firstborn of these as an occasion in which to signal his opposition to the diplomatic revolution that Chilon appears to have initiated and that his own son by Chilon's kinswoman would later seek to extend, and he did so by the simple expedient of naming the infant Dorieus—"the Dorian." It is telling that—a few decades thereafter, when Cleomenes was king—another figure in the Peloponnesus, almost certainly a Spartan, is recorded as having named his son Philachaios—"Friend of the Achaean"—for this says much about the ideological divide opened up at Lacedaemon over this question.[58]

That so radical a shift in policy should initially produce such a divide makes good sense. There is, moreover, reason to suspect that it had, at least in the short term, untoward domestic consequences. In the wake of her reconquest of Messenia, Lacedaemon's citizen population appears to have grown dramatically; and, in time, the number of Spartiates apparently came to exceed the number of available allotments. It is only on this presumption that Sparta's astonishing aggressiveness is fully intelligible. Lacedaemon's aim had not just been to seize the Tegean plain. The Spartans had brought with them fetters. Their goal was to reduce the population of Tegea to servitude; and, to Spartiates who were bereft, they evidently intended to distribute allotments of land and helots to work it. To befriend the Tegeans, then, was not just to renounce territorial claims. It was to leave in the lurch those among the citizens' sons who had been shorted in life's lottery. This must have left some at Sparta exceedingly discontent, and it is worth asking whether something might not have been done by way of compensation on behalf of Spartiate offspring left by the city unprovided.

As it happens, in the immediate aftermath of this abrupt change in Spartan foreign policy, there is clear-cut archaeological evidence for internal migration within Laconia on a considerable scale. It was in the mid-sixth century that individual farmsteads, villas, and hamlets first appeared in districts hitherto unsettled, located on the margins of the Spartan plain and elsewhere in Laconia.[59]

Moreover, four decades subsequent to Chilon's ephorate—some years after Anaxandridas had died and Cleomenes had been chosen as his successor in preference to Dorieus—the latter was given the authority to found a colony, and there appears to have been no shortage of Spartiates willing to join the living embodiment of the old "Dorian" policy in this intrinsically risky endeavor.[60] The change in Sparta's posture with regard to her neighbors appears to have had as its consequence not only the emergence of new settlements in the hinterland of Laconia but also a colonial enterprise reminiscent of the one mounted in 706 by the so-called *Partheníai*.

In retrospect—whatever misgivings Anaxandridas and the land-hungry among his compatriots may have harbored—no one can gainsay the wisdom of or the grand strategic vision underpinning Sparta's new policy. For, if ever there was a satiated power, Lacedaemon was it. When the Spartans first invaded the upper Pamisos valley, they may well have had only booty in mind. When, however, they set out to recover that land in the wake of the seventh-century Messenian revolt, they were committing themselves to a monumental quest. There were never more than nine or ten thousand Spartiates. Messenia was, by Greek standards, vast; and there were no natural barriers within the region favorable to permanently sequestering a part of it. To reconquer and then retain the Stenyklaros plain, the Spartans discovered that they had to seize and administer Messenia in its entirety. Given the number of helots that they had to police, the fact that in Messenia these helots saw themselves as a people in bondage, and the overall geopolitical situation, the Spartans could not hope to hold the region indefinitely unless they could find a way to turn their fellow Peloponnesians—the Arcadians, first of all—into faithful allies.

The old "Dorian" policy of conquest and enslavement would no longer do. Lacedaemon did not have and would never have the manpower with which to pursue it. The "Achaean" policy of overthrowing tyranny, of sponsoring oligarchy, and providing protection in return for allegiance was for Sparta the only way forward; and, when implemented, it turned out to be a phenomenal success. For, by this means, the Lacedaemonians managed to draw into alliance every major city in the Peloponnesus apart from Argos;[61] and an elaborate system of cart roads, built on a single gauge with an eye to linking the ancient political communities of that great peninsula, survives in fragments to this day as mute testimony to the magnificence of Sparta's achievement.[62] If Chilon really was the architect of Lacedaemon's hegemony within the Peloponnesus, as we have reason to suppose, and if *Mēdèn ágan* was the advice he gave his countrymen, he fully deserved to be considered one of the Seven Sages of Greece.

CONCLUSION
A Grand Strategy for Lacedaemon

HERODOTUS once described Sparta as a *kósmos,* and Plutarch later followed his lead. It was not always such. But, in the course of the archaic period, with the establishment there of the condition of good order and lawfulness that the ancients from Homer, Hesiod, Tyrtaeus, and Alcman on called *eunomía,* this is precisely what Lacedaemon became: a meticulously, more or less coherently ordered whole—apt to elicit admiration.[1] As a ruling order, the Spartiates constituted a seigneurial class blessed with leisure and devoted to a common way of life centered on the fostering of certain manly virtues. They made music together, these Spartans. There was very little that they did alone. Together they sang and they danced, they worked out, they competed in sports, they boxed and wrestled, they hunted, they dined, they cracked jokes, and they took their repose. Theirs was a rough-and-tumble world, but it was not bereft of refinement and it was not characterized by an ethos of grim austerity, as some have supposed.[2] Theirs was, in fact, a life of great privilege and pleasure enlivened by a spirit of rivalry as fierce as it was friendly. The manner in which they mixed music with gymnastic and fellowship with competition caused them to be credited with *eudaimonía*—the happiness and success that everyone craved—and it made them the envy of Hellas.[3] This gentlemanly modus vivendi had, however, one precondition: Lacedaemon's continued dominion over Laconia and Messenia and her brutal subjection of the helots on both sides of Mount Taygetus.

The grand strategy the Lacedaemonians gradually articulated in defense of the way of life they so cherished was all-encompassing, as successful grand strategies often are.[4] Of necessity, it had domestic consequences on a considerable scale. As we have seen, its dictates go a long way toward explaining the Spartans' aversion to commerce; their practice of infanticide; their provision for every citizen of an equal allotment of land and of servants to work it; the city's sumptuary laws; their sharing of slaves, horses, and hounds; their intense piety; the subjection of their male offspring to an elaborate system of education and indoctrination; their use of music and poetry to instill a civic spirit; their practice of pederasty; the rigors and discipline to which they habitually subjected themselves; and, of course, their constant preparation for war. It accounts as well for the articulation over time within Lacedaemon of a mixed regime graced with elaborate balances and checks. To sustain their dominion in Laconia and Messenia and to maintain the helots in bondage, the Spartans had to eschew faction; foster among themselves the same opinions, passions, and interests; and employ—above all, in times of strain—procedures, recognized as fair and just, by which to reach a stable political consensus consistent with the dictates of prudence.

Not surprisingly, this grand strategy had serious consequences for Lacedaemon's posture in the international sphere as well. The Spartans' perch was precarious. The Corinthian leader who compared their polity with a stream was right. Rivers really do grow in strength as other streams empty into them, and the like could be said of the Lacedaemonians: "There, in the place where they emerge, they are alone; but as they continue and gather cities under their control, they become more numerous and harder to fight."[5] Even when their population was at its height, the Spartans were few in number, and the territory they ruled was comparatively vast. The underlings they exploited were astonishingly numerous and apt to be rebellious. In Messenia, if not also in Laconia, the helots saw themselves as a people in bondage, and geography did not favor the haughty men who kept them in that condition. The Spartans could look to the *períoikoi* for support, and this they did. But the latter were not all that numerous, and it was never entirely certain that they could be relied on. They, too, had to be overawed. In the long run, the Spartans could not sustain their way of life if they did not recruit allies outside their stronghold in the southern Peloponnesus.

As we have seen, it took the Lacedaemonians some time to sort out in full the implications of their position. Early on, at least, trial and error governed their approach to the formulation of policy. But by the middle of the sixth century, Chilon and others had come to recognize that, if their compatriots did not find some way to leverage the manpower of their neighbors, they would themselves someday come a cropper. And so the Spartiates reluctantly aban-doned the dream of further expansion, repositioned themselves as defenders of Arcadian autonomy, and presented themselves to the Hellenic world as the scourge of tyranny, the champions of liberty, the friends of oligarchy, and the heirs of Agamemnon. It was under this banner that they rearranged the affairs of their fellow Peloponnesians to their liking and founded a grand alliance de-signed to keep their Argive enemies out, the helots down, and the Arcadians, above all others, in.

Taken as a whole, the grand strategy of classical Lacedaemon was bril-liantly designed for the purpose it was intended to serve. It had, however, one grave defect. It presupposed that for all practical purposes, under Sparta's he-gemony, the Peloponnesus was a world unto itself—which, of course, it was . . . at the time that this strategy was first formulated.[6] If, however, there ever came a moment when a power equal to or greater than Lacedaemon appeared in force—or even threatened to appear—at or near the entrance to that great peninsula, the Spartans would have to rethink this strategy and recast it to meet an unanticipated challenge.

It was in or quite soon after the mid-540s that such a prospect first loomed in the distance on the horizon. As we shall see in the sequel to this volume, although the Spartans were by no means slow to take note of the challenge they faced, they were exceedingly cautious in the mode of proceeding that they then adopted.

Appendix 1
Land Tenure in Archaic Sparta

WE can be reasonably confident that, in the middle of the fourth century, land at Lacedaemon was held as private property, and one was free to give or bequeath it as one wished. That is the system described and criticized by Aristotle in *The Politics* (1270a15–33)—where he speaks of these matters in the present tense and ostentatiously sidesteps referring to Lycurgus, preferring in a generic fashion to attribute the arrangements he describes to a nameless "lawgiver."[1] There can, moreover, be no doubt that private property and marked differences in wealth existed in archaic and classical Lacedaemon. Alcman, Alcaeus, and Herodotus take this for granted, and Thucydides and Xenophon provide confirming evidence for the late fifth century.[2]

There is, however, evidence for the existence of another, much more egalitarian system of land tenure in early Sparta.[3] Plutarch describes this system in various ways. In one passage in his *Life of Lycurgus* (16.1), he seems to say that Lacedaemon assigned to each newborn Spartiate boy, if he was judged healthy by the elders of his tribe, one of the nine thousand allotments of land [*klêros*] said earlier in the biography to have been created and distributed either by Lycurgus alone or by Lycurgus in part and in part also by the Agiad king Polydorus (8.2–4).[4] In his *Life of Agis* (5), however, Plutarch seems to indicate that the *klêros* ordinarily passed intact from father to son.

Plutarch's two accounts are to some degree at odds with one another. But this they have in common: a conviction that early on, thanks to political arrangements, every full-fledged member of the citizen body was guaranteed by way of public provision a competence in the form of an allotment of land, the helots to work it, and a guaranteed income.[5] With this general claim, Isocrates (11.18) appears to be in agreement, and the same can be said for Polybius (6.45, 48.3)—who, in passages in which he is clearly drawing on the diligent and well-informed fourth-century historian Ephorus, asserts that no Spartan was allowed to own more in the way of landed property than any other and that every Spartan was guaranteed a share in what he calls the *polɪtɪkè chóra.*

It does not make sense to suppose that Plutarch blindly copied one account of the land-tenure system from one source and another from another source. He was not a mere copyist slavishly following one earlier writer, then another. When he wrote on a subject, he ordinarily read a great variety of sources; he compared them with a critical eye, considering their relative plausibility; and he either chose among them on grounds he specified or left it to the reader to do the choosing.[6] In this case, it seems likely that his selection of language in the first of these passages was misleading—that, in this passage, what Plutarch meant to convey was that the elders of the tribe authorized the assignment of an allotment to the boy and that in the other passages he described the manner in which this system ordinarily operated: the transfer of the *klêros* from the father to his son. When the citizen in possession of a *klêros* had no son, possession could presumably be reassigned to the second or third son of a citizen who was blessed with an abundance of male offspring. According to Plutarch (*Mor.* 238e), only those who completed the *agōgé* could make good on this claim, and anyone of citizen birth who successfully did so had the right to an allotment.[7]

Such an arrangement was proposed by the Athenian Stranger in Plato's *Laws* (5.745b–e, 11.923c–924a); and, like other institutions suggested by Plato's chief interlocutor, it may well be a variation on a Spartan original. One might, of course, argue that the Stranger's failure to make explicit reference to Lacedaemon in the pertinent passages proves that no such arrangement ever existed at Sparta,[8] and it is true that the Athenian Stranger sometimes acknowledges to his Spartan and Cretan companions the source of his inspiration. But he does not always do so, especially when his debt would have been obvious to well-informed contemporaries;[9] and we must remember that *The Laws* is a dialogue, not a treatise, and that its author was not a pedant eager to establish his bona fides by footnoting his sources, but a great artist intent on achieving in his description of the conversation a measure of dramatic verisimilitude. Plutarch (*Agis* 5) tells us that, in the aftermath of the Peloponnesian War, a Spartan ephor named Epitadeus quarreled with his son and, in order to be able to take vengeance on the young man, secured the passage of a law allowing each Spartan to give or bequeath his *klêros* to anyone he chose.[10] If this actually happened, it would explain why the description of land tenure at Sparta in Aristotle's *Politics* differs so markedly from that provided by Plutarch in his *Lycurgus,* and it might also explain the silence of the Athenian Stranger. If the institution he took as his model was one abandoned by Sparta some decades before and if that decision was then and remained thereafter controversial (as would surely have been the case), proposing its adoption might, in the circumstances, be somewhat socially awkward. Expressly indicating that he was embracing a set of practices recently jettisoned by Lacedaemon might be regarded as a frontal assault on the fatherland of one of his companions. As any careful reader of the dialogue will notice, in his criticism of Sparta, the Athenian Stranger walks a fine line, and Megillus, his Spartan companion, occasionally displays irritation.

One might, of course, object that the depiction of Lacedaemon as an economically egalitarian polity in Isocrates, Polybius, and Plutarch is at odds with the reality depicted in Alcman, Herodotus, Thucydides, and Xenophon. There can be no doubt that Polybius' brief account is one-sided and incomplete, and the story told by Plutarch in the *Lycurgus* is, at least with regard to the legendary Lycurgus, overly schematic and in this particular misleading. But I also think that the two visions of Lacedaemon conveyed in these two sets of sources can be reconciled.

Aristotle is known to have composed a work on Lacedaemon along the lines of his *Politeía of the Athenians.* As I have suggested in the prologue to this volume, he displays in his *Politics* a keen interest in the political, social, and economic dimensions of the Spartan regime and way of life, and it stands to reason that in his monograph on Lacedaemon he would have addressed the political, social, and economic development of early Lacedaemon in the manner in which he addressed Athens' evolution in these regards in his *Politeía of the Athenians.* Moreover, as I also pointed out, the excerpts that survive confirm this presumption. If the land tenure system at Sparta had a history, as it undoubtedly did, we can be confident that Aristotle described it in detail.

This matters a great deal, for, thanks to his epitomator Heracleides Lembos (373.12 [Dilts]), we know two things—that, in this lost work, Aristotle observed that at Lacedaemon it was considered shameful to sell one's land [*gê*], and that he also reported that it was forbidden to sell one's *archaîa moîra* (F611.12 [Rose]=Tits. 143.1.2.12 [Gigon]). There are those who argue that the latter phrase refers not to an "ancestral allotment" of land as such but to the rent, if that is the proper word, paid to each Spartan citizen time out of mind by the helots who worked land communally owned.[11] For our purposes here, however, it matters not one whit whether the phrase refers to a *klêros* as such or to the share of its product paid the citizen to whom it had been assigned. What matters is that Aristotle appears to have described an arrangement for provision, likely to have been egalitarian in character, existing alongside a system of private property in land—an arrangement designed to provide those without an inherited estate with a competence sufficient to allow them to perform their duties as full-fledged citizens.[12]

We know that Plutarch read and, in his *Life of Lycurgus,* drew quite heavily Aristotle's *Polıteía of the Lacedaemonians.* We have excellent reason to suppose that he regarded its testimony on any number of matters as dispositive, and in his *Moralia* (238e–f) there is a passage that echoes Aristotle's discussion of the *archaîa moîra.* Moreover, there is another passage, this one in his *Life of Agis* (5.6), in which he mentions a citizen's land [*gê*] and his *klêros* in such a manner as to suggest he is speaking of two different things. I find it hard to believe that, in his *Life of Lycurgus* and in his *Lives of Agis and Cleomenes,* he would have attributed to early Sparta a system of communal or quasi-communal property if Aristotle in his treatise on Sparta gave such a presumption no sanction. Moreover, as we have seen, Plutarch with the story that he tells concerning the legislation sponsored by the ephor Epitadeus provides an explanation for the disappearance of this system of communal or quasi-communal property.[13] This story is also apt to be derivative from Aristotle's account of political development at Sparta, and it may have been told as well in Ephorus' discussion of the decay of the Spartan regime after the Peloponnesian War.[14]

On the face of it, then, the following conclusions, advanced in this volume, would appear to be reasonable: that there was always private property at Lacedaemon and that there was never a general redistribution of land, but that at some point early in the archaic period—perhaps when they conquered the Helos plain, perhaps only at the time of their reconquest of Messenia—the Spartans began setting aside conquered land and helots sufficient to work it as a guarantee that Lacedaemonian warriors with little or no inherited property would in the future possess the resources requisite for serving the city.[15] There is nothing strange in their having made such an arrangement, and it fits rather well what we can surmise regarding practices elsewhere in Hellas in the archaic period.[16] Moreover, a strikingly similar system of land tenure was later instituted in comparable circumstances in Egypt by Ptolemy I after the death of Alexander, and over time the system of fiefs he established in the Fayum with an eye to providing himself and his heirs with a reliable army gave way, and a system of private ownership corresponding to the aspirations of the landholders gradually replaced it, just as appears to have happened in Lacedaemon at the end of the Peloponnesian War.[17]

Against the supposition that prior to the mid-fifth century much of the land at Sparta was communally owned but assigned to individual warriors expected to defend the political community, we must weigh the silence of Herodotus, Thucydides, and Xenophon—which would have considerable weight if they elsewhere showed the keen interest in systems of land tenure that is so visible in Plato, Ephorus, and Aristotle. But such an interest they do not evidence—which means that their silence on this matter tells us a great deal about their predilections and next to nothing about arrangements at Sparta.[18]

There is, however, one other objection to the hypothesis presented here; and, to the unsuspecting glance, it would appear to have considerable force. The population of Spartiates at the time of the Persian Wars was eight thousand or more (Hdt. 7.234). That in Aristotle's day was under one thousand (*Pol.* 1270a29–31). Aristotle explains the dearth of Spartan manpower [*oliganthrōpía*] in his own time with an eye to the system of private land tenure in existence in his own day, and his argument is cogent (1270a11–18). As he suggests, in an agrarian setting in which partitive inheritance is the norm, family ambition really is apt to induce those with property to marry their offspring to others similarly situated; and, where servile labor is plentiful, partitive inheritance creates an incentive for married couples to limit childbearing. In consequence, property is likely to gradually become concentrated— which, at Sparta, would result in a steady decline in the number of those eligible to be citizens who possess a competence sufficient to support them in their status as full-time warriors and to enable them to make the requisite contribution to the *sussitía* (1271a26–36). Were this demographic trend evident only after the Peloponnesian War, it would be explicable as a product of the law of Epitadeus, and it would not be necessary to discuss the matter here. But, in fact, the decline in the Spartan population may have been more dramatic in the fifth century than it was in the fourth.

In 480, there were, as we have just seen, roughly eight thousand Spartans; and a year later, after losing two hundred ninety-eight men at Thermopylae

(Hdt. 7.202, 205.2, 223.2–225.3, 229–33, 9.71.2–4), Lacedaemon was able to send an army outside the Peloponnesus to Plataea made up of two-thirds of the surviving adult male Spartiates, in which there were five thousand Spartans (9.10). Sixty-one years later, in 418, at a time of desperation, the Spartans dispatched an even greater proportion of their available manpower—five-sixths this time, rather than two-thirds—to fight nearer home at Mantineia (Thuc. 5.64.2–3). If Thucydides' figures for the size of the Lacedaemonian army at Mantineia (5.68) are to be believed and if, as we have reason to expect, Spartans made up roughly the same proportion (ca. 41 percent) in the *lóchoi* deployed as they apparently had in the force chosen a few years earlier by lot from those units to occupy Sphacteria (4.8.9, 38.5),[19] the city was, six decades after Plataea, able to field fewer than fifteen hundred full citizens in the *lóchoi* and another three hundred *hippeîs* as the king's bodyguard and had an adult male citizen body of no more than twenty-one hundred.

It is, of course, possible that Thucydides is in error, and many scholars have argued that the number of *lóchoi* present and, therefore, the number of men in the army proper should be doubled.[20] Their incredulity is understandable, but, given the evident pride animating Thucydides' claim to have penetrated the veil of secrecy concealing such matters at Lacedaemon and to have achieved precision concerning this matter, the argument they advance is hard to swallow. Realizing this, another scholar has suggested that the Spartiates and the *períoikoi* were brigaded separately at Mantineia, as they had been at Plataea, and that Thucydides erred only in failing to report the presence of the latter.[21] This, too, seems a stretch. It is contrary to what seems to have been the case at Sphacteria, and it requires that we suppose Thucydides careless in his description of the Lacedaemonian force as a whole. On either hypothesis, however, the number of Spartans in the army at Mantineia will have been roughly thirty-three hundred and the number of full citizens just over thirty-nine hundred. Forty-seven years thereafter, in 371, in the army dispatched to Leuctra, there were only seven hundred Spartans (Xen. *Hell.* 6.4.15). They constituted two-thirds of Lacedaemon's available citizen manpower (6.1.1), which accords well with Aristotle's claim (*Pol.* 1270a31–33) that, in his time, twenty or so years thereafter, there were fewer than one thousand Spartans. How, one might ask, can this development be explained without resort to the species of analysis provided by Aristotle? How can it be explained if, in the sixth and fifth centuries, there was a communal or quasi-communal system of land tenure in place alongside the system of private property?

To this apparently compelling objection, there is, in fact, an answer. It does not matter whether the decline in population that took place between 479 and 418 was just over 51 percent or just under 74 percent. Either way, it was too dramatic to be explained in terms of the process described by Aristotle. For this to have happened, there had to have been something else at work, something much more dramatic, something other than a gradual concentration of property, and we know what it was.[22] In the period stretching from 480 to 460, the Spartans suffered severe losses. Two hundred ninety-eight died at Thermopylae in 480, as we have seen, and another ninety-one lost their lives at Plataea the following year (Hdt. 9.70). There may have been losses when Leotychides campaigned in Thessaly not long thereafter (6.72), and there were surely serious losses at Tegea and Dipaea, in the 460s, when the Spartans faced exceedingly difficult odds in battling their own allies (9.35, Isoc. 6.99).

Even more to the point, however, in 465, there was a severe earthquake and there were aftershocks in Laconia (Thuc. 1.101.2, 128.1, 2.27.2, 3.54.5, 4.56.2). The epicenter appears to have been in the vicinity of Sparta. We are told that these seismic events left only five houses standing at Lacedaemon (Plut. *Cim.* 16.4–5, Cic. *De div.* 1.112, Pliny *NH* 2.191, Ael. *VH* 6.7.2, Polyaen. 1.41.3), and Diodorus Siculus (11.63, 15.66.4), almost certainly following Ephorus of Cumae, asserts that more than twenty thousand Lacedaemonians, including a majority of the Spartiates, lost their lives—many of them when their homes collapsed on them. In the aftermath, he tells us, there were "few" Spartiates left, and the city of Sparta was "bereft of men." Among those who died were, we are told, the ephebes in their very late teens. If we assume, first, that women and small children were more likely to be in their homes when the earthquakes struck, as seems highly likely, and, second, that Spartans were reluctant to accept within their ranks half-breeds fathered by citizens on helot mothers, as seems probable, the earthquakes are apt for a time to have affected fertility as well.[23]

If my intuition in this last regard is correct, the resulting shortage of eligible Spartiate women would help explain a phenomenon unprecedented as far as we can tell: to wit, the sudden appearance in our sources of children, born to Spartan fathers of some prominence in the first two decades after the earthquakes, who were classified as *móthakes* rather than as prospective citizens and reared in the *agógē* without being guaranteed admission into the ranks of the *hómoioi*—some of whom were, nonetheless, admitted and later rose to high rank. There is good reason to suppose that Gylippus and Lysander, who are known to have had Spartan fathers, and the navarch Callicratidas, who probably did, were the half-breeds, the sons of helot mothers.[24]

To the story of the earthquakes and their consequences, we can add that, in their aftermath, there was a helot revolt that caught the Lacedaemonians flat-footed (Thuc. 1.101.2–3, 128.1, 2.27.2, 3.54.5, 4.56.2; Diod. 11.63–64). We also hear of an isolated group of three hundred infantrymen being massacred, who may have been Spartans; and there was major battle near Mount Ithome that may well have eventuated in a considerable loss of Spartiate lives (Hdt. 9.35, 64).

It is striking that in the early 450s—when the Lacedaemonians led a Peloponnesian army of ten thousand hoplites against the Phocians who were attacking Doris, which the Spartans considered their ancestral homeland—they could manage to send with the ten thousand only fifteen hundred Lacedaemonian hoplites (Thuc. 1.107.2). If this force was entirely Spartiate and constituted two-thirds of the levy, as appears to have been the norm for such expeditions, and if we suppose that the three hundred *hippeîs* guarding the regent Nicomedes son of Cleombrotus were not included in Thucydides' count, there were in that year not many more than two thousand five hundred fifty adult male Spartiates left—and it cannot have helped the situation that the battle against the Athenians at Tanagra, which followed, was hard fought and that the Spartans and their allies (as well as the Athenians) suffered heavy losses (Thuc. 1.107.3–108.2). If, on the other hand, the Lacedaemonian contingent was evenly divided between Spartiates and *períoikoi*, as it had been at Plataea, and if the seven hundred fifty Spartan hoplites sent constituted two-thirds of the levy, there would have been about fifteen hundred adult male Spartiates left.

The sudden character of this plunge in population is also strikingly visible on the ground. Prior to the 465, Lacedaemon appears to have suffered from overpopulation. Aristotle was told that there had once been as many as ten thousand Spartans (*Pol.* 1270a34–39); and, although he intimates a measure of skepticism about this number, there are reasons to suspect that his informant was, in fact, correct. There is certainly evidence for land hunger in sixth-century Lacedaemon. Early in that century, when the Spartans made a concerted attempt to conquer Tegea, their aim was to divide the territory among their citizens and make helots of the Arcadians (Hdt. 1.66). Moreover, as I point out in Chapter 4—after the Lacedaemonians decided to abandon the attempt at further expansion, to reach an accommodation with the Tegeans, and draw them into an alliance—there is archaeological evidence for internal colonization within Laconia, in which marginal land on the edge of the central plain was brought into cultivation. At this time, the number of young men at Spartan evidently exceeded the number of available allotments.

In the late fifth century, decades after the earthquakes and helot revolt, the Spartans were extremely careful to conserve manpower (Thuc. 4.15, 108, 117, 5.15). In the late archaic period, however, they were profligate with this resource. In the 540s, for example, they were perfectly willing to sacrifice three hundred men in the Battle of Champions (Hdt. 1.82), and the same was true at the time of Thermopylae (7.205). Moreover, ca. 514, when they allowed Dorieus to mount a colonial expedition, there was apparently no shortage of citizens willing to join in, and no measures were taken to prevent their departure (5.42). That 465 marked a dramatic turning point is evident from the fact that, in the wake of that date, the Spartans suddenly ceased to cultivate the marginal land on the edge of the central plain.[25] What we know of the scale and scope and what we can surmise regarding the character of the Spartan losses in the 470s and the 460s is more than adequate to explain the dearth of Spartan manpower in 418. Indeed, it is perfectly possible that, well before 418, the Spartan population had begun to recover. If we take the higher of the two estimates for the size of the Spartiate force at Mantineia, the Spartan contingent within the army fielded by Lacedaemon in 418 was considerably larger than it would have been had the battle taken place forty years before. Even if we were to opt for the lower estimate—the one that accords best with the available evidence—there would be no need to suppose that Sparta experienced a further drop in her population in the interval between the early 450s and 418.

Of course, it is perfectly conceivable that Lacedaemon suffered another great demographic shock at the end of the 430s and the beginning of the 420s when the plague devastated Athens, eliminating a quarter of her cavalrymen, a third of the city's hoplites, and an untold proportion of Athenian rowers, women, and children (Thuc. 2.47.3–54.5, 3.87.1–3). Thucydides (2.54.5) believed that no community within the Peloponnesus was affected by the plague in any significant way, and this was no doubt true of Corinth, which he knew exceptionally well.[26] But we are told by the geographer Pausanias (2.32.6, 8.41.7–9, 10.11.5) that the plague struck Troezen and Cleonae and that it also threatened Phigaleia deep in Arcadia. Moreover, it is clear from Thucydides' testimony concerning the size of the Lacedaemonian forces at Mantineia (5.68.2) that the Spartans were secretive in the extreme, especially when it

came to demographic matters. If they suffered great losses early in the Peloponnesian War as a consequence of the plague, they would almost certainly
have gone out of their way to conceal the fact.[27] It is, moreover, puzzling that,
in 420, when the ambassadors of Argos negotiated an abortive truce with the
authorities at Sparta, in which, at their insistence, the settlement of the cities'
long-standing dispute over Cynouria by a second battle of champions was deliberately left open as an option, the document included a clause specifying
that neither city could issue a challenge while the other was at war *or suffering
from a plague* (Thuc. 5.41.2). The reference to the plague in this clause was, to
say the least, unusual, and one must wonder what occasioned its inclusion at
this time. In the surviving evidence for the fifth century, the only plague of any
real importance mentioned is the one that beset Athens;[28] and one usually
does not provide for contingencies with which one is wholly unfamiliar.

The fact that Lacedaemon's population did not dramatically bounce back
in the years following 418 but declined further instead suggests that we should
not be quick to dismiss Plutarch's account of the activities of the ephor Epitadeus, which would have paved the way for the process described by Aristotle.
It is also worth noting that, throughout history, subreplacement fertility has
been common among privileged groups intent on maintaining their high
standing. This is particularly true where patriarchy is not the norm and well-
to-do women exercise considerable leverage—which was the case at Lacedaemon in the time of Plato and Aristotle, as I point out in Chapter 1. Those, such
as Xenophon, who argued that, in her social dynamics, the Sparta of his day
was quite different from what Lacedaemon had been in earlier times, may have
been on the mark. The earthquakes left the Spartiates of both sexes—those,
that is, who survived that catastrophe and the helot revolt that followed it—in
possession of an abundance of land and helots to work it. In response to their
new situation, the women and men of Sparta may have gradually adopted a
reproductive strategy different from the one that had prevailed in the past,
and the law successfully promoted by Epitadeus may have been a reflection of
a change in ethos that had silently crept in. Such is certainly the impression
given by the ancient sources.[29]

There is, to be sure, another possibility. Some scholars are inclined to dismiss the testimony found in Polybius, Plutarch, and the other ancient writers
who make similar claims. These reflect, they say, the propaganda generated in
support of the revolutionary program developed in third-century Sparta by
the Eurypontid king Agis and his younger admirer the Agiad king Cleomenes.

Polybius and Plutarch were misled, they claim, by the historian Phylarchus and by the Stoic Sphaerus of Borysthenes, who tutored Cleomenes in his youth, later returned to Lacedaemon to advise him with regard to the *agōgḗ* and the *sussitía,* and at some point wrote tracts on the Spartan regime.

There can be no doubt that Polybius and Plutarch drew on Phylarchus, and the latter appears to have read Sphaerus as well. It is, moreover, evident that their treatments of Agis and Cleomenes reflect in some measure what Phylarchus reported. That Phylarchus was sympathetic to the Spartan revolution seems clear enough,[30] but the focus of his narrative was not Lacedaemon as such. His subject was the history of Greece more generally in the period stretching from the death of Pyrrhus of Epirus to that of Cleomenes of Sparta, and we have no reason to think that he wrote about early Sparta at all.[31] Sphaerus did address the Lacedaemonian *politeía,* and he wrote a treatise on Lycurgus and Socrates, but there is no reason to suppose that he misrepresented developments for partisan purposes. The two fragments of his work on Sparta that do survive suggest on his part an attempt to provide a scrupulously accurate and detailed scholarly description of the evolution of Spartan mores, manners, and laws.[32]

It is, moreover, clear that Polybius and Plutarch read as well the work of Aratus, who was decidedly hostile to the revolutionary program developed by these two kings; and, for Spartan institutions and their development in the archaic and classical period, they had a host of other, earlier, more authoritative sources on which to draw—including not only Xenophon, Ephorus, and Plato but, at least in the case of Plutarch, Aristotle's *Politics,* his *Politeía of the Lacedaemonians,* as well as the works of his students Theophrastus and Dicaearchus. That confusion entered in, that in the oral tradition concerning eighth- and seventh-century Lacedaemon there was a telescoping and conflation of developments, that Polybius and Plutarch present a simplified, overly rational account of archaic and classical Lacedaemonian property relations there can be no doubt. But that they were fed an elaborate line by Phylarchus, by Sphaerus, or anyone else and fell for it hook, line, and sinker—this really is a stretch. There surely was a connection between the tales told about Lycurgus and the program of Agis and Cleomenes. But it makes far more sense to suppose that the two kings were inspired by a mildly confused, overly schematic, simplified, but more or less accurate account of the shape things took in Lacedaemon's heyday than to believe, as these scholars do, that the Sparta these two kings sought to restore was nothing more than a figment of the historical or philosophical imagination and that what Polybius, Plutarch, and others have to report concerning property relations at Lacedaemon in earlier times is a product of the propaganda generated during the abortive third-century revolution.[33]

Herodotus is the first surviving writer to have written about Lacedaemon. He described her as being possessed of a *politeía* (9.34.1), and he termed it a *kósmos* (1.65.4).[34] In other words, from the outset, it was recognized as distinctive—at least in part because it was a beautiful, elegantly ordered whole. This order was, moreover, noteworthy for its coherence and consistency, and it derived its coherence and consistency from a single set of principles, which I have tried to make visible in the first two chapters of this book. One additional reason for accepting the testimony of the ancient sources concerning property relations at Sparta is that the picture they draw fits in well with everything else that we are told about the fiercely communal character of Spartan life. After all, if the Spartans came to be called *hoi hómoioi,* there had to be a reason.[35]

Appendix 2
The *Néoi* at Sparta

WITHIN the ordinary Greek city, it was customary to refer to those under thirty as *hoi néoi*, "the young men" (Xen. *Mem.* 1.2.35; Polyb. 4.20.7); and we know that, at Sparta, those under that age were subject to special restrictions: Plut. *Lyc.* 25.1. This has led scholars to presume that the *néoi* referred to at Plut. *Lyc.* 15.7–8 are Spartiates in their twenties.[1] However, in classifying citizens among the youth [*neótēs*], as in so many other things, Sparta appears to have been an exception to the rule.[2] Xenophon's assertion (*Ages.* 1.6) that Agesilaus was "still young [*éti néos*]" when he became king in about 400 would otherwise make no sense given the fact (*Hell.* 5.4.13) that he was over sixty in 379 and well into his eighties and had been king for more than forty years when he died in or shortly after 360 (*Ages.* 2.28; Plut. *Ages.* 36.3, 40.3). This peculiar technical use of the term *néos* and its cognates by the Spartans almost certainly underlies the report which Diodorus (13.76.2) drew on in claiming that Kallikratidas was quite young [*néos*] when he became navarch in 407/406; and Plutarch (*Lyc.* 22.1–6) clearly uses these terms in this fashion as well. The *néoi* or, as they are sometimes (e.g., Xen. *Hell.* 3.3.8–9) called, the *neóteroi* appear to have been distinguished from the *presbúteroi* of classical Sparta in much the same fashion as the *iuniores* were distinguished from the *seniores* of ancient Rome. The fact, then, that all the men under forty-five slept with their tent-mates helps explain why so many Greeks looked on Sparta as an armed camp. If the comparative data gathered by ethnologists are any guide, Henri Jeanmaire may be correct in arguing that the young men of a set of *sussitía* shared sleeping quarters.[3] This would, in any case, stand to reason. Not all of the fifteen or so men who belonged to a particular mess will have been under forty-five, and the remainder will have spent their nights at home. It is conceivable, but, I think, improbable that a man graduated from the *néoi* when he reached the age of fifty (rather than forty-five).[4]

Abbreviations and Short Titles

In the notes, I have adopted the standard abbreviations for classical texts and inscriptions, for books of the Bible, and for modern journals and books provided in *The Oxford Classical Dictionary,* 4th edition revised, ed. Simon Hornblower, Antony Spawforth, and Esther Eidinow (Oxford: Oxford University Press, 2012); *The Chicago Manual of Style,* 15th edition (Chicago: University of Chicago Press, 2003), 15.50–53; and the bibliographical annual *L'Année Philologique.* Where possible, the ancient texts are cited by the divisions and subdivisions employed by the author or introduced by subsequent editors (that is, by book, part, chapter, section number, paragraph, act, scene, line, Stephanus page, or by page and line number). Cross-references to other parts of this volume refer to the pertinent chapter and specify whether the material referenced can be found above or below.

Unless otherwise indicated, all of the translations are my own. I transliterate the Greek, using undotted i's where no accent is required, adding macrons, accents, circumflexes, and so on. When others—in titles or statements quoted—transliterate in a different manner, I leave their transliterations as they had them.

For other works frequently cited, the following abbreviations and short titles have been employed:

ASI	*Ancient Society and Institutions: Studies Presented to Victor Ehrenberg,* ed. Ernst Badian (Oxford: Basil Blackwell, 1966).
Birgalias, *OES*	Nikos Birgalias, *L'Odyssée de l'éducation spartiate* (Athens: St. D. Basilopoulos, 1999).
Cartledge, *Agesilaos*	Paul Cartledge, *Agesilaos and the Crisis of Sparta* (Baltimore: Johns Hopkins University Press, 1987).
Cartledge, *SL*	Paul Cartledge, *Sparta and Lakonia: A Regional History, 1300–362 BC,* second edition (London: Routledge and Kegan Paul, 2002).
Cartledge, *SR*	Paul Cartledge, *Spartan Reflections* (Berkeley: University of California Press, 2001).

CASPTP   *The Contribution of Ancient Sparta to Political Thought and Practice,*
                  ed. Paul Cartledge, Nikos Birgalias, and Kostas Buraselis (Athens:
                  Alexandria Publications, 2007).

Cawkwell, *CC*   George L. Cawkwell, *Cyrene to Chaeronea: Selected Essays on Ancient
                  Greek History* (Oxford: Oxford University Press, 2011).

CSTS   *Classical Sparta: Techniques behind Her Success,* ed. Anton Powell
                  (Norman: University of Oklahoma Press, 1988).

Ducat, *Hilotes* Jean Ducat, *Les Hilotes* (Athens and Paris: École Française d'Athènes/
                  De Boccard, 1990).

Ducat, *SE*   Jean Ducat, *Spartan Education: Youth and Society in the Classical
                  Period,* tr. Emma Stafford, P.-J. Shaw, and Anton Powell (Swansea:
                  Classical Press of Wales, 2006).

FS   *Das Frühe Sparta,* ed. Andreas Luther, Mischa Meier, and Lukas
                  Thommen (Stuttgart: Franz Steiner Verlag, 2006).

Greenhalgh, *EGW* P. A. L. Greenhalgh, *Early Greek Warfare: Horsemen and Chariots in
                  the Homeric and Archaic Ages* (Cambridge: Cambridge University
                  Press, 1973).

HMLM   *Helots and Their Masters in Laconia and Messenia: Histories,
                  Ideologies, Structures,* ed. Nino Luraghi and Susan E. Alcock
                  (Washington, DC: Center for Hellenic Studies, 2003).

Hodkinson, *PWCS* Stephen Hodkinson, *Property and Wealth in Classical Sparta*
                  (London: Duckworth, 2000).

Kennell, *GV*   Nigel M. Kennell, *The Gymnasium of Virtue: Education and Culture
                  in Ancient Sparta* (Chapel Hill: University of North Carolina Press,
                  1995).

Kõiv, *ATEGH*   Mait Kõiv, *Ancient Tradition and Early Greek History: The Origins of
                  States in Early Archaic Sparta, Argos and Corinth* (Tallinn: Avita, 2003).

Kõiv, *STAS*   Matt Kõiv, "Sanctuaries and Traditions in Ancient Sparta," in
                  *Cultures in Comparison: Religion and Politics in Ancient Mediterra-
                  nean Regions,* ed. Thomas R. Kämmerer and Matt Kõiv (Münster:
                  Ugarit-Verlag, 2015), 25–66.

Lipka, *XSC*   Michael Lipka, *Xenophon's Spartan Constitution: Introduction, Text,
                  Commentary* (Berlin: De Gruyter, 2002).

MacDowell, *SL*   Douglas M. MacDowell, *Spartan Law* (Edinburgh: Scottish Aca-
                  demic Press, 1986).

MB   *Men of Bronze: Hoplite Warfare in Ancient Greece,* ed. Donald Kagan
                  and Gregory F. Viggiano (Princeton, NJ: Princeton University Press,
                  2013).

Mosshammer, *CE* Alden A. Mosshammer, *The Chronicle of Eusebius and Greek Chronographic Tradition* (Lewisburg, PA: Bucknell University Press, 1979).

Philolakōn *Philolakōn: Lakonian Studies in Honour of Hector Catling,* ed. Jan Motyka Sanders (London: British School at Athens, 1992).

Pomeroy, *SWo* Sarah B. Pomeroy, *Spartan Women* (Oxford: Oxford University Press, 2002).

Rahe, *PC* Paul A. Rahe, *The Grand Strategy of Classical Sparta: The Persian Challenge* (New Haven, CT: Yale University Press, 2015).

Rahe, *RAM* Paul A. Rahe, *Republics Ancient and Modern: Classical Republicanism and the American Revolution* (Chapel Hill: University of North Carolina Press, 1992), cited by book, chapter, and section, which correspond with volume, chapter, and section in the three-volume paperback edition published in 1994.

SAGT W. Kendrick Pritchett, *Studies in Ancient Greek Topography* (Berkeley: University of California Press, 1965–89; Amsterdam: J. C. Gieben, 1991–92).

SBM *Sparta: Beyond the Mirage,* ed. Anton Powell and Stephen Hodkinson (Swansea: Classical Press of Wales, 2002).

SBP *Sparta: The Body Politic,* ed. Anton Powell and Stephen Hodkinson (Swansea: Classical Press of Wales, 2010).

SCA *Sparta: Comparative Approaches,* ed. Stephen Hodkinson (Swansea: Classical Press of Wales, 2009).

SNS *Sparta: New Perspectives,* ed. Stephen Hodkinson and Anton Powell (Swansea: Classical Press of Wales, 1999).

SpartSoc *Spartan Society,* ed. Thomas J. Figueira (Swansea: Classical Press of Wales, 2004).

SS *The Shadow of Sparta,* ed. Anton Powell and Stephen Hodkinson (New York: Routledge, 1994).

SW *Sparta and War,* ed. Stephen Hodkinson and Anton Powell (Swansea: Classical Press of Wales, 2006).

Toynbee, *SPGH* Arnold J. Toynbee, *Some Problems of Greek History* (Oxford: Oxford University Press, 1969).

van Wees, *GW* Hans van Wees, *Greek Warfare: Myths and Realities* (London: Duckworth, 2004).

Wade-Gery, *EGH* Henry Theodore Wade-Gery, *Essays in Greek History* (Oxford: Basil Blackwell, 1958).

Notes

Introduction

1. Thuc. 4.1–23, 26–37.

2. Thuc. 4.38–40, 5.16–24.

3. Thuc. 5.24.2, 34.2.

4. Spartan *politeía:* Hdt. 9.33–35 (esp. 34.1).

5. For the word's range of meanings and the manner in which it is deployed in the fifth and fourth centuries, see Ramón Martínez Fernández, "*Politeia:* Un Nombre para la democracia," *Helmantica* 26 (1975): 357–75.

6. In this connection, see Seth Benardete, *Herodotean Inquiries* (The Hague: Martinus Nijhoff, 1969), and Rosalind Thomas, *Herodotus in Context: Ethnography, Science and the Art of Persuasion* (Cambridge: Cambridge University Press, 2000). For one part of the story, see Stanley Rosen, "Philosophy and Revolution," in Rosen, *The Quarrel between Philosophy and Poetry* (New York: Routledge, 1988), 27–55.

7. Contest of regimes: cf. Thuc. 1.18.1, 68–69, 71.1–3, 132.4, 4.126.2, 5.31.6, 68.2. with 1.70, 127.3, 2.16.2, 36–46, 3.55.3, 8.53.3, 74.3, 76.5, 89.2, 97.2, and see Leo Strauss, *The City and Man* (Chicago: Rand McNally, 1964), 139–241; Clifford Orwin, *The Humanity of Thucydides* (Princeton, NJ: Princeton University Press, 1994); and Paul A. Rahe, "Thucydides' Critique of *Realpolitik,*" *Security Studies* 5:2 (Winter 1995): 105–41, reprinted in *Roots of Realism: Philosophical and Historical Dimensions,* ed. Benjamin Frankel (London: Frank Cass, 1996), 105–41. Note also Thuc. 1.115.2, 4.76.5, 5.4.3, 6.104.2, 7.55.2.

8. Ephorus as a historian of hegemonic regimes and their decay: Arnaldo Momigliano, "L'Egemonia tebana in Senofonte e in Eforo," *Atene e Roma* 3rd ser., 2 (1935): 101–17, reprinted in Momigliano, *Terza contributo alla storia degli studi classici e del mondo antico* I (Rome: Edizioni di storia e di letteratura, 1966), 347–65; John M. Wickersham, *Hegemony and Greek Historians* (Lanham, MD: Rowman & Littlefield, 1993), 119–50; Guido Schepens, "Historiographical Problems in Ephorus," in *Historiographia antiqua: Commentationes Lovanienses in honorem W. Peremans septuagenarii editae,* ed. C. Prins (Louvain: Louvain University Press, 1977), 95–118; Giovanni Parmeggiani, "Dalla *ktisis* alla *truphē:* Una lettura di storia milesia in Eforo di Cuma (note a Eph. *FGrHist* 70 FF 127, 183)," in *Sungraphé: Materiali e appunti per lo studio della storia e della letteratura antica,* ed. Delfino Ambaglio (Como: New Press, 2000), II 83–92, and "Diodoro e la crisi delle egemonie nel IV secolo a.C.," in *Diodoro e l'altra Grecia: Macedonia, Occidente, Ellenismo nella Biblioteca storica,* ed. Cinzia Bearzot and Franca Landucci (Milan: Vita e Pensiero, 2005), 67–103; and Paul Christesen, "Spartans and Scythians, a Meeting of Mirages: The Portrayal of the Lycurgan *Politeia* in Ephorus' *Histories,*" in *SBP,* 211–63.

9. It is hard to see how anyone who has read the ancient political analysts with the sympathetic attention and care they deserve could conclude that they "lacked a 'conceptual framework' for the understanding . . . of long-range social change": cf. Moses I. Finley, "The Ancient Historian and His Sources," in Finley, *Ancient History: Evidence and Models* (London: Chatto & Windus, 1985), 7–26 (at 18, 26). For an elegant inquiry into long-range social and political change self-consciously pursued in accord with Aristotelian principles, see Claude Nicolet, *The World of the Citizen in Republican Rome,* trans. P. S. Falla (Berkeley: University of California Press, 1980).

10. See Schol. Pl. *Leg.* 1.625b and Isoc. 7.14.

11. This explains the prominence of *paideía* as a theme in both *The Republic* and *The Laws:* cf. Pl. *Resp.* 2.376c–4.445a, 6.487b–497a, 7.518b–541b, 8.548a–b, 554a–b, 559b–c, 10.600a–608b with *Leg.* 1.641b–2.674c, 3.693d–701b, 4.722b–9.880e, 11.920a–12.962e.

12. Cf. Arist. *Pol.* 1263b36–37 with 1276a8–b15.

13. Cf. Polyb. 6.19–58 with Xen. *Cyr.* 1.2.15. See *Vect.* 1.1; Pl. *Resp.* 8.544d–e, *Leg.* 4.711b–712a; Isoc. 2.31, 3.37, 7.14; Cic. *Rep.* 1.31.47, 5.3.5–5.7 (with *Leg.* 1.4.14–6.19, 3.1.2). See also Leo Strauss, *Natural Right and History* (Chicago: University of Chicago Press, 1974), 135–38.

14. In this connection, see Pl. *Ep.* 7.336d–337d.

15. After reading Pl. *Resp.* 8.543c–9.592b and *Leg.* 3.689e–701b, 4.712b–715d, note 1.631d–632c, 3.696c–698a, 4.707a–d, 711b–d, and consider 6.752b–768e in light of 5.734e–735a, 6.751a–b, and 7.822d–824a (esp. 823a); then, cf. Arist. *Pol.* 1273a39–b1 and 1278b6–15 with 1295a40–b2; consider 1328b2–23 (esp. 13–14, 22–23—where I am inclined to adopt the reading of Lambinus) in light of 1328a35–b1; and see *Rh.* 1365b21–1366a22. And finally, note *Pol.* 1264a24–1266b38, 1276b1–13, 1277a12–b32, 1283a3–42, 1288a6–b4, 1289a10–25, 1292b11–21, 1294a9–14, 1297a14–b34, 1311a8–20, 1317a40–b17, 1323a14–1342b34; and see Cic. *Leg.* 3.12.28–14.32.

16. See Alexander Hamilton, James Madison, and John Jay, *The Federalist,* ed. Jacob E. Cook (Middletown, CT: Wesleyan University Press, 1961), no. 1.

17. After reading Arist. *Pol.* 1273a39–b1, 1278b6–15, 1289a10–25, 1292b11–21, 1295a40–b2, 1328b2–23, 1328a35–b1, and the rest of the material collected in note 15, above, cf. Pl. *Leg.* 3.683e with 686b, 4.709a–710d, 5.747c–e, 6.757d–758a, 780b; Cic. *Rep.* 2.33.57. In this connection, consider Pl. *Leg.* 10.886c–910d. Cf. *Resp.* 3.414c–4.427c, 5.449a–466d, 7.540b–541d with *Leg.* 5.739a–e. Cf. *Leg.* 4.713e–714a with *Resp.* 5.473c–474a and 9.591d–592b; then, cf. *Resp.* 7.515c–516b with *Phd.* 99d–100a, *Leg.* 10.897d–e, and Xen. *Mem.* 4.3.14, 7.7. Note Pl. *Meno* 86e and *Resp.* 8.546a–547a.

18. Lacedaemonian *kósmos:* Hdt. 1.65.4, Thuc. 1.84.3, Plut. *Lyc.* 29.1. Herodotus uses the word *kósmos* and its cognates to describe not only the elegant order that the gods impose on "all things" (2.52.1), but also court protocol among the Medes (1.99.1) and Persians (8.67); the outfit reserved for infants (1.113.2); the military discipline that distinguishes an army or navy in formation from a mob charging or fleeing in disarray (3.13.1, 8.60, 86, 9.59.2, 65.1, 66.3, 69.1); the proper arrangement of a bridge of boats (7.36.4); propriety in the conduct of foreign affairs (8.142.2); good manners and orderliness in the consumption of food (8.117.2); and finery in female garb (3.1.3–4, 5.92η.3), jewelry (3.22.2), dining hall furnishings (3.123.1), tree ornaments (7.31), and military equipment (7.83.2). For the most part, Thucydides and those whose speeches he presents use the term in speaking of military discipline and orderliness on the battlefield or the lack thereof: 2.11.9, 89.9, 3.77.2, 108.3, 4.126.6, 5.66.2, 6.72.5, 7.23.3, 40.3, 84.3, 8.99. But the term is also used to describe political orders, such as the moderate oligarchy at Thebes (4.76.2), the democracy at Athens (8.48.4, 67.3), and the short-lived oligarchy of the four hundred there (8.72.2). It is also used as a term of approval, indicating that a particular practice or policy is deemed honorable (1.5.2, 33.2). On one occasion, it is employed to refer to the orderly practices that allow for public deliberation (6.18.6); and, on another, its absence is used metaphorically to describe the disorderly manner in which the plague dispatched Athenians (2.52.2).

19. Spartan *eunomía:* consider Tyrtaeus F2 (West) in light of Hom. *Od.* 17.487, Hes. *Theog.* 901–3, and Alcman F64 (PMG), and see Pind. *Pyth.* 5.63–81, F189 (Bowra), Hdt. 1.65–66, Thuc. 1.18.1, Diod. 7.12 with Antony Andrewes, *"Eunomía,"* CQ 32:2 (April 1938): 89–102. Solon's legislation was, according to his own testimony, aimed at achieving in Athens what the Spartans had accomplished: F4.30–32 (West). See also Aeschin. 1.5, 3.6. In this connection, see Edward M. Harris, "Solon and the Spirit of the Laws in Archaic and Classical Greece," in *Solon of Athens: New*

Historical and Philological Approaches, ed. Josine H. Blok and André P. M. H. Lardinois (Leiden: Brill, 2006), 290–318.

Prologue

1. This prologue and the two chapters immediately following are for the most part drawn from Paul A. Rahe, *Republics Ancient and Modern: Classical Republicanism and the American Revolution* (Chapel Hill: University of North Carolina Press, 1992), I.ii.2, v–vi. I am grateful to to the University of North Carolina Press for giving me permission to reprint this material here.

2. Cf. Pl. *Leg.* 3.693d–e with 4.712d–e; then, cf. Arist. *Pol.* 1294b13–41 with 1293b7–1294a29. For the context of Aristotle's remarks, see 1289a26–1294b41 and 1299b20–30. See also 1270b17–25. Cf. Isoc. 7.61 with Dem. 20.107–8. See the analysis attributed to Archytas of Tarentum in Stob. *Flor.* 4.1.138 (Hense). Note also Stephen Hodkinson, "The Imaginary Spartan *Politeia,*" in *The Imaginary Polis,* ed. Mogens Herman Hansen (Copenhagen: Det Kongelige Danske Videnskabernes Selskab, 2005), 222–81 (at 227–44), whose exploration of ancient opinion is far less dismissive than his title and the titles of the chapter's subsections would lead one to expect.

3. See Elizabeth Rawson, *The Spartan Tradition in European Thought* (Oxford: Clarendon Press, 1969), 139–367. For the pre-French Revolution context, see Rahe, *RAM,* II–III. See also Paul Cartledge, "The Socratics' Sparta and Rousseau's," in *SNS,* 311–37, and Ian Macgregor Morris, "The Paradigm of Democracy: Sparta in Enlightenment Thought," in *SpartSoc,* 339–62. Victor Ehrenberg's 1934 radio address "A Totalitarian State" is particularly interesting: *Aspects of the Ancient World* (Oxford: Basil Blackwell, 1946), 94–104. See also Henri Irénée Marrou, *A History of Education in Antiquity* (New York: Sheed and Ward, 1956), 22–25, and even more recently, Richard Jenkyns, *The Victorians and Ancient Greece* (Oxford: Basil Blackwell, 1980), 225. For many, Athens was to be the liberal ideal: Nicole Loraux and Pierre Vidal-Naquet, "La Formation de l'Athènes bourgeoise: Essai d'historiographie 1750–1870," in *Classical Influences on Western Thought A.D. 1650–1870,* ed. R. R. Bolgar (Cambridge: Cambridge University Press, 1979), 169–222.

4. Oxford: Antony Andrewes, "The Government of Classical Sparta," in *ASI,* 1–21 (at 1). Cambridge: Moses I. Finley, "Sparta and Spartan Society," in Finley, *Economy and Society in Ancient Greece,* ed. Brent D. Shaw and Richard P. Saller (London: Chatto & Windus, 1981), 24–40 (at 33). The presumption that the Spartans were unquestionably obedient is itself questionable: see Hdt. 9.53–55, Thuc. 5.65–73.

5. *Tês politeías tò kruptón:* Thuc. 5.68.2. Range of possible solutions wide: Antony Andrewes, *Eirene* 12 (1974): 139.

6. The pioneers were François Ollier, *Le Mirage spartiate* (Paris: Les Belles Lettres, 1933–43); Eugène Napoléon Tigerstedt, *The Legend of Sparta in Classical Antiquity* (Stockholm: Almqvist & Wiksell, 1965–74); and Rawson, *The Spartan Tradition in European Thought,* 12–115.

7. Cf. Michael Flower, "The Invention of Tradition in Classical and Hellenistic Sparta," in *SBM,* 191–217 (esp. 194–202), which is a useful, if unwitting, reductio ad absurdum of the current scholarly propensities, with the refreshing defense of oral tradition mounted by Mait Kõiv, *ATEGH,* passim (esp. 9–34); "The Origins, Development, and Reliability of the Ancient Tradition about the Formation of the Spartan Constitution," *Historia* 54:3 (2005): 233–64; and *STAS,* 25–66. See the Ph.D. dissertation of Timothy Donald Doran, "Demographic Fluctuation and Institutional Response in Sparta" (University of California at Berkeley, 2011). Detailed discussion of a single vexed question central to this larger debate: Appendix 1, below.

8. David Hume, "Of Commerce," in *Essays Moral, Political, and Literary,* ed. Eugene F. Miller, revised edition (Indianapolis: Liberty Fund, 1985), 259.

9. Consider Diog. Laert. 2.54 in light of Plut. *Ages.* 20.2 and *Mor.* 212b, and see Xen. *Hell.* 5.3.9. In this connection, see Noreen Humble, "Xenophon's Sons in Sparta? Perspectives on *Xenoi* in the Spartan Upbringing," in *SpartSoc,* 231–50. Cf. Kennell, *GV,* 113–14, who asserts that the word *agōgḗ* was a Hellenistic coinage, with Ephorus *FGrH* 70 F113, 119, which shows that the term was already in use by the mid-fourth century, if not long before. The word may well at times have been used in the same fashion as the Latin term *disciplina* (Livy 45.28.4), as Ducat, *SE,* xii–xiii, 69–71 argues. But, as the latter of the two passages from Ephorus suggests, *paideía* was the

heart of the matter, and, from the outset, the term was also employed more narrowly as a synonym for that.

10. The prose and poetic *politeîai* Critias penned concerning the Lacedaemonians survive only in scattered fragments. If these are typical of what he wrote, his account of Spartan practices and institutions was even more detailed and precise than that provided by Xenophon; and although he may well have misjudged Lacedaemon, he did not misrepresent her form of government and way of life: Lipka, *XSC,* 19–20.

11. Spartan king: consider Ephorus *FGrH* 70 F118 (ap. Strabo 8.5.5)—a badly corrupt snippet, where with Ephraim David I read *perì* rather than *katà*—in light of Arist. *Pol.* 1301b19–21 and Paus. 2.19.1; note Xen. *Hell.* 3.5.25, Diod. 14.89, Plut. *Lys.* 30.1, and Paus. 3.5.6; and see Ephraim David, "The Pamphlet of Pausanias," *PP* 34 (1979): 94–116; Hodkinson, *PWCS,* 28–29; and Lipka, *XSC,* 23–24. See also Daniel Tober, "*POLITEIAI* and Spartan Local History," *Historia* 59:4 (2010): 412–31. Cf. Massimo Nafissi, *La Nascita del Kosmos: Studi sulla storia e la società di Sparta* (Naples: Edizioni Scientifiche Italiane, 1991), 57–62; Hans van Wees, "Tyrtaeus' *Eunomia:* Nothing to Do with the Great Rhetra," in *SNS,* 1–41; Andreas Luther, *Könige und Ephoren: Untersuchungen zur spartanischen Verfassungsgeschichte* (Frankfurt am Main: Antike Verlag, 2004), 21–59; and Ducat, *SE,* 42–45.

12. Thibron: consider Arist. *Pol.* 1333b17–19 in light of Xen. *An.* 7.8.24, *Hell.* 3.1.4–10, 2.1, 4.8.17–22; Diod. 14.36.1–37.4, 38.2, 99.1. Xenophon is said by Plutarch (*Mor.* 345e) to have published his *Anabasis* under the pseudonym Themistogenes of Syracuse, and there is reason to think that this claim may be true: Xen. *Hell.* 3.1.2. It is, therefore, perfectly possible that he did something similar when he released his *Lakedaimoníōn Politeía* to the copyists. But I doubt that he would have appropriated the name of Thibron, a man whom he despised; and I have trouble believing that, had he done so, such a maneuver would have fooled Aristotle, who knew the world of the Socratics rather well. No one else even mentions the work Aristotle attributes to the Spartan. Cf. Marcello Lupi, "Tibrone, Senofonte e le *Lakedaimonion Politeiai* del IV Secolo (a Proposito di Aristotele, *Politica* 1333B)," in *La Politica di Aristotele e la storiographica locale,* ed. Marina Polito and Clara Talamo (Rome: Edizioni TORED, 2010), 131–55, with Lipka, *XSC,* 22–23.

13. Cf. Rosalind Thomas, *Literacy and Orality in Ancient Greece* (Cambridge: Cambridge University Press, 1992), 136–37, with Ellen G. Millender, "Spartan Literacy Revisited," *ClAnt* 20:1 (April 2001): 121–64. We do not know whether Spartans were taught their letters privately or by instructors supported by the city. There is no evidence bearing on this question. Like Paul Cartledge, *NECJ* 34:2 (May 2007): 149–50, I find it hard to believe that the teaching of a skill necessary for the performance of a Spartan's duties as a citizen was left to private initiative. Cf., however, Ducat, *SE,* 119–37.

14. See Giovanni Parmeggiani, "*Isotimia:* Considerazioni sulla storia e sulla storiografia su Sparta in età arcaica e classica," *RSA* 34 (2004): 73–127, and Paul Christesen, "Spartans and Scythians, a Meeting of Mirages: The Portrayal of the Lycurgan *Politeia* in Ephorus' *Histories,*" in *SBP,* 211–63. In this endeavor, Ephorus drew on the pamphlet of the king Pausanias: Strabo 8.5.5 with David, "The Pamphlet of Pausanias," 109–11.

15. See Edmond Lévy, "La Sparte de Platon," *Ktèma* 30 (2005): 217–36. Lacedaemon is a constant presence in Plato's *Laws:* see Glenn R. Morrow, *Plato's Cretan City: A Historical Interpretation of the Laws* (Princeton, NJ: Princeton University Press, 1960); Anton Powell, "Plato and Sparta: Modes of Rule and of Non-Rational Persuasion in the *Laws,*" in *SS,* 273–321; Ducat, *SE,* 53–61; and Mark J. Lutz, *Divine Law and Political Philosophy in Plato's Laws* (Dekalb: Northern Illinois University Press, 2012), 54–89.

16. This is especially true of his account in that work of Sparta: see Eckhart Schütrumpf, "Aristotle on Sparta," in *SS,* 323–45.

17. See Tigerstedt, *The Legend of Sparta in Classical Antiquity,* I 283–84.

18. See Ephraim David, "Aristotle and Sparta," *AncSoc* 13/14 (1982–83): 67–103, and Thomas J. Figueira, "Spartan 'Constitutions' and the Enduring Image of the Spartan Ethos," in *CASPTP,* 143–57. Even if one accepts at face value the argument advanced by David L. Toye, "Aristotle's Other *Politeiai:* Was the *Athenaion Politeia* Atypical?" *CJ* 94:3 (February–March 1999): 235–53, that Aristotle's sources for the political development of most of the Greek cities he studied were grossly inadequate, this argument does not apply to Lacedaemon, as he readily concedes.

19. *Suda* s.v. *Dıkaíarchos.* There are no grounds for supposing that Dicaearchus' treatise was not taken up by the Lacedaemonians until the Roman period, as Tigerstedt, *The Legend of Sparta in Classical Antiquity,* I 586, n. 651, suggests, and Kennell, *GV,* 19, vigorously asserts; and it is most unlikely that this was the case: see K. M. T. Chrimes, *Ancient Sparta: A Re-examination of the Evidence* (Manchester: Manchester University Press, 1949), 7; Edmond Lévy, "Remarques préliminaires sur l'éducation spartiate," *Ktèma* 22 (1997): 151–60 (at 154, n. 16); Hodkinson, *PWCS,* 62, n. 19; and Ducat, *SE,* 177, n. 43. At every stage in their history, the Spartans, who were proud of their heritage, would have welcomed such a work.

20. Cf. Kennell, *GV,* passim (esp. 5–48), who emphatically denies that there was any substantial continuity between the civic *paideía* given the Spartiates in the classical age and the *agōgē* of the Hellenistic and Roman periods, with Lévy, "Remarques préliminaires sur l'éducation spartiate," 151–60, and Ducat, *SE,* ix–xvii, who quite rightly assert that the available evidence suggests the contrary. Note Paul Cartledge's review of the last-mentioned work: *NECJ* 34:2 (May 2007): 149–50.

21. Cicero on Sparta: cf. *Flacc.* 25.63 with *Tusc.* 2.14.34.

22. Ephorus' hostility to Sparta: Massimiliano Pavan, "La teoresia storica di Diodoro Siculo," *RAL* 16 (1961): 19–51. 117–50 (esp. 31–32). Regarding Xenophon, the argument advanced by Leo Strauss, "The Spirit of Sparta and the Taste of Xenophon," *Social Research* 6 (1939): 502–36; W. E. Higgins, *Xenophon the Athenian: The Problem of the Individual and the Society of the Polis* (Albany: State University of New York Press, 1977), 65–82, 115–22; and Gerald Proietti, *Xenophon's Sparta: An Introduction* (Leiden: E. J. Brill, 1987), has now been taken up by a number of classicists: see Chapter 1, note 78, below. Cf. Ollier, *Le Mirage spartiate,* I 372–440, and Tigerstedt, *The Legend of Sparta in Classical Antiquity,* I 159–79, who envisage Xenophon as a more or less unabashed admirer of Lacedaemon. This view still has its adherents: cf. Guido Schepens, "À la Recherché d'Agésilas le roi de Sparte dans le jugement des historiens du IVe siècle av. J.-C.," *REG* 118:1 (January–June 2005): 31–78 (at 43–62), with Noreen Humble, "True History: Xenophon's *Agesilaus* and the Encomiastic Genre," forthcoming in *Xenophon and Sparta: New Perspectives,* ed. Anton Powell and Nicolas Richer (Swansea: Classical Press of Wales, n.d.).

23. See, for example, Pl. *Leg.* 1.630d–631b, 3.688a–d, with Lévy, "La Sparte de Platon," 217–36, and Lutz, *Divine Law and Political Philosophy in Plato's Laws,* 54–89; then, consider Arist. *Pol.* 1269b12–1271b19, 1333b5–1334b5, 1337a11–1339a10. As David, "Aristotle and Sparta," 67–103, points out, on this matter, the two philosophers were generally in agreement. For careful, recent reexaminations of Aristotle's critique, see Elisabeth Hermann-Otto, "Verfassung und Gesellschaft Spartas in der Kritik des Aristoteles," *Historia* 47:1 (1st Quarter 1998): 18–40, and Edmond Lévy, "Le Régime lacédémonien dans la *Politique* d'Aristote: Une Réflexion sur le pouvoir et l'ordre social chez les Grecs," in *Images et représentations du pouvoir et de l'ordre sociale dans l'antiquité,* ed. Michel Molin (Paris: De Boccard, 2001), 57–72. For a summary account of the criticism these figures direct at Lacedaemon, see Chapters 1 and 2, below. Cf. Ollier, *Le Mirage spartiate,* I 139–371, who dismisses as a bigoted aristocrat any ancient observer who is in any way critical of the direct democracies of antiquity and in any way admiring of Lacedaemon; and Tigerstedt, *The Legend of Sparta in Classical Antiquity,* I 241–304, who takes note of the criticism directed at Lacedaemon but does not have a just estimate of its significance, with Ducat, *SE,* 50–64, 140–41, and Hodkinson, "The Imaginary Spartan *Politeia,*" 227–32, 249–54, 259–61, who have a better understanding and appreciation of the central concerns of the two philosophers.

24. Cf. Hodkinson, *PWCS,* 19–112, who recognizes that the Socratics were critics of Sparta and who then goes on to argue that Theophrastus, Dicaearchus, Heracleides, Sphaerus, and the like ignored what the men they most admired had to say, with Figueria, "Spartan 'Constitutions' and the Enduring Image of the Spartan Ethos," 143–57.

25. See Noreen Humble, "Xenophon, Aristotle and Plutarch on Sparta," in *CASPTP,* 291–300.

26. One could easily apply to Plutarch's lives of Lycurgus and Numa the argument developed with regard to his paired lives of two other legendary founders by Christopher B. R. Pelling, "'Making Myth Look Like History': Plato in Plutarch's *Theseus-Romulus,*" in *Plutarco, Platón y Aristóteles,* ed. Aurelio Pérez Jiménez, José García López, and Rosa María Aguilar (Madrid: Ediciones Clasicas, 1999), 431–43, reprinted as "'Making Myth Look Like History': Plutarch's *Theseus-Romulus,*" in Pelling, *Plutarch and History: Eighteen Studies* (London: Duckworth, 2002), 171–95.

27. Customary discernment and caution: Christopher B. R. Pelling, "Plutarch's Adaptation of His Source Material," *JHS* 100 (1980): 127–40, reprinted in Pelling, *Plutarch and History*, 91–115. Note the difficulty that Claude Mossé, "L'Image de Sparte dans les *Vies parallèles* de Plutarque," in *CASPTP*, 303–13, has in squaring what we know concerning Plutarch's consistently careful, judicious treatment of the evidence available to him with the thesis that, in his treatment of Lacedaemon, the biographer somehow resolutely ignored that evidence. For a corrective, see Willem den Boer, *Laconian Studies* (Amsterdam: North Holland Publishing, 1954), 221, who observes, "Modern historians, though possessing no more material for interpretation than Plutarch, have all too often disposed of the customs related by him as ridiculous concoctions offered by him or his sources, and in so doing they have shown less modesty and historical discernment than Plutarch commanded." Plutarch's debt to Plato and Aristotle is obvious and well known. On what he owed Xenophon, see Philip Stadter, " 'Staying Up Late': Plutarch's Reading of Xenophon," in *Xenophon: Ethical Principles and Historical Enquiry*, ed. Fiona Hobden and Christopher Tuplin (Leiden: Brill, 2012), 43–62.

28. Adam Ferguson, *An Essay on the History of Civil Society*, ed. Duncan Forbes (Edinburgh: Edinburgh University Press, 1966), 159.

29. For a thorough survey of the issues and of the literature published on this subject prior to the 1970s, see Pavel Oliva, *Sparta and Her Social Problems* (Amsterdam: Adolf M. Hakkert, 1971); for a more recent survey, see Jean Ducat, "Sparte archaïque et classique: Structures économiques, sociales, politiques (1965–1982)," *REG* 96 (1983): 194–225. I cite, selectively, the more recent literature in the notes below.

Chapter 1. *Paideía*

1. This chapter and the succeeding chapter should serve, in part, as a refutation of Stephen Hodkinson's contention that Lacedaemon was an ordinary *pólis*, which requires that, to a very considerable extent, one disregard the sources: cf. Mogens Herman Hansen, "Was Sparta a Normal or an Exceptional Polis?" with Stephen Hodkinson, "Was Sparta an Exceptional Polis?"; and see Mogens Herman Hansen and Stephen Hodkinson, "Spartan Exceptionalism? Continuing the Debate," all in *SCA*, 385–493.

2. Ethnographic description of Sparta: Hdt. 1.65.1–67.6, 82–83, 2.80, 5.39–42, 6.52–60, 106.1–107.1, 7.102–4, 206–9, 8.72, 9.7–11, 82, 85, with Rosalind Thomas, *Herodotus in Context: Ethnography, Science and the Art of Persuasion* (Cambridge: Cambridge University Press, 2000), 102–34. Cf. Ellen Millender, "Herodotus and Spartan Despotism," in *SBM*, 1–62, and "The Spartan Dyarchy: A Comparative Perspective," in *SCA*, 1–67 (at 1–18), who exaggerates Herodotus' insistence on Lacedaemonian alterity and then treats his observations as an echo of anti-Spartan Athenian prejudice, with Edmond Lévy, "La Sparte de Hérodote," *Ktèma* 24 (1999): 123–34, who thinks him highly favorable to Lacedaemon and who takes his good humor in this regard as a sign that Sparta was not as severe as it would become. I see no reason to entertain either hypothesis or to suppose the historian's assessment anything other than nuanced, balanced, and sound.

3. See Thuc. 1.77.6 and Xen. *Lac. Pol.* 1–10 with Ducat, *SE*, 1–22. Note also Pl. *Leg.* 1.634d–e and Dem. 20.106

4. City into camp, etc.: Pl. *Leg.* 2.666e, Isoc. 6.81, Plut. *Lyc.* 24.1. See Arist. *Pol.* 1324b5–9. In this connection, see also Pl. *Leg.* 1.625c–626c, 628e, 633a–d, 3.688a–d. Cf. Stephen Hodkinson, "Was Classical Sparta a Military Society?" in *SW*, 111–62. Prohibitions against travel and visitation: Ar. *Av.* 1012–13; Thuc. 1.144.2, 2.39.1; Xen. *Lac. Pol.* 14.4; Pl. *Prt.* 342c–d; Isoc. 11.18; Arist. F538 (Rose) = F543 (Gigon); Plut. *Lyc.* 27.6–9, *Agis* 10.3–8, *Mor.* 238d–e with Stefan Rebenich, "Fremdenfeindlichkeit in Sparta? Überlegungen zur Tradition des Spartanischen Xenelasie," *Klio* 80 (1998): 336–59, and Thomas J. Figueira, "Xenelasia and Social Control in Classical Sparta," *CQ* n. s. 53:1 (May 2003): 44–74. Note, however, Xen. *Mem.* 1.2.6. Pl. *Leg.* 12.949e–953e is a commentary on and critique of this Spartan practice. Note the ironical discussion at Pl. *Prt.* 342a–d. See David Whitehead, "The Lakonian Key," *CQ* n.s. 40:1 (1990): 267–68. Intensive patriotism: Thomas Babington Macaulay, *The History of England* (Philadelphia: E. H. Butler & Co., 1861), I 273. Rarely

imitated, universally admired: Xen. *Lac. Pol.* 10.8, Arist. *Pol.* 1337a26–32. See also Joseph. *Ap.* 2.225. For an extended meditation on the *pólis* as a species of political community, see Rahe, *RAM*, I.i–vii. For further discussion of the reasons why Lacedaemon inspired wonder and admiration, see Paul Christesen, "Utopia on the Eurotas: Economic Aspects of the Spartan Mirage," in *Spart-Soc*, 309–37.

    5. Pythagoras and Herodotus on faction: Aristox. F8 (Müller *FHG* II 273), Hdt. 8.3.1.

    6. Antidotes to faction: Alexander Hamilton, James Madison, and John Jay, *The Federalist*, ed. Jacob E. Cook (Middletown, CT: Wesleyan University Press, 1961), no. 10. *Homónoia:* Democr. *Vorsokr.*[6] 68 B250; Lys. 18.17; Xen. *Mem.* 4.4.16; Pl. *Resp.* 1.351a–352a, *Alc.* I 126b–127d; Anaximenes *Rh.* 1424b15–18 (Fuhrmann); Arist. *Eth. Eud.* 1241a15–34, *Eth. Nic.* 1155a22–26, 1167a22–b16, *Pol.* 1330a9–23. See also Thuc. 8.75.2, 93.3; Andoc. 1.140; Lys. 2.63; Aeneas Tacticus 14.1; Hyper. F27 (Jensen); Arist. *Pol.* 1306a9; Paus. 5.14.9. Free vs. commercial *agorá:* Arist. *Pol.* 1331a30–b3. Greek attitude toward commerce: Rahe, *RAM*, I.i–iii.

    7. No coins; flat, iron ingots used instead; silver and gold outlawed: Xen. *Lac. Pol.* 7.5–6; [Pl.] *Eryxias* 400b; Plut. *Lyc.* 9.1–3, *Lys.* 17, *Mor.* 226d; Just. *Epit.* 3.2.11–12; Porph. *Abst.* 4.3; Poll. *Onom.* 7.105, 9.79. Note the measures adopted in Plato's Cretan city: *Leg.* 5.741e–744a. See Thomas J. Figueira, "Iron Money and the Ideology of Consumption at Sparta," in *SBM*, 137–70. Citizens barred from commerce and the mechanical arts: Xen. *Lac. Pol.* 7.1–2; Isoc. 11.18; Plut. *Lyc.* 24.2, *Ages.* 26.6–9, *Mor.* 214b, 239d; Polyaen. 2.1.7; Ael. *VH* 6.6. See also Plut. *Lyc.* 9.4–9, *Mor.* 226d. Extreme lack of respect for mechanical arts: Hdt. 2.167. Given the absence of metics, the necessary arts and crafts were presumably practiced by landless *períoikoi* and by some of the helots (Plut. *Comp. Lyc. et Num.* 2.7) as well: see R. T. Ridley, "The Economic Activities of the Perioikoi," *Mnemosyne*, 4th ser., 27 (1974): 281–92, which needs amendment in light of the rejoinder by Guy Berthiaume, "Citoyens spécialistes à Sparte," *Mnemosyne*, 4th ser., 29 (1976): 360–64. For another view, see Paul Cartledge, "Did Spartan Citizens Ever Practice a Manual Tekhne?" *LCM* 1 (1976): 115–19. Note the measures which the Athenian Stranger devised for Magnesia: Pl. *Leg.* 5.743c–744a, 8.847d–e, 849c–d. Men under thirty barred from *agorá:* Plut. *Lyc.* 25.1 (with Arist. *Pol.* 1278a25–26). Servants of Ares, craftsmen of war: Plut. *Comp. Lyc. et Num.* 2.6. Seek reputation for valor: Thuc. 6.11.6. Trained to secure infantry victory: Xen. *Hell.* 7.1.8.

    8. Horse-breeding: Paus. 6.2.1. Scrutiny of newborns and infanticide: Plut. *Lyc.* 16.1–3 with Pomeroy, *SWo,* 34–37, and the unpublished Ph.D. dissertation of Timothy Donald Doran, "Demographic Fluctuation and Institutional Response in Sparta" (University of California at Berkeley, 2011), passim (esp. 23–53, 70–77). Note Pierre Roussel, "L'Exposition des enfants à Sparte," *REA* 45 (1943): 5–17, and Marc Huys, "The Spartan Practice of Selective Infanticide and Its Parallels in Ancient Utopian Tradition," *AncSoc* 27 (1996): 47–74. Cf. Stefan Link, "Zur Aussetzung neugeborener Kinder in Sparta," *Tyche* 3 (1998): 153–64, and Marcello Lupi, *L'Ordine delle generazioni: Classi di età e costumi matrimoniali nell'antica Sparta* (Bari: Edipuglia, 2000), 47–137.

    9. Equal allotment of land and helots to work it: consider Plut. *Lyc.* 8.2–4, 16.1–3, *Lyc. et Num.* 2.10–11, *Sol.* 16.1–3, *Mor.* 226b, 231e, 238e; Polyb. 6.45.3, 48.3; Just. *Epit.* 3.3.3; Porph. *Abst.* 4.3 in light of Aristotle F611.12 (Rose) = Tits. 143.1.2.12 (Gigon) and Isoc. 11.18, and see Pl. *Leg.* 3.684d–e, 5.736c–e and Isoc. 6.20, 12.179, 259 with Appendix 1, below. On the helots in particular, see Detlef Lotze, *Metaxù Eleuthérōn kaì Doúlōn: Studien zur Rechtsstellungunfreier Landbevölkerungen in Griechenland bis zum 4. Jahrhundert v. Chr* (Berlin: Akademie Verlag, 1959), 38–47; Jean Ducat, "Aspects de l'hilotisme," *AncSoc* 9 (1978): 5–46, "Le Mépris des hilotes," *Annales (ESC)* 29 (1974): 1451–64, and *Hilotes*, which should be read with an eye to Paul Cartledge's review: *CPh* 87:3 (July 1992): 260–63; and Stephen Hodkinson, "Spartiates, Helots and the Direction of the Agrarian Economy: Towards an Understanding of Helotage in Comparative Perspective," in *HMLM*, 248–85. Origins and secondary literature: see Chapter 3, below.

    10. For the existence of and the rationale behind the regulations determining the rent to be paid, see Plut. *Mor.* 239e. For the precise amount paid to each Spartan master and for its distribution within the household, see Plut. *Lyc.* 8.7. The portion reserved for the wife corresponds closely with the monthly contribution made by her husband to the common mess: cf. Plut. *Lyc.* 12.3, who has converted the Laconian into Attic measures, with Dicaearchus F72 (Wehrli) ap. Ath. 4.141c. See also Porph. *Abst.* 4.4. This portion was roughly what a soldier or slave could expect in rations:

see Hom. *Od.* 19.27; Hdt. 7.187.2; Thuc. 4.16.1; Polyb. 6.39.3; Diog. Laert. 8.18; Ath. 3.98e, 6.272b. The annual rent from the allotment seems to have been adequate for about seven persons. See Detlef Lotze, "Zu Einigen Aspekten des Spartanischen Agrarsystems," *JWG* 2 (1971): 63–76. For admirably elaborate, if highly speculative, attempts to calculate the needs of such a household, the needs of the helots required for its support, and the productivity of the land in Messenia likely to have been allocated for this purpose, see Thomas J. Figueira, "Mess Contributions and Subsistence at Sparta," *TAPhA* 114 (1984): 87–109; "Population Patterns in Late Archaic and Classical Sparta," *TAPhA* 116 (1986): 165–213; and "The Demography of the Spartan Helots," in *HMLM,* 193–239, as well as Henk W. Singor, "Spartan Lots and Helot Rents," in *De Agricultura: In Memoriam Pieter Willem de Neeve (1945–1990),* ed. Heleen Sancisi-Weerdenburg, R. J. Vander Spek, H. C. Teitler, and H. T. Wallinga (Amsterdam: J. C. Gieben, 1993), 31–60, and Hodkinson, *PWCS,* 369–98. See also Walter Scheidel, "Helot Numbers: A Simplified Model," in *HMLM,* 240–47. Earlier studies include Ulrich Kahrstedt, "Die Spartanische Agrarwirtschaft," *Hermes* 54 (1919): 279–94, and Auguste François Victor Jardé, *Les Céréales dans l'antiquité grecque* (Paris: Boccard, 1925), 107–22. Cf. Arist. *Pol.* 1264a24–36 for Aristotle's criticism of the similar arrangement in Plato's *Republic.*

11. Martial arts and civil courage: Arist. *Pol.* 1264a9–11, Plut. *Mor.* 239d–e. For the emphasis on courage, see Thuc. 2.39.1, Pl. *Leg.* 2.667a. Caring for selves and possession of fields: Plut. *Mor.* 217a. Josephus on activity and aim: *Ap.* 2.228–31.

12. Masters, seigneurs, leisured gentlemen: Arist. *Pol.* 1269a34–b12, *Rh.* 1367a28–33; Plut. *Lyc.* 24.2. See also Isoc. 11.20. All of the Spartans *kaloì kagathoí:* Thuc. 4.40.2 with Félix Bourriot, "*Kaloi kagathoi, Kalokagathia* à Sparte aux époques archaïque et classique," *Historia* 45:2 (2nd Quarter 1996): 129–40, and Philip Davies, "*Kalos Kagathos* and Scholarly Perceptions of Spartan Society," *Historia* 62:3 (July 2013): 259–79. Spartans as *hómoioi:* Xen. *Hell.* 3.3.5, *Lac. Pol.* 10.7, 13.1, *An.* 4.6.16; Arist. *Pol.* 1306b30; Dem. 20.107. See Hdt. 3.55.1, 7.234.2, 9.62.3 and Thuc. 4.40.2, who use the word playfully as an adjective in contexts where Sparta is being discussed. Something of the sort may be in the background as well at Solon F36.18–20 (West). See also Xen. *Hell.* 3.3.11, Pl. *Leg.* 3.696a–b, Isoc. 7.61. Property and faction: cf. James Madison, *The Federalist,* no. 10, with Pl. *Leg.* 5.744d–745b and Arist. *Pol.* 1295b1–1296a21. Two types of landed property (private and not) at Lacedaemon: Arist. F611.12 (Rose) = Tit. 143.1.2.12 (Gigon) ap. Heraclid. Lemb. 373.12 (Dilts). It was illegal to sell one's civic allotment and shameful to sell one's privately owned farm. Note Plut. *Mor.* 238e–f. For further discussion, see Appendix 1.

13. Sparta exceptional in regard to public education of children, supervision of citizens: Arist. *Eth. Nic.* 1180a24–26, *Pol.* 1337a31–32. Rich and poor subject to same regimen: Thuc. 1.6.4, Xen. *Lac. Pol.* 2–4, Pl. *Leg.* 2.666e–667a, Plut. *Lyc.* 16.4–25.9. Same garb, athletic nudity: Thuc. 1.6.4, Xen. *Lac. Pol.* 7.3, Pl. *Resp.* 5.452c, with Ephraim David, "Sparta and the Politics of Nudity," in *SBP,* 137–63. *Sussítion:* Xen. *Lac. Pol.* 5; Isoc. 11.18; Arist. *Pol.* 1263b36–1264a1, F611.13 (Rose) = Tit. 143.1.2.13 (Gigon) ap. Heraclid. Lemb. 373.13 (Dilts); Plut. *Lyc.* 10, 12, *Mor.* 226d–227a, 236f; Porph. *Abst.* 4.4. See Pl. *Leg.* 8.842b. See also Alcman F98 (PMG) and Plut. *Mor.* 218d who call it the *andreîon.* Note also Just. *Epit.* 3.3.4. See Monika Lavrencic, *Spartanische Küche: Das Gemeinschaftsmahl der Männer in Sparta* (Vienna: Böhlau, 1993), and Adam Rabinowitz, "Drinking from the Same Cup: Sparta and Late Archaic Commensality," in *SCA,* 113–91.

14. Dowries forbidden: Plut. *Mor.* 227f–228a and Just. *Epit.* 3.3.8, who seem to be describing the situation prior to the general liberalization of property law which took place in the fourth century. For this development, see Plut. *Agis* 5.3–7 and Arist. *Pol.* 1270a15–26. Note also the emphasis which Justin places on the manner in which the absence of dowries limits the leverage of the wife and enables the husband to impose a discipline on her. Women inherit, magistrates fine gold diggers: Plut. *Lys.* 30.6, *Mor.* 230a; Ael. *VH* 3.10, 6.4, 10.15. Consider Pollux's reference (*Onom.* 3.48) to *díkē kakogamíou* in light of Plut. *Lys.* 30.7. One should read Plut. *Ages.* 2.6 and *Mor.* 1d in light of Ath. 13.566a–b. See also 13.555c, Stob. *Flor.* 4.22.16 (Hense). There is reason to suspect that, in this regard, Spartan arrangements regarding the inheritance of private property may have been similar to those at Gortyn—where, even when there were surviving sons, a daughter was entitled to inherit half a son's portion of the property left by their parents: see Chapter 2, note 33, below. Sumptuary laws: Plut. *Lyc.* 13.5–7 (with Xen. *Ages.* 8.7), 27.1–5, *Mor.* 189e, 227c. See Arist. F611.13 (Rose) = Tit. 143.1.2.13 (Gigon) ap. Heraclid. Lemb. 373.13 (Dilts). There was evidently some sort of dress code as well, and it applied to both women (Arist. F611.13 [Rose] = Tit.

143.1.2.13 [Gigon] ap. Heraclid. Lemb. 373.13 [Dilts]) and men (*Pol.* 1294b25–29; Plut. *Mor.* 237b, 239c; Just. *Epit.* 3.3.5). See also Plut. *Lyc.* 10.3. For an overview, see Hodkinson, *PWCS*, 209–70.

15. Exception made for breeding and racing of horses: see the material collected by G. E. M. de Ste. Croix, *The Origins of the Peloponnesian War* (Ithaca: Cornell University Press, 1972), 137–38 (with 354–55), and consider Hodkinson, *PWCS*, 303–33. Late formation of standing force of cavalry: Thuc. 4.55. Military employment, see Xen. *Hell.* 6.4.10–11. Free use of servants, horses, and hounds: Xen. *Lac. Pol.* 6.3–4, Arist. *Pol.* 1263a33–39. Common way of life: Thuc. 1.6.4, Xen. *Lac. Pol.* 7.3–4, Arist. *Pol.* 1294b19–29.

16. Old helots of Achaean stock: Chapter 3, note 32, below.

17. Selective recruitment of freed helots as soldiers: Ronald F. Willetts, "The *Neodamodeis*," *CPh* 49 (1954): 27–32; Yvon Garlan, "Les Esclaves grecques en temps de guerre," in *Actes de colloque d'histoire sociale 1970* (Paris: Annales Littéraires de l'Université de Besançon, 1972), 29–62 (esp. 40–48); Karl-Wilhelm Welwei, *Unfreie im antiken Kriegsdienst* (Wiesbaden: Franz Steiner Verlag, 1974–77) I: *Athen und Sparta*, 108–74; Teresa Alfieri Tonini, "Il problema dei *neodamodeis* nell'ambito della società spartana," *RIL* 109 (1975): 305–16; Umberto Cozzoli, "Sparta e l'affrancamento degli iloti nel V e nel IV secolo," in *Sesta miscellanea greca e romana* (Rome: Istituto Italiano per la Storia Antica, 1978), 213–32; and Ducat, *Hilotes*, 155–73. In this connection, one should perhaps also consider Detlef Lotze, "Mothakes," *Historia* 11:4 (October 1962): 427–35.

18. Helot threat: consider Xen. *Hell.* 3.3.4–7; Pl. *Leg.* 6.776c–d, 777b–d; Arist. *Pol.* 1264a32–36, 1269a34–1269b12, 1272b16–22 (with 1330a25–28). To assess the impact on Spartan policy of the fear to which the helot danger gave rise, one should read Hdt. 7.235 (with Xen. *Hell.* 4.8.8, Diod. 14.84.5); Thuc. 4.3–5, 8–23, 26–41, 53–57, 5.35, 39.2–3, 44.3, 56.2–3, 115.2, 6.105.2, 7.18.3, 26.2, 86.3; Diod. 13.64.5–7 in light of Critias *Vorsokr.*[6] 88 B37; Thuc. 4.80 (with 1.132.4, 4.6, 41.3, 55.1, 5.14.3, 23.3, 35.6–7, and Borimir Jordan, "The Ceremony of the Helots in Thucydides, IV, 80," *AC* 59 [1990]: 37–69); Xen. *Lac. Pol.* 12.4; Plut. *Lyc.* 28, *Sol.* 22.1–3. The fact that the Spartans found the means to contain the helot threat should not be taken as evidence that it was not at all times serious: cf. Arlette Roobaert, "Le Danger hilote?" *Ktèma* 2 (1977): 141–55; James T. Chambers, "On Messenian and Laconian Helots in the Fifth Century B.C.," *The Historian* 40 (1977–78): 271–85; Manfred Clauss, *Sparta: Eine Einführung in seine Geschichte und Zivilisation* (Munich: C. H. Beck, 1983), 109–15; Richard J. A. Talbert, "The Role of the Helots in the Class Struggle at Sparta," *Historia* 38:1 (1st Quarter 1989): 22–40; Ducat, *Hilotes*, 105–82; Michael Whitby, "Two Shadows: Images of Spartans and Helots," in *SS*, 87–126, who give the ancient evidence regarding this matter short shrift, with Paul Cartledge, "Richard Talbert's Revision of the Spartan-Helot Struggle: A Reply," *Historia* 40:3 (1991): 379–81; Stefan Link, *Der Kosmos Sparta: Recht und Sitte in klassischer Zeit* (Darmstadt: Wissenschaftliche Buchgesellschaft, 1994), 1–9; Elisabeth Herrmann-Otto, "Verfassung und Gesellschaft Spartas in der Kritik des Aristoteles," *Historia* 47:1 (1998): 18–40 (at 22–25); and Ernst Baltrusch, "Mythos oder Wirklichkeit? Die Helotengefahr und der Peloponnesische Bund," *HZ* 272:1 (February 2001): 1–24, who rightly insist on regarding it as dispositive. Timidity of Laconian helots seized by Thebans: Plut. *Lyc.* 28.10. At the time of the great earthquakes of the 460s, even the old helots of Laconia rose up (note Thuc. 1.128.1, 132.4; then compare Diod. 11.63–64 and Plut. *Cim.* 16.4–8, 17.3 with Paus. 3.11.8; see also Plut. *Lyc.* 28.12); and after the Theban defeat of Sparta at Leuctra, many of the Laconian helots joined the invaders of Laconia: see Ephraim David, "Revolutionary Agitation in Sparta after Leuctra," *Athenaeum* 68 (1980): 299–308. Note also Thuc. 7.26.2. Hostile force lying in wait: Arist. *Pol.* 1269b36–39. In general, see Ducat, "Aspects de l'hilotisme," 5–46 (esp. 24–38); Paul Cartledge, "Rebels and *Sambos* in Classical Greece: A Comparative View," in Cartledge, *SR*, 127–52; and Dorothy M. Figueira and Thomas J. Figueira, "The Colonial 'Subject' and the Ideology of Subjection in Lakōnikē: Tasting Laconian Wine Behind Lacanian Labels," in *SCA*, 305–30.

19. Messenian helots as nation in bondage hostile to masters, prone to revolt: consider Xen. *Hell.* 3.3.4–7; Pl. *Leg.* 6.776c–d, 777b–d; Arist. *Pol.* 1269a34–1269b12, 1272b17–22 (with 1330a25–28); Ath. 6.264f–265a in light of Thuc. 1.101.2, and see Chapters 3 and 4, below, where I address the scholarly disputes concerning the ethnogenesis of the Messenians. Jean Ducat understates the threat posed by the Laconian helots, but he is nonetheless correct in emphasizing the role played in Messenia by the national question: see *Hilotes*, 105–73.

20. Argive threat: Arist. *Pol.* 1269a39–1269b5. The recent discovery of a new fragment of

Tyrtaeus (*POxy.* 3316 = F23a [West]) confirms the contention of Pausanias (2.24.7, 3.2.2–3, 7.3–6, 4.5.1–3, 10.1, 6–7, 11.1–8, 14.1, 8, 15.7, 17.2, 7, 8.27.1) that Argos was already hostile to Sparta in the very early years of the archaic period. Note also Xen. *Hell.* 3.5.11, Strabo 8.4.10.

21. Helots of two regions greatly outnumber the Spartans: Hdt. 9.10.1, 28.2, 29.1, 61.2. The precise numbers are disputed: see the demographic studies cited in note 10, above. Note also Xen. *Hell.* 3.3.4–5. Even after Messenia had become independent, the helots remained numerous. Plutarch (*Cleom.* 18.3) claims that Aetolians invading the region in the third century were able to run off with fifty thousand slaves; the observation made by one Spartan that these invaders had helped the city by lightening her burden suggests that virtually all of those taken were helots. The extent of that burden in earlier times helps explain the intensity of the Spartan eagerness to conserve manpower, especially after 465: Hdt. 7.205.2; Thuc. 4.15, 19.1, 5.15; Diod. 13.52.3; Androtion *FGrH* 324 F44; Plut. *Ages.* 30.

22. *Períoikoi* loyal only out of fear: Xen. *Hell.* 3.3.6. Note the manner in which they comported themselves when the opportunity for rebellion presented itself: Thuc. 1.101.2; Xen. *Hell.* 6.5.25, 32, 7.2.2, *Ages.* 2.24; Plut. *Ages.* 32.12. See also Cartledge, *SL,* 153–66, and David, "Revolutionary Agitation in Sparta after Leuctra," 299–308. Cf. Graham Shipley, "*Perioikos:* The Discovery of Classical Lakonia," in *Philolakōn,* 211–26. Allies often disaffected and sometimes hostile: Christina Wolff, *Sparta und die peloponnesische Staatenwelt in archaischer und klassischer Zeit* (Munich: Herbert Utz Verlag, 2010). Note also Rahe, *PC,* Chapters 4 and 5. I treat this question in detail in *The Grand Strategy of Classical Sparta: The Athenian Challenge,* forthcoming.

23. Corinthian leader on Spartan weakness nearer home: Xen. *Hell.* 4.2.11–12. Demographic decline: Appendix 1. Single defeat apt to endanger: consider Xen. *Hell.* 7.1.10, Arist. *Pol.* 1270a29–34, in light of Charles-Louis de Secondat, baron de La Brède et de Montesquieu, *Considérations sur les causes de la grandeur des Romains et de leur décadence* 18.52–60, in *Œuvres complètes de Montesquieu* II (Oxford: Voltaire Foundation, 2000), 235.

24. Fear as a fundamental passion: Thucydides (cf. 8.40.2 with 24.4) hints at this. So does Isocrates (12.177–81). See Lys. 33.7 with Preston H. Epps, "Fear in Spartan Character," *CPh* 28 (1933): 12–29. For the salutary effect of such fear, see Pl. *Leg.* 3.699c, Arist. *Pol.* 1308a24–30. What the helot threat did for the citizens of Sparta, the Etruscans, Samnites, Gauls, and Carthaginians accomplished for the Roman aristocracy: cf. Sall. *Iug.* 41.3 with Jochen Martin, "Dynasteia," in *Historische Semantik und Begriffsgeschichte,* ed. Reinhart Koselleck (Stuttgart: Klett-Cotta, 1978), 228–41. Slow to go to war: Thuc. 1.23.6, 68–71, 88, 118.2, 5.107, 109. Caution on the field of battle: Hdt. 9.46–48 and Thuc. 5.63–65. When successful in routing the foe, the Spartans were more concerned with minimizing their own losses than with making their victory complete. Thus, where the Athenians were inclined to charge forward, press home their advantage, and slaughter or capture as many as possible of those who had taken to heel, the Spartans tended to hold back and to remain in formation under the protection afforded by their phalanx: cf. Thuc. 1.70.2–5 with 5.73.4, and see Paus. 4.8.11; Plut. *Lyc.* 22.9–10, *Mor.* 228f. For similar reasons, the Lacedaemonians were prohibited from dispersing to strip the bodies of the enemy dead: Plut. *Mor.* 228f–229a and Ael. *VH* 6.6. Interests confused with honor: cf. the charge made at Thuc. 5.105.3–4 with the pattern of behavior evidenced at 3.52–68. Distrust and deceit: Hdt. 9.54.1 with Alfred S. Bradford, "The Duplicitous Spartan," in *SS,* 59–85, and Andrew J. Bayliss, "Using Few Words Wisely? 'Laconic Swearing' and Spartan Duplicity," in *SCA,* 231–60. The Spartans were even supposed to have invented the stratagem of securing victory by bribing key figures on the enemy side: Paus 4.17.2. Note also Plut. *Ages.* 32.14, *Marc.* 22.9–10, *Mor.* 238f: it was considered more glorious to win by trickery than in a pitched battle. Temple to *Phóbos:* Plut. *Cleom.* 9.1–2 with Ernst Bernert, *RE* s.v. Phobos XX:1 (1941): 309–18, and Marie-Madeleine Mactoux, "Phobos à Sparte," *RHR* 210:3 (1993): 259–304.

25. Imbued with a fear of the gods: Paus. 3.5.8. The evidence for Spartan piety is ubiquitous: see Hdt. 1.65–70, 5.42–46, 62–75, 90–93, 6.52–86, 105–7, 120 (cf. Pl. *Leg.* 3.698c–e, Paus. 4.15.2, Strabo 8.4.9), 7.133–37, 204–6, 220–21, 239, 8.141, 9.7–11, 19, 33–38, 61–62, 64–65, 73, 78–81, 85; Thuc. 1.103, 112, 118, 126–34, 2.74, 3.14–15, 92, 4.5, 118, 5.16–18, 23, 30, 49–50, 54, 75–76, 82, 116, 6.95, 7.18, 8.6; Xen. *Hell.* 3.1.17–19, 23–24, 2.21–31, 3.1–5, 4.3–4, 6, 11, 15, 18, 23, 5.5, 23–25, 4.2.20, 3.14, 21, 5.1–2, 11, 6.10, 7.2–5, 7, 5.1.29, 33, 3.14, 19, 27, 4.37, 41, 47, 49, 6.4.2–3 (cf. 7–8), 15–16, 5.12, 17–18, 7.1.31, 34, *Lac. Pol.* 8.5, 13.2–5, 8–9, 15.2–5, 9, *Ages.* 1.2, 10–13, 27,

31, 2.13–15, 17, 3.2–5, 8.7, 11.1–2, 8, 16. For an overview, see Robert Parker, "Spartan Religion," in *CSTS*, 142–72; Michael A. Flower, "Spartan 'Religion' and Greek 'Religion,'" in *SCA*, 193–229; Anton Powell, "Divination, Royalty and Insecurity in Classical Sparta," in *SBP*, 85–135; and Nicolas Richer, *La Religion des Spartiates: Croyances et cultes dans l'Antiquité* (Paris: Les Belles Lettres, 2012). For an intriguing attempt partially to explain why the Spartans were so exceptionally pious, see Paul Cartledge, "Seismicity and Spartan Society," *LCM* 1 (1976): 25–28. Note Stephen Hodkinson, "Social Order and the Conflict of Values in Classical Sparta," *Chiron* 13 (1983): 239–81 (at 273–76).

26. Laws made by gods: Pl. *Leg.* 1.634d–e. Menelaus: Soph. *Aj.* 1073–84. Importance of *aidōs*: Nicolas Richer, "*Aidōs* at Sparta," tr. Emma Stafford, in *SNS*, 91–115. *Enōmotía*: Hdt. 1.65.5; Thuc. 5.66.3, 67.3, 68.3; Xen. *Lac. Pol.* 11.4, *An.* 3.4.21, 4.3.26, *Hell.* 6.4.12; Timaeus *Lexicon of Words in Plato* s.v. *enōmotía*; *Suda* s.v. *enōmotía*; *Etym. Magn.* s.v. *enōmotía*; Phot. *Bibl.* s.v. *enōmotía* with Arnold J. Toynbee, "The Enomotia," in Toynbee, *SPGH*, 368–71, and Hans van Wees, "'The Oath of the Sworn Bands': The Acharnae Stela, the Oath of Plataea and Archaic Spartan Warfare," in *FS*, 125–64 (esp. 125–35).

27. Though originally published in 1912, Martin Nilsson's essay on this subject, "Die Grundlagen des spartanischen Lebens," in Nilsson, *Opuscula Selecta* (Lund: Gleerup, 1951–52), II 826–69, remains valuable—particularly for its discussion of the similar institutions to be found in the tribes of Africa and the South Seas. See also Henri Jeanmaire, *Couroi et courètes: Essai sur l'éducation spartiate et sur les rites d'adolescence dans l'antiquité hellénique* (Lille: Bibliothèque Universitaire, 1939), 147–227, 463–588, with Louis Gernet, "Structures sociales et rites d'adolescence dans la Grèce antique," in Gernet, *Les Grecs sans miracle,* ed. Riccardo di Donato (Paris: Maspero, 1983), 201–11. Recent work paying particular attention to the relevant anthropological literature includes Angelo Brelich, *Paides e parthenoi* (Rome: Edizioni dell' Ateneo 1969), I 113–207; Pierre Vidal-Naquet, "The Black Hunter and the Origin of the Athenian *Ephebia*" and "Recipes for Greek Adolescence," in Vidal-Naquet, *The Black Hunter: Forms of Thought and Forms of Society in the Greek World,* trans. Andrew Szegedy-Maszak (Baltimore: Johns Hopkins University Press, 1986), 106–56; Jean-Pierre Vernant, "Between Shame and Glory: The Identity of the Young Spartan Warrior," in Vernant, *Mortals and Immortals: Collected Essays,* ed. Froma I. Zeitlin (Princeton, NJ: Princeton University Press, 1991), 220–43; and Marcello Lupi, "Sparta Compared: Ethnographic Perspectives in Spartan Studies," in *SBM*, 305–22. Cf. Kennell, *GV*, who is inclined to throw out much of the available evidence, with Ducat, *SE*, passim, who demonstrates its value. For the reasons why, throughout this work, I persist in using the term *agōgḗ* to refer to the system of *paideía* established in archaic and classical Sparta; see the Prologue, note 9, above

28. Herd of boys: Pl. *Leg.* 2.666e–667a, Plut. *Lyc.* 16.7–9. See also Xen. *Lac. Pol.* 2.1–11. Absorption into political community: Plut. *Lyc.* 24.1 with Jean-Jacques Rousseau, *Du Contrat social* 2.7, in *Œuvres complètes de Rousseau,* ed. Bernard Gagnebin and Marcel Raymond (Paris: Bibliothèque de Pléiade, 1959–1969), III 381–82. There is no evidence to justify Ducat's conviction (*SE,* 119–37, 261) that the *paîdes* slept at home and remained a part of the *oîkos*.

29. Dances, poetry, songs: Plut. *Lyc.* 21, 24.5 with Birgalias, *OES*, 185–219. For the dances, see Henri Jeanmaire, "La Cryptie lacédémonienne," *REG* 26 (1913): 143 n. 2, and Soteroula Constantinidou, "Dionysiac Elements in Spartan Cult Dances," *Phoenix* 52:1/2 (Spring–Summer 1998): 15–30. Note Paus. 3.11.9. Athletics, mock battles, dancing, musical contests: Thuc. 5.69.2–70, Polyb. 4.20.6, Val. Max. 2.6.2, Plut. *Mor.* 238b, Ath. 14.630e–631c (with 627b–d, 628e–f). Cf. Pl. *Leg.* 1.633b–c, 2.654a–662c. One should probably interpret what we are told (Paus. 3.14.8–10, Cic. *Tusc.* 5.27.77, Lucian *Anach.* 38, Plut. *Mor.* 290d) of the mock battles among the Spartan youth in light of the parallel discussion in Ephorus (*FGrH* 70 F149 [ap. Strabo 10.4.18, 20]) and Aristotle (F611.15 [Rose] = Tit. 143.1.3.15 [Gigon] ap. Heraclid. Lemb. 374.15 [Dilts]) regarding the practice on Crete. It is clearly not fortuitous that, at Sparta, flute playing was an hereditary office: cf. Hdt. 6.60 with Thuc. 5.70. See, in this connection, Everett L. Wheeler, "*Hoplomachia* and Greek Dances in Arms," *GRBS* 23 (1982): 223–33, and "The *Hoplomachoi* and Vegetius' Spartan Drillmasters," *Chiron* 13 (1983): 1–20. Short rations, theft, and punishment: Xen. *Lac. Pol.* 2.6, *An.* 4.6.14–16; Plut. *Lyc.* 17.5–8, *Mor.* 237e–f with Birgalias, *OES*, 81–95.

30. Boy and fox: Plut. *Lyc.* 18.1, *Mor.* 234a–b. Fox meat a delicacy: Galen *De aliment. fac.* 3.1.665 [*CMG*], Oreib. 2.68.11 [*CMG*]. Cf. Jean Ducat, "L'Enfant spartiate et le renardeau," *REG*

117:1 (January–June 2004): 125–40, and *SE*, 192, with Stefan Link, "Snatching and Keeping: The Motif of Taking in Spartan Culture," in *SpartSoc*, 1–24.

31. Music central: Ath. 14.632f–633a. Pindar on Spartan choirs: F189 (Bowra). Terpander on spears, music, and justice at Lacedaemon: F6 (Bergk) should be read with Hellanicus *FGrH* 4 F85; Plut. *Mor.* 1134b–c, 1146b–c; Ath. 14.635f. See also Arist. F545 (Rose) = F551 (Gigon). Alcman on cithara and swords: F41 (PMG). Pratinus on Laconian taste for choruses: F2 (PMG).

32. Great festivals of Sparta: see Felix Bölte, "Zu Lakonischen Festen," *RhM* 78 (1929): 124–43; Michael Pettersson, *Cults of Apollo at Sparta: The Hyakinthia, the Gymnopaidiai, and the Karneia* (Stockholm: Paul Åströms Forlag, 1992); Ducat, *SE*, 249–79; and Richer, *La Religion des Spartiates*, 343–559. In this connection, one should also consult Jeanmaire, *Couroi et courètes*, 513–40; Angelo Brelich, *Guerre, agoni et culti nella Grecia arcaica* (Bonn: R. Habelt, 1961), esp. 22–39, 74–84; and Jean-Pierre Vernant, "Une Divinité des marges: Artémis Orthia," in *Recherches sur les cultes grecs et l'occident* II (Naples: Centre Jean Bérard, 1984), 13–28. Music vs. *stásis*: Plut. *Mor.* 1146b–c with 779a. In judging what may seem an extravagant claim, one should consider the parallel testimony of Polybius concerning Arcadia: 4.17.3–21.12. Pindar on poetry and *eunomía*: *Pyth.* 5.63–81. Lacedaemonian neglect of musical techniques and focus on utility: Arist. *Pol.* 1339b2–4. See also Pl. *Leg.* 2.659d–661d, 666e. Charms of army camp and Spartan expertise: Xen. *An.* 4.8.25–28.

33. Total subordination of the individual to the community: Pl. *Resp.* 2.375b–403c, 10.606e–608b, *Leg.* 2.654c–671a, 3.700a–701b, 4.719b–e, 7.801a–804b, 810b–813a, 817a–d, 8.829c–e, 10.890a, 11.935e–936b, 12.941b.

34. Johann Peter Eckermann, *Gespräche mit Goethe* (Jena: E. Diederichs, 1905), II 298–99.

35. Plutarch on focus of Spartan poetry: *Lyc.* 21.2. See also *Mor.* 238a–b, Ath. 14.632f–633a. Homer regarded as depicting Ionian way of life: Pl. *Leg.* 3.680c–e. Plato treats Tyrtaeus as the poet supreme in Lacedaemon: *Leg.* 1.629a–630d, 2.666e–667a, 9.858e. See Dio Chrys. *Orat.* 2.29. Lycurgus' discovery and propagation of the Homeric epics: Plut. *Lyc.* 4.5. Poems chanted on march: cf. Ath. 14.630f with Thuc. 5.69.2, and see Plut. *Mor.* 238b. After dinner, singing of Tyrtaeus: Philochorus *FGrH* 328 F216.

36. Sons of Heracles: Tyrtaeus F2 (West). Land of milk and honey: cf. Deut. 8.7–8 with Eur. F1083 (Nauck²). The rigor of Spartan life caused some Jews to suppose that Spartan law derived from Abraham: 1 Macc. 12; Joseph. *AJ* 12.225–27, 13.164–70. See Michael S. Ginsburg, "Sparta and Judaea," *CPh* 29:2 (April 1934): 117–22.

37. Oracle: Tyrtaeus F4 (West). For the historical significance of this oracle, see the discussion of the Great Rhetra in Chapter 4, below.

38. Helots: Tyrtaeus F5–7 (West).

39. Consider Myron of Priene *FGrH* 106 F2 in light of Theognis 53–58 (West); Ar. *Nub.* 69–72, *Lys.* 1150–56, *Eccl.* 720–24; and Poll. *Onom.* 7.68, and see Plut. *Lyc.* 28.8–11, *Demetr.* 1, *Mor.* 239a–b. In this connection, one should read Pl. *Leg.* 7.816d–e. Note also Theopomp. *FGrH* 115 F13. Plutarch (*Comp. Lyc. et Num.* 1.10) describes the treatment of the helots as "savage and contrary to custom in the extreme." See Ducat, "Le Mépris des hilotes," 1451–64, and *Hilotes*, 107–27, 178–80; Ephraim David, "Laughter in Spartan Society," in *CSTS*, 1–25; and Figueira and Figueira, "The Colonial 'Subject' and the Ideology of Subjection in Lakōnikē," 305–30.

40. For an overview, read Xen. *Lac. Pol.* 2–3, *An.* 4.6.14–15, 4.8.25 (with 4.7.16); Isoc. 12.211–17; Paus. 3.16.7–11; Plut. *Lyc.* 16–18, 21, 28, *Mor.* 237a–238d, 239d; Lucian *Anach.* 38; Ael. *VH* 7 (with Stat. *Theb.* 4.233, Philostr. *VA* 6.20, Tert. *Ad Martyras* 4, Libanius *Or.* 1.23, and Themistius *Or.* 21.250a); and Hesychius s.v. *Boúa, Bouagór,* in conjunction with R. C. Bosanquet, "Excavations at Sparta, 1906: 5. The Sanctuary of Artemis Orthia," *ABSA* 12 (1905–6): 303–17 (esp. 312–17); K. M. T. Chrimes, *Ancient Sparta: A Re-examination of the Evidence* (Manchester: Manchester University Press, 1949), 84–136; and Françoise Frontisi-Ducroux, "La *Bomolochia*: Autour de l'embuscade à l'autel," in *Recherches sur les cultes grecs et l'Occident* II (Naples: Centre Jean Bérard, 1984), 29–49. For evidence pertinent to the dances and the masks worn, consider Hdt. 6.129–30; Ar. *Nub.* 553–56, *Eq.* 697, *Lys.* 82, 1242–76, 1296–1308, *Plut.* 279 (all with the attendant scholia); Schol. Eur. *Hec.* 934; Xen. *Hell.* 4.5.11, *Ages.* 2.17 (with *An.* 6.1.11); Sosibius *FGrH* 595 F7 (ap. Ath. 14.621d–f); Verg. *G.* 2.487–88; Lucian *Salt.* 10–12; Libanius *Or.* 64.17; Ath. 14.629f–631d, 15.678c; Poll. *Onom.* 4.99–107 (with Ar. *Nub.* 540–48 and the attendant scholia,

Theophr. *Char.* 6.3, Paus. 6.22.1), 150–51 (with Ar. *Plut.* 1050–94); Hesychius s .v. *Brudalícha, Brullıchıstaí, deıkēlıstaí* (with Plut. *Ages.* 21.8, *Mor.* 212f, and Schol. Ap. Rhod. *Argon.* 1.746), *thermastrís, kalabís, kórdax, kordakízeıa, kordakısmoí, koruthalístrıaı* (with Ath. 4.139a–b), *kulínthıon, kúnthıon, kúrıthra, kurıttoí, turbasía,* and Phot. *Bibl.* s.v. *kallabís, móthōn* (with Ath. 14.618c), in light of R. M. Dawkins, "Excavations at Sparta, 1906: 6. Remains of the Archaic Greek Period," and R. C. Bosanquet, "7. The Cult of Orthia as Illustrated by the Finds," *ABSA* 12 (1905–6): 318–30 (esp. 324–26), 331–43 (esp. 338–43); Guy Dickins, "The Terracotta Masks," in *The Sanctuary of Artemis Orthia at Sparta,* ed. R. M. Dawkins (London: Macmillan, 1929), 163–86 (with plates xlvii–lxii); and Arthur Pickard-Cambridge, *Dithyramb, Tragedy and Comedy,* second edition, rev. T. B. L. Webster (Oxford: Oxford University Press, 1962), 132–87 (esp. 132–37, 162–69). After digesting this material, peruse Pl. *Resp.* 3.412e–414a and *Leg.* 1.633a–2.674c (esp. 671b–d), 7.812b–817d (esp. 815c–d, 816d–e), note Ephraim David, "Sparta's Social Hair," *Eranos* 90 (1992): 11–21; ponder the seminal discussion of Jean-Pierre Vernant, "Between Shame and Glory: The Identity of the Young Spartan Warrior," 220–43; and see Ducat, *SE,* 139–222, 249–79. Note, in this connection, Jean-Pierre Vernant and Françoise Frontisi-Ducroux, "Features of the Mask in Ancient Greece," in Jean-Pierre Vernant and Pierre Vidal-Naquet, *Myth and Tragedy in Ancient Greece,* trans. Janet Lloyd (New York: Zone Books, 1988), 189–206 (esp. 195–201), and Jane Burr Carter, "The Masks of Ortheia," *AJA* 91:3 (July 1987): 355–83. For comparative data from other Greek cities, see Françoise Frontisi-Ducroux, "L'Homme, le cerf, et le berger: Chemins grecs de la civilité," *TR* 4 (1983): 53–76, and Denise Fourgous, "Gloire et infamie des seigneurs de l'Eubée," *Metis* 2 (1987): 5–30; and consider H. J. Rose, "Greek Rites of Stealing," *HThR* 34 (1941): 1–5, with Hdt. 3.48. Spartans free in fullest sense of the word: Critias *Vorsokr.*[6] 88 B37.

41. Tyrtaeus F10 (West). Good for stirring up the *néoı:* Plut. *Cleom.* 2.4 with Appendix 2, below. Cf. Plut. *Mor.* 235f with 959a–b.

42. Tyrtaeus F11 (West).

43. Cf. Tyrtaeus F12 (West) with Hom. *Il.* 11.784 (cf. 6.208–9) and *Od.* 1.1–3. See, in particular, Werner Jaeger, "Tyrtaeus on True Arete," in Jaeger, *Five Essays,* tr. Adele M. Fiske (Montreal: Mario Casalini, 1966), 103–42. See also H. James Shey, "Tyrtaeus and the Art of Propaganda," *Arethusa* 9 (1976): 5–28; Charles Fuqua, "Tyrtaeus and the Cult of Heroes," *GRBS* 22 (1981): 215–26; and Theodore A. Tarkow, "Tyrtaeus 9D: The Role of Poetry in the New Sparta," *AC* 52 (1983): 48–69.

44. Tyrtaeus F12.1–9 (West).

45. Tyrtaeus F12.10–22 (West).

46. Cf. Hom. *Il.* 22.38–76 with Tyrtaeus F10.23–27 (West). See P. A. L. Greenhalgh, "Patriotism in the Homeric World," *Historia* 21:4 (4th Quarter 1972): 528–37.

47. Burial of ordinary Spartans: Arist. F611.13 (Rose) = Tit. 143.1.2.13 (Gigon) ap. Heraclid. Lemb. 373.13 (Dilts). Burial of champions: see, for example, Paus. 3.12.9, 14.1, and note R. Ball, "Herodotos' List of the Spartans Who Died at Thermopylai," *MusAfr* 5 (1976): 1–8, and W. R. Connor, "Pausanias 3.14.1: A Sidelight on Spartan History, C. 440 B.C.," *TAPhA* 109 (1979): 21–27. Only those who died in battle had their names inscribed on their tombstones: consider *IG* V i 701–3, 706–7 in light of Plut. *Lyc.* 27.3, *Mor.* 238d, and see Franz Willemsen, "Zu den Lakedämoniergräbern im Kerameikos," *MDAI(A)* 92 (1977): 117–57. Those who distinguished themselves in so dying might receive the prize of valor [*arısteîa*] and even become the subject of song: see Pritchett, *GSW,* II 285; note Plut. *Lyc.* 21.2 and Ael. *VH* 6.6; and consider Bölte, "Zu Lakonischen Festen," 124–32 (esp. 130 n. 6), and Henry Theodore Wade-Gery, "A Note on the Origin of the Spartan Gymnopaidiai," *CQ* 43:1/2 (January–April 1949): 79–81 (esp. 80 n. 4), in conjunction with Hdt. 1.82. See Hodkinson, *PWCS,* 237–70, and Polly Low, "Commemorating the Spartan War-Dead," in *SW,* 85–109.

48. Tyrtaeus F12.23–34 (West). Note Xen. *Hell.* 5.4.33.

49. Tyrtaeus F12.35–44 (West). There were formal mechanisms for selecting those who had distinguished themselves: consider Hdt. 8.124 and Thuc. 2.25.2 in light of David M. Lewis, *Sparta and Persia* (Leiden: Brill, 1977), 42 n. 102, and see Plut. *Ages.* 34.8–11 (with Ael. *VH* 6.3 and Polyaen. 2.9), 35.1–2.

50. Ritual preparations for combat designed to discomfit the foe: cf. Hdt. 7.208–9 with 1.82, and see Xen. *Lac. Pol.* 11.3, 13.8; Plut. *Mor.* 238f; Ael. *VH* 6.6. According to Tacitus (*Germ.* 38), the

Suevi wore their hair long for similar reasons and their chiefs prepared for battle in a similar fashion. Wine imbibed before battle: Xen. *Hell.* 6.4.8 with Plut. *Dion* 30.5. Hereditary flute players and march: Hdt. 6.60 with Thuc. 5.70, Plut. *Mor.* 238b, with note 29, above. Paean: Aesch. *Sept.* 270; Thuc. 5.70; Diod. 5.34.5; Plut. *Lyc.* 21.4, 22.5–7, *Mor.* 238b with Pritchett, *GSW,* I 105–8. Role of intoxicants in war: John Keegan, *The Face of Battle* (New York: Viking Press, 1976), 113–14, 181–82, 241, 326. Royal sacrifice to Muses on eve of battle: Plut. *Lyc.* 21.7, *Mor.* 238b. In this connection, see also Dio Chrys. *Or.* 2.31M, 92R; Val. Max. 2.6.2.

51. Overpopulation: Chapter 4 and Appendix 1, below. The decline in population that took place in and after 465 may well have altered the rigor of the selection process, as Henk W. Singor, "Admission to the *Syssitia* in Fifth-Century Sparta," in *SNS,* 67–89, suggests.

52. Martin Nilsson's reconstruction in 1912 ("Die Grundlagen des spartanischen Lebens," 826–69 [esp. 826–49]) of the stages of the *agōgḗ* needs adjustment in light of the arguments and evidence presented by Aubrey Diller, "A New Source on the Spartan *Ephebeia*," *AJPh* 62 (1941): 499–501; Chrimes, *Ancient Sparta,* 84–117; C. M. Tazelaar, "PAIDES KAI EPHEBOI: Some Notes on the Spartan Stages of Youth," *Mnemosyne,* 4th ser., 20:2 (1967): 127–53; Hodkinson, "Social Order and the Conflict of Values in Classical Sparta," 249–50; MacDowell, *SL,* 159–67; Dirk-Achim Kukofka, "Die *Paidískoi* im System der spartanischen Altersklassen," *Philologus* 137:3 (1993): 197–205; Kennell, *GV,* 28–142; Lupi, *L'Ordine delle generazioni,* 27–64; and Ducat, *SE,* 69–222. Cf. Albert Billheimer, "Tà déka aph hébēs," *TAPhA* 77 (1946): 214–20, and H. I. Marrou, "Les Classes d'âge de la jeunesse spartiate," *REA* 48 (1946): 216–330. For a useful survey of the range of opinion in the past, see Birgalias, *OES,* 59–70. For comparative material, see Heinrich Schurtz, *Altersklassen und Männerbünde: Eine Darstellung der Grundformen der Gesellschaft* (Berlin: G. Reimer, 1902); Bernardo Bernardi, *Age Class Systems: Social Institutions and Polities Based on Age,* trans. David I. Kertzer (Cambridge: Cambridge University Press, 1985); and Robert Sallares, *The Ecology of the Ancient Greek World* (London: Duckworth, 1991), 160–92.

53. For the stages through which Spartan boys advanced and the ages in which they completed each stage, cf. Xen. *Lac. Pol.* 2–4 with *Hell.* 5.4.32; see Plut. *Lyc.* 16.1–2, 7, 12, 17.3–4, 22.1–6; and consider the evidence contained in the so-called Herodotus and Strabo glosses (which are conveniently reprinted by MacDowell, *SL,* 161) in light of the literature cited in note 52, above. I have followed Ducat, *SE,* 69–117, except in two particulars—first, where his argument seems to me to depart from the evidence suggesting that the class of *eirénes* was constituted by *tà déka aph hébēs* (those between *hḗbē* and thirty), evidence, let me add, which he fully cites; and, second, where his argument is at odds with the evidence strongly suggesting that, at Lacedaemon, the terms *néoi* and *hēbôntes* were used to refer to men in the age group stretching from twenty to forty-five (evidence I cite in Appendix 2, below). The existence of a formal *dokimasía* by the magistrates stands to reason and can be inferred from occasional allusions in the ancient texts. We are told of the scrutiny that took place shortly after a child's birth (Plut. *Lyc.* 16.1–2); there is evidence (Ael. *VH* 6.3, which should be read with Plut. *Ages.* 34.8–11) suggesting that, at one or more stages in the course of his education, each *paîs* could expect to be given a formal looking over. That he would again be subjected to scrutiny when he became a *paidískos* also stands to reason and can be inferred from Xenophon's reference (*Hell.* 5.4.25) to someone who had just graduated *ek paídōn* as *eudokimṓtatos;* and Plutarch's reference (*Lyc.* 17.1) to *hoi eudokímoi néoi* suggests that those who entered adulthood and came to be called *hoi hēbôntes* or *hoi néoi* were once again put through a *dokimasía.* Consider Xenophon's use of the words *adókimoi* and *eudokímos* at *Lac. Pol.* 3.3, 13.8 with this possibility in mind, and see Willem den Boer, *Laconian Studies* (Amsterdam: North Holland Publishing, 1954), 284–88, in light of Appendix 2 and note 60, below. Note also Xen. *Hell.* 5.4.32, which suggests what we would in any case assume: that formal judgments were reached at each major interval.

54. Vigorous training, tests of strength and courage: Plut. *Lyc.* 16.7–19.13 with Xen. *Lac. Pol.* 2.1, *Hell.* 5.4.32. *Krupteía:* Pl. *Leg.* 1.633b–c (with the scholia); Arist. F538, 611.10 (Rose) = F543, Tit. 143.1.2.10 (Gigon) ap. Heraclid. Lemb. 373.10 (Dilts); Plut. *Lyc.* 28.2–4, *Cleom.* 28.4. See Just. *Epit.* 3.3.6–7. Jeanmaire, "La Cryptie lacédémonienne," 121–50, elucidates the nature of this institution by drawing attention to African parallels. Consider Jeanmaire, *Couroi et courètes,* 510, 550–69; and Chrimes, *Ancient Sparta,* 374–76, in light of Arnold Van Gennep, *The Rites of Passage,* trans. Monika B. Vizedom and Gabrielle L. Caffee (Chicago: University of Chicago Press, 1961),

and see Edmond Lévy, "La Kryptie et ses contradictions," *Ktèma* 13 (1988): 245–53; Birgalias, *OES,* 97–126 ; and Ducat, *SE,* 281–309, 319–32 (on which, see the judicious remarks of Paul Cartledge: *NECJ* 34:2 [May 2007]: 149–50). I am persuaded neither by Plutarch (*Lyc.* 28.12–13) that Lycurgus could not have devised so brutal an institution and that it must therefore have been invented after the great helot revolt of 465 nor by Jacqueline Christien, "Les Temps d'une vie," *Métis* 12 (1997): 45–79 (at 70–72), that the institution was not invented until the liberation of Messenia, and I suspect that it belongs in "the ghost year" between childhood and adulthood identified by Tazelaar, "PAIDES KAI EPHEBOI," 127–53; Kukofka, "Die *Paidískoi* im System der spartanischen Altersklassen," 197–205; and Ducat, *SE,* 94–98. With regard to *PLondon* No. 187, see note 57, below.

55. Lacedaemon for a time populous: Chapter 4 and Appendix 1, below. Completion of *agōgế,* acceptance into *sussıtíon,* and citizenship: Xen. *Lac. Pol.* 10.7; Plut. *Mor.* 235b, 238e. Taking up of allotment: Plut. *Mor.* 238e, Teles F3.15 [Hense], with Arist. *Pol.* 1271a26–36. *Hupomeíones:* Xen. *Hell.* 3.3.6.

56. Composition of *sussıtíon:* Plut. *Lyc.* 12.3, Porph. *Abst.* 4.4. Cf. Schol. Pl. *Leg.* 1.633a, where the number of members mentioned is ten, and Plut. *Agis* 8.4, where the reinstituted *sussıtíon* of the late third century is to include hundreds of members. Blackball: Plut. *Lyc.* 12.9–11. Military function: consider Hdt. 1.65.6; Plut. *Mor.* 226d–e; Polyaen. 2.1.15, 3.11, in light of Xen. *Cyr.* 2.1.28. The members were called tentmates [*súskēnoı*]: Xen. *Lac. Pol.* 7.4, 9.4, 15.5. See also Pl. *Leg.* 1.625c–626b, 633a, and Singor, "Admission to the *Syssitia* in Fifth-Century Sparta," 67–89. *Políteuma:* Persaeus *FGrH* 584 F2. Decorum: consider Critias *Vorsokr.*[6] 88 B32–37; Xen. *Lac. Pol.* 5.2–8; Pl. *Leg.* 1.637a (with 639d–e); Sosibius *FGrH* 595 F19; Dion. Hal. 2.23.3; Plut *Lyc.* 12, 25.4 (with *Cleom.* 9.1), *Mor.* 224d; and Ath. 141a–e in light of Nick R. E. Fisher, "Drink, *Hybris* and the Promotion of Harmony in Sparta," in *CSTS,* 26–50; Stefan Link, " 'Durch diese Tür geht kein Wort hinaus!' (Plut. Lyk. 12, 8)," *Laverna* 9 (1998): 82–112; and Ephraim David, "Sparta's *Kosmos* of Silence," in *SNS,* 117–46. Note also David, "Laughter in Spartan Society," 1–4. See also Hdt. 6.84.

57. *Néos* until forty-five: Appendix 2, below. Magisterial inspection every ten days: Agatharchides of Cnidus F86 F10. Punished if found to be fat: Ael. *VH* 14.7. Nights spent with the *sussıtíon:* Plut. *Lyc.* 15.7–9 with Xen. *Lac. Pol.* 1.5, Plut. *Mor.* 228a–b, *Suda* s.v. *Lukoûrgos.* Garrisons: H. W. Parke, "The Evidence for Harmosts in Laconia," *Hermathena* 46 (1931): 31–38. The institution of the *agronómoı* devised by Plato (*Leg.* 6.762e–763c, 778d–779a) would appear to be a close imitation of the arrangement described in a fragment surviving from an ancient medical work (*PLondon* No. 187)—which was discussed long ago by Paul Girard, "Sur la Cryptie des Lacédémoniens," *REG* 11 (1898): 31–38, and "*Krypteia,*" in *Dictionnaire des antiquités grecques et romaines d'après les textes et les monuments,* ed. Charles Victor Daremberg and Edmond Saglio (Graz: Akademische Druck- und Verlagsanstalt, 1962–63), III:1 871–73, who confused the system of garrisons and patrols described therein with the *krupteía;* and which has more recently been reexamined by Ducat, *SE,* 309–19, who doubts whether it has to do with Sparta at all. With Girard, I believe that the reference in the papyrus to Agesilaus as a *Lákōn* suggests that the subject is Lacedaemon. While in his twenties and still an *eırến,* if I am correct, a Spartan could expect to spend two years in garrison duty and on patrol in the manner described. Without some such arrangement, it is inconceivable that the Spartans could have maintained their dominion—particularly that in Messenia (above, at note 54). Although the Athenian ephebes performed some functions comparable to those performed by the Spartans doing garrison service (Aeschin. 2.167, Arist. *Ath. Pol.* 42.2–5), they had more in common with the Spartans undergoing the *krupteía:* see Vidal-Naquet, "The Black Hunter and the Origin of the Athenian *Ephebia,*" 106–28; John J. Winkler, "The Ephebes' Song: *Tragōidia* and *Polis,*" in *Nothing to Do with Dionysos? Athenian Drama in Its Social Context,* ed. John J. Winkler and Froma I. Zeitlin (Princeton: Princeton University Press, 1990), 20–62; and Pierre Vidal-Naquet, "The Black Hunter Revisited," *PCPhS* 212 (1986): 126–44. Cf. Arist. *Pol.* 1331a19–23, 1331b14–17, which is an adaptation of Spartan practice to the needs of a walled city.

58. Dion. Hal. *Ant. Rom.* 2.23.3. For the *sussıtíon* as a religious institution, note Alcman's use of the word *thíasos* in connection with the *andreîon:* F98 (PMG).

59. *Hıppágretaı* and *hıppeîs:* Xen. *Lac. Pol.* 4.3–4. See Hdt. 1.67.5, 8.124.3; Thuc. 5.72.4; Xen. *Hell.* 3.3.9–11, 6.4.14 (where, with Stephanus, I read *hıppeîs* rather than *híppoı*); Ephorus *FGrH* 70 F149 (ap. Strabo 10.4.18); Dion. Hal. *Ant. Rom.* 2.13.4; Plut. *Lyc.* 25.6, *Mor.* 231b; Stob. *Flor.* 4.1.138 (Hense); Hesych. s.v. *hıppagrétas.* It is in this connection that one should read Pl. *Prt.*

342b–c, *Grg.* 515e. See also Jeanmaire, *Couroi et courètes,* 542–50, and Thomas J. Figueria, "The Spartan *Hippeis,*" in *SW,* 57–84. Cf. Thuc. 4.55 and Xen. *Hell.* 4.4.10–12 with Ephorus *FGrH* 70 F149: the three hundred *hippeîs* were apparently not a cavalry unit in the strict sense, but rather an elite infantry unit that accompanied the king—perhaps at first on horseback—to and from engagements: see Greenhalgh, *EGW,* 94–95 and Chapter 3, below. Victory in the Olympic Games apparently guaranteed election by the *hippagrétai:* consider Xen. *Hell.* 2.4.33 in light of Plut. *Lyc.* 22.8. During the march of Xenophon's Ten Thousand to the sea, the Spartan Cheirisophus appears to have organized a similar elite unit: Xen. *An.* 3.4.43. Note the various groups of three hundred Spartan warriors mentioned in the sources: Hdt. 1.82.3, 7.202, 205.2 (which should be read with 220.3–4), 9.64.2; Xen. *Hell.* 6.5.31. Institutions of similar import are instanced elsewhere: see Marcel Detienne, "La Phalange: Problèmes et controverses," in *Problèmes de la guerre en Grèce ancienne,* ed. Jean-Pierre Vernant (Paris: Mouton, 1968), 134–42; Pritchett, *GSW,* II 221–25; and Geneviève Hoffmann, "Les Choisis: Un Ordre dans la cité grecque?" *Droit et cultures* 9–10 (1985): 15–26, and note Tac. *Germ.* 13.3–14.1. For an overview, see J. E. Lendon, "Spartan Honor," in *Polis and Polemos: Essays on Politics, War, and History in Ancient Greece,* ed. Charles D. Hamilton and Peter Krentz (Claremont, CA: Regina Books, 1997), 105–26.

60. *Agathoergoí:* Hdt. 1.67.5 with David Whitehead, "Ephorus(?) on the Spartan Constitution," *CQ* n. s. 55:1 (May 2005): 299–301. There is no evidence specifying when a Spartiate ceased to be a *hēbôn.* In ordinary speech, the term is used to refer to those who have become adults but have not yet reached old age: see Tazelaar, "PAIDES KAI EPHEBOI," 143–46, 150. Most scholars, nonetheless, assume that a man would leave the royal bodyguard when he reached his thirtieth birthday: see, most recently, ibid. 150; Hodkinson, "Social Order and Conflict of Values in Classical Sparta," 242, 244–47; MacDowell, *SL,* 66–68; and Cartledge, *Agesilaos,* 204–5. There are two reasons for doubting that this was the case. There is evidence that the Spartans employed the terms *néoi* and *neôteroi* to distinguish warriors under the age of forty-five from the *presbúteroi* (below, Appendix 2); and in the *Hellenica* (3.3.8–11), Xenophon appears to use both terms, as synonyms for *hēbôntes,* to designate the *hippeîs* commanded by the *hippagrétai.* Furthermore, in the *Lakedaimoníôn Politeía* (4.3), he not only tells us that the *hippagrétai* were chosen from among the *hēbôntes;* he adds that they were selected from among the *akmázontes.* In ordinary Greek parlance, the last-mentioned term would normally be used to refer to a man over thirty years in age: Pl. *Resp.* 5.460e–461a. It is hard to believe that a people notorious for being inclined to honor their elders would think that a man had reached his *akmḗ* earlier than that, and it is even harder to believe that they would be willing to entrust the royal guard to the command of men so young.

61. Eligible for magistracies: Xen.*Lac. Pol.* 4.6–7 with 2.2. Eligible for permission to travel abroad: Isoc. 11.18, Pl. *Prt.* 342c–d. If my hypothesis as to the central importance of a man's forty-fifth birthday is correct (Appendix 2), the exclusion of all but *presbúteroi* from political office would be yet another sign of the exaggerated respect that the Spartans showed to those of advanced age. Note that it was contrary to custom [*paranómōs*] for the Spartans to send *hēbôntes* abroad as governors [*árchontes*] of allied cities: Thuc. 4.132.3. In this connection, see Arist. *Pol.* 1332b12–1333a16.

62. Bachelors subject to civic disabilities and rituals of harassment and humiliation: Clearchus of Soli F73 (Wehrli); Plut. *Lyc.* 15.1–3, *Lys.* 30.7, *Mor.* 227e–f; Stob. *Flor.* 67.16; Poll. *Onom.* 3.48, 8.40, read in light of Xen. *Lac. Pol.* 1.6. Cf. Hdt. 2.80.1, Xen. *Lac. Pol.* 9.4–6. Clandestine nocturnal visits to wives: Xen. *Lac. Pol.* 1.5; Plut. *Lyc.* 15.6–10, *Mor.* 228a should be read in conjunction with Appendix 2, below. Relations within Spartan marriages: Nilsson, "Die Grundlagen des spartanischen Lebens," 849–62. Cf. Lupi, *L'Ordine delle generazioni,* 65–194, with Nigel Kennell, "Age-Class Societies in Ancient Greece," *AC* 43 (2013): 1–73 (esp. 24–42), and see Pomeroy, *SWo,* 33–71.

63. Wife-sharing: Xen. *Lac. Pol.* 1.7–9, Plut. *Lyc.* 15.12–13, Nicolaus of Damascus *FGrH* 90 F103Z. Fraternal polyandry: Polyb. 12.6b.8. Marriage for procreation only: Plut. *Comp. Lyc. et Num.* 4.1. *Apatheía* with regard to wife: 3.4. Matrimony slighted: Joseph. *Ap.* 2.273. See Stavros Perentidis, "Réflexions sur la polyandrie à Sparte dans l'antiquité," *RD* 75:1 (1997): 7–31, and "Sur la polyandrie, la parenté, et la définition du mariage à Sparte," in *Parenté et société dans le monde grec de l'Antiquité à l'âge moderne,* ed. Alain Bresson et al. (Paris: Diffusion du Boccard, 2006), 131–52. Note Ludwig Ziehen, "Das spartanische Bevölkerungsproblem," *Hermes* 68 (1933): 218–37, who suspects that polyandry was a reaction to the sexual imbalance produced at Lacedaemon

by the earthquakes of 465; Hodkinson, *PWCS,* 81–82, 103, 123, 371–72, 406–7, 420, 438–40, who envisages it as a strategy aimed at preventing a division of the family patrimony; and Pomeroy, *SWo,* 37–39, 46–49, who draws attention to the manner in which polyandry strengthened the power of women.

64. Εἰσπνήλας: Theoc. 12.13 and Callim. F68 (Pfeiffer) with the scholia. See also Plut. *Cleom.* 3.2; Ael. *VH* 3.10, 12; and Hesych. s.v. *empneî.* In this connection, one should note Xenophon's use of *empnein* at *Symp.* 4.15. Patron, protector, friend: Plut. *Lyc.* 16.12–18.9, *Mor.* 237b–c; Ael. *VH* 3.10, 12. For an overview, see Paul Cartledge, "The Politics of Spartan Pederasty," in Cartledge, *SR,* 91–105; Kenneth J. Dover, "Greek Homosexuality and Initiation," in *The Greeks and Their Legacy: Prose Literature, History, Society, Transmission, Influence* (Oxford: Basil Blackwell, 1988), 115–34 (esp. 123–24); Birgalias, *OES,* 221–52; Ducat, *SE,* 164–68, 196–201; and Stefan Link, "Education and Pederasty in Spartan and Cretan Society," in *SCA,* 89–111. See also Brelich, *Paides e parthenoi,* I 113–26; and Claude Calame, *Les Choeurs de jeunes filles en Grèce archaïque* (Rome: L'Ateneo and Bizarri, 1977), I 350–57. It is perhaps worth adding that it is quite possible, but by no means certain, that the Spartans followed the Thessalian practice (Theoc. 12.14) of using the term *aΐtas* or "hearer" to designate the *erómenos;* they are known to have used the term in the archaic period for describing young girls: Alkman F34 (Page) with scholia.

65. Surrogate father, expected role: Cic. *Rep.* 4.3.3, Plut. *Lyc.* 18.8–9, Ael. *VH* 3.10. Rules of decorum and eventual abandonment of passive for active role: cf. Xen. *Lac. Pol.* 2.12–14, whose treatment of the relations between the two as Platonic may be ironic, with Ar. *Lys.* 1173–74; Pl. *Leg.* 1.636a–b, 8.836b–c; Mart. 4.55.6–7; Photius s.v. *kusolákōn,* whose testimony belies Xenophon's claim; and see Cic. *Rep.* 4.4.4, who reports that the law allowed the two to embrace and to share a bed but not to remove their cloaks. Ritual abduction of bride, dressed as man, her hair cut short in manner of boy: Plut. *Lyc.* 15.4–6, 16.11 with Annalisa Paradiso, "Osservazioni sulla cerimonia nuziale spartana," *QS* 24 (1986): 137–53. Cf. the Argive law concerning married women adorned with beards: Plut. *Mor.* 245f. At Lacedaemon, the abduction could be more than a ritual: Hdt. 6.65.2. It is also possible that there was a pre-marital period in which young Spartans had sexual relations of a sort with maidens in the same fashion as each did with his *paɪdɪká,* as Hagnon of Tarsus (Ath. 13.602d–e) contended. Cf. Lupi, *L'Ordine delle generazioni,* 65–194, who regards the practice of pederasty and the treatment of these maidens as elements in an elaborate system of population control, with Kennell, "Age-Class Societies in Ancient Greece," 24–42. Political character of institution and Australian/Melanesian analogue: Rahe, *RAM,* I.iv.6.

66. Indifference regarding wife: Plut. *Comp. Lyc. et Num.* 3.1–4. Membership of pederastic pair in same *sussítíon:* Pl. *Leg.* 1.636a–b. Stationed in close proximity but not alongside one another in the battle line: Xen. *Symp.* 8.35. Note *Hell.* 4.8.37–39, where the *paɪdɪká* in question may well be a Spartiate. Sacrifice to Eros before drawing up phalanx: Sosicrates *FGrH* 461 F7 ap. Ath. 13.561e–f. It can hardly be an accident that Plato equates Spartan practice in these matters with that on Crete: consider *Leg.* 8.836b–c in light of Ephorus *FGrH* 70 F149. Victory, safety, and pederasty: consider Ath. 13.561e–f in light of Onasander 24. In this connection, see Daniel Ogden, "Homosexuality and Warfare in Ancient Greece," in *Battle in Antiquity,* ed. Alan B. Lloyd (Swansea: Classical Press of Wales, 2009), 107–68 (esp. 117–19, 139–47).

67. Cf. the principle to which Antigone in public appeals (Soph. *Ant.* 1–10, 21–38, 69–77, 80–81, 83, 86–87, 89, 93–97, 448, 450–70, 499–507, 937–43) with that to which, in the same setting, Kreon appeals (162–210, 280–314, 449, 473–96, 635–80); note the character of their exchange (508–25); consider the initial attitude of the chorus and that attributed to the people of Thebes (582–634, 683–733, 781–805, 817–22); note the focus of Antigone's soliloquy (891–928); and see Bernard Knox, *The Heroic Temper: Studies in Sophoclean Tragedy* (Berkeley: University of California Press, 1964), 91–116. Fundamental and ineliminable though this tension may be, many scholars are oblivious to it: see, for example, Cynthia Patterson, *The Family in Greek History* (Cambridge, MA: Harvard University Press, 1998).

68. Consider Letter of 31 October 1823 to A. Coray, in *The Writings of Thomas Jefferson,* ed. Andrew A. Lipscomb and Albert Ellery Bergh (Washington, DC: Thomas Jefferson Memorial Association, 1903–7), XV 482, in light of Charles-Louis de Secondat, baron de La Brède et de Montesquieu, *L'Esprit des lois* 1.5.2, in *Œuvres complètes de Montesquieu,* ed. Roger Caillois (Paris: Bibliothèque de la Pléiade, 1949–51). In eighteenth-century France, Jefferson's opinion was widely

held: Elizabeth Rawson, *The Spartan Tradition in European Thought* (Oxford: Clarendon Press, 1969), 256–60.

69. Groups smaller than ten are often ineffective; those larger than twenty are subject to faction: note the findings of E. J. Hobsbawm, *Primitive Rebels: Studies in Archaic Forms of Social Movements in the Nineteenth and Twentieth Centuries* (New York: W. W. Norton, 1965), 18–19, and *Bandits,* second edition (New York: Pantheon Books, 1981), 16, 20. Col. Nicholas G. L. Hammond served behind the German lines in Macedonia during World War II. In a conversation held on the twenty-second of March 1981, he remarked to me that in 1943 the standard number of men assigned to a unit within the ELAS guerrilla army was fifteen. As the leaders of that body of soldiers understood, one critical factor is that the men be familiars in the full sense of the term: see S. L. A. Marshall, *Men Against Fire: The Problem of Battle Command in Future War* (New York: William Morrow, 1947), 42, 123–56; Edward A. Shils and Morris Janowitz, "Cohesion and Disintegration in the Wehrmacht in World War II," *Public Opinion Quarterly* 12 (Summer 1948): 280–315; Robert J. Rielly, "Confronting the Tiger: Small Unit Cohesion in Battle," *Military Review* 80 (2000): 61–65, and Leonard Wong, Thomas A. Colditz, Raymond A. Millen, and Terence M. Potter, *Why They Fight: Combat Motivation in the Iraq War* (Carlisle Barracks, PA: Strategic Studies Institute, 2003). A sense of shared mission is no doubt essential as well: cf. Robert J. MacCoun, Elizabeth Kier, and Aaron Belkin, "Does Social Cohesion Determine Motivation in Combat? An Old Question with an Old Answer," *Armed Forces and Society* 32:4 (July 2006): 646–54, who think social cohesion inconsequential in comparison with a sense of shared commitment to the unit's mission, with Michael Desch, *Power and Military Effectiveness: The Fallacy of Democratic Triumphalism* (Baltimore, MD: Johns Hopkins University Press, 2008), 159–63.

70. Spartiates never more numerous than nine or ten thousand: Arist. *Pol.* 1270a36–37; Plut. *Lyc.* 8.3, 16.1. Spartan mother's demand: *Mor.* 241f. According to Stobaeus (*Flor.* 3.7.29–30 [Hense]), Aristotle attributed this famous admonition to Gorgo, the daughter of Cleomenes and wife of Leonidas, who figures prominently in Herodotus' narrative (5.51, 7.205, 239); with one exception, it is elsewhere attributed to an unnamed Spartan mother sending her son off to battle. I see no reason to doubt that Aristotle could have been Stobaeus' source, and I am therefore less inclined than some scholars to suppose that, in his text, Aristotle is a corruption for Ariston. For the most recent discussion of this scholarly problem, and for a useful list of the passages in which this admonition figures, see Mason Hammond, "A Famous *Exemplum* of Spartan Toughness," *CJ* 75 (1979–80): 97–109. For an examination of the larger issues, see Thomas J. Figueira, "Gynecocracy: How Women Policed Masculine Behavior in Archaic and Classical Sparta," in *SBP,* 265–96.

71. See Hdt. 7.101–4, which should perhaps be read in light of Timaeus *Lexicon of Words in Plato* s.v. *enōmotía; Suda* s.v. *enōmotía; Etym. Magn.* s.v. *enōmotía;* Phot. *Bibl.* s.v. *enōmotía.* Cf. Ellen Millender, "*Nómos Despótēs*: Spartan Obedience and Athenian Lawfulness in Fifth-Century Thought," in *Oikistes: Studies in Constitutions, Colonies, and Military Power in the Ancient World,* ed. Vanessa B. Gorman and Eric W. Robinson (Leiden: Brill, 2002), 33–59, who reads this passage ironically not as a well-informed and, for the most part, admiring description of the foundations of Spartan steadfastness but as an echo of the criticism that Pericles is said by Thucydides to have directed at Lacedaemon in the Funeral Oration (which she takes as a reflection of Thucydides' own considered opinion).

72. Mothers and sons: Plut. *Mor.* 240c–242b with Bella Zweig, "The Only Women Who Give Birth to Men: A Gynocentric, Cross-Cultural View of Woman in Ancient Sparta," in *Women's Power, Man's Game,* ed. Mary Deforest (Wauconda, IL: Bolchazy-Carducci Publishers, 1993), 32–53, and Pomeroy, *SWo,* 57–63. Fathers and sons: Xen. *Lac. Pol.* 6.1–2; *IG* V i 213, 255. As will become clear, I do not believe that to explain this one needs to suppose that, after a Spartan reached the age of seven, the *oîkos* continued in practice to loom large within his daily experience. It is, in my opinion, deprivation that produced this fierce reaction. Cf., however, Ducat, *SE,* 119–37 (with 92, 261).

73. Corruption and bribery, Hdt. 3.148, 5.51.2, 6.50.2, 72, 82.1, 8.5.1; Thuc. 1.76.4, 95, 109.2, 2.21.1 (note Plut. *Per.* 22.2 and Diod. 13.106.10), 128–30, 5.16.3, 8.45.3, 50.3; Ephorus *FGrH* 70 F193; and Plut. *Per.* 22.4, *Lys.* 16.1–17.1 in light of Thuc. 1.77.6; Eur. *And.* 451; Ar. *Pax* 623–24; Xen. *Lac. Pol.* 14; and Arist. *Pol.* 1270b6–12, 1271a1–5, F544 (Rose) = F 430, 550 (Gigon). Note Pausanias' expectations at Thuc. 1.131.2. An exception to the rule was deemed worthy of note:

Thuc. 4.81. In this connection, see K. L. Noethlichs, "Bestechung, Bestechlichkeit und die Rolle des Geldes in der spartanischen Aussen- und Innenpolitik vom 7. bis 2. Jh. v. Chr.," *Historia* 36:2 (2nd Quarter 1987): 129–70. Cf., however, Hodkinson, *PWCS,* 19–20.

74. Violence to human nature: Rousseau, *Du Contrat social* 2.7, in *Œuvres complètes de Rousseau,* III 381–82. Rousseau made the same point in even stronger terms in his initial draft of this work: ibid., III 313. From the constant constraint imposed on the individual Spartan, Rousseau argued, "there was born in him an ardent love of the fatherland which was always the strongest or rather the unique passion of the Spartiates, and which made of them beings above humanity."

75. Man-subduing: Simonides F111 (PMG), which foreshadows the testimony later found in Thuc. 1.84.3, 2.39.1–2; Xen. *Hell.* 7.1.8; Pl. *Leg.* 1.633b. Ducat, *SE,* 35–36, to the contrary notwithstanding, it makes no sense to suppose that the unnamed sources for Simonides' deployment of this epithet, to whom Plutarch (*Ages.* 1.3) alludes, erred in supposing that, in describing Lacedaemon as *damasímbrotos,* Simonides was speaking of the impact of the Spartan *politeía* on the citizens of Lacedaemon. They presumably had in their possession the poem in which Simonides employed the term and knew perfectly well what he had in mind. In any case, the poet who was the first surviving writer to discuss Lycurgus and his achievements (Simonides F628 [PMG]) can hardly be supposed incapable of making the observation attributed to him.

76. Dion. Hal. *Ant. Rom.* 20.13. For evidence confirming Dionysius' claim concerning the attitude of the Athenians, see Dem. 18.132, 22.51–52.

77. Toil, victory, honor: Pl. *Alc.* I 122c7. Cf. *Resp.* 8.548c. With Nicholas Denyer, "Introduction," in Plato, *Alcibiades,* ed. Nicholas Denyer (Cambridge: Cambridge University Press, 2001), 1–29 (14–26), I take the first of these two dialogues to be an authentic work of Plato.

78. See Christopher J. Tuplin, *The Failings of Empire: A Reading of Xenophon Hellenica 2.3.11–7.5.27* (Stuttgart: Franz Steiner Verlag, 1993), and "Xenophon, Sparta and the *Cyropaedia,*" in *SS,* 127–81, and note Godfrey Hutchinson, *Sparta: Unfit for Empire* (London: Frontline Books, 2014). Then, consider Noreen Humble, "*Sophrosyne* and the Spartans in Xenophon," in *SNS,* 339–53, in light of Noreen Humble, "Was Sōphrosynē Ever a Spartan Virtue?" in *SBM,* 85–109, and see Noreen Humble, "The Author, Date and Purpose of Chapter 14 in the *Lakedaimoniōn Politeía,*" in *Xenophon and His World,* ed. Christopher J. Tuplin (Stuttgart: Franz Steiner Verlag, 2004), 215–28; "Why the Spartans Fight So Well . . . Even in Disorder: Xenophon's View," in *SW,* 219–33; "The Renaissance Reception of Xenophon's *Spartan Constitution:* Preliminary Observations," in *Xenophon: Ethical Principles and Historical Enquiry,* ed. Fiona Hobden and Christopher Tuplin (Leiden: Brill, 2012), 63–88; and "True History: Xenophon's *Agesilaus* and the Encomiastic Genre," forthcoming in *Xenophon and Sparta: New Perspectives,* ed. Anton Powell and Nicolas Richer (Swansea: Classical Press of Wales, n.d.), as well as Stephen Hodkinson, "The Imaginary Spartan *Politeia,*" in *The Imaginary Polis,* ed. Mogens Herman Hansen (Copenhagen: Det Kongelige DanskeVidenskabernes Selskab, 2005), 222–81 (at 238–44, 245–49, 259, 268); and Ellen Millender, "Spartan 'Friendship' and Xenophon's Crafting of the *Anabasis,*" in *Xenophon: Ethical Principles and Historical Enquiry,* 377–425.

79. Spartan love of money: Pl. *Resp.* 8.544c read in light of 545a, 548a. See also Isoc. 8.95–96, 11.20; Plut. *Mor.* 239e–f. Widespread disobedience of law against possession of silver and gold: Pl. *Alc.* I 122e–123a. See *Hipp. Maj.* 283d. Individual Spartans were known to have large sums on deposit in Arcadia and at Delphi: Posidonius *FGrH* 87 F48c and Plut. *Lys.* 18.2. Houses as private nests where great expenditures made: Pl. *Resp.* 8.548a–b. See also Diod. 15.65.5, Paus. 9.14.6. Stocked with valuables: Xen. *Hell.* 6.5.27. Plato as critic of Lacedaemon: Edmond Lévy, "La Sparte de Platon," *Ktèma* 30 (2005): 217–36.

80. Aristotle on sumptuary laws: F611.13 (Rose) = Tit. 143.1.2.13 (Gigon) ap. Heraclid. Lemb. 373.13 (Dilts). Charges Spartans covetous of wealth and subject to intemperate, luxury-loving women: *Pol.* 1269b12–1270a14, 1271a18, 1271b17. On the lack of self-control exhibited by Spartan women, see also Pl. *Leg.* 1.637c, 6.780d–781d, 7.804c–806c, and note Dion. Hal. *Ant. Rom.* 2.24.6, Plut. *Comp. Lyc. et Num.* 3.5–9. See James Redfield, "The Women of Sparta," *CJ* 73 (1977–78): 146–61; Alfred S. Bradford, "Gynaikokratoumenoi: Did Spartan Women Rule Spartan Men," *AncW* 14 (1986): 13–18; Barton Kunstler, "Family Dynamics and Female Power in Ancient Sparta," *Helios* 13:2 (1986): 31–48; Maria H. Dettenhofer, "Die Frauen von Sparta: Gesellschaftliche Position und politische Relevanz," *Klio* 75 (1993): 61–75; and Paul Cartledge, "Spartan Wives:

Liberty or License?" in Cartledge, *SR,* 106–26. Ellen Millender, "Athenian Ideology and the Empowered Spartan Woman," in *SNS,* 355–91, and Stephen Hodkinson, "Female Property Ownership and Empowerment in Classical and Hellenistic Sparta," in *SpartSoc,* 103–36, may be right in some measure in suspecting that the ancient testimony concerning Spartan women, which is largely Athenian, reflects bias and hostility. But this does not mean that this testimony is wholly or even largely inaccurate. For a thorough review of the evidence for the lives of women at Lacedaemon, see Pomeroy, *SWo,* passim. Note Xen. *Hell.* 6.5.28. The example set by Lacedaemon in this particular has on occasion stirred interest outside the ranks of classicists: see, for example, Simone de Beauvoir, *The Second Sex* (New York: Knopf, 1952), 82.

81. Law of Epitadeus: Plut. *Agis* 5.3–7 with Appendix 1. Oracle warning love of money to destroy Lacedaemon: Arist. F544 (Rose) = F430, 550 (Gigon), Diod. 7.12.5, Plut. *Mor.* 239f. For additional citations, see Joseph Fontenrose, *The Delphic Oracle: Its Responses and Operations with a Catalogue of Responses* (Berkeley: University of California Press, 1978), 272: Q10.

82. Isocrates on the Lacedaemonian fear of reproach: 6.59. Three hundred who accompany Leonidas mature men with surviving sons: Hdt. 7.205.2 read in light of 220.3–4.

83. Cowards put to death: Lycurg. 1.129–30.

84. Cowards expelled from *hómoioi,* shunned, degraded: Xen. *Lac. Pol.* 9.4–6, 10.7; Plut. *Ages.* 30.2–4. Fate of those Spartans dispatched to Thermopylae but not killed: cf. Hdt. 7.232 with 229–31, 9.71. In this connection, see Tyrtaeus F11.14 (West) with Plut. *Ages.* 30.2–4, and consider David, "Laughter in Spartan Society," 1–25 (esp. 13–17), and Jean Ducat, "The Spartan 'Tremblers,'" in *SW,* 1–55.

85. Hdt. 1.82. Site of battle: Paus. 2.38.6–7 with W. Kendrick Pritchett, "Pausanias' Anigraia Route and Anthene," in *SAGT,* III 102–42; "Pseudo-Skylax and Pausanias on the Thyreatis," in *SAGT,* VI 91–101; and "A Road on Mount Zavitsa," in *SAGT* VII, 169–77. After reading Chapter 3, note 3, below, cf. Noel Robertson, *Festivals and Legends: The Formation of Greek Cities in the Light of Public Ritual* (Toronto: University of Toronto Press, 1992), 179–207, who treats the Battle of Champions as a figment of the aetiological imagination, with J. Kendrick Pritchett, "Aetiology sans Topography: 2. Thyreatis and the Battle of Champions," in *Thucydides' Pentekontaetia and Other Essays* (Amsterdam: J. C. Gieben, 1995), 228–62.

86. Xenophon on Lechaeum: *Hell.* 4.5.11–19 (esp. 14).

87. Lacedaemonian contingent at Sphacteria: Thuc. 4.37–40.

88. Spartan treatment of men taken prisoner at Sphacteria: Thuc. 5.34.2, Diod. 12.76.1. See Thuc. 4.19.1, 108.7, 5.15–24.

89. Agesilaus' handling of survivors of battle of Leuctra: Plut. *Ages.* 30.2–6, *Mor.* 191c; Polyaen. *Strat.* 2.1.13.

90. Spartan conduct in the wake of Leuctra: Xen. *Hell.* 6.4.16. See Plut. *Ages.* 29. Xenophon reports much the same phenomenon in connection with the disaster at Lechaeum: *Hell.* 4.5.10.

91. Pericles on Spartan preeminence in efforts to promote civil courage: Thuc. 2.39.1. Institutions at Sparta promote *homónoia:* Xen. *Mem.* 3.5.15–16; Isoc. 12.177–79, 258–59; Dem. 20.107–8; Polyb. 6.48.2–5; Diod. 7.12.2–4. Note also Xen. *Ages.* 1.4, Lys. 33.7, Dem. 20.107–8, Polyb. 6.46.6–8. In this connection, see Arist. *Pol.* 1306a9–12. General Will: Rousseau, *Du Contrat social* 1.6–2.7, 3.10, 4.1, in *Œuvres complètes de Rousseau,* III 360–84, 421–23, 437–39.

Chapter 2. *Polıteía*

1. See Lewis Namier, *The Structure of Politics at the Accession of George III,* second edition (London: Macmillan, 1957), x–xi, first published in 1929.

2. This aspect of Namier's argument has attracted considerable criticism: see Harvey C. Mansfield, Jr., "Sir Lewis Namier Considered," *Journal of British Studies* 2 (November 1962): 28–55; cf. Robert Walcott, " 'Sir Lewis Namier Considered' Considered," ibid. 3:2 (May 1964): 85–108, with Mansfield, "Sir Lewis Namier Again Considered," ibid. 3:2 (May 1964): 109–19; and note Quentin Skinner, "The Principles and Practice of Opposition: The Case of Bolingbroke versus Walpole," in *Historical Perspectives: Studies in English Thought and Society in Honour of J. H. Plumb,* ed. Neil McKendrick (London: Europa, 1974), 93–128.

3. See Rahe, *RAM*, passim.

4. This term was introduced by Machiavelli, who used *lo stato* to allude to "command over men," and it reached its full development in the political science of Thomas Hobbes, who would have accepted Max Weber's definition of the state as that entity which "(successfully) claims the *monopoly of the legitimate use of physical force* within a given territory": cf. J. H. Hexter, "The Predatory Vision: Niccolò Machiavelli. *Il Principe* and *lo stato*," in Hexter, *The Vision of Politics on the Eve of the Reformation: More, Machiavelli, and Seyssel* (New York: Basic Books, 1973), 150–78, and Harvey C. Mansfield, Jr., "On the Impersonality of the Modern State: A Comment on Machiavelli's Use of *Stato*," *APSR* 77 (1983): 849–57, with Max Weber, "Politics as a Vocation," *From Max Weber: Essays in Sociology* (New York: Oxford University Press, 1946), 78, and see Quentin Skinner, "The State," in *Political Innovation and Conceptual Change*, ed. Terence Ball, James Farr, and Russell L. Hanson (Cambridge : Cambridge University Press, 1989), 90–131. The state is an abstract entity constituted by power; and to the extent that it has a tangible existence, it is indistinguishable from the arms by which that power is exerted—the police forces, the standing army, and the bureaucracy that make up the permanent government in every modern polity. The state is never synonymous with the body politic, and it is never itself a true community. This is evident enough from the manner in which it is consistently coupled with and distinguished from the individual, the church, and society. In this connection, one would do well to ponder Nietzsche's observation that "State is the name of the coldest of all the cold monsters. Coldly as well does it lie; and this lie creeps out of its mouth: 'I, the State, am the People.'" As Nietzsche goes on to suggest, it is "a Faith and a Love," not the State, that constitute a People. See Friedrich Nietzsche, *Also Sprach Zarathustra* 1, "Vom neuen Götzen," in Nietzsche, *Werke*, fifth edition, ed. Karl Schlechta (Munich: Carl Hanser Verlag, 1966), II 313. This theme has been taken up recently and treated from an anthropological perspective by Moshe Berent, "Hobbes and the Greek Tongues," *HPTh* 17:1 (Spring 1996): 36–59; "Stasis, or the Greek Invention of Politics," *HPTh* 19:3 (Autumn 1998): 331–62; and "Anthropology and the Classics: War, Violence and the Stateless Polis," *CQ* n.s. 50:1 (2000): 257–89. Cf. Mogens Herman Hansen, "Was the Polis a State or a Stateless Society?" in *Even More Studies in the Ancient Greek Polis*, ed. Thomas H. Nielsen (Stuttgart: Franz Steiner, 2002), 17–47, with Moshe Berent, "In Search of the Greek State: A Rejoinder to M. H. Hansen," *Polis: The Journal for the Society of Greek Political Thought* 21:1/2 (2004): 107–46. As Peter L. P. Simpson, *Political Illiberalism: A Defense of Freedom* (New Brunswick, NJ: Transaction Publishers, 2015), 3–5, points out, the only ancient analogues to the modern state with its bureaucracy and mercenary, standing army were the despotisms found in China and the Near East and the principate established by Augustus.

5. Pure democracy: Alexander Hamilton, James Madison, and John Jay, *The Federalist,* ed. Jacob E. Cook (Middletown, CT: Wesleyan University Press, 1961), no. 10. *Pólis* the men: the references are collected by Charles Forster Smith, "What Constitutes a State," *CJ* 2:7 (May 1907): 299–302. Alcaeus: F112.10 and F426 (Lobel-Page).

6. Inscriptions identify polity with citizens: *GHI* 1–2. In contrast, the Near Eastern texts customarily refer to those whom we are inclined to call the Babylonians as "the people of the territory of the city of Babylon." See Fritz Schachermeyr, "La Formation de la cité grecque," *Diogène* 4 (1953): 22–39 (esp. 30–33). Identity of soldier and civilian: Yvon Garlan, *War in the Ancient World: A Social History* (London: Chatto & Windus, 1975), 86–103. See also Xen. *Vect.* 2.3–4. Land and citizenship: Michel Austin and Pierre Vidal-Naquet, *Economic and Social History of Ancient Greece* (Berkeley: University of California Press, 1980), 95–99. It took a special decree of the assembly to extend this right to a noncitizen: Jan Pečírka, *The Formula for the Grant of Enktesis in Attic Inscriptions* (Prague: Universita Karlova, 1966).

7. For an example of the confusion that inevitably arises when one attempts to introduce the state-society distinction into an analysis of a Greek *pólis*, see Stephen Hodkinson, "The Imaginary Spartan *Politeia*," in *The Imaginary Polis*, ed. Mogens Herman Hansen (Copenhagen: Det Kongelige Danske Videnskabernes Selskab, 2005), 222–81 (esp. 244–63).

8. Note Arist. *Pol.* 1280a25–1281a4, see [Dem.] 25.16–17, and consider Ferdinand Tönnies, *Community and Association* (London: Routledge and Kegan Paul, 1955). The failure to grasp the importance of Tönnies's distinction for understanding the Greek *pólis* can lead one to attribute a

confusion to Aristotle where none exists: R. G. Mulgan, *Aristotle's Political Theory: An Introduction for Students of Political Theory* (Oxford: Oxford University Press, 1977), 13–37.

9. As Aristotle on one occasion (*Eth. Nic.* 1162a16–29) acknowledged, the household is more natural than the *pólis* because it is prior to and more necessary than the political community. If he elsewhere (*Pol.* 1253a18–29) denies this, it is because the household lacks self-sufficiency [*autárkeıa*] and can therefore survive and do its proper work in promoting virtue only as part of a much larger unit. The confusion caused by Aristotle's two statements is purely semantic in origin: from the perspective of efficient causation, the household holds priority; from that of final causation, the *pólis* is first. The household is a prerequisite for life; the *pólıs*, for the good life. The inevitable tension between this private community and the public community is the background for the dramatic action of Aeschylus' *Eumenides,* Sophocles' *Antigone,* and Aristophanes' *Clouds.* It is no accident that Aristophanes' *Ecclesiazusae* makes no mention of procreation: a city without households would be a city that paid little or no attention to the rearing of children. For a defense of the household, see Aristotle's critique (*Pol.* 1261a4–1264b25) of Plato's abolition of the household in *The Republic.* Note also *Eth. Eud.* 1242a21–26. Consider Jean-Pierre Vernant, "Marriage," in Vernant, *Myth and Society in Ancient Greece,* sixth edition, tr. Janet Lloyd (New York: Zone Books, 1988), 55–77, in light of Emile Benveniste, *Indo-European Language and Society,* tr. Elizabeth Palmaer (Coral Gables, FL: University of Miami Press, 1973), 193–97, and see Sally C. Humphreys, "*Oikos* and *Polis,*" "Public and Private Interests in Classical Athens," and "The Family in Classical Athens: Search for a Perspective," in Humphreys, *The Family, Women and Death: Comparative Studies* (London: Routledge and Kegan Paul, 1983), 1–32, 58–78.

10. See Adam Ferguson, *An Essay on the History of Civil Society,* ed. Duncan Forbes (Edinburgh: Edinburgh University Press, 1966), 160–61, and Jean-Jacques Rousseau, *Du Contrat social* 2.3, in *Œuvres complètes de Rousseau,* ed. Bernard Gagnebin and Marcel Raymond (Paris: Bibliothèque de Pléiade, 1959–1969), III 372.

11. See Harvey C. Mansfield, Jr., *Statesmanship and Party Government: A Study of Burke and Bolingbroke* (Chicago: University of Chicago Press, 1965), and John Brewer, *Party Ideology and Popular Politics at the Accession of George III* (Cambridge: Cambridge University Press, 1976), 55–95.

12. "The many" and "the few": Pl. *Resp.* 6.489b–500e, Thuc. 3.82.1. "The commoners" and "the notables": Arist. *Ath. Pol.* 34.3. "The mob" and "the gentlemen both noble and good": Thuc. 7.8.2, Pl. *Resp.* 8.569a4. "Those about Thucydides" and "the friends" of Pericles, Cimon, and Lysander: Plut. *Per.* 10.1–3, 14.1, *Lys.* 17.6. See also Lys. 12.64, Xen. *Hell.* 6.4.18. *Hetaıría:* Thuc. 3.82, Lys. 12.55, Isoc. 4.79, Pl. *Resp.* 2.365d, Arist. *Pol.* 1272b34.

13. Give and take of political struggle, fleeting factions: e.g., Thuc. 5.46.4, Plut. *Lys.* 17.6, Xen. *Hell.* 5.4.25. Political disputation: Peter A. Brunt, "Spartan Policy and Strategy in the Archidamian War," *Phoenix* 19:4 (Winter 1965): 255–80 (at 278–80). Note Plut. *Ages.* 5.3–4. Citizens greedy for honor: Arist. *Pol.* 1271a4. Legislator's intention: Plut. *Ages.* 5.5. See Xen. *Cyr.* 8.2.26–28 and Dem. 20.108. For the dark side of *phılotımía,* see Hdt. 3.53.4; Eur. *Phoen.* 531–67, *IA* 337–42, 527; Ar. *Thesm.* 383–94, *Ran.* 280–82, 675–85; Thuc. 2.65.7, 3.82.8, 8.89.3; Lys. 14.21; Isoc. 3.18, 12.81–82; Pl. *Resp.* 8.548c–550b, 9.586c; Dem. 8.71; Arist. *Eth. Nic.* 1107b21–34, 1125b1–25. For an extreme view, see Men. F620 (Koerte³) = F534 (Kock).

14. Pindar preaches moderation: F198 (Bowra). For the source, see Plut. *Mor.* 457b. I have followed Plutarch's editors Pohlenz and Sieveking in adopting the reading *hístasın*—which is found in manuscripts G, X3, and S2—rather than the more common *è stásın.* Channeling *phılotımía:* Lys. 16.18–21, 19.55–57, 21.22–25, 26.3; Isoc. 2.29–30, 6.35–36, 8.93, 18.61; Isae. 7.35–40; Pl. *Symp.* 178d–e, *Ep.* 7.338d–e; Dem. 18.257, 19.223, 20.5–6, 21.159–67, 28.22, 42.24–25, 45.66–67, 50.64, 51.22; Aeschin. 1.129, 196, 2.105, 3.19–20; Lycurg. 1.15, 140; Arist. *Pol.* 1324a29–32. In this connection, see also Aeschin. 1.160.

15. Mixed regime: Arist. *Pol.* 1270b17–25, 1294b13–41. See also Pl. *Leg.* 691d–e, Polyb. 6.3–10, Cic. *Rep.* 2.23. Note Xen. *Hell.* 7.1.32. For a general discussion, see Édouard Will, Claude Mossé, and Paul Goukowsky, *Le Monde grec et l'orient* (Paris: Presses Universitaires de France, 1972–75), I 438–44. See also Antony Andrewes, "The Government of Classical Sparta," in *ASI,* 1–21; Stefan Link, *Der Kosmos Sparta: Recht und Sitte in klassischer Zeit* (Darmstadt: Wissenschaftliche Buchgesellschaft, 1994), 54–79; and Hodkinson, "The Imaginary Spartan *Politeia,*" 227–44.

16. For an overview, see Paul Cloché, "Sur le rôle des rois de Sparte," *LEC* 17 (1949): 113–38, 343–81; Carol G. Thomas, "On the Role of the Spartan Kings," *Historia* 23:3 (3rd Quarter 1974): 257–70; Bernard Sergent, "La Répresentation spartiate de la royauté," *RHR* 189 (1976): 3–52; and Pierre Carlier, *La Royauté en Grèce avant Alexandre* (Strasbourg: Association pour l'étude de la civilisation romane, 1984), 240–324, and "À Propos de la double royauté spartiate," in *CASPTP,* 49–60. Note also Ellen Millender, "Herodotus and Spartan Despotism," in *SBM,* 1–62, and "The Spartan Dyarchy: A Comparative Perspective," in *SCA,* 1–67, as well as Anton Powell, "Divination, Royalty and Insecurity in Classical Sparta," in *SBP,* 85–135.

17. Kings hold office for life: Polyb. 6.45.50. Escape the *agōgē*: Plut. *Ages.* 1.1–5. Cf. Stob. *Flor.* 3.40.8 (Hense). Take meals outside the barracks: Xen. *Hell.* 5.3.20. Belong to *gerousía*: Hdt. 6.57.5, Thuc. 1.20.3, Arist. *Pol.* 1270b35–1271a6, Plut. *Lyc.* 5.10–14, 26. Herodotus appears to claim that each king had two votes, but Thucydides denies that this was the case. While the king was a minor, a regent [*pródikos*]—usually the nearest agnatic male relative—exercised his prerogatives: see Xen. *Hell.* 4.2.9, Paus. 3.4.9, Plut. *Lyc.* 3, Hesychius s.v. *prodikeîn.* One should probably interpret Paus. 3.6.2–3 in this light. There is reason to suspect that Herodotus' discussion (6.56–58) of the kings' powers draws on a Spartan document listing their prerogatives: Carlier, *La Royauté en Grèce avant Alexandre,* 250–52. Sacrifice on city's behalf: Xen. *Lac. Pol.* 15.2. See also Hdt. 6.56. Command Spartan army and forces of Peloponnesian League: Hdt. 5.74–75, 6.48–50, 9.10.2; Xen. *Lac. Pol.* 15.2. In an emergency, of course, another man could stand in for a king: Herodotus (7.137.2, 8.42.2) mentions two such occasions during the Persian Wars and alludes to their exceptional character by drawing attention to the fact that the commanders were not members of either royal house. Able to wage war as they wished, sacrilege to resist authority to do so: cf. Hdt. 5.70–75 and 6.49–51, 61–74 with 6.56. Hereditary generals with life tenure: Arist. *Pol.* 1271a18–26, 39–40, 1285a3–10, 14–15, 1285b26–35. See also Just. *Epit.* 3.3.2. Shared command: Rahe, *PC,* chapters 2 and 4.

18. Lacedaemonians and Heraclids from Sparta: Hdt. 8.114.2; cf. Thuc. 1.12.3. The two were bound by a compact: Xen. *Lac. Pol.* 15.1 with Lipka, *XSC,* 234. Note also the connection with the Dioscuri: Hdt. 5.75.2. Since the kings were not, strictly speaking, Lacedaemonians at all, it is a mistake to draw general conclusions concerning the Spartiates as a whole from stories told about the two *basileîs,* as Hodkinson, *PWCS,* 209–368, is wont to do.

19. For the Arcadians, see Hdt. 8.73.1 (which should be read with 2.171.2–3 and Thuc. 1.2.3), Hellanicus *FGrH* 4 F161, Xen. *Hell.* 7.1.23, Dem. 19.261, Paus. 5.1.1, Cic. *Rep.* 3.15.25, Schol. D. Ael. Aristid. *Panath.* 103.16 (Dindorf) with Maria Pretzler, "Arcadia: Ethnicity and Politics in the Fifth and Fourth Centuries BCE," in *The Politics of Ethnicity and the Crisis of the Peloponnesian League,* ed. Peter Funke and Nino Luraghi (Washington, DC: Center for Hellenic Studies, 2009), 86–109 (at 87–91). For the Athenians, see Hdt. 7.161.3 (with 8.55); Eur. *Ion* 29–30, 589–92 (with 20–21, 265–70, 999–1000), F360 (Nauck[2]); Ar. *Vesp.* 1075–80; Thuc. 1.2.5–6, 2.36.1; Lys. 2.17; Pl. *Menex.* 237d, 239a, 245d–e, *Ti.* 23d–e, *Criti.* 109c–e; Isoc. 4.23–25, 12.124–25; Dem. 19.261, 60.4; Lycurg. 1.41 (with 21, 47–48, 85); Hyper. 6.7 (Jensen); Paus. 2.14.4; Cic. *Rep.* 3.15.25; Ael. Aristid. *Panath.* 30 (Lenz/Behr); Schol. D. Ael. Aristid. *Panath.* 103.14 and 16 (Dindorf); Harpocration s.v. *autochthónes.*

20. Laconia's "old helots" Achaean in origin: with Chapter 3, note 32, below. Sparta and the Heraclid claim: Hdt. 5.43. For further allusions to the import of descent from Heracles and Zeus, see 1.7, 13–14, 91, 7.208, 8.137, 9.26–27, 33; Thuc. 5.16.2; Xen. *Lac. Pol.* 15.2. In this connection, see Walter Burkert, "Demaratos, Astrabakos und Herakles: Königsmythos und Politik zur Zeit der Perserkriege (Herodot 6, 67–60)," *MH* 22 (1965): 166–77, and Ulrich Huttner, *Die politische Rolle der Heraklesgestalt im griechischen Herrschertum* (Stuttgart: Franz Steiner Verlag, 1997), 48–58. For further discussion, see Chapter 3, below.

21. *Basileús* sacrosanct: Plut. *Agis* 19.9. Majestic burial rites: Xen. *Hell.* 3.3.1. For the import of these burial rites, see Hans Schaefer, "Das Eidolon des Leonidas," in *Charites: Studien zur Altertumswissenschaft,* ed. Konrad Schauenburg (Bonn: Athenaeum, 1957), 223–33, and Cartledge, *Agesilaos,* 331–43. Demigods: Xen. *Lac. Pol.* 15.9. According to Aristotle (F611.10 [Rose] = Tit. 143.1.2.10 [Gigon] ap. Heraclid. Lemb. 373.10 [Dilts]), nothing was sold for three days and the market was strewn with chaff. See also Tyrtaeus F7 (West), Hdt. 6.58–59, Paus. 4.14.4–5.

22. New *basileús* normally eldest surviving son of predecessor: Hdt. 5.39.1–42.2, Xen. *Hell.*

3.3.2, Nep. *Ages.* 1.2–5, Plut. *Ages.* 1.1–5, Paus. 3.6.2–3. The royal title descended, as directly as possible, down the male line. Where the legitimacy of an heir was in dispute, Delphi might be consulted, but the decision lay in principle with the *pólis* and with its magistrates: Hdt. 6.61–66; Xen. *Hell.* 3.3.1–4; Paus. 3.6.2–3, 8.8–10 with Brenda Griffith-Williams, "The Succession to the Spartan Kingship, 520–400 BC," *BICS* 54:2 (December 2011): 43–58. At succession, cancellation of debts, reenactment of founding choral dances and sacrifices: Hdt. 6.59, Thuc. 5.16.3. Current kings as *archágetai*: Plut. *Lyc.* 6.2–3. For the meaning, see Tyrtaeus' paraphrase of the oracle: F4 (West). For the term *archagétēs*, see Pind. *Ol.* 7.79 (with 30); *GHI* 1.5.11, 26; Eur. *Or.* 555; Thuc. 6.3.1; Pl. *Lys.* 205d; Xen. *Hell.* 6.3.6, 7.3.12; Ephorus *FGrH* 70 F118; Arist. *Ath. Pol.* 21.5–6; Polyb. 34.1.3 (ap. Strabo 10.3.5); *ICr* III iii A; *IDelos* nos. 30, 35 (with Fernand Robert, "Le Sanctuaire de l'archégète ANIOS à Delos," *RA* 41 [1953]: 8–40; and with Georges Daux, "Chronique des fouilles et découvertes archéologique en Grèce en 1961," *BCH* 86 [1962]: 629–978 [at 959–62], and "Chronique des fouilles et découvertes archéologiques en Grèce en 1962," *BCH* 87 [1963]: 689–878 [at 862–69]); Strabo 14.1.46; Paus. 10.4.10; Plut. *Arist.* 11.3, *Demetr.* 53, *Mor.* 163b–c. See also Irad Malkin, *Religion and Colonization in Ancient Greece* (Leiden: Brill, 1987), 241–50. Obsession with legitimacy: Hdt. 5.39–41, 6.61–70; Xen. *Hell.* 3.3.1–4. Heraclids barred from having offspring by any woman from abroad: Plut. *Agis* 11.2. I see no reason to accept the view, advanced by Cartledge, *Agesilaos,* 96, that the prohibition against a Heraclid's having children *ek gunaikòs allodapês* is a prohibition against marrying anyone not of Heraclid stock. There is no evidence suggesting that the descendants of Heracles were a separate caste; in ordinary circumstances, the pertinent adjective refers to those from foreign parts; and, in the passage cited, the prohibition under discussion here is linked with another barring settlement abroad on pain of death. Moreover, it is most unlikely that the Spartans were worried that a son born to a non-Heraclid woman would somehow not be a Heraclid. What the Spartans did, of course, fear was the corrupting influence of foreigners. And, believing, as they did, that their own right to Laconia and Messenia rested on a divinely sanctioned Heraclid claim, they were terrified at the prospect that a legitimate claimant to either throne might be born abroad to a foreign woman, reared among an alien people, and groomed as a champion against Lacedaemon. In this connection, consider Hdt. 6.74.1–75.1 in conjunction with W. P. Wallace, "Kleomenes, Marathon, the Helots, and Arkadia," *JHS* 74 (1954): 32–35.

23. Conduct of sacrifices: Arist. *Pol.* 1285a3–7; Xen. *Lac. Pol.* 13.2–5, 8, 11. On campaign absolute sway: Hdt. 9.10.3, Xen. *Hell.* 5.4.15 (with 25), and Arist. *Pol.* 1285a7–9 (with Plut. *Ages.* 32.6–11), and note Thuc. 5.66.2–4, 8.3, 5. Word law: Thuc. 5.60 (cf. 63), 71–72. The discussion of royal patronage here recapitulates in brief an argument advanced in my unpublished Ph.D. dissertation: see Paul A. Rahe, "Lysander and the Spartan Settlement, 407–403 B.C." (Yale University 1977). As Cartledge, *Agesilaos,* 99–112, 139–59, 242–73, has more recently shown, Agesilaus made ample use of the patronage power available to the king. The same was presumably true of Cleomenes son of Anaxandridas: see Rahe, *PC,* chapters 2 and 4.

24. To get some feel for the role that a king or regent could play in the making of foreign policy, one need only survey Herodotus (3.148, 5.49–54, 6.50–84, 9.106 [with 90–91, 104]), Thucydides (1.79–85, 94–96, 128–35, 2.12–13, 18, 71–75, 5.16–17, 19, 59–60, 63, 8.5, 8, 70–71), and Xenophon (*Hell.* 2.2.11–13, 4.28–39, 3.2.21–31 [with Paus. 3.8.3–6, Plut. *Mor.* 835f, Lys. 18.10–12], 4.2–29, 5.17–25, 4.1.1–2.8, 3.1–23, 4.19–5.18, 6.1–7.7, 5.1.32–34, 2.3–7, 32, 37, 3.8–25, 4.13–18, 20–41, 47–59, 6.3.18–20, 4.1–16, 5.3–5, 12–21, 7.5.9–14). *Xenía* and *proxenía:* Gabriel Herman, *Ritualised Friendship and the Greek City* (Cambridge: Cambridge University Press, 1987), and Lynette G. Mitchell, *Greeks Bearing Gifts: The Public Use of Private Relationships in the Greek World, 435–323 BC* (Cambridge: Cambridge University Press, 2002). For further evidence, see Gabriel Herman, "Nikias, Epimenides, and the Question of Omissions in Thucydides," *CQ* n.s. 39:1 (1989): 83–93, and "Patterns of Name Diffusion Within the Greek World and Beyond," *CQ* n.s. 40:2 (1990): 349–63. Lacedaemon alone not betrayed to Philip of Macedon by treachery: Paus. 7.10.1–3. Royal selection of Sparta's *próxenoi* abroad likely: Paus. 3.8.4. Royal selection of cities' *próxenoi* at Lacedaemon: Hdt. 6.57.2. Possible ratification of choice by these cities: *IG* II² 106. In practice, *proxenía,* like the relationship of *xenía* on which it was modeled, tended to be hereditary both at Sparta (Pl. *Leg.* 1.642b–c) and abroad (Thuc. 6.89.2). I see no reason to accept the suggestion advanced by D. J. Mosley, "Spartan Kings and Proxeny," *Athenaeum,* 2nd ser. 49 (1971): 433–

35, that the royal prerogative in this sphere was merely meant to supplement the arrangements made on their own behalf by other communities.

25. Royal selection of *Púthioi:* Hdt. 6.57, Xen. *Lac. Pol.* 15.5, Cic. *Div.* 1.43.95, *Suda* s.v. *Púthioi.* In this connection, see also Plut. *Pel.* 21.3. Royal manipulation of religion for political purposes: note Polyb. 10.2.8–13 and August. *De civ. D.* 2.16, and see Hdt. 6.61–70, 73–76. 82; Thuc. 5.16.2.

26. See Rahe, *PC,* chapter 4.

27. Road network and its maintenance: Hdt. 6.57.4 with Giannēs Y. A. Pikoulas, *To Hodıko Dıktyo tēs Lakōnıkēs* (Athens: Ēoros, 2012). As I suggest in the text, it is by no means certain that the two kings concerned themselves solely with the roads built within Laconia and Messenia. Elsewhere Pikoulas quite plausibly suggests that the Lacedaemonians and their allies, working in tandem, may have been responsible for the elaborate network of cart roads constructed throughout the Peloponnesus in the archaic period: Chapter 4, note 62, below.

28. Oversight over adoptions and marriages of heiresses unbetrothed: Hdt. 6.57.4–5. Herodotus' use of the verb *hıknéetaı* in this passage suggests that, in choosing a husband for a Spartan *patroûchos,* the kings were expected to abide by certain principles of law or policy, but everything that we know about the position accorded the family within the Lacedaemonian polity militates against the view, advanced by Evanghelos Karabélias, "L'Épiclérat à Sparte," in *Studi in onore di Arnaldo Biscardi* (Milan: Istituto editoriale Cisalpino, 1982), II 469–80, that they would ordinarily follow the Athenian practice and award her to her nearest surviving male relation. It is worth noticing that Herodotus' characterization of the power exercised by the kings in this sphere precludes the possibility that their decisions were subject to review by a higher authority. I am inclined to suppose that—at least in the period prior to the passage of Epitadeus' law—the kings were expected to award a *patroûchos* to the younger son of a Spartan who was not in a position to inherit his father's public allotment.

29. Thomas Babington Macaulay, "Leigh Hunt," in Macaulay, *Critical, Historical, and Miscellaneous Essays* (New York: Hurd & Houghton, 1860), IV 362.

30. Athenian wag: Plut. *Ages.* 15.7. See Pl. *Resp.* 8.548a–b, Arist. *Pol.* 1270b33–35.

31. Spartan houses: cf. Plut. *Lyc.* 13.5–7, *Mor.* 189e, 227c, 285c, 997c–d, and F62 (Sandbach) with Xen. *Ages.* 8.7, and see Pl. *Resp.* 8.548a–b.

32. Arist. *Pol.* 1270a26–29 with Pomeroy, *SWo,* 84–85. I find Stephen Hodkinson's attempt, "Land Tenure and Inheritance in Classical Sparta," *CQ* n.s. 36:2 (1986): 378–406 (at 394–98), to reconcile this passage with Hdt. 6.57.4–5 as implausible as his earlier insistence (378–79, 384–85) that Plut. *Lyc.* 8.3–6 and 16.1 cannot be reconciled with *Agis* 5.3–7. See Appendix 1.

33. Law of Epitadeus: Plut. *Agis* 5.3–7 with Appendix 1. For the results, see Arist. *Pol.* 1270a18–21. In this connection, note Pl. *Leg.* 11.922a–929e (esp. 922d–923b). Citizenship and *sussıtíon* contribution: Arist. *Pol.* 1271a26–36. Greed of Spartan notables, dowries, concentration of property in hands of heiresses: 1270a15–26, 1307a34–36. In this connection, note also 1269b–1270a14, 1271a18, 1271b17. Dowries were forbidden in earlier times: Plut. *Mor.* 227f–228a, Just. *Epit.* 3.3.8. It is worth noting that Justin explicitly links the prohibition of dowries with the husband's capacity to keep his wife under control. Stephen Hodkinson's suggestion ("Land Tenure and Inheritance in Classical Sparta," 394–95, 398–404) that the daughter of a Spartan had inheritance rights comparable to those of her counterpart at Gortyn seems quite plausible (at least with regard to the private property of her parents); and, as he points out, such a supposition makes sense of the proportion of land that came to be concentrated in the hands of Sparta's women in Aristotle's day (after, I would insist, the public allotment had come to be treated, in effect, as private property). From the outset, the rules of inheritance will no doubt have affected the pattern of marriage alliances and encouraged restrictions on the number of offspring within the small circle of families which possessed an abundance of private property. After the public allotments were in effect privatized, this behavior seems to have become universal. See Hodkinson, "Inheritance, Marriage and Demography: Perspectives upon the Success and Decline of Classical Sparta," in *CSTS,* 79–121 (esp. 82–95, 109–14), and *PWCS,* 65–149, 399–445.

34. Royal land in towns of *períoıkoı:* Xen. *Lac. Pol.* 15.3. Proportion of booty, claim on hides and chines of sacrificed animals, piglet from every litter: cf. Hdt. 9.81 with Phylarchus *FGrH* 81

F56, and see Hdt. 6.56. Tax receipts and flow of gold and silver from abroad: Pl. *Alc.* I 123a–b with Strabo 8.5.4.

35. Royal capacity to work harm: Arist. *Pol.* 1272b38–1273a2.

36. The literature on this subject is considerable. See, most recently, Nicolas Richer, *Les Éphores: Études sur l'histoire et sur l'image de Sparte (VIIIe–IIIe siècles avant Jésus-Christ* (Paris: Publications de la Sorbonne, 1998), 153–521, and Stefan Sommer, *Das Ephorat: Garant des spartanischen Kosmos* (St. Katharinen: Scripta Mercaturae Verlag, 2001), 16–78. Note Andreas Luther, *Könige und Ephoren: Untersuchungen zur spartanischen Verfassungsgeschichte* (Frankfurt am Main: Antike Verlag, 2004).

37. Ephors like Roman tribunes: Cic. *Rep.* 2.33.57–58, *Leg.* 3.7.15–16; and Rousseau, *Du Contrat social* 4.5, in *Œuvres complètes de Rousseau,* III 454.

38. Iteration unknown, presumably forbidden: H. D. Westlake, "Reelection to the Ephorate?" *GRBS* 17 (1976): 343–52, and Richer, *Les Éphores,* 304–9. Office for only a year: cf. Xen. *Ages.* 1.36, Arist. *Pol.* 1272a6–7, Paus. 3.11.2, and Plut. *Ages.* 4.3 with Xen. *Hell.* 2.3.9–10. Majority vote, power almost unchecked: 2.3.34, 4.29. Note Arist. F611.10 (Rose) = Tit. 143.1.2.10 (Gigon) ap. Heraclid. Lemb. 373.10 (Dilts). *Eúthuna:* Plut. *Agis* 12.1. Cf. Arist. *Rh.* 1419a31 with *Pol.* 1271a6–8. Whether the retiring ephors were jailed while their conduct was under review, as seems to have been the case with the *basileîs* at Cumae, is unknown: Plut. *Mor.* 291f–292a. For the procedures followed in Athens, see Arist. *Ath. Pol.* 4.2, 48.3–5, 54.2, with Rhodes, *CAAP,* 114–15, 155, 313, 316–18, 547–48, 560–64, 597–99.

39. Ephors summon little assembly: Xen. *Hell.* 3.3.8. *Gerousía* juxtaposed with "common assembly": Diod. 11.50. The context leaves little doubt that we should identify Xenophon's "little assembly" with the ephors and *gerousía*. His point is that the ephors, instead of summoning the *gerousía* proper, unobtrusively consulted those of the *gérontes* who happened to be nearby. If they had called a formal meeting of the *gerousía*, they might have tipped off Cinadon's conspirators that something was afoot. See also Hdt. 5.40. Some scholars believe that the Spartans held a great assembly once a year and argue that "the little assembly" was the regular monthly meeting of the *ekklēsía* mentioned by Schol. Thuc. 1.67.3: cf. W. G. G. Forrest, *CR* 83 (1969): 197 n. 1, and Walter Burkert, "Apellai und Apollon," *RhM* 118 (1975): 1–21 (esp. 8–10). On the basis of Ephorus *FGrH* 70 F149 (ap. Strabo 10.4.18) and the analysis attributed to Archytas of Tarentum in Stob. *Flor.* 4.1.138 (Hense), a number of scholars conclude that the *hippeîs* constituted "the little assembly": cf. Henri Jeanmaire, *Couroi et courètes: Essai sur l'éducation spartiate et sur les rites d'adolescence dans l'antiquité hellénique* (Lille: Bibliothèque Universitaire, 1939), 544–45; Marcel Détienne, "La Phalange: Problèmes et controverses," in *Problèmes de la guerre en Grèce ancienne,* ed. Jean-Pierre Vernant (Paris: Seuil, 1968), 119–42 (at 135–40); and Geneviève Hoffmann, "Les Choisis: Un Ordre dans la cité grecque?" *Droit et cultures* 9–10 (1985): 15–26 (at 21).

40. Summoning of common assembly: Xen. *Hell.* 2.2.19, Plut. *Agis* 9.1, read in light of Diod. 11.50. Introduction of laws, decrees, and declarations of war and peace through *gerousía:* Xen. *Hell.* 2.2.19, 5.2.11–24; Plut. *Agis* 5.3–4, 8.1–9.1. Regular monthly meetings of common assembly: Schol. Thuc. 1.67.3 with Plut. *Lyc.* 6.1–4, Hdt. 6.57.2. In this connection, one should consider Burkert, "Apellai und Apollon," 1–21. For the role played by the *gerousía,* see Diod. 11.50, Plut. *Lyc.* 6. See Henry Theodore Wade-Gery, "The Spartan Rhetra in Plutarch *Lycurgus* VI: A. Plutarch's Text," *CQ* 37:1/2 (January–April 1943): 62–72, reprinted in Wade-Gery, *EGH,* 37–54. A. H. M. Jones provides a useful discussion of the issues in "The Lycurgan Rhetra," in *ASI,* 165–75. To the secondary literature he cites, one should add W. G. Forrest, "Legislation in Sparta," *Phoenix* 21:1 (Spring 1967): 11–19; Edmond Lévy, "La Grande *Rhètra,*" *Ktèma* 2 (1977): 86–103, and Françoise Ruzé, "Le Conseil et l'assemblée dans la grande *Rhètra* de Sparte," *REG* 104 (1991): 15–30. I am not persuaded by Richer's recent attempt, *Les Éphores,* 93–115, to find mention of the ephors in the Great Rhetra's account of the procedures governing the operations of the Spartan assembly. Ephor presides, chooses proposal presenter: Plut. *Mor.* 214b, 801b–c. Puts question, rules which side has majority: Thuc. 1.87.1–2. Decisions by "ephors and assembly": Xen. *Hell.* 2.4.38, 3.2.23, 4.6.3. See Andrewes, "The Government of Classical Sparta," 13–14, and Jones, "The Lycurgan Rhetra," 165–75. See also Hdt. 5.40. *Kúrios* within regime: Arist. *Pol.* 1322b12–16.

41. Ephors regulate foreign visitation and citizen sojourns abroad: Thuc. 1.144.2, 6.88.9, 8.12.1–3; Xen. *Lac. Pol.* 14.4; Plut. *Lyc.* 27.6–9, *Agis* 10.3–8 should be read in light of Hdt. 3.148.2;

Thuc. 1.131.1–2; Xen. *Hell.* 2.2.13, 19; Plut. *Lys.* 19.7–21.1. Receive embassies, conduct negotiations, decide when to place matters before authorities: Thuc. 5.36–38, 6.88.7–93.3, 8.5–6 should be read in light of Hdt. 3.46, 148.2, 6.106, 9.6–11; Thuc. 1.90.5; Xen. *Hell.* 2.2.11–13, 17–19, 4.28–29, 35–38, 3.1.1, 5.2.9, 11–24; Theopomp. *FGrH* 115 F85; Polyb. 4.34; Plut. *Them.* 19.1–3, *Cim.* 6.3, *Lys.* 14.5–8. The appointment of a harmost: Xen. *Hell.* 4.8.32. The supersession of a commander: Xen. *Hell.* 2.4.28–29. Orders to commanders: Thuc. 1.131.1–2; Xen. *Hell.* 3.1.1, 7, 2.12; Plut. *Lys.* 19. See also Thuc. 8.6.3, 12.1–3; Xen. *Hell.* 3.2.6–7, 5.4.24. Needless to say, a strong king could influence the choices made: Plut. *Mor.* 212d. Army called up: Xen. *Hell.* 3.2.23–25, 5.6, 4.2.9, 5.3.13, 4.47, 6.4.17, 5.10. For a full discussion, see Andrewes, "The Government of Classical Sparta," 10–12 and notes: sometimes the ephors were implementing a decision of the assembly; at other times, they were no doubt acting on their own authority. Similarly, sometimes the assembly picked the commander; at other times this detail seems to have been left to the ephors: Hdt. 9.10; Thuc. 8.12; Xen. *Hell.* 2.4.29, 5.1.33, 4.14, *An.* 2.6.2. Age groups for march determined: *Lac. Pol.* 11.2, *Hell.* 6.4.17.

42. Enforcement of sumptuary laws, censorship of music and poetry: Plut. *Agis* 10.5–8, Ael. *VH* 14.7. Inspection of the *néoi* and their bedding: Agatharchides *FGrH* 86 F10, Ael. *VH* 14.7. Appointment of *hippágretai:* Xen. *Lac. Pol.* 4.3–4. Control of treasury, oversight of tax collection: Plut. *Agis* 16.1. Receive proceeds from sale of prisoners and booty: Diod. 13.106.8–9, Plut. *Lys.* 16. The Spartans normally sold captured men and goods on the spot. The proceeds were public property: Pritchett, *GSW,* I 85–92. Intercalation of months: Plut. *Agis* 16.1.

43. Annual declaration of war on helots and use of *krupteía:* Arist. F538, 611.10 (Rose) = F543, Tit. 143.1.2.10 (Gigon) ap. Heraclid. Lemb. 373.10 (Dilts), Plut. *Lyc.* 28.7. For the murder of helots, see Thuc. 4.80, Myron of Priene *FGrH* 106 F2. Cf. Annalisa Paradiso, "The Logic of Terror: Thucydides, Spartan Duplicity and an Improbable Massacre," with David Harvey, "The Clandestine Massacre of the Helots (Thucydides 4.80)," both in *SpartSoc,* 179–217. Most scholars doubt Isocrates' assertion (12.181) that the ephors could execute *períoikoi* without trial. I am hesitant to reject his statement out of hand. Decree specifying obedience to the law, compliance with customs, and shaving of upper lip: consider Arist. F539 (Rose) = F545 (Gigon) in light of Ath. 4.143a, and see Plut. *Cleom.* 9.3. See Humfrey Michell, *Sparta* (Cambridge: Cambridge University Press, 1964), 126 n. 5.

44. Conduct of *eúthuna:* Arist. *Pol.* 1271a6–8. That they examined the magistrates of the preceding year and not their fellow magistrates follows from their examining the ephors of the preceding year. Authority to suspend fellow officials: Xen. *Lac. Pol.* 8.4. Individually judge civil suits: Arist. *Pol.* 1275b8–10. Moral censors and criminal justices authorized to impose fines: Xen. *Lac. Pol.* 8.4, Arist. *Pol.* 1270b28–31. Role in capital cases: Xen. *Lac. Pol.* 10.2; Arist. *Pol.* 1270b39–40, 1273a19–20, 1275b10, 1294b33–34; Plut. *Lyc.* 26.2, *Mor.* 217a–b should all be read in light of Paus. 3.5.2, which shows the ephors joining the *gerousía* in a capital case involving a king. For a conduct of the *anákrisis* and prosecution by the ephors, see Thuc. 1.95.3–5, 131; Xen. *Hell.* 5.4.24, *Lac. Pol.* 8.4; and the new Theophrastus fragment: John J. Keaney, "Theophrastus on Greek Judicial Procedure," *TAPhA* 104 (1974): 179–94 (at 189–91). See also Robert J. Bonner and Gertrude Smith, "Administration of Justice in Sparta," *CPh* 37 (1942): 113–29. Note the appearance of a king in a judicial role: Plut. *Mor.* 213d.

45. Ephors alone seated in presence of the kings: Xen. *Lac. Pol.* 15.6, Nicolaus of Damascus F114.16 (*FHG* Müller III 459), Plut. *Mor.* 217c. Cf. Arist. F611.10 (Rose) = Tit. 143.1.2.10 (Gigon) ap. Heraclid. Lemb. 373.10 (Dilts). Can summon kings, jail, and fine for misconduct: Thuc. 1.131; Nep. *Paus.* 3.5; Plut. *Lyc.* 12.5 (read in light of *Mor.* 226f–227a), *Lys.* 30.1, *Ages.* 2.6, 4.2–5.4, *Cleom.* 10, *Mor.* 1d, 482d. The king was required by law to answer the third summons. See also Thuc. 5.63, Ephorus *FGrH* 70 F193. Whether these last two references record the work of the ephors remains unclear. There must have been some limit to the fines they could impose: an extremely large fine was tantamount to banishment. Two ephors accompany king on campaign, give advice: Xen. *Lac. Pol.* 13.5. See Hdt. 9.76.3, Xen. *Hell.* 2.4.36. When the expedition took the king far away from Lacedaemon for an extended period, the city could send a board of advisors [*súmbouloi*] in addition or, more likely, instead: Xen. *Hell.* 3.4.2, 20, 4.1.5, 5.3.8. When the judgment of a king inspired distrust, the same procedure could be followed even when the struggle was nearer home: Thuc. 5.63.

46. Ruled by laws and ephors: Plut. *Mor.* 211c. Compact with the *pólis:* Xen. *Lac. Pol.* 15.1. Royal oath to maintain *nómoi:* Nicolaus of Damascus F114.16 (*FHG* Müller III 459). Monthly exchange of oaths with kings: Xen. *Lac. Pol.* 15.7. Shooting star and suspension of king: Plut. *Agis* 11 with H. W. Parke, "The Deposing of Spartan Kings," *CQ* 39:3/4 (July–October 1945): 106–12.

47. Ephors can arrest and indict kings on capital charges: Hdt. 6.82, Thuc. 1.131, Plut. *Agis* 18–19. Fate of fifth-century kings: G. E. M. Ste. Croix, *The Origins of the Peloponnesian War* (Ithaca: Cornell University Press, 1972), 350–53, and Powell, "Divination, Royalty and Insecurity in Classical Sparta," 85–135.

48. Herodotus (6.75, 85, 7.205) places Cleomenes' death and Leonidas' succession shortly before the battle of Marathon in 490. When Leonidas' reign came to an abrupt end at Thermopylae in 480 (7.224), Pleistarchus—his son by Cleomenes' daughter Gorgo (5.48, 7.205, 239)—became king. Pleistarchus was a minor at the time of the battle of Plataea in 479 (9.10) and remained so for a considerable time thereafter (Thuc. 1.132). His mother Gorgo was only eight or nine years old in 499 at the time of the Ionian Revolt (Hdt. 5.51) and cannot have given birth to a child before 493 at the earliest. See Darrel W. Amundsen and Carol Jean Diers, "The Age of Menarche in Classical Greece and Rome," *Human Biology* 41:1 (February 1969): 125–32. Indeed, since the Spartans did not normally marry off their daughters at menarche, but usually waited a few years until they were fully grown (Plut. *Lyc.* 15.4), it is probable that Gorgo did not marry Leonidas much, if at all before 490. This suggests that Pleistarchus reached the age of thirty and took on the full responsibilities of kingship (cf. Xen. *Mem.* 1.2.35 with Mary White, "Some Agiad Dates: Pausanias and His Sons," *JHS* 84 [1964]: 140–52 [at 140–41]) only shortly before his death—which took place sometime before the battle of Tanagra in 458 or 457 when Pleistoanax had already succeeded him (Thuc. 1.107.2; *HCT*, I 270). This supposition is confirmed by Pausanias' report (3.5.1) that Pleistarchus died very soon after taking up the kingship. Cf. Diod. 13.75.1 with White, "Some Agiad Dates," 140 n. 3. According to Theophrastus (Plut. *Ages.* 2.6, *Mor.* 1d), Archidamus was once fined for choosing too short a wife. See also Ath. 13.566a–b, and note Pollux' reference (*Onom.* 3.48) to *díkē kakogamíou.* I do not share the skepticism of Andrewes, "The Government of Classical Sparta," 19 n. 17; Ste. Croix, *The Origins of the Peloponnesian War,* 352; and Cartledge, *Agesilaos,* 20, regarding this anecdote. The Spartans had every reason to concern themselves with the physical qualities of the offspring of their kings. Cf. Thuc. 2.18 with 5.63: Archidamus courted disaster in 431.

49. Theophrastus' testimony: Keaney, "Theophrastus on Greek Judicial Procedure," 181–82. Cf. Xen. *Lac. Pol.* 4 with Moses I. Finley, "Sparta and Spartan Society," in Finley, *Economy and Society in Ancient Greece,* ed. Brent D. Shaw and Richard P. Saller (London: Chatto & Windus, 1981), 32–33. Role political jealousy could play in trials: Plut. *Mor.* 775c–e.

50. Kings court ephors: Arist. *Pol.* 1270b13–17. Aware of vulnerability: Xen. *Ages.* 1.36. Polybius on royal spirit of obedience: 23.11.4. Powers akin to those of tyrants: Xen. *Lac. Pol.* 8.4, Pl. *Leg.* 4.712d2–e5, Arist. *Pol.* 1270b14.

51. Chance governs selection of ephors: Pl. *Leg.* 3.692a with Paul A. Rahe, "The Selection of Ephors at Sparta," *Historia* 29:4 (4th Quarter 1980): 385–401. The defense of the orthodox view that the ephors were directly elected, advanced by Peter J. Rhodes, "The Selection of Ephors at Sparta," *Historia* 30:4 (4th Quarter 1981): 498–502; Richer, *Les Éphores,* 271–300; and Sommer, *Das Ephorat,* 22–23, leaves unexplained Plato's testimony, which gibes well with the observations of Aristotle (*Pol.* 1270b8–10, 20–29) and is clearly not intended as a description of the peculiar circumstances of the fourth century. If the ephors and the *gérontes* were selected in the same fashion, as these scholars suppose, it would be impossible to explain why the outcomes differed, as we shall soon see, so dramatically.

52. For the relationship, in general, between favors accepted and dependency, see Xen. *Cyr.* 5.5.25–34. For a Spartan king's practice of the art of gaining adherents in this fashion, see Plut. *Ages.* 20.6, *Mor.* 212d. In this connection, note Xen. *Hell.* 5.4.15–34, 6.4.14. Ephors nonentities: Arist. *Pol.* 1270b20–29. In Aristotle's day, poor and easily bribed: 1270b8–10. Kings can await board more favorable or more easily corrupted: e. g., Plut. *Ages.* 4.3–6. A king could deal with his opponents by the same means: Cic. *QFr.* 1.2.7; Plut. *Ages.* 5.2–4, 20.6, *Mor.* 212d, 482d. Note Xen. *Ages.* 11.11–12. Overwhelming authority if two kings united: Hdt. 6.56, Plut. *Agis* 12.2–3. As Carlier, "À Propos de la double royauté spartiate," 49–60, argues, the fact that Sparta was a dyarchy, not a monarchy, was crucial for her political development.

53. Brutus on the virtues of dyarchy: Dion Hal. *Ant. Rom.* 4.73.4.

54. Royal rivalry: Hdt. 6.52.8, Arist. *Pol.* 1271a25–26. See also Plut. *Mor.* 215f. Foreign clients of differing political persuasions in Phlius (Xen. *Hell.* 5.3.10–17, 20–25; cf. Diod. 15.19.4), Mantineia (Xen. *Hell.* 5.2.1–7, 6.5.4), and Elis (3.2.21–31, Paus. 3.8.3–6, Plut. *Mor.* 835f, Lys. 18.10–12). Note also the ties linking Agesilaus with leading figures at Tegea: Xen. *Hell.* 6.4.18, *Ages.* 2.23. In this connection, see Ernst Baltrusch, "Polis und Gastfreundschaft: Die Grundlagen der spartanischen Aussenpolitik," in *FS*, 165–91. Factions sometimes grouped about the two thrones: e.g., Xen. *Hell.* 5.4.25.

55. See Rahe, *PC*, Chapter 4.

56. Sthenelaidas vs. Archidamus: Thuc. 1.79–88. Pleistoanax was then in exile (Thuc. 5.16 with Plut. *Per.* 22.3) and his son Pausanias was a minor (Thuc. 3.26). In light of what we know concerning the career of Pleistoanax both before (Plut. *Per.* 22.1–3) and after (Thuc. 5.16) his exile and of what we know concerning Pausanias' subsequent activities (Plut. *Lys.* 21.1–7, Xen. *Hell.* 2.4.29–43, Diod. 14.33.5–7, Paus. 3.5.1–3, Lys. 18.10–12), it seems unlikely that Pleistoanax' younger sibling Cleomenes, who served as Pausanias' regent, was in favor of war or could have swung the adherents of his brother and nephew behind a policy that must have been repugnant to them. This cannot, however, be ruled out as a possibility. For another view, see W. Robert Connor, "Pausanias 3.14.1: A Sidelight on Spartan History, C. 440 B.C.," *TAPhA* 109 (1979): 21–27.

57. Character of regime mix: Plut. *Dion* 53.4. Master of the many: Dem. 20.10. Power of the *gérontes:* Dion. Hal. *Ant. Rom.* 2.14.2.

58. Membership in *gerousía* prize allotted to virtue: Dem. 20.107, Arist. *Pol.* 1270b23–25. Highest honor in city: Plut. *Lyc.* 26. Prestige associated with membership: *Mor.* 801b–c.

59. Drawn from aristocracy: consider Hdt. 9.85.2—where all of the manuscripts, in reading *hiréas* and not *irénes*, point to the existence at Lacedaemon of a sacerdotal aristocracy—in conjunction with Pierre Brulé and Laurent Piolot, "Women's Way of Death: Fatal Childbirth or *Hierai?* Commemorative Stones at Sparta and Plutarch, *Lycurgus*, 27.3," tr. Anton Powell, in *SpartSoc,* 151–78; then, note Aristotle's claim (*Pol.* 1294b19–29) that the *gerousía* was, for all intents and purposes, reserved for the *kaloì kagathoí;* consider his employment (1306a18–19) of the word *dunasteutiké*—which was ordinarily used to single out narrow, clan-based aristocracies—to describe the process by which the *gérontes* were selected; and see Rahe, "The Selection of Ephors at Sparta," 386–87 (with notes). Popular acclamation and life tenure: Plut. *Lyc.* 26.1–5, *Ages.* 4.3; Polyb. 6.45.5. Power to set agenda and annul assembly decisions that go beyond agenda: Plut. *Lyc.* 6, *Agis* 8–9 with Forrest, "Legislation in Sparta," 11–19. Service with ephors on juries in capital cases: Paus. 3.5.3, Plut. *Mor.* 217b, Arist. *Pol.* 1275b10. Augurs: Cic. *Div.* 1.43.95–96.

60. See Ephraim David, "The Trial of Spartan Kings," *RIDA,* 3rd ser., 32 (1985): 131–40.

61. Candidates canvass for office: Arist. *Pol.* 1271a10–18. *Gérontes* preside over disposition of all public affairs: Isoc. 12.154. Factions and their election: Nikos Birgalias, "La *Gerousía* et *les gérontes* de Sparte," *Ktèma* 32 (2007): 341–49.

62. Guardian of the constitution: Just. *Epit.* 3.3.2, Isoc. 12.154. Comparable role played by England's House of Lords: *The Records of the Federal Convention of 1787,* ed. Max Farrand (New Haven, CT: Yale University Press, 1911–37), I 288–89, 309–10: 18 June 1787.

63. Aristotle on the young: *Rh.* 1389a2–b12.

64. Aristotle on the old: *Rh.* 1389b13–1390a22. Cf. Soph. *Aj.* 1328–67 with 678–83.

65. Young excluded from political responsibilities: Thuc. 4.132.3. This did not preclude their holding subordinate leadership positions within the *agōgḗ:* see, for example, Xen. *Lac. Pol.* 2.1–14 (esp. 2, 5, 8, 11), Plut. *Lyc.* 16.8, 17.2–18.7 with Ducat, *SE,* 69–117. War for the young, deliberation for the old: Arist. *Pol.* 1329a2–17. Exaggerated respect paid to age: Hdt. 2.80.1; Xen. *Mem.* 3.5.15; Plut. *Lyc.* 15.2–3, 20.15, *Mor.* 227f, 232f, 235c–f, 237d; Just. *Epit.* 3.3.9 with Ephraim David, *Old Age in Sparta* (Amsterdam: Adolf M. Hakkert, 1991). Cf. Plato's depiction of Athens: *Resp.* 8.562e–563d.

66. Old well-suited to be censors: Plut. *Mor.* 795e–796a. Punished for failure to discipline wrongdoing on the part of the young: 237c. See also *Lyc.* 17.1–2.

67. Hetoimaridas: Diod. 11.50. On rare occasions, the division between young and old could even become a ground for civil strife in a city: Polyb. 4.53.3–55.6.

68. Well-mixed regime: Arist. *Pol.* 1294b13–41. Egalitarian socioeconomic arrangements:

Isoc. 7.61, 12.178–79. Political egalitarianism: 7.61. In this connection, one might wish to ponder Aristotle's discussion of the fashion in which the distribution of offices within a polity can be at odds or in tension with its *agōgē* and ethos: *Pol.* 1292b11–20.

69. Instability of mixed regimes: Tac. *Ann.* 4.33. Sparta a well-constituted *civitas: Dial.* 40. See *Ann.* 3.26–27 with *Hist.* 2.38.

70. John Stuart Mill, "Grote's History of Greece [I]," in *The Collected Works of John Stuart Mill,* ed. John M. Robson et al. (Toronto: University of Toronto Press, 1963–91), XI 302–3.

71. Xenophon's oblique criticism of Sparta: see Chapter 1, note 78, above. Plato as critic of Lacedaemon: *Leg.* 1.625c9–631b1, 3.688a–d with Edmond Lévy, "La Sparte de Platon," *Ktèma* 30 (2005): 217–36, and Mark J. Lutz, *Divine Law and Political Philosophy in Plato's Laws* (Dekalb: Northern Illinois University Press, 2012), 54–89. Aristotle also: *Pol.* 1271a41–1271b9, 1325a5–8, 1333a30–1334b5, 1338b9–38.

72. Lycurgus among the best lawgivers: Arist. *Pol.* 1296a18–21. Turned tyranny into an aristocracy: 1316a29–34 with 1271b24–27. Rightly made provision for moral formation of citizens: *Eth. Nic.* 1180a21–32, *Pol.* 1337a11–32. Deserved even more honor than accorded: Arist. F534 (Rose) = F544 (Gigon). Spartans flourish under laws of Lycurgus: Arist. *Rh.* 1398b17–18. As Joe Sachs, "Translator's Preface," in Aristotle, *The Politics,* tr. Joe Sachs (Newburyport, MA: Focus Philosophical Library, 2012), vii–xi (esp. ix–x), demonstrates, Aristotle's treatment of Lacedaemon is complex, extremely nuanced, critical, and appreciative.

Chapter 3. Conquest

1. See Iris Murdoch, *The Nice and the Good* (London: Penguin, 1978), 171.

2. Cf., for example, Robin Osborne, *Greece in the Making, 1200–479 B.C.* (London: Routledge, 1996); Jonathan Hall, *A History of the Archaic Greek World, ca. 1200–479 BCE* (Oxford: Wiley-Blackwell, 2007); and Massimo Nafissi, "Sparta," in *A Companion to Archaic Greece,* ed. Kurt A. Raaflaub and Hans van Wees (Malden, MA: Wiley-Blackwell, 2009), 117–37, who provides a useful summary of the view of early Spartan history that I think mistaken.

3. Cf. Noel Robertson, *Festivals and Legends: The Formation of Greek Cities in the Light of Public Ritual* (Toronto: University of Toronto Press, 1992), 147–252, who, in treating Spartan festivals, denies the commonsense view that events frequently gave rise to ritual and contends, instead, that with regard to the archaic period ritual repeatedly gave rise to pseudo-historical events, with Kõiv, *STAS,* 25–66, who argues that more often than not Spartan rituals commemorate genuine historical events.

4. See Kõiv, *ATEGH,* 3–34, who surveys and analyzes the secondary literature and evidence germane to the weighing of communal oral traditions. For the pertinence of his analysis to the study of early Lacedaemon, see ibid., 35–215; Mait Kõiv, "The Origins, Development, and Reliability of the Ancient Tradition about the Formation of the Spartan Constitution," *Historia* 54:3 (2005): 233–64; and *STAS,* 25–66.

5. *Phúsis* vs. *nómos:* Hdt. 7.101–5 (esp. 102.1, 103.4, 104.4–5). *Nómos* king of all: Hdt. 3.38, Pindar F16 (Maehler). Kinship entirely fictive: Jonathan M. Hall, *Ethnic Identity in Greek Antiquity* (Cambridge: Cambridge University Press, 1997); *Hellenicity: Between Ethnicity and Culture* (Chicago: University of Chicago Press, 2002); and "The Dorianization of the Messenians," in *HMLM,* 142–68, as well as Thomas J. Figueira, "The Evolution of Messenian Identity," in *SNS,* 211–44; and Nino Luraghi, *The Ancient Messenians: Construction of Ethnicity and Memory* (Cambridge: Cambridge University Press, 2008), 1–248.

6. See Luigi Luca Cavalli-Sforza, Paolo Menozzi, and Alberto Piazza, *The History and Geography of Human Genes* (Princeton, NJ: Princeton University Press, 1994), passim (esp. 3–157, 372–82). For a less technical and more accessible treatment, see Luigi Luca Cavalli-Sforza, *Genes, Peoples and Languages,* tr. Mark Seielstad (New York: North Point Press, 2000). For a particularly telling example, see Isabel Mendizabal et al., "Reconstructing the Population History of European Romani from Genome-wide Data," *Current Biology* 22:24 (6 December 2012): 2342–49. No less telling is the case of the ancient Etruscans. The oral tradition (Hdt. 1.94.5–7) asserting that they were a kinship community and that they immigrated into Italy from Asia Minor is now borne out

by the linguistic evidence and by human and bovine DNA studies: note Robert S. P. Beekes, *The Origins of the Etruscans* (Amsterdam: Koninklijke Nederlandes Akademievan Wetenschappen, 2003); then, see Cristiano Vernesi et al., "The Etruscans: A Population-Genetic Study," *American Journal of Human Genetics* 74:4 (April 2004): 694–704; Alessandro Achilli et al., "Mitochondrial DNA Variation of Modern Tuscans Supports the Near Eastern Origin of Etruscans," *American Journal of Human Genetics* 80:4 (April 2007): 759–68; and Marco Pellechia et al., "The Mystery of Etruscan Origins: Novel Clues from *Bos taurus* Mitochondrial DNA," *Proceedings of the Royal Society: Biological Sciences* 274 (2007): 1175–79. For another case where a DNA study confirms a group's oral traditions about its biological origins, see Mark Thomas et al., "Y Chromosomes Traveling South: The Cohen Modal Haplotype and the Origins of the Lemba—the 'Black Jews of Southern Africa,'" *American Journal of Human Genetics* 66:2 (February 2000): 674–86.

7. The broad claims to the contrary advanced by some classicists on the basis of Jan M. Vansina, *The Oral Tradition: A Study in Historical Methodology,* tr. H. M. Wright (Chicago: Aldine, 1965), and *Oral Tradition as History* (Madison: University of Wisconsin Press, 1985), should be taken with a large grain of salt. Among other things, as Kõiv, *ATEGH,* 9–34; "The Origins, Development, and Reliability of the Ancient Tradition about the Formation of the Spartan Constitution," 233–64; and *STAS,* 25–66, points out, Vansina's findings suggest that oral traditions having to do with the formation and reshaping of communities often have staying power.

8. Spartan fascination with genealogy: Pl. *Hipp. Maj.* 285b7–286a5. Cf. Rosalind Thomas, *Literacy and Orality in Ancient Greece* (Cambridge: Cambridge University Press, 1992), 108–13, who underestimates, in my judgment, the degree to which cultural imperatives in early Greece encouraged the well-born to cherish and pass on family lore, with James Allan Stewart Evans, *The Beginnings of History: Herodotus and the Persian Wars* (Toronto: University of Toronto Press, 2006), 271–89.

9. See *IACP,* passim.

10. See Oswyn Murray, "Herodotus and Oral History" and "Herodotus and Oral History Reconsidered," as well as Rosalind Thomas, "Herodotus' Histories and the Floating Gap," all in *The Historian's Craft in the Age of Herodotus,* ed. Nino Luraghi (Oxford: Oxford University Press, 2001), 16–44, 198–210, 314–25.

11. See Joachim Latacz, *Troy and Homer: Towards a Solution of an Old Mystery,* tr. Kevin Windle and Rosh Ireland (Oxford: Oxford University Press, 2004). See also Louise Schofield, *The Mycenaeans* (Los Angeles: J. Paul Getty Museum, 2007), 186–97, and Jorrit M. Kelder, *The Kingdom of Mycenae: A Great Kingdom in the Late Bronze Age Aegean* (Besthesda, MD: CDL Press, 2010).

12. Date posited for the end of the Trojan War: Eratosth. *FGrH* 241 F1. Isocrates' Archidamus (6.16–33) elegantly summarizes the legend. See also Apollod. *Bibl.* 2.8.2–4 and Diod. 4.37.3–4, 57–58, 7.8–9. For further details, see Tyrtaeus F3.12–15, 11.1–2 (West); Pindar *Pyth.* 1.62–65; *Isthm.* 9.3–4; Hdt. 1.56.2–3, 6.52.1, 8.31, 9.26.2–5, 27.2; Thuc. 1.9.2, 12.3, 107.2, 3.92.3; Ephorus *FGrH* 70 F121; Isoc. 12.255; Strabo 9.4.7; Paus. 5.1, 8.5.1–6; Steph. Byz. s.v. *Naúpaktos.* For a complete collection of the ancient *testimonia,* see Friedrich Prinz, *Gründungsmythen und Sagenchronologie* (Munich: C. H. Beck, 1979), 420–50.

13. Legends dovetail: Hdt. 2.171.2–3, 8.73; Xen. *Hell.* 7.1.23; Strabo 8.7.1; Paus. 2.18.2, 38.1, 3.2.1, 5.1.1–2, 7.1.1–9, 6.1–2, 18.5.

14. See Oscar Broneer, "The Cyclopean Wall on the Isthmus of Corinth and Its Bearing on Late Bronze Age Archaeology," *Hesperia* 35:4 (October–December 1966): 346–62, and "The Cyclopean Wall on the Isthmus of Corinth, Addendum," *Hesperia* 37:1 (January–March 1968): 26–35. For a brief summary, see James Wiseman, *The Land of the Ancient Corinthians* (Göteborg: P. Åström, 1978), 59–60. For the context, see also Schofield, *The Mycenaeans,* 186–97.

15. Roughly speaking, wherever in Greece the ancient traditions speak of there being interlopers who conquered the local population subsequent to the fall of Troy, the latter later reappear as subjects of the former: consider the examples of this species of subjection collected by Hans van Wees, "Conquerors and Serfs: Wars of Conquest and Forced Labour in Archaic Greece," in *HMLM,* 33–80.

16. For a further discussion of the historical value of the legends pertaining to Greece in and after the Bronze Age, see Margalit Finkelberg, *Greeks and Pre-Greeks: Aegean Prehistory and Greek Heroic Tradition* (Cambridge: Cambridge University Press, 2010).

17. Genealogies: Hdt. 7.204, 8.131; Paus. 3.2–10.

18. The English translations of Hdt. 8.131.3 need correction in one particular. The manuscript tradition, which strongly favors reading "two" where these translations opt for "seven," is now supported by *POxy* 2390, which shows that Leotychidas son of Anaxilas was once king, as Plut. *Mor.* 224c–d and *Lyc.* 13.7 also suggest. In this connection, see George L. Huxley, *Early Sparta* (London: Faber & Faber, 1962), 117–19; W. G. G. Forrest, *A History of Sparta, 950–192 B.C.,* second edition (London: Hutchinson University Library, 1980), 13–23; David P. Henige, *The Chronology of Oral Tradition: Quest for a Chimera* (Oxford: Clarendon Press, 1974), 207–13; Paul Cartledge, *SL,* 293–98; John F. Lazenby, *The Spartan Army* (Warminster, UK: Aris & Phillips, 1985), 64–66; Martin L. West, "Alcman and the Spartan Royalty," *ZPE* 91 (1992): 1–7; and Paul Christesen, *Olympic Victor Lists and Ancient Greek History* (Cambridge: Cambridge University Press, 2007), 505–7.

19. Amyclae avoids destruction: Paus. 3.2.6, Servius ad Verg. *Aen.* 10.564. Pindar on pre-Dorian Amyclae: *Pyth.* 1.65, 11.32, *Nem.* 11.34. Evidence suggesting kingship at Amyclae: Paus. 4.7.8, 10.9.5. In assessing what archaeology has to teach us about Lacedaemon, Laconia, and Spartan colonization in this period, I have profited from reading Paul Cartledge, *SL,* 3–137, and "Early Lacedaeimon: The Making of a Conquest State," in *Philolakōn,* 49–55, as well as *Continuity and Change in a Greek Rural Landscape: The Laconia Survey,* ed. William Cavanagh, Joost Crouwel, and Graham Shipley (London: British School at Athens, 1996–2002); William G. Cavanagh, Christopher B. Mee, and Peter James *The Laconia Rural Sites Project* (London: British School at Athens, 2005); and the summary account provided by Nigel Kennell and Nino Luraghi, "Laconia and Messenia," in *A Companion to Archaic Greece,* 239–54.

20. Victor Parker, "Zur Datierung der Dorischen Wanderung," *MH* 52 (1995): 130–54, may, of course, be correct in arguing that the Dorians did not arrive until the tenth century.

21. Thucydides' warning: 1.10.2–3.

22. Pastoral features in Carneia: Ath. 4.141e–f with Michael Pettersson, *Cults of Apollo at Sparta: The Hyakinthia, the Gymnopaidiai, and the Karneia* (Stockholm: Paul Åströms Förlag, 1992), 57–72; Irad Malkin, *Myth and Territory in the Spartan Mediterranean* (Cambridge: Cambridge University Press, 1994), 149–58; and Nicolas Richer, *La Religion des Spartiates: Croyances et cultes dans l'Antiquité* (Paris: Les Belles Lettres, 2012), 423–56. Cattle-raiding: Paus. 4.4.5–8, 7.1–2. Note Thuc. 1.5, and consider Hdt. 2.152 along with the numerous references in Homer to raiding by sea and by land: *Il.* 1.121–26, 366–69, 2.688–93, 6.414–28, 9.405–9, 11.660–762, 18.509–40, *Od.* 9.39–61, 14. 83–88, 211–75, 16.418–27. See Alastar Jackson, "War and Raids for Booty in the World of Odysseus," in *War and Society in the Greek World,* ed. John Rich and Graham Shipley (London: Routledge, 1993), 64–76.

23. Evidence for the four villages near acropolis: Paus. 3.16.9–10, *IG* V i 674–88. Agiad kings—senior branch: Hdt. 6.51.1–52.7. Buried in Pitana: Paus. 3.14.1–2. Eurypontid kings—homes and graves in Limnai: 3.12.8; cf. Hdt. 6.69.3 with Paus. 3.16.6–7. Marshy area near Eurotas: Strabo 8.5.1.

24. Five *lóchoi:* Arist. F541 (Rose) = F546 (Gigon). No longer the pattern in the late fifth century: Thuc. 5.68.3. Passing comment: Hdt. 9.53 with Henry Theodore Wade-Gery, "The Spartan Rhetra in Plutarch's *Lycurgus* VI: C. What Is the Rhetra?" *CQ* 38:3/4 (July–October 1944), 115–26, reprinted in Wade-Gery, *EGH,* 66–85, and Cartledge, *Agesilaos,* 427–31. Cf. Lazenby, *The Spartan Army,* 3–64 (esp. 48–52). Thucydides (1.20.4) to the contrary notwithstanding, there is no reason to gainsay Herodotus' testimony. He had visited the village to which he attributes the pertinent *lóchos* (Hdt. 3.55.2); and by Thucydides' day—almost certainly as a consequence of a precipitous decline in the number of Spartiates (Appendix 1, below) that the Lacedaemonians, with their instinct for secrecy (Thuc. 5.68.2, Plut. *Lyc.* 20.9), will not have wished to divulge to a stranger—the Spartan army had undergone a reorganization (Thuc. 5.68.3), regarding which the Athenian historian is apt to have been kept quite ignorant. Note also Herodian 4.8.3.

25. Epigraphical evidence from Roman period: *IG* V i 675, to be read with Kennell, *GV,* 162–69, who, rightly in my opinion, argues that the *neopólitai* mentioned therein are Amyclaeans.

26. Amyclae discussed: Pind. *Pyth.* 1.65, 11.32, *Nem.* 11.34, *Isthm.* 7.12–15; Xen. *Hell.* 4.5.11; Arist. F532 (Rose) = F539 (Gigon). Pitana mentioned: *POxy* 2389 F35 (a commentary reflecting a reference to the village on Alcman's part); Pindar *Ol.* 6.78–31; Hdt. 3.55.2, 9.53; Eur. *Tro.* 1110–13;

Thuc. 1.20.4. Peace of Nicias inscription set up at Amyclae: 5.18.10–11. Note 5.41.2–3. The silence of the sources concerning Mesoa, Limnai, and Konosoura has led one scholar recently to take an absence of evidence as evidence of absence and to suggest that, in the archaic and classical periods, the three villages did not as such exist, and that the land they occupied was a part of Pitana, which was the name used to describe the entire area located about the acropolis: see Marcello Lupi, "Amompharetos, the *Lochos* of Pitane and the Spartan System of Villages," in *SW*, 185–218.

27. Herodotus' king lists: 7.204, 8.131. Struggle pitting Pitana and Mesoa against Limnai and Konosoura: Paus. 3.16.9–10.

28. Amyclae once independent: Pind. *Isthm.* 7.12–15, Arist. F532 (Rose) = F539 (Gigon), Paus. 3.2.6. Cult of Apollo Hyakinthia peculiar to Amyclae: Xen. *Hell.* 4.5.11 with Pettersson, *Cults of Apollo at Sparta*, 9–41, and Richer, *La Religion des Spartiates*, 343–82. Amyclaeans excluded from Artemis Orthia cult: Paus. 3.16.9.

29. Pausanias reliable: Christian Habicht, *Pausanias' Guide to Ancient Greece* (Berkeley: University of California Press, 1985); Andrew R. Meadows, "Pausanias and the Historiography of Classical Sparta," *CQ* n.s. 45:1 (1995): 92–113; and Paul Cartledge, "Sparta's Pausanias: Another Laconian Past," in *Pausanias: Travel and Memory in Roman Greece*, ed. Susan E. Alcock, John F. Cherry, and Jaś Elsner (New York: Oxford University Press, 2001), 167–72. Note, however, Maria Pretzler, "Pausanias and Oral Tradition," *CQ* n.s. 55:1 (May 2005): 235–49, who rightly sees that he relies on local oral traditions and—wrongly in my opinion—doubts their veracity. Note also Jaś Elsner, "Pausanias: A Greek Pilgrim in the Roman World," *P&P* 135 (1992): 5–29, and "Pausanias: A Pilgrim in the Roman World. Postscript, 2003," in *Studies in Ancient Greek and Roman Society*, ed. Robin Osborne (Cambridge: Past and Present Publications, 2004), 282–85; Susan E. Alcock, "Landscapes of Memory and the Authority of Pausanias," in *Pausanias Historien*, ed. Jean Bingen (Geneva: Fondation Hardt, 1996), 241–76; and Maria Pretzler, *Pausanias: Travel Writing in Greece* (London: Duckworth, 2007), and "Pausanias' *Description of Greece*: Back to the Roots of Greek Culture," in *Mediterranean Travels: Writing Self and Other from the Ancient World to Contemporary Society*, ed. Patrick Crowley, Noreen Humble, and Silvia Ross (London: Legenda, 2011), 32–46. Support of Delphi, destruction of Aigys, seizure of Eurotas headwaters: Paus. 3.21.3, 8.35.3–4. Invasion of Cynouria: 3.2.5, 7.2.

30. Conquest of Pharis, Geronthrae, Amyclae: Paus. 3.2.6, 7.4 with Victor Parker, "Some Dates in Early Spartan History," *Klio* 75 (1993): 45–60 (at 45–48). Teleklos on Nedon River and at Pherae: Nepos *Conon* 1.1, Strabo 8.4.4, Paus. 3.2.6. Killed at sanctuary of Artemis Limnatis: Strabo 6.3.3; Diod. 15.66.3; Paus. 3.2.6, 7.4, 4.4.2–3, 31.3–4.

31. See Graham Shipley, "*Perioikos:* The Discovery of Classical Lakonia," in *Philolakōn*, 211–26, and "Sparta and Its Perioikic Neighbors: A Century of Reassessment," *Hermathena* 181 (2006): 51–82; Jonathan M. Hall, "Sparta, Lakedaimon, and the Nature of Perioikic Dependency," in *Further Studies in the Ancient Greek Polis*, ed. Pernille Flensted-Jensen (Stuttgart: Franz Steiner Verlag, 2000), 73–89; Norbert Mertens, "*ouk homoîoi, agathoì dé:* The *Perioikoi* in the Classical Lakedaeimonian *Polis*," in *SBM*, 285–303; Mogens Herman Hansen, "The Perioikic Poleis of Lakedaimon," in *Once Again: Studies in the Ancient Greek Polis* (Stuttgart: Franz Steiner Verlag, 2004), 149–64; Julián Gallego, "The Lakedaimonian *Perioikoi:* Military Subordination and Cultural Dependence," in *Esclavage antique et discriminations socio-culturelles*, ed. Vasilis I. Anastasiadis and Panagiotis N. Doukellis (Bern: Peter Lang, 2005), 33–57; and Jean Ducat, "Le Statut des périèques lacédémoniens," *Ktèma* 33 (2008): 1–86.

32. Alcamenes conquers Helos: Paus. 3.2.7. Rich soil of nearby plain: Polyb. 5.19.7. The claim advanced by Theopompus of Chios (*FGrH* 115 F122) that the old helots of Laconia were descended from the Achaeans of an earlier age is perfectly compatible with Hellanicus *FGrH* 4 F188; Ephorus *FGrH* 70 F117; Paus. 3.2.7, 20.6; and Harpocration s.v. *heilōteúein*, as Theopompus' own testimony elsewhere (*FGrH* 115 F13) makes clear. Apart from Antiochus of Syracuse's claim (*FGrH* 555 F13) that the Spartans made helots of citizens who refused to fight in the First Messenian War, there is not a shred of evidence to support Nino Luraghi's rejection of the ancient tradition that the helots of Laconia were a conquered people: Luraghi, "Helotic Slavery Reconsidered," in *SBM*, 227–48 (esp. 236–38, 240–42), and "The Imaginary Conquest of the Helots," in *HMLM*, 109–41. Nor is his claim true that the subjection of conquered peoples was in antiquity unparalleled. It was, in fact, commonplace, as van Wees, "Conquerors and Serfs," 33–80, demonstrates. See

also Karl-Wilhelm Welwei, "Überlegungen zur frühen Helotie in Lakonien," in *FS,* 29–41, and Kõiv, *ATEGH,* 149–59. For a recent attempt to make sense of the term helot, see Timothy Barnes, "A Note on the Etymology of *Heílotes,*" in *SCA,* 286–87.

33. The fact that, in *The Iliad* (2.581–90, 9.150–53, 292–94), Homer mentions a series of places in southern Laconia and in the Mani and no place to the north of Sparta itself as belonging to Lacedaemon may be an indication of the situation in the early archaic period—as Lukas Thommen, "Das Territorium des frühen Sparta," in *FS,* 15–28, suspects. But it may, instead, reflect the geopolitics of the Mycenaean period, as the recent discovery of a Mycenaean palace at Agios Vasileios near Xirokambi strongly suggests: see Chapter 4, note 27, below.

34. Alcamenes and Nikandros launch First Messenian War: Paus. 4.4.4–5.10. Lasts twenty years, Theopompus finishes: Tyrtaeus F5 (West); Paus. 4.6.5, 13.6, 15.2–3.

35. Olympic games founded in 776: Eratosth. *FGrH* 241 F1; Paus. 5.4.5–6, 8.5–9.6; Euseb. *Chron.* 1.191–94 (Schoene-Petermann). Literary evidence weighed in light of the archaeological record: Catherine Morgan, *Athletes and Oracles: The Transformation of Olympia and Delphi in the Eighth Century BC* (Cambridge: Cambridge University Press, 1990), 1–147. Last Messenian, first Spartan victory in footrace: Paus. 5.8.6, Euseb. *Chron.* 1.195–96 (Schoene-Petermann). Pausanias' dates for the First Messenian War: 4.5.10, 4.12.7–13.7, with Mosshammer, *CE,* 204–9.

36. Pausanias' chronology worthless: Victor Parker, "The Dates of the Messenian Wars," *Chiron* 12 (1991): 25–47; Pamela-Jane Shaw, "Olympiad Chronology and 'Early' Spartan History," in *SNS,* 273–209 (at 275–82), and *Discrepancies in Olympiad Dating and Chronological Problems of Archaic Peloponnesian History* (Stuttgart: Franz Steiner Verlag, 2003), 100–144; and Christesen, *Olympic Victor Lists and Ancient Greek History,* 112–22, 482–87. Case for dating the First Messenian War to the early seventh century: Mischa Meier, *Aristokraten und Damoden: Untersuchungen zur inneren Entwicklung Spartas im 7. Jahrhundert v. Chr. und zur politischen Funktion der Dichtung des Tyrtaios* (Stuttgart: Franz Steiner Verlag, 1998), 18–185.

37. Cf. Walter Scheidel, "The Greek Demographic Expansion: Models and Comparisons," *JHS* 123 (2000): 120–40, whose doubts seem to me unjustified. Early in the archaic period, conditions in Greece were not unlike those in North America in the eighteenth century, where, as Scheidel acknowledges, the population doubled every twenty-five years. That there would in time be overshoot goes without saying, and this may explain the colonial movement of the eighth, seventh, and sixth centuries.

38. Minyan saga: Pind. *Pyth.* 4 (esp. 250–61), 5.63–76; Paus. 3.1.7–8; Hdt. 4.145.2–149.2. Dorian tribes: Hom. *Od.* 19.177, Tyrtaeus F19.8 (West). Triphylia: Strabo 8.3.3, 19 with Thomas Heine Nielsen, "Triphylia," in *IACP,* 540–46.

39. Lemnos and Imbros, Amyclae, then Crete: Conon *FGrH* 26 F1.36, Plut. *Mor.* 247d.

40. *Partheníai:* Arist. *Pol.* 1306b29–31, Antiochus of Syracuse *FGrH* 555 F 13, Ephorus of Cumae *FGrH* 70 F216, Diod. 8.21, Paus. 10.10.6, Polyaen. *Strat.* 2.14.2. Taras founded in 706: Euseb. *Chron.* p. 91 (Helm). Note Bjorn Quiller, "Reconstructing the Spartan Partheniai: Many Guesses and a Few Facts," *SO* 71 (1996): 34–41, and see Massimo Naffisi, "From Sparta to Taras: *Nomima, Ktisis,* and Relationships between Colony and Mother City," in *SNS,* 245–72, for an intelligent discussion of the evidence and the recent scholarship. Note also Marcello Lupi, *L'Ordine delle generazioni: Classi di età e costumi matrimoniali nell'antica Sparta* (Bari: Edipuglia, 2000), 171–94 (which should be read in light of ibid., 47–169).

41. Turmoil in early Lacedaemon: Thuc. 1.18.1. Thera, Melos, Lyktos, Gortyn, Taras: Malkin, *Myth and Territory in the Spartan Mediterranean,* 67–142. For an intelligent overview of this early period that pays close attention to the various strands in the oral tradition, see Kõiv, *ATEGH,* 69–140.

42. Early generosity in incorporating strangers: Ephorus *FGrH* 70 F118 and Arist. *Pol.* 1270a34–37.

43. Agamemnon and Achilles: Hom. *Il.* 1.8–303.

44. Chariots deployed in Homer as prestige vehicles: Greenhalgh, *EGW,* 1–39, and Robert E. Gaebel, *Cavalry Operations in the Ancient Greek World* (Norman: University of Oklahoma Press, 2002), 19–60. I do not mean to suggest that there is anything odd about the use of chariots as prestige vehicles: J. K. Anderson, "Homeric, British and Cyrenaic Chariots," *AJA* 69:4 (October 1965): 349–52, and "Greek Chariot-Borne and Mounted Infantry," *AJA* 79:3 (July 1975): 175–87.

But the fact that the Mycenaean depictions of chariots show neither bowmen nor spearmen operating in combat from these platforms does not mean that chariots were not used by the Mycenaeans as they were used in Egypt, Assyria, Babylonia, and the Hittite lands. The argument advanced by Joost H. Crouwel, *Chariots and Other Means of Land Transport in Bronze Age Greece* (Amsterdam: Allard Pierson Series, 1981), on the basis of these depictions needs to be adjusted in light of the evidence from the Hittite texts for the deployment by the Achaeans of chariots on a grand scale in combat within Asia Minor: see Aht3 (CTH147) §12, in *The Ahhiyawa Texts,* ed. and tr. Gary Beckman, Trevor Bryce, and Eric Cline (Atlanta: Society of Biblical Literature, 2011), 81. There are passages suggesting Homer's awareness of the manner in which chariots were used for combat in Bronze Age Asia Minor, but they are few: see *Il.* 4.293–309, 5.9–20, 8.114–23, 11.150–54, 289, 531–42, 15.352–54, 16.377–428, 809–15. Cf. van Wees, *GW,* 158–60, whose defense of Homer concedes the basic point.

45. Awareness of the advantages of fighting in formation: Hom. *Il.* 2.553–55, 4.293–325, 13.125–35, 16.169–217. Fighting at the Argive trench: 12.1–471, 13.39–14.134, 15.262–746. Struggle for Patroclus' body: 17.352–65. Open-field combat: 4.419–7.282, 8.53–334, 11.15–847, 14.361–15.3, 16.218–20, 257–17.761, 20.156–22.374.

46. See Greenhalgh, *EGW,* 40–145; Anderson, "Greek Chariot-Borne and Mounted Infantry," 175–87; Crouwel, *Chariots and Other Wheeled Vehicles in Iron Age Greece,* esp. 53–65, 102–8; and Robin Archer, "Chariotry to Cavalry: Developments in the Early First Millennium," in *New Perspectives on Ancient Warfare,* ed. Garret G. Fagan and Matthew Trundle (Leiden: Brill, 2010), 57–79. Where the terrain was favorable, as it was on Cyprus, chariots continued to be used in a military context: Hdt. 5.113.

47. Thesis that literary imperatives hide reality of mass combat: Joachim Latacz, *Kampfparänese, Kampfdarstellung und Kampfwirklichkeit in der Ilias, bei Kallinos und Tyrtaios* (Munich: Verlag C. H. Beck, 1977), to be read with Rüdiger Leimbach's severely critical review, *Gnomon* 52:5 (1980): 418–25; Pritchett, *GSW,* IV 7–33; and Kurt Raaflaub, "Homeric Warriors and Battles: Trying to Resolve Old Problems," *CW* 101:4 (Summer, 2008), 469–83. Sarpedon's analysis: Hom. *Il.* 12.309–28 with Ian Morris, "The Use and Abuse of Homer," *ClAnt* 5:1 (April 1986): 81–138, and Susanne Ebbinghaus, "Protector of the City, or the Art of Storage in Early Greece," *JHS* 125 (2005): 51–72. For a more plausible view of Homer's account of battle, see Hans van Wees, "Kings in Combat: Battles and Heroes in the *Iliad,*" *CQ* n.s. 38:1 (1988): 1–24, and "The Homeric Way of War: The *Iliad* and the Hoplite Phalanx," *G&R* 41 (1994): 1–18, 131–55; "Heroes, Knights and Nutters: Warrior Mentality in Homer," in *Battle in Antiquity,* ed. Alan B. Lloyd (Swansea: Classical Press of Wales, 1996), 1–86; "Homeric Warfare," in *A New Companion to Homer,* ed. Ian Morris and Barry Powell (Leiden: Brill, 1997), 668–93; and *GW,* 153–65. See also Anthony M. Snodgrass, "The 'Hoplite Reform' Revisited," in Snodgrass, *Archaeology and the Emergence of Greece* (Ithaca, NY: Cornell University Press, 2006), 344–59; Paul A. Cartledge, "The Birth of the Hoplite: Sparta's Contribution to Early Greek Military Organization," in Cartledge *SR,* 153–66 (at 153–58); J. E. Lendon, *Soldiers and Ghosts: A History of Battle in Classical Antiquity* (New Haven: Yale University Press, 2005), 20–38; and Everett L. Wheeler, "Land Battles," in *CHGRW,* I 186–223 (at 193–95). There is, as Cartledge, "The Birth of the Hoplite," 157, puts it, "all the difference in the world between mass military action, even decisive mass military action," of the sort now thought to be found in Homer, "and regular engagements between massed ranks of hoplite phalanxes."

48. Hoplite phalanx on eve of Persian Wars: Hdt. 7.9β. See also Thuc. 4.92; Xen. *Mem.* 3.1.8; Arr. *Tact.* 12.2; Polyb. 13.3.2–6, 18.29–31. For the manner in which being arrayed in files ruled out combat avoidance and for the vital importance in battle of good order [*eutaxía*], as opposed to disorder [*ataxía*], see Jason Crowley, *The Psychology of the Athenian Hoplite: The Culture of Combat in Classical Athens* (Cambridge: Cambridge University Press, 2012), 49–66.

49. Archaeological evidence: Anthony M. Snodgrass, *Arms and Armour of the Greeks* (Ithaca, NY: Cornell University Press, 1967), 41–45, 48–77; *Archaic Greece: Age of Experiment* (London: J. M. Dent, 1980), 105–7; and "Setting the Frame Chronologically," in *MB,* 85–94; C. W. J. Eliot and Mary Eliot, "The Lechaion Cemetery near Corinth," *Hesperia* 37 (1968): 345–67 (at Plate 102, 2); John B. Salmon, "Political Hoplites?" *JHS* 97 (1977): 84–101; and Meral Akurgal, "Eine protokorinthische Oinochoe aus Erythrai," *Istanbuler Mitteilungen* 42 (1992): 83–96. Hoplite figurines dedicated at Lacedaemon: A. J. B. Wace, "The Lead Figurines," in *The Sanctuary of Artemis Orthia*

at Sparta, ed. R. M. Dawkins (London: Macmillan, 1929), 249–84, and John Boardman, "Artemis Orthia and Chronology," *ABSA* 58 (1963): 1–7. Function of flute: Thuc. 5.70; Plut. *Mor.* 210f; Ath. 14.627d; Polyaen. *Strat.* 1.10.1, *Excerpta* 18.1. Cf. Hans van Wees's fanciful reinterpretation of the Chigi vase, which resolutely ignores the difficulties encountered by vase painters intent on depicting the hoplite phalanx, in "The Development of the Hoplite Phalanx: Iconography and Reality in the Seventh Century," in *War and Violence in Ancient Greece,* ed. Hans van Wees (London: Duckworth, 2000), 125–66 (at 134–46), and in *GW,* 166–83, with the much more sensible discussion of the iconography in Adam Schwartz, *Reinstating the Hoplite: Arms, Armour and Phalanx Fighting in Archaic and Classical Greece* (Stuttgart: Franz Steiner Verlag, 2009), 123–35. See also Jeffrey M. Hurwit, "Reading the Chigi Vase," *Hesperia* 71 (2002): 1–22.

50. Function of *aspís:* Arist. *Pol.* 1297b19–20. Nomenclature: cf. John F. Lazenby and David Whitehead, "The Myth of the Hoplite's *Hoplon,*" *CQ* n.s. 46:1 (1996): 27–33, with Schwartz, *Reinstating the Hoplite,* 25–27.

51. Fate of hoplites caught outside the phalanx: Hdt. 9.69.2; Thuc. 3.97–98, 4.32–36, 5.10; Xen. *Hell.* 4.2.16–23, 5.11–17. Hoplite enslaved to his *hópla:* Eur. *HF* 190. Cf. Anthony M. Snodgrass, "The Hoplite Reform and History," in Snodgrass, *Archaeology and the Emergence of Greece,* 309–30 (at 312–15); van Wees, "The Development of the Hoplite Phalanx," 125–66; and Peter Krentz, "Warfare and Hoplites," in *The Cambridge Companion to Archaic Greece,* ed. H. Alan Shapiro (Cambridge: Cambridge University Press, 2007), 61–84, with Cartledge, "The Birth of the Hoplite," 153–66; Adam Schwartz, "The Early Hoplite Phalanx: Order or Disarray," *C&M* 53 (2002): 31–64, *Reinstating the Hoplite,* 27–54, and "Large Weapons, Small Greeks: The Practical Limitations of Hoplite Weapons and Equipment," in *MB,* 157–75; and Gregory F. Viggiano, "The Hoplite Revolution and the Rise of the Polis," in *MB,* 112–33 (at 113–20); then, see Christopher A. Matthew, *A Storm of Spears: Understanding the Greek Hoplite at War* (Havertown, PA: Casemate Publishers, 2012), 39–59, 168–237. Note also Scott Rusch, *Sparta at War: Strategy, Tactics, and Campaigns, 550–362 BC* (London: Frontline Books, 2011), 16–18, and Fernando Echeverría Rey, "*Taktikè Technè:* The Neglected Element in Classical 'Hoplite' Battles," *AncSoc* 41 (2011): 45–82. The arguments concerning what hoplites could do when not wearing the panoply advanced by Louis Rawlings, "Alternative Agonies: Hoplite Martial and Combat Experiences Beyond the Phalanx," in *War and Violence in Ancient Greece,* 233–59, do not, for the most part, bear on the question being discussed here.

52. Function of *aspís:* Thuc. 5.71.1, Plut. *Mor.* 220a. Note also Diod. 12.62.5, Plut. *Pel.* 1.10. For a highly plausible reconstruction of the manner in which hoplites actually fought, see Victor D. Hanson, *The Western Way of War: Infantry Battle in Classical Greece,* second edition (Berkeley: University of California Press, 2009), and *Hoplites: The Classical Greek Battle Experience,* ed. Victor D. Hanson (London: Routledge, 1991). See also Marcel Detienne, "La Phalange: Problèmes et controverses," in *Problèmes de la guerre en Grèce ancienne,* ed. Jean-Pierre Vernant (The Hague: Mouton, 1968), 119–42; Pritchett, *GSW,* IV 33–93; Wheeler, "Land Battles," 186–223; Schwartz, *Reinstating the Hoplite,* 38–45, 146–234; and Allen Pittman, "'With Your Shield or on It': Combat Applications of the Greek Hoplite Spear and Shield," in *The Cutting Edge: Studies in Ancient and Medieval Combat,* ed. Barry Molloy (Stroud, Gloucestershire: Tempus, 2007), 64–76. Although there is much to be learned from studies subsequent to those by Hanson, for the reasons indicated in the text, I am not persuaded by the attacks on his assertion that hoplites normally fought in close formation and that battles frequently culminated in a mass shove [*ōthismós*]: cf. George L. Cawkwell, *Philip of Macedon* (London: Faber & Faber, 1978), 150–53, and "Orthodoxy and Hoplites," *CQ* n.s. 39:2 (1989): 375–89, reprinted in Cawkwell, *CC,* 416–37; and Peter Krentz, "The Nature of Hoplite Battle, " *ClAnt* 4 (1985): 50–61, "Fighting by the Rules: The Invention of the Hoplite *Agôn,*" *Hesperia* 71 (2002): 23–39, "Warfare and Hoplites," 61–84, and "Hoplite Hell: How Hoplites Fought," in *MB,* 134–56, as well as Adrian K. Goldsworthy; "The Othismos, Myths and Heresies: The Nature of Hoplite Battle," *War in History* 4 (1997): 1–26, and van Wees, "The Development of the Hoplite Phalanx," 125–66, and *GW,* 166–97, with A. J. Holladay, "Hoplites and Heresies," *JHS* 102 (1982): 94–103; Robert D. Luginbill, "*Othismos:* The Importance of the Mass-Shove in Hoplite Warfare," *Phoenix* 48:1 (Spring 1994): 51–61; Paul Bardunias, "The Mechanics of Hoplite Battle: Storm of Spears and Press of Shields," *Ancient Warfare, Special Issue 3: The Battle of Marathon* (2011): 60–68; and Crowley, *The Psychology of the Athenian Hoplite,* 49–66. The

dispute is summarized in Donald Kagan and Gregory F. Viggiano, "The Hoplite Debate," in *MB*, 1–56.

53. Virtues of single-grip shield: Schwartz, *Reinstating the Hoplite*, 35–37. Armband-and-rim-grip shield and phalanx inseparable: Paul A. Cartledge, "The Birth of the Hoplite," 158, and "Hoplitai/Politai: Refighting Ancient Battles," in *MB*, 74–84 (esp. 77–78); and Viggiano, "The Hoplite Revolution and the Rise of the Polis," 113–20.

54. Thud of missiles: Alcaeus F140.10 (Lobel-Page), Archilochus F139.6 (West), Callinus F1.14 (West). Note F1.5, 9–11. Archers sheltering behind the shields of the heavily armed: Hom. *Il.* 4.112–15, 8.255–72, 15.440–44. Light-armed troops doing the same: Tyrtaeus F11.35–38 (West). Skirmishing: F19.19–20, 23a.10–14 (West). Van Wees, who rightly cites this evidence and draws attention to the pertinent vase paintings, fails to recognize that the survival of outmoded tactics has no bearing on the crucial question: cf. van Wees, "The Development of the Hoplite Phalanx," 125–66, and *GW*, 166–83

55. Rejection of Homeric understanding of human excellence, front ranks of phalanx protecting those behind: Tyrtaeus F12 (West). Fence of shields: F19 (West). Depiction of hoplite warfare: F11 (West). Cf. van Wees, "The Development of the Hoplite Phalanx," 149–52, who tries to read the phalanx out of Tyrtaeus' battle descriptions, with Schwartz, *Reinstating the Hoplite*, 115–23, who shows that this cannot be done. The argument that Jason Crowley, *The Psychology of the Athenian Hoplite*, passim, makes concerning the Athenians can be extended to Lacedaemonians as well. In this connection, see Robert D. Luginbill, "Tyrtaeus 12 West: Come Join the Spartan Army," *CQ* n.s. 52:2 (2002): 405–14.

56. Aristocracies based on horsemen: Arist. *Pol.* 1289b33–40, 1297b1–27. See also 1321a5–11. It is almost universally assumed that Aristotle has true cavalry in mind, but it is perfectly possible that he is thinking of horse-borne raiders and infantrymen. *Hippobótai* of Chalcis and *Hippeîs* of Eretria: Arist *Ath. Pol.* 15.2; Hdt. 5.77.2, 600.1.

57. Thebes and chariots: Soph. *Ant.* 149, 844–45. The elite Theban unit of "charioteers and footmen" mentioned by Diod. 12.701.1 would appear to be, like the *hippeîs* of Lacedaemon, a relic of an earlier epoch. Narrow aristocracy [*dunasteía olígōn*] at Thebes: Thuc. 3.62 with Hdt. 9.15–16, 86–88; Plut. *Arist.* 18.7.

58. On this particular point, see Josho J. Brouwers, "From Horsemen to Hoplites: Some Remarks on Archaic Greek Warfare," *BABesch* 82:2 (2007): 305–19 (at 309–16), and *Henchmen of Ares: Warriors and Warfare in Early Greece* (Rotterdam: Karwansaray Publishers, 2013), 40–103. In this connection, note Ioannis Georganas, "Weapons and Warfare in Early Iron Age Thessaly," *Mediterranean Archaeology and Archaeometry* 5:2 (2005): 63–74.

59. One-half of Messenian harvest extracted each year: Tyrtaeus F6 (West), Paus. 4.14.4–5. Homeric analogue: *Il.* 18.509–12, 22.111–28, with Henk W. Singor, "Spartan Lots and Helot Rents," in *De Agricultura: In Memoriam Pieter Willem de Neeve (1945–1990)*, ed. Heleen Sancisi-Weerdenburg, R. J. Vander Spek, H. C. Teitler, and H. T. Wallinga (Amsterdam: J. C. Gieben, 1993), 31–60 (at 42–45), and Stefan Link, *Das Frühe Sparta: Untersuchungen zur spartanischen Staatsbildung im 7. und 6. Jahrhundert v. Chr.* (St. Katharinen: Scripta Mercaturae Verlag, 2000), 31–58.

60. Argive shields: Snodgrass, *Arms and Armour of the Greeks*, 54–55, 67–68, and Pierre Amandry, "Le Bouclier d'Argos," *BCH* 107 (1983): 627–34, with Plin. *NH* 7.200; Apoll. *Bibl.* 2.2.1–2; Dion. Hal. *Ant. Rom.* 4.16.2; Paus. 2.25.7, 8.50.1; *POxy* 10.1241. In this connection, see Irene Ringwood Arnold, "The Shield of Argos," *AJA* 41 (1937): 436–40.

61. Panoply tombs at Argos: Paul Courbin, "Une Tombe géometrique d'Argos," *BCH* 81 (1957): 322–86 (at 340–67), and Evangelia Protonotariou-Deilaki, "Arkhaiotites kai mnimeia: Argolidokorinthias," *AD* 26 (1971): 68–84 (esp. 81–82, Figure 13) and 27 (1973): 80–122 (esp. 99, Plate 95). If no shield was found in any of these tombs, it was presumably because the practice of adding bronze rims, emblems, and facings to the wooden shields did not begin until the last third of the seventh century: see Peter Bol, *Argivische Schilde* (Berlin: Walter de Gruyter, 1989).

62. Argives and Arcadians aid Messenians in First Messenian War: Paus. 4.10.7–11.8, 8.5.10. Cynouria dispute: 3.2.2–3, 7.3. Nikandros and Asinaeans ravage the Argolid: 3.7.4. Battle of Hysiae: 2.24.7 with Mosshammer, *CE*, 223–24 (with n. 8). Pheidon of Argos: Arist. *Pol.* 1310b16–28 and Ephorus *FGrH* 70 F115 with Antony Andrewes, "The Corinthian Actaeon and Pheidon of

Argos," *CQ* 43:1/2 (January–April 1949): 70–78, and Salmon, "Political Hoplites?" 92–93. Cf., however, Mait Kõiv, "The Dating of Pheidon in Antiquity," *Klio* 83 (2001): 327–47, and Hall, *A History of the Archaic Greek World,* 144–54. Oracle: Palatine Anthology 14.73. After reading note 3, above, cf. Robertson, *Festivals and Legends,* 147–65, 208–16, who treats the battle of Hysiae as a figment of the etiological imagination, with J. Kendrick Pritchett, "Aetiology sans Topography: 1. Kenchreai and the Battle of Hysiai," in *Thucydides' Pentekontaetia and Other Essays* (Amsterdam: J. C. Gieben, 1995), 207–28. Cf. also Shaw, "Olympiad Chronology and 'Early' Spartan History," 282–94, and *Discrepancies in Olympiad Dating and Chronological Problems of Archaic Peloponnesian History,* 158–88, who proposes to redate the battle of Hysiae to the early fifth century.

63. Mercenaries as innovators: John Hale, "Not Patriots, Not Farmers, Not Amateurs: Greek Soldiers of Fortune and the Origins of Hoplite Warfare," in *MB,* 176–93, building on Wolf-Dietrich Niemeier, "Archaic Greeks in the Orient: Textual and Archaeological Evidence," *BASO* 322 (2001): 11–32, and Nino Luraghi, "Traders, Pirates, Warriors: The Proto-History of Greek Mercenary Soldiers in the Eastern Mediterranean," *Phoenix* 60:1 (Spring–Summer 2006): 21–47. Aristocrats pioneer: Snodgrass, "The Hoplite Reform and History," 309–30.

64. Political consequences of democratization of warfare: Arist. *Pol.* 1297b1–27 with Martin P. Nilsson, "Die Hoplitentaktik and das Staatswesen," *Klio* 22 (1929): 240–49; Hilda L. Lorimer, "The Hoplite Phalanx with Special Reference to the Poems of Archilochus and Tyrtaeus," *ABSA* 42 (1947): 76–138; Paul A. Cartledge, "Hoplites and Heroes: Sparta's Contribution to the Technique of Ancient Warfare," *JHS* 97 (1977): 11–27; Salmon, "Political Hoplites?" 84–101; and Victor Davis Hanson, *The Other Greeks: The Family Farm and the Agrarian Roots of Western Civilization* (New York: Free Press, 1995). Tyrants associated with war, at odds with the traditional aristocracy, and favorable to the *dêmos:* Arist. *Pol.* 1305a7–28, 1310b12–16 with Antony Andrewes, *The Greek Tyrants* (London: Hutchinson University Library, 1956). Cf. George L. Cawkwell, "Early Greek Tyranny and the People," *CQ* n.s. 45:1 (1995): 73–86, reprinted in Cawkwell, *CC,* 33–53. I am not inclined willfully to ignore the evidence concerning tyranny provided by Herodotus, Aristotle, and other classical sources: cf., however, Greg Anderson, "Before *Tyrannoi* Were Tyrants: Rethinking a Chapter of Early Greek History," *ClAnt* 24:2 (October 2005): 173–222. As Lendon, *Soldiers and Ghosts,* 402, rightly recognizes, to reject the hypothesis advanced by Nilsson, Lorimer, Cartledge, Salmon, and Hanson, one would have to suppose that "Aristotle knew less about the period in question than we do" because "he had no archeologists to help him." The critique of Aristotle along these lines advanced by Hans van Wees, "Tyrants, Oligarchs and Citizen Militias," in *Army and Power in the Ancient World,* ed. Angelos Chaniotis and Pierre Ducrey (Stuttgart: Franz Steiner Verlag, 2002), 61–82, is ill-grounded: both on the implausible presumption that, if Aristotle fails to provide documentation in *The Politics,* it is because he has no knowledge of particulars, and on a systematic misreading of the argument the peripatetic actually makes. The passages that van Wees thinks contradictory can easily be reconciled with one another—and with the available archaeological and literary evidence. Before assessing the propensity, now fashionable, to reject the judgments of Aristotle on such matters, one should consider the care that he took to collect accurate information: see George L. Huxley, "On Aristotle's Historical Methods," *GRBS* 13:2 (Summer 1972): 157–69, and "Aristotle as Antiquary," *GRBS* 14:3 (Fall 1973): 271–86. Note also James Day and Mortimer Chambers, *Aristotle's History of Athenian Democracy* (Berkeley: University of California Press, 1962), passim (esp. 5–23). The argument articulated by David L. Toye, "Aristotle's Other *Politeiai:* Was the *Athenaion Politeia* Atypical?" *CJ* 94:3 (February–March 1999): 235–53, for the view that Aristotle's sources for the political development of most of the Greek cities he studied were grossly inadequate suffers from two grave weaknesses. It leaves unexplained why Aristotle nonetheless bothered with the enterprise, and it presupposes what we do not know: that the surviving fragments of Aristotle's *politeíai* are representative of the works from which they were drawn; that Aristotle's students did not go on research expeditions for the purposing of collecting local traditions in the cities studied; and that there were few, if any, local histories and chronicles of which we now have no knowledge. Our ignorance today can hardly be indicative of the evidence then available to the peripatetic and his students.

65. Hesiod's posture of deference: *Op.* 8–9, 27–39, 174–285, *Theog.* 79–93. Thersites' fate: Hom. *Il.* 2.211–78.

66. Plato on the thoughts of an impecunious hoplite ranged alongside a rich weakling: *Resp.*

8.556b–e. As should be clear, for my purposes here, it does not matter one whit whether the hoplites of the archaic period were for the most part smallholders—as, Hanson contends, they were—or gentleman farmers, as some now think: cf. Hanson, *The Other Greeks,* with Lin Foxhall, "The Control of the Attic Landscape," in *Agriculture in Ancient Greece,* ed. Berit Wells (Stockholm: Paul Åströms Forlag, 1992), 155–59, "A View from the Top: Evaluating the Solonian Property Classes," in *The Development of the Polis in Archaic Greece,* ed. Lynnette G. Mitchell and Peter J. Rhodes (London: Routledge, 1997), 113–36, and "Can We See the 'Hoplite Revolution' on the Ground? Archaeological Landscapes, Material Culture, and Social Status in Early Greece," in *MB,* 194–221; and Hans van Wees, "The Myth of the Middle Class Army: Military and Social Status in Ancient Athens," in *War as a Cultural and Social Force: Essays on Warfare in Antiquity,* ed. Tønnes Bekker-Nielsen and Lise Hannestad (Copenhagen: Det kongelige Danske Videnskabernes Selskab, 2001), 45–71, "Mass and Elite in Solon's Athens: The Property Classes Revisited," in *Solon of Athens: New Historical and Philological Approaches,* ed. Josine H. Blok and André P. M. H. Lardinois (Leiden: Brill, 2006), 351–89, and "Farmers and Hoplites: Models of Historical Development," in *MB,* 222–55; then, see G. E. M. de Ste. Croix, "The Solonian Census Classes and the Qualifications for Cavalry and Hoplite Service," in Ste. Croix, *Athenian Democratic Origins and Other Essays,* ed. David Harvey and Robert Parker (New York: Oxford University Press, 2005), 5–72. In the circumstances, this is a socioeconomic distinction without a political difference, for it is hard to see why either group would have been willing to defer to the horsey set. For a corrective, see Cartledge, "Hoplitai/Politai: Refighting Ancient Battles," 74–84; Viggiano, "The Hoplite Revolution and the Rise of the Polis," 112–33; and Victor Davis Hanson, "The Hoplite Narrative," in *MB,* 256–75. To reconcile the unorthodox Marxist analysis of the family farm as a new and hitherto unnoticed mode of production that Hanson articulates in *The Other Greeks* with Lendon's admirable account —*Soldiers and Ghosts,* 20–90—of the aristocratic ethos driving hoplite warfare and of the manner in which the "passive courage" expected of the hoplite came to substitute for the prowess of the Homeric *prómachos,* one would need only adjust Hanson's depiction of the hoplite ethos in modest ways with an eye to the presence of slaves on the estates of most hoplites and then consider the fact that his smallholders, for all of their apparent ordinariness, nonetheless constituted what Tocqueville once aptly called "an aristocracy of masters": see my review of his book in *AJPh* 118:3 (Autumn 1997): 459–62; and, on this particular point, consider Michael H. Jameson, "Agriculture and Slavery in Classical Athens," *CJ* 73:2 (December 1977–January 1978): 122–45, and "Agricultural Labor in Ancient Greece," in *Agriculture in Ancient Greece,* 135–46, as well as Lin Foxhall, "Access to Resources in Classical Greece: The Egalitarianism of the Polis in Practice," in *Money, Labour and Land,* ed. Paul Cartledge, Edward E. Cohen, and Lin Foxhall (London: Routledge, 2002), 209–20, and "Culture, Landscapes, and Identities in the Mediterranean World," *MHR* 18:2 (2003): 75–92, who make a strong case for a reliance on dependent labor on the part of those smallholders who possessed enough land to be able to serve in the phalanx. The survey data Foxhall cites, however, casts little light on the archaic period, as she acknowledges; and, unless one is willing to take an absence of evidence as evidence for absence, it is insufficient as a support for her implausible claim that the colonization movement had nothing to do with land hunger. Moreover, her attempt to evade the evidence, both literary and archaeological, that there was a modicum of equality in colonial land distribution is not at all persuasive. For a corrective to her argument that early Greece was radically inegalitarian, which is to a considerable degree consistent with Hanson's argument, see the discussion of Greek egalitarianism in Ian Morris, *Archaeology as Cultural History: Words and Things in Iron Age Greece* (Oxford: Blackwell, 2000), 109–312, who—by deliberately ignoring what can be learned from Aristotle and by quarantining archaic aristocratic discourse as countercultural—nonetheless overstates the case for an early egalitarianism and underestimates the time that it took for equality to become the norm.

67. Spartan adjustment to brute fact of hoplite warfare: Cartledge, "Hoplites and Heroes," 24–27.

68. Laconia as Peloponnesian acropolis: Diod. 14.82.4. Euripides on Laconia: F1083 (Nauck²).

69. Size of Spartan domain: Cartledge, *SL,* 6. Two-fifths of Peloponnesus: Thuc. 1.10.2.

70. Terpander of Lesbos sings of justice at the Carneia in 676: Hellanicus *FGrH* 4 F85, Sosibius *FGrH* 595 F3. See W. G. G. Forrest, "The Date of the Lykourgan Reforms in Sparta," *Phoenix* 17:3 (Autumn 1963): 157–79. Cf. Arnold J. Toynbee, "Sparta's Constitutional Development," and

"The Dating of the Adoption, in the Hellenic World in General and at Sparta in Particular, of the Various Components of the Hoplite Equipment, and the Dating of the Adoption of Phalanx-Tactics," in Toynbee, *SPGH*, 213–49 (at 221–39), 250–60, who recognizes that the sociopolitical reform instituted at Lacedaemon must have been a consequence of the military revolution, but dates the latter and, therefore, the former to the latter part of the seventh century.

71. Thaletas of Gortyn at Carneia in 676: Philodemos *De Musica* 85–86 (Kemke). Plays prominent role in founding Gymnopaidiai: Plut. *Mor.* 1134b–c. Foundation occasioned by Spartan defeat: Henry Theodore Wade-Gery, "A Note on the Origin of the Spartan Gymnopaidiai," *CQ* 43:1/2 (January–April 1949): 79–81; Pettersson, *Cults of Apollo at Sparta*, 42–56; and Richer, *La Religion des Spartiates*, 383–422. On Hysiae, see note 62, above.

72. Outbreak of Second Messenian War, role of Argives and Arcadians: Tyrtaeus F5.6, 23a (West); Apollod. *FGrH* 244 F334; Paus. 3.3.1–5, 4.15.1–17.9. Note Arist. *Pol.* 1269a39–1269b5.

73. Tyrtaeus' war fought by "fathers of our fathers": F5.6 (West). Pausanias dates outbreak of Second Messenian War to 685: 4.15.1, 23.4. In this connection, see Mosshammer, *CE*, 204–9.

74. Initial stage of Second Messenian War: Paus. 4.15.2–17.9, 22.6–7, 8.5.13; Kallisthenes *FGrH* 124 F23; Polyb. 4.33.5–6; Plut. *Mor.* 548f. Tyrtaeus on Battle of the Great Trench: F9, 23a (West). See Schol. Arist. *Eth. Nic.* 1116b. Aristocrates lived two generations before Periander of Corinth and is said to have ruled over almost all of Arcadia: Diog. Laert. 1.94. Aristomenes retreats to Eira on the Neda River near Phigaleia and conducts guerrilla war: Paus. 4.15.4–23.4, 26.6, 33.4–6 with Mattias N. Valmin, *Études topographiques sur la Messénie ancienne* (Lund: Carl Blom, 1930), 118–20. Flight 287 years before Epaminondas' liberation of Messenia: 4.26.3–27.11.

75. Flight of Aristomenes, daughter marries Damagetus of Ialysos: Paus. 4.24.1–3. Diagoridae: Pind. *Olymp.* 7; Thuc. 8.35.1, 44, 52, 84.2–3; Xen. *Hell.* 1.1.2, 5.19; Diod. 13.38.5–6, 45.1–6; Paus. 6.6.2, 7.1–7. Aristomenes' death at Rhodes at time of reign in Lydia of Ardys son of Gyges: 4.24.2–3. Pindar's failure to mention the descent of the Diagoridae from Aristomenes would weigh against the story told by Pausanias only if it could be shown that, in 490 in the larger Greek world, one's descent from a failed Messenian leader would have been a source of pride. Cf. Henry Theodore Wade-Gery, "The 'Rhianos Hypothesis,'" in *ASI*, 289–302, who is, I think, too quick to dismiss Pausanias' testimony concerning the Diagorid connection. Pausanias' error concerning the number of generations separating Damagetus and the Diagoridae of the fifth and fourth centuries is an indication of genealogical confusion of the sort to be expected and nothing more.

76. Cf. Lionel Pearson, "The Pseudo-History of Messenia and Its Authors," *Historia* 11:4 (October 1962): 397–426; Daniel Ogden, *Aristomenes of Messene: Legends of Sparta's Nemesis* (Swansea: Classical Press of Wales, 2004); and Nino Luraghi, *The Ancient Messenians: Construction of Ethnicity and Memory* (Cambridge: Cambridge University Press, 2008), 1–248 (esp. 88–92), who seem to think the stories pure retrojection from quite late.

77. Marriage of Hagnagora and Thrayx of Phigaleia: Rhianos *FGrH* 265 F40, Paus. 4.24.1. Capture of Phigaleia, its liberation with the help of one hundred citizens of Oresthasion, monument at Phigaleia in their honor: 8.39.3–5, 41.1; Polyaen. 6.27.2. Descendants of Tharyx still prominent in the mid-fourth century: Wade-Gery, "The 'Rhianos Hypothesis,'" 292–97. Note also Arnold J. Toynbee, "Sparta's Conquest of Laconia and Messenia," in Toynbee, *SPGH*, 164–88 (at 186, n. 2). After reading note 3, above, cf. Robertson, *Festivals and Legends*, 219–52, with J. Kendrick Pritchett, "Aetiology sans Topography: 3. Phigaleia and the Oresthasians and 4. The Ithomaia and the Messenian Wars," in Pritchett, *Thucydides' Pentekontaetia and Other Essays*, 262–79.

78. Helot families: Thuc. 1.103.1–3. Helot households and settlements: Diod. 12.67.4, Strabo 8.5.4, Xen. *Hell.* 3.3.5. For a succinct account of what archaeology has to teach us about Messenia in the age stretching from the Mycenaean period through the period of Spartan domination, see Ann B. Harrison and Nigel Spencer, "After the Palace: The Early 'History' of Messenia," in *Sandy Pylos: An Archaeological History from Nestor to Navarino*, ed. Jack L. Davis (Austin: University of Texas Press, 1998), 147–62 (at 158–62).

79. Shared cults: Maddalena L. Zunino, *Hiera Messeniaka; La Storia religiosa della Messenia dall'età micenea all'età ellenistica* (Udine: Forum, 1997). Memory and the oppressed: L. R. Shero, "Aristomenes the Messenian," *TAPhA* 69 (1938): 500–531, and Susan E. Alcock, "The Pseudo-History of Messenia Unplugged," *TAPhA* 129 (1999): 333–41, "The Peculiar Book IV and the Problem of the Messenian Past," in *Pausanias: Travel and Memory in Roman Greece*, 143–53, and

Archaeologies of the Greek Past: Landscape, Monuments and Memories (Cambridge: Cambridge University Press, 2002), 132–75. Daniel Ogden's analysis of the tales told concerning Aristomenes needs to be reconsidered in light of Alcock's sensible suspicion that there lies at their core the outlines of a true story: see Ogden, *Aristomenes of Messene*, 1–127.

Chapter 4. Politics and Geopolitics

1. Disputed date for Lycurgus. Time of Leobatas: Hdt. 1.65.4. Time of Charillos: Simonides F628 (PMG), Schol. Pl. *Resp.* 10.599d–e, *Suda* s.v. *Lukoûrgos*, Arist. *Pol.* 1271b24–26. Hieronymus of Rhodes and others claim time of Terpander and Thaletas: Ath. 14.635e–f, Arist. *Pol.* 1274a29, Plut. *Lyc.* 4.1–3. Note also Mosshammer, *CE*, 173–91.

2. Lycurgus and ephorate: Hdt. 1.65.4–5, Pl. *Ep.* 8.345a–c. Theopompus and ephorate: Arist. *Pol.* 1313a26–28. See also Pl. *Leg.* 3.691d–692a. Even Xenophon (*Lac. Pol.* 8.3) hints that Lycurgus was not solely responsible. For a comprehensive survey of the ancient *testimonia* and of modern opinion, see Nicolas Richer, *Les Éphores: Études sur l'histoire et sur l'image de Sparte (VIIIème–IIIème siècles avant Jésus-Christ)* (Paris: Publications de la Sorbonne, 1998), 13–20, and note Stefan Sommer, *Das Ephorat: Garant des spartanischen Kosmos* (St. Katharinen: Scripta Mercaturae Verlag, 2001), 3–16.

3. Lycurgus, Polydorus, and public land allotments: Plut. *Lyc.* 8, *Mor.* 231.

4. Great Rhetra attributed variously to Lycurgus and to Theopompus and Polydorus: Tyrtaeus F4 (West), Plut. *Lyc.* 6. Workings of the assembly: Chapter 2, note 40, above, and the attendant text. See Henry Theodore Wade-Gery, "The Spartan Rhetra in Plutarch *Lycurgus* VI: B. The *Eynomia* of Tyrtaios," *CQ* 38:1/2 (January–April 1944): 1–9, reprinted in *EGH*, 54–66. For a recent review of the role played by Tyrtaeus, see Mischa Meier, *Aristokraten und Damoden: Untersuchungen zur inneren Entwicklung Spartas im 7. Jahrhundert v. Chr. und zur politischen Funktion der Dichtung des Tyrtaios* (Stuttgart: Franz Steiner Verlag, 1998), passim (esp. 186–328). As should be clear, I am not persuaded by those who deny that Tyrtaeus is alluding to the Great Rhetra: cf. Hans van Wees, "Tyrtaeus' *Eunomia*: Nothing to Do with the Great Rhetra," in *SNS*, 1–41, with Mischa Meier, "Tyrtaios fr. 1ᴮ G/P bzw. fr. °14 G/P (= fr. 4 W) und die große Rhetra—kein Zusammenhang?" *GFA* 5 (2002): 65–87. Hans van Wees's response, "Gute Ordnung ohne Grosse Rhetra: Noch einmal zu Tyrtaios' *Eunomia*," *GFA* 5 (2002): 89–103, is not compelling, as Stefan Link, "Eunomie im Schoss der Rhetra? Zum Verhältnis von Tyrt. frgm. 14 W und Plut. *Lyk.* 6, 2 und 8," *GFA* 6 (2003): 141–50, points out. Nor can I regard the Great Rhetra as a forgery: cf. Massimo Nafissi, "The Great *Rhetra* (Plut. *Lyc.* 6): A Retrospective and Intentional Construct?" in *Intentional History: Spinning Time in Ancient Greece*, ed. Lin Foxhall, Hans-Joachim Gehrke, and Nino Luragi (Stuttgart: Franz Steiner Verlag, 2010), 89–119. Nor am I inclined to doubt that the Great Rhetra was an archaic document and to redate the fragments attributed to Tyrtaeus to the late fifth century: cf. Andreas Luther, *Könige und Ephoren: Untersuchungen zur spartanischen Verfassungsgeschichte* (Frankfurt am Main: Antike Verlag, 2004), 21–93. Note, however, Christopher A. Faraone, "Stanzaic Structure and Responsion in the Elegiac Poetry of Tyrtaeus," *Mnemosyne*, 4th ser., 59:1 (2006): 19–52. For a proper appreciation of the oral traditions on which our written sources ground themselves, see Mait Kõiv, *ATEGH*, 9–215; "The Origins, Development, and Reliability of the Ancient Tradition about the Formation of the Spartan Constitution," *Historia* 54:3 (2005): 233–64; and *STAS*, 25–66.

5. Aristotle's sensitivity to the defects of the oral tradition: F611.9 (Rose) = Tit. 143.1.2.9 (Gigon) ap. Heraclid. Lemb. 372.9 (Dilts). Resort to shorthand, evidence for circumspection and discrimination in attribution: F611.10 (Rose) = Tit. 143.1.2.10 (Gigon) ap. Heraclid. Lemb. 373.10 (Dilts), *Pol.* 1269a29–1271b31, 1273b33–35, 1274a22–30, 1296a18–21 with Raymond Weil, *Aristote et l'histoire: Essai sur la Politique* (Paris: Librairie C. Klincksieck, 1960), 243–44; Richer, *Les Éphores,* 58–59; and Edmond Lévy, "Le Régime lacédémonien dans la *Politique* d'Aristote: Une Réflexion sur le pouvoir et l'ordre social chez les Grecs," in *Images et représentations du pouvoir et de l'ordre sociale dans l'antiquité,* ed. Michel Molin (Paris: De Boccard, 2001), 57–72 (at 59–61).

6. Two lawgivers named Lycurgus: Timaeus of Tauromenium *FGrH* 566 F 127.

7. First, see Henry Theodore Wade-Gery, "The Spartan Rhetra in Plutarch *Lycurgus* VI: B.

The *Eynomia* of Tyrtaios," *CQ* 38:1/2 (January–April 1944): 1–9 and "The Spartan Rhetra in Plutarch, *Lycurgus* VI: C. What Is the Rhetra?" *CQ* 38:3/4 (July–October 1944): 115–26, reprinted in Wade-Gery, *EGH,* 54–85. Then, consider W. G. G. Forrest, "The Date of the Lykourgan Reforms in Sparta," *Phoenix* 17:3 (Autumn 1963): 157–79, and *A History of Sparta, 950–192 B.C.,* second edition (London: Hutchinson University Library, 1980), 40–68.

8. Paus. 3.2.5.

9. List of ephors eponymous: Timaeus of Tauromenium *FGrH* 566 T10 and Apollod. *FGrH* 244 F335a with Robert Sherk, "The Eponymous Officials of Greek Cities: Mainland Greece and the Adjacent Islands," *ZPE* 84 (1990): 231–95 (at 241–43). List supposed a late invention: Richer, *Les Éphores,* 67–73. Ephors at Thera: *IG* XII iii 322, 326, 330, 336. Ephors at Taras: *SEG* XL 901 read in light of *IG* XIV 645 and *SEG* XXX 1162–70. Presence at Taras evidence for existence of ephorate in eighth-century Lacedaemon: Arnold J. Toynbee, "Sparta's Constitutional Development," in Toynbee, *SPGH,* 213–49 (at 218–19, n. 6). Unsupported claim that Spartan institutions adopted abroad long after colonies founded: Massimo Nafissi, *La Nascita del Kosmos: Studi sulla storia e la società di Sparta* (Naples: Edizioni Scientifiche Italiane, 1991), 114–15, n. 57, and "From Sparta to Taras: *Nomima, Ktiseis* and Relationships Between Colony and Mother City," in *SNS,* 245–72 (at 247–49), as well as Sommer, *Das Ephorat,* 11–12.

10. Elected archons at Athens: *Epit. Her.* 1 [Kenyon], Arist. *Ath. Pol.* 3.1–4. Eupatrid aristocracy dominant there: Plut. *Thes.* 25.1–2; Arist. *Ath. Pol.* 3.1–6, 8.2, 13.2; Poll. *Onom.* 8.111 with Henry Theodore Wade-Gery, "Eupatridai, Archons, and Areopagus," *CQ* 25:1–2 (January and April 1931): 1–11, 77–89, reprinted in Wade-Gery, *EGH,* 86–115. Cf. Thomas J. Figueira, "The Ten Archontes of 579/8 at Athens," *Hesperia* 53:4 (October–December 1984): 447–73, who believes that the term *eupatrid* is indicative of partisan approval and political aspiration and does not, as Wade-Gery argues and I believe, denote a caste analogous to the Roman patricians. Shift from Bacchiad kingship at Corinth to annual magistrate chosen from Bacchiad clan: Diod. 7.9, Paus. 2.4.4, Hdt. 5.92β.1, Euseb. *Chron.* 1.220–22 (Schoene-Petermann). Prerogatives of Heraclid kings at Argos sharply reduced: Paus. 2.19.2 in light of Arist. *Pol.* 1310b26–27.

11. Lycurgus curbs powers of nephew Charillos at Sparta: Ephorus *FGrH* 70 F147–49; Arist. F611.10 (Rose) = Tit. 143.1.2.10 (Gigon) ap. Heraclid. Lemb. 372.10 (Dilts), *Pol.* 1271b20–31, 1316a30–34; Plut. *Lyc.* 3–5.

12. Spartan *politeía:* Hdt. 9.33–35 (esp. 34.1). Rule of law first emerges on Crete: *ML* no. 2 with Lilian H. Jeffery, *Archaic Greece: The City States, c. 700–500 B.C.* (New York: St. Martin's Press, 1976), 188–95. Hereditary monarch at Thera: Hdt. 4.147–50, *IG* XII iii 762, Paus. 3.1.7–8. Also at Taras: Hdt. 3.136.2. Board of ephors at Thera: *IG* XII iii 322, 326, 330, 336. Cyrene founded as colony of Thera ca. 630: Hdt. 4.150–67, *ML* no. 5 (with Paus. 3.14.2–3). Euhesperides as colony of Cyrene: Theotimos *FGrH* 470 F1. In existence by about 600: Ahmed Buzaian and John A. Lloyd, "Early Urbanism in Cyrenaica: New Evidence from Euesperides (Benghazi)," *LibStud* 27 (1996): 129–52. See also Hdt. 4.204. *Gerousía* at Cyrene and Euhesperides: *SEG* IX 1 (with Hdt. 4.165.1), XVIII 772 with Peter M. Fraser, "An Inscription from Euesperides," *Bulletin, société royale d'archéologie d'Alexandrie* 39 (1951): 132–43 and "Corrigendum," ibid. (1953): 62, as well as Simon Hornblower, *Thucydides and Pindar: Historical Narrative and the World of Epinikian Poetry* (Oxford: Oxford University Press, 2005), 246–47, and *CT,* III 641. Note Thuc. 7.50.1–2. Officeholding on Thera restricted to descendants of original settlers: Arist. *Pol.* 1290b7–14. Possibility that there were helots on the island: Ove Hansen, "Were the Native Inhabitants of Thera Called Helots by the Spartan Colonists?" *AJPh* 105:3 (Autumn 1984): 326–27.

13. Selection of ephors akin to lottery: Pl. *Leg.* 3.692a. *Hoi túchontes* chosen: Arist. *Pol.* 1270b29.

14. Three ephors, not five, at Thera (*IG* XII iii 330, 336), Taras (cf. *SEG* XL 901 with *IG* XIV 645 and *SEG* XXX 1162–70), Geronthrae (*IG* V i 1114), Taenarum (*IG* V i 1240–41), and probably Kardamyle (*IG* V i 1331). Spartan army once based on three Dorian tribes: Tyrtaeus F19 (West), Paus. 4.7.8.

15. Five arbitrators: Plut. *Sol.* 10.6. Five *sunktístai* appointed for colony: Hdt. 5.46. Five judges at Plataea: Thuc. 3.52.3. In Roman times, if not also in the classical period, five *Bídaioi* presided over the ritual conflict of the ephebes at Platanistas: Paus. 3.11.2.

16. Tribal reforms at Corinth: John B. Salmon, *Wealthy Corinth: A History of the City to 338 B.C.* (Oxford: Clarendon Press, 1984), 205–9, 413–19, and "Cleisthenes (of Athens) and Corinth," in *Herodotus and His World: Essays from a Conference in Memory of George Forrest,* ed. Peter Derow and Robert Parker (Oxford: Oxford University Press, 2003), 219–34. On Samos: Graham Shipley, *A History of Samos, 800–188 B.C.* (Oxford: Clarendon Press, 1987), 287–89, and Aideen Carty, *Polycrates, Tyrant of Samos: New Light on Archaic Greece* (Stuttgart: Franz Steiner Verlag, 2015), 41–42. At Eretria: Denis Knoepfler, "Le Territoire d'Érétrie et l'organisation politique de la cité (*démoi, chōroi, phylai*)," in *The Polis as an Urban Centre and as a Political Community,* ed. Mogens Herman Hansen (Copenhagen: Munksgaard, 1997), 352–449, and Keith G. Walker, *Archaic Eretria: A Political and Social History from the Earliest Times to 490 BC* (London: Routledge, 2004), 239–55. At Athens: Hdt. 5.66–69 and Arist. *Ath. Pol.* 20–21 with Phillip Brook Manville, *The Origins of Citizenship in Ancient Athens* (Princeton, NJ: Princeton University Press, 1990). At Cyrene: Hdt. 4.160–64 and Arist. *Pol.* 1319b19–26 with Eric W. Robinson, *The First Democracies: Early Popular Government Outside Athens* (Stuttgart: Franz Steiner Verlag, 1997), 105–8. At Rome: Tim J. Cornell, *The Beginnings of Rome: Italy and Rome from the Bronze Age to the Punic Wars (c. 1000–264 BC)* (London: Routledge, 1995), 173–97, and Christopher Smith, *Early Rome and Latium: Economy and Society, c. 1000–500 BC* (Oxford: Clarendon Press, 1996), 196–210. For an overview, see Nicholas F. Jones, *Public Organization in Ancient Greece: A Documentary Study* (Philadelphia: American Philosophical Society, 1987), and James L. O'Neil, *The Origins and Development of Ancient Greek Democracy* (Lanham, MD: Rowman & Littlefield, 1995), 161–73. Case for Sparta: Wade-Gery, "The Spartan Rhetra in Plutarch's *Lycurgus* VI: C. What Is the Rhetra?" 115–26, reprinted in Wade-Gery, *EGH,* 66–85, and Cartledge, *Agesilaos,* 427–31.

17. Theopompus succeeded by grandson: Paus. 3.7.6, 4.15.3. King at end of First Messenian War: Tyrtaeus F5 (West), Paus. 4.6.4–5. Alive but incapacitated at time of Hysiae: 2.24.7, 3.7.5. Great Rhetra and procedure for arraying citizens by tribes and villages: Tyrtaeus F4 (West), Plut. *Lyc.* 6 with Wade-Gery, "The Spartan Rhetra in Plutarch's *Lycurgus* VI: C. What Is the Rhetra?" 117–26, reprinted in Wade-Gery, *EGH,* 70–85. Organization of the Carneia: Hesych. s.v. *Karneâtai.*

18. Social discontent, food shortage, and pressure for land redistribution at Sparta during Messenian revolt: Tyrtaeus F1 (West) with Arist. *Pol.* 1306b36–1307a2, Paus. 4.18.1–3.

19. My reconstruction differs from that advanced by Kõiv, *ATEGH,* 148–215, and "The Origins, Development, and Reliability of the Ancient Tradition about the Formation of the Spartan Constitution," 233–64, in one important particular. He wants to credit a Lycurgus who lived before the First Messenian War with the Great Rhetra and the establishment of the Spartan *kósmos* more generally. I believe that the Great Rhetra and many of the other distinctive Spartan institutions were the work of Theopompus, Polydorus, and their immediate successors in the seventh century and that, in a fashion perfectly consistent with the working of oral tradition, these were attributed to the eighth-century lawgiver.

20. Polydorus assassinated: Paus. 3.3.2–3. Image on ephors' seal of office: 3.11.10.

21. Late development of Spartan institutions and practices: Nafissi, *La Nascita del Kosmos,* 11–150; Lukas Thommen, *Lakedaimonion Politeia: Die Entstehung der Spartanischen Verfassung* (Stuttgart: Franz Steiner Verlag, 1996), 115–46, and *Sparta: Vefassungs- und Sozialgeschichte einer griechischen Polis* (Stuttgart: Verlag J. B. Metzler, 2003); Stephen Hodkinson, "The Development of Spartan Society and Institutions in the Archaic Period," in *The Development of the Polis in Archaic Greece* (Abingdon: Routledge, 1997), 83–102; Jacqueline Christien, "Les Temps d'une vie," *Métis* 12 (1997): 45–79; Dean A. Miller, "The Spartan Kingship: Some Extended Notes on Complex Duality," *Arethusa* 31:1 (1998): 1–17; Stefan Link, *Das Frühe Sparta: Untersuchungen zur spartanischen Staatsbildung im 7. und 6. Jahrhundert v. Chr.* (St. Katharinen: Scripta Mercaturae Verlag, 2000); and Michael Flower, "The Invention of Tradition in Classical and Hellenistic Sparta," in *SBM,* 191–217. Ducat, *Hilotes,* 140–44, even suggests that the Messenians were not made helots until the fifth century.

22. *Damasímbrotos:* Simonides F111 (PMG). *Eunomía:* Tyrtaeus F2 (West). Common way of life established early on: see, for example, Simonides F628 (PMG), Hdt. 1.65.2–4, Thuc. 1.6.4, Plut. *Lyc.* 2–26.

23. See Birgalias, *OES,* 343–65, and Mischa Meier, "Wann Enstand das *Homoios*-Ideal in

Sparta?" in *FS,* 113–24, who rightly, in my judgment, locate the crucial developments in the context of Sparta's seventh-century reconquest of Messenia. In this connection, see also Meier, *Aristokraten und Damoden,* 186–324.

24. Milesian notable at Sparta: Hdt. 5.49–51.

25. Geographical challenges: Felix Bölte, RE s.v. Sparta: C. Geographie (1929): III A:2 1294–1373 (at 1343–47); W. Kendrick Pritchett, "Greek Section of Peutinger Table," in *SAGT,* III 197–288 (at 258–61), "The Topography of Tyrtaios and the Messenian Wars," in *SAGT,* V 1–68 (with the attendant plates), and "Pausanias' Derai of the Second Messenian War," in *SAGT,* VII 179–81; Jacqueline Christien, "Promenades en Laconie," *DHA* 15 (1989): 75–105, "Les Liaisons entre Sparte et son territoire malgré l'encadrement montagneux," in *Montagnes, fleuves, forêts dans l'histoire: Barrières ou lignes de convergence?* ed. Jean-François Bergier (St. Katharinen: Scripta Mercaturae Verlag, 1989), 14–44, and "The Lacedaemonian State: Fortifications, Frontiers, and Historical Problems," in *SW,* 163–83; and Giannēs Y. A. Pikoulas, "Hē Denthelıātıs kaì tò hodıkó tēs díktyo (Schólıa stèn *IG* V i 1431)," in *Praktıkà toû 3. Topıkoû Sınedríou Messēnıakōn Spoudōn* (Athens: Peloponnesiaka Supplement No. 18, 1991), 279–88. For a synoptic view of the road system developed by Lacedaemon, see Giannēs Y. A. Pikoulas, *To Hodıko Dıktyo tēs Lakōnıkēs* (Athens: Ēoros, 2012), passim (esp. 111–36, 393–435, 456–59, 492–502, 562–64). All of this should be read in light of W. Kendrick Pritchett, "Ancient Greek Roads," in *SAGT,* III 143–96 (esp. 167–94).

26. Hom. *Od.* 3.477–4.2.

27. See Vassilis Aravantinos and Adamanti Vasilogramvrou, "The First Linear B Documents from Agios Vasileios (Laconia)," in *Études mycéniennes, 2010: Actes du XIIIe colloque international sur les textes égéens,* ed. Pierre Carlier et al. (Pisa: Fabrizio Serra Editore, 2012), 42–54. According to more recent reports in the press, the palace had ten rooms.

28. Leuctron: Thuc. 5.54.1; Xen. *Hell.* 6.5.24; Paus. 8.27.4; Plut. *Cleom.* 6.2, *Pelop.* 20.4. For the road, see W. Kendrick Pritchett, "Pausanias' Road from Megalopolis to the Lakonian Frontier," in *SAGT,* V 69–76 (with the attendant plates).

29. Location of Oresthasion: Hdt. 9.11.2 and Thuc. 5.64.1–3 read in light of Paus. 8.3.1–2, 27.3, 44.1–3, with *HCT,* V 91–93, and Thomas Heine Nielsen, "Arkadia," in *IACP,* 505–39 (at 525): no. 287. Note Pherecydes *FGrH* 3 F135a, Eur. *El.* 1273–75, Thuc. 4.134.1. Early on, citizens hostile to Lacedaemon: Paus. 8.29.3, 41.1. For later uses of this route as a way into Arcadia, see Xen. *Hell.* 6.5.10–11, 7.5.9. Alcamenes at Ampheia: Paus. 4.5.8–10, 7.3. Location of Ampheia: Giannēs Y. A. Pikoulas, "Tò pólısma Ámpheıa (Paus. 4.5.9)," *Praktıkà toû 3. Diethnoûs Sunedríou Peloponnēsıakōn Spoudōn* (Athens: Peloponnesiaka Supplement No. 13:2, 1987–88), 479–85.

30. Epaminondas and Megalopolis: Diod. 15.66.1–2, 68–69, 71.6–72.4; Paus. 8.27.1–8, 9.13–14.

31. Messenians, Arcadians, Argives: Hdt. 5.49.8 with Arist. *Pol.* 1269a39–1269b5 1270a1–3.

32. Indications that early on Sicyon, Aegina, and Epidaurus recognized Argos' hegemony: Hdt. 6.92, Thuc. 5.53. Argive control of Cythera and coastline from Cynouria to Malea: Hdt. 1.82.2. Aid given Helos against Alcamenes: Paus. 3.2.7. See Matt Kõiv, "Cults, Myths and State Formation in Archaic Argos," in *When Gods Spoke: Researches and Reflections on Religious Phenomena and Artefacts,* ed. Peeter Espak, Märt Läänemets, and Vladimir Sazonov (Tartu: University of Tartu Press, 2015), 125–64 (esp. 126–40).

33. Asine from the Argolid to Messenia: Paus. 2.36.4–5, 3.7.4, 4.8.3, 14.3, 34.9–11, with Catherine Morgan and Todd Whitelaw, "Pots and Politics: Ceramic Evidence for the Rise of the Argive State," *AJA* 95:1 (January 1991): 79–108 (at 83), who point to evidence that Asine in the Argolid was sacked in the late eighth century, and Victor Parker, "Some Dates in Early Spartan History," *Klio* 75 (1993): 45–60 (at 54–56). Cf. Isabelle Ratinaud-Lachkar, "Insoumise Asiné? Pour une Mise en perspective des sources littéraires et archéologiques relatives à la destruction d'Asiné par Argos en 715 avant notre ère," *OAth* 29 (2004): 73–88, whose argument is based on the false presumption that there is no reliable evidence for Argive-Spartan enmity in the early archaic period, with Kõiv, "Cults, Myths and State Formation in Archaic Argos," 126–40.

34. Argives and Arcadians aid Messenian revolt: Tyrtaeus F23a (West).

35. Survey data and archaeological evidence: *The Minnesota Messenian Expedition: Reconstructing a Bronze Age Regional Environment,* ed. William A. McDonald and George R. Rapp, Jr. (Minneapolis: University of Minnesota Press, 1972); William A. McDonald and William D. E.

Coulson, "The Dark Age at Nichoria: A Perspective," in *Excavations at Nichoria in Southwest Greece: Volume III: Dark Age and Byzantine Occupation,* ed. William A. McDonald and William D. E. Coulson (Minneapolis: University of Minnesota Press, 1983), 316–29; Susan E. Alcock, "A Simple Case of Exploitation? The Helots of Messenia," in *Money, Labour, and Land: Approaches to the Economics of Ancient Greece,* ed. Paul Cartledge, Edward E. Cohen, and Lin Foxhall (London: Routledge, 2002), 185–99; and Susan E. Alcock, Andrea M. Berlin, Ann B. Harrison, Sebastian Heath, Nigel Spencer, and David L. Stone, "Pylos Regional Archaeological Project. Part VII: Historical Messenia. Geometric through Late Roman," *Hesperia* 74:2 (April–June, 2005): 147–209.

 36. Ethnic identity of Messenians supposed a late development: Thomas J. Figueira, "The Evolution of Messenian Identity," in *SNS,* 211–44, and Nino Luraghi, *The Ancient Messenians: Construction of Ethnicity and Memory* (Cambridge: Cambridge University Press, 2008), 1–248. To save his highly persuasive argument that the revolt of 465, the subsequent establishment of a helot refugee population at Naupactus, and the later interaction between the Athenians, that population at Naupactus, the helots of Messenia, and the Spartans had a considerable impact on the manner in which the Messenians in later times understood themselves, Figueira need only to amend that argument by conceding the truth of Thucydides' observation (1.101.2) that "most of the helots" who rose up in 465 "were the descendants of the ancient Messenians who had earlier been reduced to subjection" and by acknowledging what the fifth-century evidence quite strongly suggests: that the helots of Messenia who revolted in 464 already had a strong sense of their identity as a nation in bondage. As I have argued from the outset, ethnogenesis does not take place in a vacuum, and ethnic identity is always in flux.

 37. Fighting near Pylos in time of Anaxandros: Paus. 3.3.4, 7.6, 14.4. Fighting in the time of Leotychidas I: Rhianos *FGrH* 265 F43, Paus. 4.15.2. Messenia subjugated 230 years before Epaminondas liberates it: Plut. *Mor.* 194b, Ael. *VH* 13.42.

 38. Nauplians settled at Mothone: Paus. 4.24.4, 27.8, 35.2. One hundred communities of *períoikoi:* Androtion *FGrH* 324 F49. For an overview, see Cartledge, *SL;* Graham Shipley, "Messenia," in *IACP,* 547–68; and the secondary literature cited in Chapter 3, note 31. On the *períoikoi,* note also Franz Hampl, "Die Lakedaemonischen Perioeken," *Hermes* 72 (1937): 1–49, and Graham Shipley, "'The Other Lakedaimonians': The Dependent Perioikic *Poleis* of Laconia and Messenia," in *The Polis as an Urban Centre and as a Political Community,* 189–281.

 39. See Ann B. Harrison and Nigel Spencer, "After the Palace: The Early 'History' of Messenia," in *Sandy Pylos: An Archaeological History from Nestor to Navarino,* ed. Jack L. Davis (Austin: University of Texas Press, 1998), 147–62 (at 158–62), and see Stephen Hodkinson, "Spartiates, Helots and the Direction of the Agrarian Economy: Towards an Understanding of Helotage in Comparative Perspective," in *HMLM,* 248–85 (esp. 263–78).

 40. Quota: Tyrtaeus F6 (West), Paus. 4.14.4–5. Quantum: Plut. *Lyc.* 8.7, *Mor.* 239e. The portion reserved for the wife corresponds closely with the monthly contribution made by her husband to the common mess: cf. Plut. *Lyc.* 12.3, who has converted the Laconian into Attic measures, with Dicaearchus F72 (Wehrli) ap. Ath. 4.141c. See also Porph. *Abst.* 4.4. Cf. Stephen Hodkinson, "Sharecropping and Sparta's Economic Exploitation of the Helots," in *Philolakōn,* 123–34, who thinks that the shift from sharecropping to the payment of a rent took place much, much later. For additional bibliography, see Chapter 1, note 10, above.

 41. Overseers: Hodkinson, "Spartiates, Helots and the Direction of the Agrarian Economy," 263–78, who draws attention to Hesychius s.v. *mnōionómoi,* which he rightly suggests that we read in light of Hybrias ap. Ath. 15.695f–696a. I do not doubt that there were helots in subordinate positions who colluded with the authorities, as Hodkinson suggests. But I suspect that the *mnōionómoi,* who are described by Hesychius as *tōn Eilótōn árchontes,* were Spartan magistrates assigned to manage the subject population [*mnōía*].

 42. Policy of secrecy: Thuc. 5.68.2. Survey work in search of archaic and classical fortifications within Messenia and on its borders is needed, I believe, analogous to that undertaken by Jacqueline Christien, "The Lacedaemonian State: Fortifications, Frontiers, and Historical Problems," 163–83, with regard to the fortifications built by the Spartans along Laconia's east coast during the Peloponnesian War and those constructed by the Messenians and their allies on the western slope of Mount Taygetus after their liberation by Epaminondas. I would not be surprised to learn that the latter forts had Spartan predecessors.

43. Battle lost near Orchomenos: Theopompus of Chios *FGrH* 115 F69 with D. M. Leahy, "The Spartan Defeat at Orchomenus," *Phoenix* 12:4 (Winter 1958): 141–65.

44. Spartans defeated by Tegeans in Battle of the Fetters: Hdt. 1.66, Deinias of Argos *FGrH* 306 F4.

45. Lichas and bones of Orestes: Hdt. 1.67–68; Paus. 3.11.10, 8.54.4. Some think Orestes' bones must have been found not at Tegea, as Herodotus claims, but at the strategic site of Oresthasion (above, note 29), a few miles east of the road from Sparta through Arcadia to Messenia: see, for example, George L. Huxley, "Bones for Orestes," *GRBS* 20:2 (1979): 145–48. I regard this hypothesis as intriguing and attractive but unproven.

46. Except regarding Tegea, Spartans successful in reign of Leon and Hegesikles: Hdt. 1.65.1. Hegemony achieved under Anaxandridas and Ariston: 1.67.1, 68.6. See Arnold J. Toynbee, "Sparta's Conquest of Laconia and Messenia," in Toynbee, *SPGH,* 164–88 (at 182–85).

47. Meltas' achievements and fate: Diod. 7.13.2; Paus. 2.19.2; Plut. *Mor.* 340c, 396c. In this connection, see Antony Andrewes, "Ephoros Book I and the Kings of Argos," *CQ* n. s. 1:1/2 (January–April 1951): 39–45.

48. Bones of Teisamenos: Paus. 7.1.8 with D. M. Leahy, "The Bones of Tisamenus," *Historia* 4:1 (1955): 26–38.

49. Heirs to Agamemnon: Hdt. 7.153.1, 159 with Deborah D. Boedeker, "Hero Cult and Politics in Herodotus: The Bones of Orestes," in *Cultural Poetics in Archaic Greece: Cult, Performance, Politics,* ed. Carol Dougherty and Leslie Kurke (Cambridge: Cambridge University Press, 1993), 164–77; Barbara McCauley, "Heroes and Power: The Politics of Bone Transferal," in *Ancient Greek Hero Cult* (Stockholm: Paul Åströms Förlag, 1999), 85–98; David D. Phillips, "The Bones of Orestes and Spartan Foreign Policy," in *Gestures: Essays in Ancient History, Literature, and Philosophy Presented to Alan L. Boegehold,* ed. Geoffrey W. Bakewell and James P. Sickinger (Oxford: Oxbow Books, 2003), 301–16; and Karl-Wilhelm Welwei, "Orestes at Sparta: The Political Significance of the Grave of the Hero," in *SpartSoc,* 219–30.

50. Runaway Messenians once made Tegean citizens: Polyb. 4.33.5. Refugees expelled in wake of Spartan alliance: Arist. F592 (Rose) = F609 (Gigon) with Felix Jacoby, "*Chrēstoús Poieîn* (Aristotle fr. 592R)," *CQ* 38:1/2 (January–April 1944): 15–16, and Toynbee, "Sparta's Conquest of Laconia and Messenia," 186, n. 2. Note Kallisthenes *FGrH* 124 F23. Cf. George L. Cawkwell, "Sparta and Her Allies in the Sixth Century," *CQ* n. s. 43:2 (1993): 364–76 (at 368–70), reprinted in Cawkwell, *CC,* 54–73; Thomas Braun, "*Chrēstoús Poieîn,*" *CQ* n. s. 44:1 (1994): 40–45; Thomas Heine Nielsen, *Arkadia and Its Poleis in the Archaic and Classical Periods* (Göttingen: Vandenhoeck & Ruprecht, 2002), 188–90, 393–94; and Thommen, *Sparta,* 53, who give the treaty a fifth-century date. To do so, one would have to suppose what we know to be untrue: that the helot threat first presented itself at the time of the earthquakes in the mid-fifth century.

51. Stone monument: Arist. F592 (Rose) = F609 (Gigon). Location disputed: cf. Leahy, "The Spartan Defeat at Orchomenos," 162–64 (with n. 68), with W. Kendrick Pritchett, "The Course of the Alpheios River," in *SAGT,* I 122–30, and see Henry Theodore Wade-Gery, "The 'Rhianos Hypothesis,'" in *ASI,* 289–302 (at 297–98, 302).

52. The helot threat was not the motive for the alliance with Tegea alone; it was the concern that inspired from the outset Lacedaemon's alliance system as a whole: Ernst Baltrusch, "Mythos oder Wirklichkeit? Die Helotengefahr und der Peloponnesische Bund," *HZ* 272:1 (February 2001): 1–24.

53. Spartans posture as friends of liberty, enemies to tyranny: Thuc. 1.18.1, Arist. *Pol.* 1312b7–8. Overthrow tyrants, sponsor oligarchies: Thuc. 1.19, 76.1; Arist. *Pol.* 1307b23–24. Corinthians recall to standard: Hdt. 5.92α. Sparta's policy was no doubt based on a shrewd calculation of the community's interest, but legendary it was not: cf. Rainer Bernhardt, "Die Entstehung der Legende von der tyrannenfeindlichen Aussenpolitik Spartas im sechsten und fünften Jahrhundert v. Chr.," *Historia* 36:3 (3rd Quarter 1987): 257–89, with Cawkwell, "Sparta and Her Allies in the Sixth Century," 364–76, reprinted in Cawkwell, *CC,* 54–73.

54. List of tyrants overthrown: Plut. *Mor.* 859c–d. Chilon as ephor: Diog. Laert. 1.68, Euseb. *Chron.* 2.96–97 (Schoene). Elected to *gerousía:* Arist. *Rh.* 1398b14–15. Papyrus linking Chilon with Aeschines' expulsion: *FGrH* 105 F1 with D. M. Leahy, "Chilon and Aeschines: A Further Consideration of Rylands Greek Papyrus fr. 18," *BRL* 38 (1955–1956): 406–35.

55. *Mēdèn ágan:* Arist. *Rh.* 1389b2–7. Chilon ephor at advanced age: Hdt. 1.59, Diog. Laert. 1.72. Elevates importance of office: Hdt. 1.68. Architect of new policy: Guy Dickins, "The Growth of Spartan Policy," *JHS* 32 (1912): 1–42 (at 21–26), and George L. Huxley, *Early Sparta* (London: Faber & Faber, 1962), 67–76. The available evidence justifies neither the view, recently resurrected by Nafissi, *La Nascita del Kosmos,* 31–150, that Chilon was the figure who instigated the Spartan revolution nor the contention, suggested even more recently by Thommen, *Sparta,* 59–61, that, as a statesman, he was a figment of the later imagination.

56. Childless king Anaxandridas forced to take as second wife Chilon's niece or second cousin: Hdt. 5.39–41 with 6.65.2. On this, see Simon Hornblower, "Commentary," in Herodotus, *Histories: Book V,* ed. Simon Hornblower (Cambridge: Cambridge University Press, 2013), 150–53.

57. Cleomenes insists he is an Achaean, not a Dorian: Hdt. 5.62.2–72.4 with Hornblower, "Commentary," 181–217.

58. Anaxandridas' son Dorieus: Hdt. 5.41.2–3. Likely Spartan named Philachaios: *IG* V ii 159, read in light of Posidonius *FGrH* 87 F48c. See C. H. de Carvalho Gomes, "Xouthias Son of Philakhaios: On *IG* V.2.159 and Its Possible Historical Placement," *ZPE* 108 (1995): 103–6.

59. See R. W. V. Catling, "The Survey Area from the Early Iron Age to the Classical Period (c. 1050–c. 300 BC)," in *Continuity and Change in a Greek Rural Landscape: The Laconia Survey,* ed. William G. Cavanagh, Joost Crouwel, and Graham Shipley (London: British School at Athens, 1996–2002), II 151–256.

60. Dorieus' colonial venture: Hdt. 5.42–48 with Irad Malkin, *Myth and Territory in the Spartan Mediterranean* (Cambridge: Cambridge University Press, 1994), 192–218, and Hornblower, "Commentary," 153–62.

61. Because the evidence we possess is limited and much of it comes from the period after the end of the Peloponnesian War, the character of the so-called Peloponnesian League, especially as it existed in the sixth century, is disputed: cf. Jakob A. O. Larsen, "Sparta and the Ionian Revolt: A Study of Spartan Foreign Policy and the Genesis of the Peloponnesian League," *CPh* 27:2 (April 1932): 136–50, "The Constitution of the Peloponnesian League," *CPh* 28:4 (October 1933): 257–76, and "The Constitution of the Peloponnesian League, II," *CPh* 29:1 (January 1934): 1–19; Donald Kagan, *The Outbreak of the Peloponnesian War* (Ithaca, NY: Cornell University Press, 1969), 9–30; and G. E. M. de Ste. Croix, *The Origins of the Peloponnesian War* (Ithaca, NY: Cornell University Press, 1972), 89–166, 333–42, with Cawkwell, "Sparta and Her Allies in the Sixth Century," 364–76, reprinted in Cawkwell, *CC,* 54–73; J. E. Lendon, "Thucydides and the Constitution of the Peloponnesian League," *GRBS* 35:1 (1994): 159–77; David C. Yates, "The Archaic Treaties Between Sparta and her Allies," *CQ* n.s. 55:1 (May 2005): 65–76; and Sarah Bolmarcich, "Thucydides 1.19,1 and the Peloponnesian League," *GRBS* 45:2 (2005): 5–34, and "The Date of the 'Oath of the Peloponnesian League,'" *Historia* 57:1 (2008): 65–79, and see Klaus Tausend, *Amphiktyonie und Symmachie: Formen zwischenstaatlicher Beziehungen im archaischen Griechenland* (Stuttgart: Franz Steiner Verlag, 1992), 167–80; Ernst Baltrusch, *Symmachie und Spondai: Untersuchungen zum griechischen Völkerrecht der archaischen und klassischen Zeit (8.-5. Jahrhundert v. Chr.)* (Berlin: Walter de Gruyter, 1994), 19–30, and "Mythos oder Wirklichkeit?" 1–24; and Christina Wolff, *Sparta und die peloponnesische Staatenwelt in archaischer und klassischer Zeit* (Munich: Herbert Utz Verlag, 2010). Few scholars doubt that the alliance system served to protect Sparta from helot revolts, to combat tyranny, and to sustain oligarchies in the cities allied with Sparta. Elsewhere I suggest that, initially, its members swore to follow Lacedaemon's two Heraclid kings wherever they led: Rahe, *PC,* chapters 2 and 4.

62. Sparta and her allies responsible for Peloponnesian cart-road network: Giannēs Y. A. Pikoulas, "The Road Network of Arkadia," in *Defining Ancient Arkadia,* ed. Thomas Heine Nielsen and James Roy (Copenhagen: Det Kongelige Danske Videnskabernes Selskab, 1999), 248–319 (esp. 250–57, 306–9).

Conclusion

1. Lacedaemon a *kósmos:* Hdt. 1.65.4, Plut. *Lyc.* 29.1 with the material collected in Introduction, note 18, above. See also Thuc. 1.84.3 and Gloria Ferrari, *Alcman and the Cosmos of Sparta*

(Chicago: University of Chicago Press, 2008). Spartan *eunomía:* Tyrtaeus F2 (West) with the material collected in Introduction, note 19, above.

2. The material remains cast doubt on the supposition that the Spartans ever lived lives of grim austerity: see Reinhardt Förtsch, "Spartan Art: Its Many Different Deaths," and Stephen Hodkinson, "Patterns of Bronze Dedications at Spartan Sanctuaries, c. 650–350 BC: Towards a Quantified Database of Material and Religious Investment," in *Sparta in Laconia: The Archaeology of a City and Its Countryside,* ed. William G. Cavanagh and S. E. C. Walker (London: British School at Athens, 1998), 49–63, as well as Stephen Hodkinson, "Lakonian Artistic Production and the Problem of Spartan Austerity," in *Archaic Greece: New Approaches and New Evidence,* ed. Nick R. E. Fisher and Hans Van Wees (London: Duckworth, 1998), 93–118. For a thorough and systematic examination of archaic and early classical Spartan art, see Reinhardt Förtsch, *Kunstverwendung und Kuntslegitimation im archaischen und frühklassischen Sparta* (Mainz am Rhein: Phillip von Zabern, 2001). It is, I would suggest, a mistake typifying our modern bourgeois mentality to suppose that the martial ethos propagated by Tyrtaeus required austerity and ruled out an appreciation for the beautiful.

3. Cf. Thuc. 2.37–40, where Pericles peddles to his compatriots the myth of Lacedaemonian austerity, with Critias *Vorsokr.*[6] 88 B6 and Xen. *Lac. Pol.* 1.2, 9.3, who attribute to them *eudaimonía,* and see Nicolas Richer, "*Eunomia* et *eudaimonia* à Sparte," *Dikè* 4 (2001): 13–38, and Ducat, *SE,* 336–39.

4. The term "grand strategy" was introduced in 1906 by Julian Stafford Corbett in the so-called "Green Pamphlet," which was printed as an appendix to the 1988 reprint of the book *Some Principles of Maritime Strategy* (London: Longmans, Green, & Co., 1911), wherein he elaborated on the idea without resorting to the term. The notion was taken up and first fully developed after World War I by J. F. C. Fuller, *The Reformation of War* (London: Hutchinson & Co., 1923), 211–28. For a recent discussion of its proper application to the study of ancient history, see Kimberly Kagan, "Redefining Roman Grand Strategy," *Journal of Military History* 70:2 (April 2006): 333–62 (esp. 348–50).

5. Lacedaemon like a river: Xen. *Hell.* 4.2.11–12.

6. See Victor Alonso-Troncoso, "The Idea of the Peloponnese in the Spartan Diplomatic Tradition," in *CASPTP,* 63–74.

Appendix 1. Land Tenure in Archaic Sparta

1. It is striking—as I have pointed out early on in Chapter 4, above—that, when Aristotle (*Pol.* 1270a6–7, 1271b24–27) does mention Lycurgus by name in this particular context, it is only to report what "they say" or what "is said" about his activities. As this fact suggests, it is not at all clear that Aristotle is confident that the historical Lycurgus was responsible for the institutions, apart from the *gerousía* (Plut. *Lyc.* 5.10–14 with Arist. *Pol.* 1271b25, 1316a29–34), attributed to him in other writers. Cf. Hodkinson, *PWCS,* 92–93, with Raymond Weil, *Aristote et l'histoire: Essai sur la Politique* (Paris: Librairie C. Klincksieck, 1960), 243–44; Nicolas Richer, *Les Éphores: Études sur l'histoire et sur l'image de Sparte (VIIIème–IIIème siècles avant Jésus-Christ)* (Paris: Publications de la Sorbonne, 1998), 58–59; and Edmond Lévy, "Le Régime lacédémonien dans la *Politique* d'Aristote: Une Réflexion sur le pouvoir et l'ordre social chez les Grecs," in *Images et représentations du pouvoir et de l'ordre sociale dans l'antiquité,* ed. Michel Molin (Paris: De Boccard, 2001), 57–72 (at 59–61).

2. For a brief but convincing discussion of the evidence, see Hodkinson, *PWCS,* 77–79.

3. Cf. Hodkinson, *PWCS,* 9–149 (esp. 19–64), who rejects the ancient evidence supporting Plutarch's claim that there was public provision, with Marcello Lupi, "L'*Archaia moira:* Osservazioni sul regime fondiario a partire spartano da un libro recente," *Incidenza dell'antico* 1 (2003): 151–72, and Thomas J. Figueira, "The Nature of the Spartan *Klēros,*" in *SpartSoc,* 47–76, who show not only that the evidence for public provision is reliable but also that, in the sociopolitical context of the archaic age, the practices described in our sources make perfectly good sense. What follows in this appendix is a restatement and amendment of Figueira's argument.

4. See also Plut. *Lyc. et Num.* 2.10–11, *Sol.* 16.1–3, *Mor.* 226b, 231e.

5. As Pavel Oliva, "On the Problem of the Helots," *Historica* 3 (1961): 5–34, and "Die Hel-

otenfrage in der Geschichte Spartas," in *Die Rolle der Volksmassen in der Geschichte der vorkapital-istischen Gesellschaftsformationen,* ed. Joachim Herrmann and Irmgard Sellnow (Berlin: Akademie Verlag, 1975), 109–16, repeatedly remarked, the peculiar form of property relations predominant at Sparta was intimately bound up with the peculiar status of the helots.

6. See Christopher B. R. Pelling, "Plutarch's Adaptation of His Source Material," *JHS* 100 (1980): 127–40, reprinted in Pelling, *Plutarch and History: Eighteen Studies* (London: Duckworth, 2002), 91–115.

7. Note, in this connection, Teles F3 (Hense) ap. Stob. *Flor.* 3.40.8 (Hense).

8. Cf. Cynthia Patterson, *The Family in Greek History* (Cambridge, MA: Harvard University Press, 1998), 250 n. 12, and Hodkinson, *PWCS,* 72.

9. See, for example, Ducat, *SE,* 53–57.

10. See David Asheri, "Sulla legge di Epitadeo," *Athenaeum* 39 (1961): 45–68; Pavel Oliva, *Sparta and Her Social Problems* (Amsterdam: Adolf M. Hakkert, 1971), 188–93; Jacqueline Christien, "La Loi d'Epitadeus: Un Aspect de l'histoire économique et sociale à Sparte," *RD,* 4th ser., 52 (1974): 197–221; Ephraim David, "The Conspiracy of Cinadon," *Athenaeum* 57 (1979): 239–59, and *Sparta Between Empire and Revolution (404–243 B.C.): Internal Problems and Their Impact on Contemporary Greek Consciousness* (New York: Ayer, 1981), 5–10, 43–77; and Gabriele Marasco, "La Retra di Epitadeo e la situazione sociale di Sparta nel IV secolo," *AC* 49 (1980): 131–45. Cf. Eckart Schütrumpf, "The *Rhetra* of Epitadeus: A Platonist's Fiction," *GRBS* 28:4 (1987): 441–57— who bases his argument for rejecting Plutarch's report on a demonstrably false premise: that Plut. *Agis* 5.3–7 is incompatible with the claims advanced concerning Sparta's property regime by Aristotle in *The Politics*—with the secondary literature cited in note 13, below. It is, moreover, far simpler to suppose that the deployment of Platonic political psychology in Plut. *Agis* 5.3–7 is Plutarch's work, as it surely is elsewhere in his corpus, than to accept Schütrumpf's completely unfounded assertion that the biographer mindlessly copied a fiction invented by some unidentifiable Platonist of an earlier time. Moreover, Plutarch may not be as much of a Platonist as Schütrumpf thinks: see Hugh Liebert, "Plutarch's Critique of Plato's Best Regime," *HPTh* 30:2 (Summer 2009): 251–71.

11. See John F. Lazenby, "The *Archaia Moira:* A Suggestion," *CQ* n.s. 45:1 (1995): 87–91. If Lazenby is correct in supposing that the passage in Heracleides Lembus refers to a prohibition against selling not the *klêros* itself but the *apophorá* paid by the helots working the *klêros,* what is at stake is far less likely to be the tribute in kind paid a particular Spartiate in any given month than his right to that *apophorá.*

12. This passage poses, I believe, an insuperable obstacle for the argument advanced by Stephen Hodkinson. It is not, then, surprising that he is so eager to get rid of the *archaîa moîra* that he descends into special pleading: cf. Hodkinson, *PWCS,* 85–90.

13. The claim that Aristotle's testimony in *The Politics* is incompatible with Plut. *Agis* 5.3–7 is demonstrably false: cf. Hodkinson, *PWCS,* 90–94, with Ephraim David, "Aristotle and Sparta," *AncSoc* 13–14 (1982–83): 67–103, and Lévy, "Le Régime lacédémonien dans la *Politique* d'Aristote," 59–61.

14. Aristotle as a likely source for the story concerning Epitadeus' law: Gabriele Marasco, "Aristotele come fonte di Plutarco nelle biografie di Agide e Cleomene," *Athenaeum* 56 (1978): 170–81. Although Giovanni Parmeggiani, "*Isotimia:* Considerazioni sulla storia e sulla storiografia su Sparta in età arcaica e classica," *RSA* 34 (2004): 73–127, and Paul Christesen, "Spartans and Scythians, a Meeting of Mirages: The Portrayal of the Lycurgan *Politeia* in Ephorus' *Histories,*" in *SBP,* 211–63, do not raise the possibility that Ephorus might be a source for the tale, this possibility is a logical consequence of the account they give of the historian's treatment of Sparta's decline. Ephorus was exceedingly diligent in his research: Victor Parker, "The Historian Ephorus: His Selection of Sources," *Antichthon* 38 (2004): 29–50.

15. See the stimulating discussion of Henri Jeanmaire, *Couroi et courètes: Essai sur l'éducation spartiate et sur les rites d'adolescence dans l'antiquité hellénique* (Lille: Bibliothèque Universitaire, 1939), 481–90, who treats the public allotment as a species of fief conferred on the warriors of the community.

16. Figueira, "The Nature of the Spartan *Klēros,*" 61–63, rightly harps on this point.

17. See Josef Mélèze-Modrzejewski, "Régime foncier et status social dans l'Egypt ptolé-

maïque," in *Terre et paysans dépendants dans les sociétés antiques* (Paris: Éditions du CNRS, 1979), 163–88, with Pomeroy, *SWo,* 77–82.

18. Cf. Hodkinson, *PWCS,* 19–149 (esp. 68–81), and Paul Christesen, "Utopia on the Eurotas: Economic Aspects of the Spartan Mirage," in *SpartSoc,* 309–37 (esp. 316–22).

19. See Arnold J. Toynbee, "The Six-Morai Hoplite Army," in Toynbee, *SPGH,* 373–85 (at 381–83).

20. Some think that one must double the number of *lóchoi* present: Arnold J. Toynbee, "The Growth of Sparta," *JHS* 33:2 (1913): 264–75, and "The Organization and Strength of the Lacedaemonian Army at Mantineia in 418 B.C.," in Toynbee, *SPGH,* 396–401; *HCT,* IV 110–17; Henry Theodore Wade-Gery, "The Spartan Rhetra in Plutarch's *Lycurgus* VI: C. What Is the Rhetra?" *CQ* 38:3/4 (July–October 1944): 115–26 (at 117–19), reprinted in Wade-Gery, *EGH,* 66–85 (at 71–74); John F. Lazenby, *The Spartan Army* (Warminster: Aris & Phillips, 1985), 41–44, and *The Peloponnesian War: A Military Study* (New York: Routledge, 2004), 121–22; and *CT,* III 180–82.

21. See W. G. G. Forrest, *A History of Sparta, 950–192 B.C.,* second edition (London: Hutchinson University Library, 1980), 131–37. In this connection, note Cameron Hawkins, "Spartans and *Perioikoi:* The Organization and Ideology of the Lakedaimonian Army in the Fourth Century B.C.E.," *GRBS* 51:3 (2011): 401–34, who doubts that the *períoikoi* were ever brigaded with the Spartiates.

22. Cf. Hodkinson, *PWCS,* 399–423, who tacitly acknowledges that social processes are insufficient to explain so sharp and rapid a demographic drop, with Thomas J. Figueira, "Population Patterns in Late Archaic and Classical Sparta," *TAPhA* 116 (1986): 165–213. Note as well Thomas J. Figueira, "Mess Contributions and Subsistence at Sparta," *TAPhA* 114 (1984): 87–109.

23. See Ludwig Ziehen, "Das spartanische Bevölkerungsproblem," *Hermes* 68 (1933): 218–37 (esp. 232–35, 237), and Arnold J. Toynbee, "The Earthquake of *circa* 466 or 464 B.C. at Sparta City," in Toynbee, *SPGH,* 346–52. In general, the Greeks may have been inclined to suppose that mothers contributed little, if anything to the biological makeup of their own progeny: see G. E. R. Lloyd, *Science, Folklore and Ideology: Studies in the Life Sciences in Ancient Greece* (Cambridge: Cambridge University Press, 1983), 66, 86–111. But the Spartans were clearly aware that offspring are as apt to resemble mothers as fathers. Otherwise, it would be hard to make sense of Theophrastus' report that Archidamus was fined for having married too short a wife (Plut. *Ages.* 2.6, *Mor.* 1d) and of the fact that Spartan men were reluctant to marry the sister or daughter of a coward (Xen. *Lac. Pol.* 9.4–6).

24. For the evidence and its most natural interpretation, see Detlef Lotze, "Mothakes," *Historia* 11:4 (October 1962): 427–35; Daniel Ogden, *Greek Bastardy in the Classical and Hellenistic Periods* (Oxford: Clarendon Press, 1996), 217–24; and Pomeroy, *SWo,* 96–98, 102. The argument advanced by Ducat, *Hilotes,* 166–68, makes sense as long as one presumes that the child of a helot woman acknowledged by a Spartiate father was considered free. Cf. Stephen Hodkinson, "Servile and Free Dependants of the Spartan *Oikos,*" in *Schiavi e Dipendenti nell'Ambito dell'Oikos e della Familia,* ed. Mauro Moggi and Giuseppe Cordiano (Pisa: ETS, 1997), 45–71 (esp. 55–62).

25. See R. W. V. Catling, "The Survey Area from the Early Iron Age to the Classical Period (c. 1050–c. 300 BC)," in *Continuity and Change in a Greek Rural Landscape: The Laconia Survey,* ed. William G. Cavanagh, Joost Crouwel, and Graham Shipley (London: British School at Athens, 1996–2002), II 151–256.

26. See Ronald S. Stroud, "Thucydides and Corinth," *Chiron* 24 (1994): 267–304.

27. Note the riposte attributed to Archidamus: Plut. *Lyc.* 20.9.

28. See Robert Sallares, *The Ecology of the Ancient Greek World* (Ithaca, NY: Cornell University Press, 1991), 241–66.

29. Note Xen. *Lac. Pol.* 14, and see the literature on feminine license: Pl. *Resp.* 8.548a–b, *Leg.* 1.637c, 6.780d–781d, 7.804c–806c; Arist. *Pol.* 1269b12–1270a14, 1271a18, 1271b17; Dion. Hal. *Ant. Rom.* 2.24.6; Plut. *Comp. Lyc. et Num.* 3.5–9 with Pomeroy, *SWo,* 63–71. For a fascinating discussion—grounded in the observations of S. Ryan Johnson, "Status Anxiety and Demographic Contraction of Privileged Populations," *Population and Development Review* 13:3 (September 1987): 439–70, and Philip Longman, "The Return of Patriarchy," *Foreign Policy* 153 (March–April 2006): 56–60, 62–65—see the as yet unpublished Ph.D. dissertation of Timothy Donald Doran, "Demographic Fluctuation and Institutional Response in Sparta" (University of California at

Berkeley, 2011), 78–112. I see no reason to challenge Plutarch's dating of the legal change. Cf, however, Figueira, "Population Patterns in Late Archaic and Classical Sparta," 194–96.

30. Opinions differ sharply as to whether Phylarchus' narrative is worthy of trust: see François Ollier, *Le Mirage spartiate* (Paris: Les Belles Lettres, 1933–43), II 88–93, 105–7, 196–97; Emilio Gabba, "Studi su Filarco: Le Biografie plutarchee di Agide e di Cleomene," *Athenaeum* n. s. 35 (1957): 3–55, 193–239, reprinted as Gabba, *Studi su Filarco: Le Biografie plutarchee di Agide e di Cleomene* (Pavia: Tipografia del Libro, 1957); Thomas W. Africa, *Phylarchus and the Spartan Revolution* (Berkeley: University of California Press, 1961); Eugène Napoléon Tigerstedt, *The Legend of Sparta in Classical Antiquity* (Stockholm: Almqvist & Wiksell, 1965–74), II 49–85; Paul Pédech, *Trois historiens méconnus: Théopompe, Duris, Phylarque* (Paris: Les Belles Lettres, 1989), 391–493 (esp. 428–29, 439–93); Benjamin Shimron, "Some Remarks on Phylarchus and Cleomenes III," *RFIC* 94 (1966): 452–59, and *Late Sparta: The Spartan Revolution, 243–146 B.C.* (Buffalo: Department of Classics, State University of New York, 1972), passim (esp. 9–14, 22–24, 56–60); and Paul Cartledge and Antony Spawforth, *Hellenistic and Roman Sparta: A Tale of Two Cities* (London: Routledge, 1989), 38–58.

31. This point is made by Tigerstedt, *The Legend of Sparta in Classical Antiquity,* II 81.

32. See Sphaerus *FGrH* 585 T1, T3a–b, F1–2. Cf. Ollier, *Le Mirage spartiate,* II 99–123; Tigerstedt, *The Legend of Sparta in Classical Antiquity,* II 82–85; and Kennell, *GV,* 11–12, 98–114, with Figueira, "The Nature of the Spartan *Klēros,*" 56–57. As Ducat, *SE,* 29–32, points out, there is not a shred of evidence to substantiate Kennell's claim, *GV,* 102–8, that the *Instituta Laconica* nos. 1–17 (Plut. *Mor.* 236f–238d) derive from either of the two treatises by Sphaerus in which Lacedaemon loomed large.

33. Cf. Ollier, *Le Mirage spartiate,* passim (esp. II 187–215); Tigerstedt, *The Legend of Sparta in Classical Antiquity,* passim (esp. II 113–30, 226–64); and Hodkinson, *PWCS,* passim (esp. 1–149, 399–449). The last of these three works—which is, by far, the most cogent and interesting argument for the view that they share—has been answered by Lupi, "L'*Archaia moira:* Osservazioni sul regime fondiario a partire spartano da un libro recente," 151–72; Figueira, "The Nature of the Spartan *Klēros,*" 47–76; and Pomeroy, *SWo,* 161. The argument developed by Mait Kõiv, *ATEGH,* 9–215, and "The Origins, Development, and Reliability of the Ancient Tradition about the Formation of the Spartan Constitution," *Historia* 54:3 (2005): 233–64, with regard to early Sparta applies with no less force to third-century Lacedaemon. Rhetoricians exploit existing beliefs and, when convenient, distort them for present-day purposes. It is rarely, if ever, within their power to get away with fabricating such beliefs out of whole cloth. Cf., however, Michael Flower, "The Invention of Tradition in Classical and Hellenistic Sparta," in *SBM,* 191–217 (at 194–202), who evidently thinks otherwise.

34. Spartan *politeía:* Thuc. 1.18.1, 68.1, 132.4, 4.126.2, 5.31.6, 68.2. Sparta as *kósmos:* Plut. *Lyc.* 29.1. Cf. Thuc. 4.76.2 on Thebes.

35. If one rejects the evidence that there was at one time an egalitarian property scheme at Sparta, one will be driven by the logic of one's position on this question to deny that there was anything special or unusual about Lacedaemon at all, as Stephen Hodkinson recognizes: Chapter 1, note 1, above.

Appendix 2. The *Néoi* at Sparta

1. See, for example, MacDowell, *SL,* 78–79, and Ducat, *SE,* 101–12.

2. Consider Hdt. 7.234.2, 9.10.1, 12.2 in light of Henry Theodore Wade-Gery, "The Spartan Rhetra in Plutarch's *Lycurgus* VI: C. What Is the Rhetra?" *CQ* 38:3/4 (July–October 1944): 115–26 (at 125), reprinted in Wade-Gery, *EGH,* 66–85 (at 82), and note Thucydides' use (2.8.1 and, in one manuscript, 4.80.3) of the same term; then see Cartledge, *Agesilaos,* 21.

3. See Henri Jeanmaire, *Couroi et courètes: Essai sur l'éducation spartiate et sur les rites d'adolescence dans l'antiquité hellénique* (Lille: Bibliothèque Universitaire, 1939), 483.

4. Cf., however, Thomas J. Figueira, "Mess Contributions and Subsistence at Sparta," *TAPhA* 114 (1984): 87–109 (at 101–2 n. 47), and "Population Patterns in Late Archaic and Classical Sparta," *TAPhA* 116 (1986): 165–213 (at 167–69).

Author's Note and Acknowledgments

This book—intended as the prelude to a trilogy dedicated to the study of Sparta and her conduct of diplomacy and war from the archaic period down to the second battle of Mantineia—has been a long time in gestation, and I have incurred many debts along the way. I was first introduced to ancient history by Donald Kagan when I was a freshman at Cornell University in the spring of 1968. The following year, I took a seminar he taught on the ancient Greek city and another seminar on Plato's *Republic* with Allan Bloom. After graduating from Yale University in 1971, I read *Litterae Humaniores* at Wadham College, Oxford, on a Rhodes Scholarship. It was there that my ancient history tutor W. G. G. Forrest first piqued my interest in Lacedaemon. The argument elaborated in the third and fourth chapters of this book concerning the genesis of the Spartan constitution was first broached in a tutorial paper that I wrote for him at that time.

I returned to Yale University in 1974 for graduate study. There, three years later, I completed a dissertation under the direction of Donald Kagan entitled "Lysander and the Spartan Settlement, 407–403 B.C." In the aftermath, I profited from the comments and suggestions of Antony Andrewes, who was one of my readers. It was my intention at that time to turn my thesis into a book focused on Sparta, Athens, and Persia, and I carved out of it an article on the selection of ephors at Sparta and penned another, in which I discussed the makeup of the Achaemenid Persian army at the time of Cunaxa, the tactics the Persians customarily employed, and the relative strength of Greek hoplites faced with such a challenge. But the book I had in mind I did not write.

Instead, with encouragement from Bernard Knox during the year 1980–81, in which I was a Junior Fellow at the Center for Hellenic Studies, I got side-tracked. I wrote one 1,200-page work entitled *Republics Ancient and Modern: Classical Republicanism and the American Revolution;* then, three shorter monographs—one on Machiavelli and English republicanism, another on the political philosophy of Montesquieu, and a third on modern republicanism in the thought of Montesquieu, Rousseau, and Tocqueville. In the intervening years, however, I ordinarily taught a lecture course on ancient Greek history in the fall and a seminar on some aspect of that subject in the spring, and I frequently gave thought to Lacedaemon, and to the work I had once done with George Forrest and Don Kagan.

This book and the volume that follows on Sparta and Persia constitute a belated acknowledgment of what I owe them both. The first two chapters of this volume had their origin in my dissertation and were published in a more elaborated form in the first part of *Republics Ancient and Modern.* I am grateful to the University of North Carolina Press for giving me permission to reprint this material in revised form here.

In the interim since the appearance of that study, there has been a dramatic upsurge of interest in Spartan mores, manners, and institutions and a torrent of new scholarship, much of it revisionist, some of it ingenious and highly speculative. In recasting my two chapters, I have sought to exploit what I think especially valuable in the new scholarship and to respond (mainly in the notes) to that scholarship where, as is often the case, I think it in error. In assessing both the old and the new scholarly arguments advanced concerning the multitude of questions in dispute, I have embraced the explanatory parsimony championed by William of Ockham—which is to say, I have consistently preferred the most economic account consistent with the evidence. This I have done not on the naive assumption that the most economic account is always true (which it is not), but on the more plausible presumption that it is less likely to be false than accounts that are complex, convoluted, and far-fetched. In short, although I may admire the ingenuity of Claudius Ptolemy and his successors, it is the elegance and simplicity of Copernicus, Galileo, and Newton that I prefer.

I am indebted to Victor Davis Hanson, whose books *The Western Way of War* and *The Other Greeks: The Family Farm and the Agrarian Roots of Western Civilization* clarified, as never before, the nature of hoplite warfare, its relationship with the family farm understood in an unorthodox Marxist sense as a mode of production, and the manner in which this nexus shaped the emergent *pólis* of the archaic age. As the notes to the third chapter of this volume should make clear, I have attended to the criticism recently directed at Hanson's account of hoplite warfare, and, for the most part, I have found it unconvincing. I am persuaded, however, by those among his critics who assert that gentleman farmers of middling wealth, not rich enough to own horses, came to be predominant within Hellas in the period covered by this book. What these scholars forget, however, is that, in a world dominated by aristocrats of great wealth, the political interests of gentleman farmers who are not similarly well-born and those of the smallholders singled out for attention by Hanson largely coincide.

Eugene D. Genovese also served as an inspiration. I first met him in the late 1970s when I was a beginning assistant professor. Over the years, we became good friends; and, when opportunity knocked, he and his wife Betsey agreed to be the godparents of my firstborn child. As I have pondered the helots and the role they played in the history of archaic Sparta, I have returned again and again to his books—especially, *Roll, Jordan, Roll: The World the Slaves Made* and *From Rebellion to Revolution: Afro-American Slave Revolts in the Making of the Modern World*—and to the innumerable conversations that we had in days gone by concerning slave societies and the regime imperatives they are driven to embrace.

I would also like to record my debt to Patrick Leigh Fermor. Long ago, when Peter Green learned that I was interested in the manner in which the rugged terrain in certain parts of Messenia might have facilitated banditry and resistance on the part of Lacedaemon's helots, he suggested that I contact Paddy, who had learned a thing or two about this sort of resistance while serving on Crete during the Second World War. In the summer of 1983, I followed up on this recommendation. Our meeting over a lunch at Paddy's home in Kardamyli paved the way for a series of visits, often lasting a week or more, which took place at irregular intervals over the twenty-three years following that largely liquid repast. On nearly every occasion, our conversations returned to ancient Sparta; and in 1992, when *Republics Ancient and Modern* appeared, Paddy wrote a generous appraisal of it for the *Spectator*.

I drafted the third and fourth chapters of this book in the summer of 2009, when I was a visiting fellow at the Social Philosophy and Policy Center at Bowling Green State University, and I am grateful to Ellen Frankel Paul, Fred D. Miller, Jr., and Jeffrey Paul for hosting me there. On 23 November 2009, thanks to the kind invitation of Heinrich Meier, I was able to test my perceptions regarding Lacedaemon by delivering a lecture entitled "The Spartan Way of Life" to a learned audience at a *Vortragsabend* sponsored by the Carl Friedrich von Siemens Stiftung in Munich. The final revisions of this manuscript were completed while, with added assistance from the Earhart Foundation, I was a W. Glenn Campbell and Rita Ricardo-Campbell National Fellow at the Hoover Institution on the campus of Stanford University. These were invaluable opportunities, and I am grateful for the support I received.

For the most part, however, this book was written in years in which I was teaching history at Hillsdale College. I am grateful to the Charles O. Lee and Louise K. Lee Foundation, which supports the chair I held and still hold at the college; to the trustees of the college and to its president, Larry Arnn; and to my colleagues and students there, who were always supportive. I owe a special debt to Dan Knoch, the director of the Hillsdale College library; to Maurine McCourry, who arranged for the purchase of books; and to Judy Leising and Pam Ryan, who handled interlibrary loan. I also owe a particular debt to one of my anonymous readers, who went over the manuscript with great care and made a multitude of helpful suggestions. Librarians and those who read manuscripts for academic presses are the unsung heroes of the academic world, and no one knows better than I how much we scholars owe them.

The fact that I was able to finish this book I owe to Dr. Marston Linehan, Dr. Peter Pinto, and the staff at the Clinical Center of the National Institutes of Health in Bethesda, Maryland—where in the summer of 2012 I was treated for prostate cancer and for complications attendant on surgery. Had Dr. Pinto not devised a new method for diagnosing prostate cancer, had he not done my surgery with great precision, and had he and his colleagues not found a way to eliminate the lymphocele that bedeviled me in the aftermath, I would not now be in a position to write these words.

Throughout the period in which this book was written, my four children were patient, and they and my wife kept me sane. From time to time, they brought me back to the contemporary world from classical antiquity, where, at least in my imagination, I may sometimes have seemed more at home than in the here and now.

Index of Subjects

archery in war, 87, 177, 179
aristocracy, aristocratic ethos of early Hellas,
    81–82, 89–95, 147, 152, 179–81
army, Spartan
    cavalry, 10–11, 33, 151, 158
    enōmotíai (sworn bands), 13, 153, 160
    garrison duty, 24, 114, 157
    hippeîs (royal bodyguard), 25, 32–33,
        49, 88–89, 130, 132, 157–58, 168,
        179
    hoplite warfare, 11, 19–21, 23, 27, 33,
        80–97, 114, 132–33, 152, 159,
        177–82
        aspís (hoplite shield), 84–91, 178
            antilabḗ and *pórpax*, 84–91
        hereditary flute players, 23, 155–56
        lóchos (regiment early on), 72,
            102–3, 130, 174, 192
        military revolution, 80–97, 182
        móra (regiment later), 33
        phalanx, 19–21, 23, 27, 80–97, 103,
            152, 159, 177–82

Battle of the Champions, 33, 134
Battle of the Fetters, 115, 118, 188
Battle of the Great Trench, 94, 182

cavalry in archaic Greek warfare, 81, 85,
    89–91, 176–77, 179, 181
chariot warfare in the Bronze Age and the
    archaic period, 80–81, 89–91, 98, 106,
    176–77, 179
constituent villages of Lacedaemon
        Amyclae, xviii, 71–74, 77, 79, 174–76
        cult of Apollo Hyakinthos, 74

Konosoura, 72, 74, 175
Limnai, 72, 74, 174–75
    Eurypontid residence and graves,
        72
Mesoa, 72, 74, 175
Pitana, 72–74, 174–75
    Agiad residence and graves, 72

Deuteronomy, book of, 17
Dipaea, battle of, 131
distinctive attributes of the Spartans, 1–63,
    143–72
    civic equality (status of Spartans as
        hómoioi: equals, peers), 10, 18, 24,
        32, 34, 41, 55, 131, 136, 150, 162
    eudaimonía (happiness, success), xiv,
        52, 63, 121, 190
    fear embraced, 11–13
    homónoia (likemindedness, civic
        solidarity), 7–35, 40, 59–60, 149,
        162
    kalokagathía (gentlemanliness: nobility
        and goodness), 10, 34, 150, 171
    obedience to *nómos* (custom,
        convention, law), 7, 12–13, 28–29,
        31, 50–51, 65, 160, 170, 172
    patriotism, 7–35
    public-spiritedness, 7–35, 62
    sharp distinction between the young
        and the old, 5, 11–12, 14, 19–20,
        22–24, 27, 36, 42, 49, 54–60, 67,
        75, 87, 94, 101, 119, 127, 137, 151,
        153, 155, 171, 175
    sophrosúnē (moderation, temperance),
        25, 30, 161

distinctive attributes of the Spartans (*cont.*)
  universal literacy, 3, 146, 173
  virtue, v, 1, 10, 12–13, 16, 20–22, 33,
    39–41, 52, 54, 60, 62, 88, 105, 121,
    171

ethnicity in Greece and ethnogenesis, 7, 18,
  64–69, 90, 103, 112, 118, 148, 151, 165,
  172–73, 182, 187
Exodus, book of, 17

festivals of Lacedaemon
  Carneia, 14, 93–94, 98, 103–4, 174,
    181–82, 185
  ceremonial dancing, 13–15, 18, 43,
    153–54, 166
  choirs, 13–15, 49, 121–22, 154, 169
  Gymnopaidiai, 14, 35, 93, 98, 103–4,
    154–55, 182
  Hyacinthia at Amyclae, 14, 74, 175
  masked dancers, 18, 154–55
First Messenian War, 76, 89–90, 94, 100, 103,
  109–12, 175–76, 179, 185–86
French Revolution, 2, 145

Gemeinschaft-Gesellschaft distinction, 38
grand strategy, articulation of Spartan, 6,
  11–12, 63–64, 105–6, 114–23, 152, 190
  Arcadian question, 90, 94–97, 105–23,
    179, 182, 186, 188–89
  Argive threat, 11, 33, 74, 80, 90–97,
    105, 110–12, 115–16, 119, 123,
    151–52, 175, 179–80, 182, 186–88
  bones of Orestes and Teisamenos,
    115–16, 188
  foundation of Peloponnesian League,
    42, 90, 114–23, 132, 165, 188–89
  geopolitical challenges, 93, 106–10,
    112–14, 116, 186
  hegemony acquired and exercised,
    30, 60, 76, 89–90, 114–23, 143,
    188
  helot threat, 11–12, 18, 23–24, 49, 79,
    96–97, 112–14, 116, 119, 121–23,
    132–34, 149–52, 154, 169, 175–76,
    179, 182–83, 186–88
    Messenian dimension, 11–12,
      94–97, 106–23, 132–34,
      149–52, 154, 169, 182–83,
      186–88
  overthrow of tyrants, championship of
    liberty, 116–19, 123, 188–89
  road network for carts built through-
    out Peloponnesus on single gauge,
    119–20, 189

Tegea the center of gravity, 114–18,
  132–33

hetairíai, political clubs at Athens, 40, 164
hoplite warfare in Greece, 11, 19–21, 23, 27,
  33, 80–97, 114, 132–33, 152, 159, 177–82
Hysiae, battle of, xviii, 75, 90, 93–96, 104,
  179–80, 182, 185

idiótēs (private individual, prose writer), 16,
  38
institutional arrangements within Lacedaemon, 1–63, 143–72
  absence of a state apparatus, 37–38, 163
  age classes
    eirénes (young men in their
      twenties), 23, 156–57
    hēbôntes (young men under 45),
      23–28, 49, 137–38, 155–58
    néoi (young warriors under 45),
      20, 23–28, 49, 104, 137–38,
      155–58, 169, 193
    forbidden travel abroad, 25, 158
    presbúteroi (senior men over 45),
      25–26, 51, 137–38, 158
    eligible for magistracies, 25,
      158
  agōgḗ (system of education and
    indoctrination), 3–4, 13–30, 41,
    72, 105, 122, 126, 135, 145–47,
    153–57, 165, 171–72
  archaîa moîra (ancestral allotment),
    24, 127–28, 191
  archives, 3
  booty, disposition of, 47, 49, 119, 167,
    169, 174
  burial practices, 22, 155
  coinage banned, 9, 28–32, 45, 47, 149,
    161–62
  common assembly, 2, 43, 48–49,
    54–55, 60–61, 98–99, 104, 168–69,
    171, 183
  dowries outlawed, 10, 46–47, 150, 167
  hómoioi (status of Spartiates as equals,
    peers), 10, 18, 24, 32, 34, 131, 136,
    150, 162
  infanticide, 9, 26, 122, 149
  klêros (public allotment of land), 9–12,
    24, 32, 46–47, 52, 55, 77–79, 98,
    104, 114–15, 118–19, 122, 125–36,
    149–50, 157, 162, 167, 183, 191
  krupteía (secret service, initiatory rite),
    23–25, 49, 105, 156–57, 169
  little assembly (probably ephors and
    gérontes: elders), 48, 168

oîkos (household), partial suppression
of, 25–30, 38, 153, 160
paideía (formation, education),
xiii–xv, 4, 7, 13–30, 62, 144–48,
153–57
pederasty, 26–28, 30, 105, 122, 159
aîtas (hearer), 159
eispnélas (lovers as "breathers-in"),
26–27, 159
paidiká (boy beloved), 27, 159
poetry, memorization and recitation,
13–23, 49, 122, 153–55, 169
possession of gold and silver banned,
9, 28–31, 46–47, 106, 149, 161, 168
private property in land, 10, 30, 45–47,
89, 125, 128–30, 150, 167
property regime, 9, 24, 32, 46–47,
125–36, 162, 167, 191
rules of inheritance, 10, 45, 61,
128–29, 150, 167
sacrificial practices, 23, 25, 27, 41, 43,
47, 156, 159, 165–66
shift from organization by three tribes
to organization by five villages,
102–4
sumptuary laws, 10, 31, 49, 122, 150,
161, 169
sussítion (men's mess), 10, 23–30, 33,
41, 46–49, 105, 129, 135, 137, 150,
157, 159, 167
isokratía (sharing of power), 117

javelins in archaic Greek warfare, 33, 80–81,
85, 87, 89

King James Bible, 15–16

Leuctra, battle of, 34–35, 109, 130, 151–52,
162

magistracies within Lacedaemon, 36–63,
98–106, 162–72, 183–86
agathoergoí (doers of good), 25, 102–3,
115, 158
dual kingship of Heraclids, 1, 4–5, 17,
41–54, 60–61, 69–74, 77, 79–80,
82, 101–4, 116–17, 135, 165–71,
174, 177, 184–85, 188–89
Achaean, not Dorian and not
Spartiate, 42, 165
adoption, kings oversee, 45–47,
127, 167, 182
Agiad royal line, 42, 69–74, 80, 98,
104, 106, 108–9, 117–18, 125,
134, 170, 174

senior to Eurypontids, 72
agōgḗ (system of education and
indoctrination), not subject to,
41, 165
archagétai (founders), kings as, 43,
166
barred from having children by
women from abroad, 43, 166
booty, claim on a portion, 47, 167
carriage roads constructed and
maintained, 44–45, 106–10,
119, 162, 167, 186, 189
divine right, 16, 60
Eurypontid royal line, 42, 50, 53,
69–76, 80, 90, 98, 103, 110, 134,
174
exchange of oaths with ephors each
month, 50, 170
funerals like those of demigods, 43,
165
gerousía (council of elders), kings
members of, 41, 165
heiresses, kings dispose of, 45–47,
167
hereditary succession to general-
ship with life tenure, 42–45,
165
authorized to wage war against
any territory they wished,
42, 165
legitimizes Dorian conquest of
Laconia, 42–43
list of kings, 69–71, 174
patronage, kings control, 43–47,
52, 170
próxenoi (vice-consuls), kings
appoint, 44, 166
role in foreign relations, 44–45,
52–53, 47, 166, 171
Púthioi (envoys to Delphic oracle),
kings appoint, 44, 167
resources at disposal, 47, 167–68
rivalry between two kings the
norm, 52–53, 171
sacral and sacrosanct, 22, 43, 60,
165
sacrifices, kings conduct, 23, 27,
41, 43, 47, 156, 159, 165–66
subject to trial at behest of ephors,
50–51, 170
sussítion (men's mess), kings do not
join, 41, 165
ephorate, 1, 3–4, 32, 35, 41, 48–54, 61,
89, 98, 100–104, 117, 119, 126,
128, 134, 168–71, 183–85, 188–89

magistracies within Lacedaemon (*cont.*)
  annual declaration of war on
    helots, use of young men
    undergoing *krupteía* (period
    of concealment), 49, 169
  board of five, 48
  broad judicial powers, 49–50,
    169–71
  calendar, managed by, 49, 169
  calls up army, 49, 169
  common assembly, ephors
    summon and preside, 48, 168
  compared with Roman tribunes,
    48, 168
  conducts *dokimasía* (scrutiny), 23,
    49, 156
  conducts *eúthuna* (giving of
    accounts), 48, 50, 168–69
  exchange of oaths with the kings
    each month, 50, 170
  filled by procedure akin to lottery,
    51–52, 60, 102, 118, 170, 184
  foreign policy: ephors receive
    embassies, negotiate treaties,
    appoint generals, 49, 169
  grand jury and service on jury in
    capital cases, 50–51, 54, 60,
    169–71
  harmosts, ephors appoint, 49, 169
  hippagrétai (select and command
    hippeîs, royal bodyguard),
    ephors appoint, 49, 157–58,
    169
  iteration in office almost certainly
    prohibited, 48, 51, 168
  kings court, 51, 170
  list of ephors eponymous, 100, 184
  little assembly, ephors summon,
    preside, propose measures,
    48–49, 168
  nonentities chosen, 52–53, 102,
    170, 184
  oversight and enforcement of the
    law, 49–50, 169–70
  Polydorus' image on seal of office,
    104, 185
  regulates visits to Lacedaemon and
    travel abroad, 49, 168–69
  reshaped by tribal reform, 103–4,
    185
  sale and distribution of booty, 49,
    169
  seated in presence of kings, 50,
    169
  two members accompany kings on
    campaign to observe and
    advise, 50, 169
  unchecked, quasi-tyrannical
    power, 1, 48–49, 51, 170
  gerousía (council of elders), 41, 48–50,
    53–61, 89, 101–2, 117, 165,
    168–69, 171, 184, 188, 190
    age, wealth, stature make force for
      caution and conservatism,
      54–60, 171
    direct election for life, canvassing,
      54–55, 171
    form jury with ephors for capital
      cases, 50, 54, 60, 169, 171
    function as augurs, 54, 171
    guardian of the constitution, check
      on assembly, 54, 171
    minimum age sixty, 54, 171
    prestige, 53–54, 171
    priestly caste, 54, 171
    probouleutic functions, 54, 61
    selected from nobility, 53–54,
      60–61, 89, 171
    twenty-eight elected receive "prize
      allotted to virtue," 54, 171
  harmosts (garrison commanders), 3,
    49, 157, 169
  hippagrétai (select and command
    hippeîs, royal bodyguard), 25,
    157–58, 169
  mnōionómoi (overseers of the helots),
    113–14, 187
  paidonómos (master of the boys), 25
Mantineia, first battle of, 130, 133
mercenaries in Greek warfare, 87, 91, 163, 180
mores and manners of the Spartans, 1–63,
  143–72
  agonistic ethos, 23–30, 40–41, 51–53
  aidōs (reverence, awe), 13, 25, 30, 52,
    153
  aversion to commerce, 8–9, 45, 122,
    149
  bachelors, harsh treatment of, 26, 158
  breeding of horses, 10–11, 89, 122,
    149, 151
  children, treatment of, 10, 13–30, 150
    reared as wild animals, 62
  cloaks of purple, 23, 155–56
  conduct and situation of women, 10,
    15, 18–19, 25–27, 30–31, 35,
    46–47, 79, 90, 117–18, 131, 134,
    149–50, 158–62, 167, 170, 187,
    189, 192

customary secrecy, 2–3, 114, 130, 133–34, 174, 187

eugenics, 9–10, 149

gymnasium, 10, 59, 105

long hair, 23, 155–56

marriage practices, 26–27, 159

musical culture, 14–23

philonikía (love of victory), 51

philotimía (love of honor), 40–41, 56, 164

piety with regard to the gods, 12–13, 16–17, 41–43, 105, 122, 152–53, 165

procreative strategy and demographic trajectory, 12, 23, 34, 118–19, 122, 129–34, 149–50, 152, 156, 167, 176, 192–93

   plague as possible influence, 133–34

sacrifice to Muses before battle, 23, 155–56

secret craving for wealth, susceptibility to bribery, 9, 21, 27–31, 45–47, 52, 57, 106, 149–50, 160–61, 168, 170

transhumance perhaps once a practice, 71–72, 174

tremblers (cowards), brutal treatment of, v, 20, 32–34, 43, 162

wife-sharing, 26, 117, 158–59

wine imbibed before battle, 23, 155–56

oligarchy in Greece, oligarchic, 1, 41, 60–61, 119, 123, 144

Olympic Games, 76, 95, 158, 174, 176

oral tradition, 66, 71, 99, 135, 145, 172–76, 183, 185

Peace of Nicias, 34, 73, 175

Peloponnesian League, 42, 90, 114–23, 132, 165, 188–89

Peloponnesian War, xii, 3–4, 30, 32, 46, 126–29, 134

phúsis (nature) vs. *nómos* (convention, law, custom), xiii, 65, 172

Plataea, battle of, 33, 130–32, 170

Second Messenian War, 19, 94–97, 114, 116, 182, 186

Spartan *politeía* (citizenship, constitution, regime, regimen, way of life), xii–xv, 1–63, 72–114, 121–38, 143–73, 183–85, 189–91, 193

   balances and checks, 41, 99, 122

damasímbrotos (man-subduing), 29, 105, 161, 185

designed to prevent *stásis* (partisanship, faction, civil strife), 8–10, 14, 39–41, 61, 154

emergence and formation of, 98–114

Great Rhetra, 98, 104, 146, 154, 168, 183, 185

kósmos (beautifully ordered whole), xv, 105, 121, 136, 144, 185, 189, 193

mixed regime, 41, 60–61, 122, 164, 171–72

   aristocratic element, 1, 10–12, 44, 52–55, 60–62, 66, 93, 101–5, 114, 171–72, 184

   democratic element, 1–3, 37, 41, 51, 53, 60–61, 91–92, 102–5, 144–45, 163, 180–81

   monarchical element, 1, 41, 60, 102, 104, 170

políteuma (ruling order) of Spartiates defines, xi–xiv, 1–63, 72–114, 121–38, 143–75, 182, 187, 191–92

produces *eunomía* (good order), xv, 14, 16, 52, 105, 121, 144, 154, 185, 190

shift from organization by three tribes to organization by five villages, 102–4

statelessness, 37–39, 163

totalitarian comparison, 2, 145

subordinate classes within Lacedaemon

   helots (servile sharecroppers), 9–11, 17–19, 23–24, 33, 42–43, 49, 75–76, 79, 96–97, 102, 104, 112–36, 149–54, 165, 169, 175–76, 179, 182, 184–92

      earthquake in Laconia in 465/4 and helot revolt, 97, 116, 131–34, 157, 192

      old Achaean stock in Laconia, 11, 42, 68, 75, 151, 165, 175

   hupomeíones (inferiors), 24, 157

   móthakes (half-breeds put through *agōgḗ:* system of education and indoctrination), 131, 192

   Partheníai (so-called "sons of the virgins") denied allotments, expelled, 79–80, 119, 176

   períoikoi (free "dwellers-about"), 11–12, 43, 47, 72–76, 102, 113, 122, 130–32, 149, 152, 167, 169, 175, 187, 192

Tanagra, battle of, 132, 170
Tegea, battle of, 131
Thermopylae, battle of, 28, 33, 97, 129–33, 162, 170

Trojan War, 22, 67, 71, 77, 80–81, 173
tyranny in archaic Greece, 91–92, 101–3, 180

xenía (guest-friendship) in Greece, 44, 166

Index of Persons and Places

Achaea in the Peloponnesus, Achaeans, xviii, 68, 116

Achaeans, Danaans, Argives of the Mycenaean period, 11, 20, 42, 66–71, 75–82, 108, 111, 116, 118–19, 151, 165, 175–77, 182, 189

Acharnae, deme in Attica, 153

Adrastus, legendary son of Talaus, 21

Aegean Sea, 78, 90, 100

Aegina in the Saronic Gulf, Aeginetans, 85, 110, 186

Aeschines, last Orthagorid tyrant of Sicyon, 117, 188

Aeschylus son of Euphorion, tragedian, 164

Aesop, author of *The Fables,* 31

Agesilaus son of Archidamus (II), fourth-century Eurypontid king, 34, 137, 157, 162, 166, 171

Agios Vasileios (near Xirokambi), Mycenaean palace at, 75, 107–8

Agis (II) son of Archidamus (II), fifth-century Eurypontid king of Sparta, 50

Agis (IV) son of Eudamidas (II), third-century Eurypontid king, 134–35

Aigys region within northern Taygetus, 74–75, 175

Akobos on western slopes of Taygetus, 109

Akritas, Cape, in southwestern Messenia, 75, 107, 110, 113

Alcaeus of Mytilene, lyric poet, 37, 87, 125, 163, 179

Alcidamas of Elaea, sophist, 63

Alcman of Sparta, lyric poet, xv, 11, 14, 121, 125, 127, 144, 150, 154, 157, 174, 189

Alexander the Great, 129

Alpheios River along border of Arcadia and Sparta's domain, 116, 188

Ambracia near the Ionian Sea, Ambraciots, 117

Ammianus Marcellinus, xiii

Ampheia in northeastern Messenia, 107, 109, 111, 113, 186

Anaxandridas (II), sixth-century Agiad king, 44, 70, 106, 115, 117–19, 166, 188–89

Anaxandros son of Eurykrates, seventh-century Agiad king, 70, 113, 187

Andania at mouth of Soulima valley in Messenia, xviii, 94, 107, 112

Androtion son of Andron, Atthidographer, 113, 152, 187

Antiochus of Syracuse, historian, 79, 175–76

Apollo, 14, 17, 72, 74, 90, 93, 115, 154, 174–75, 182

Aratus son of Clinias, statesman and historian, 135

Arcadia in the Central Peloponnesus, Arcadians, xviii, 42, 68, 75, 77, 90, 94–96, 105–16, 119, 123, 132–33, 154, 161, 165, 179, 182, 186, 188
  Arcadian League, 111

Archelaus, eight-century Agiad king, 70, 100

Archidamus (II) son of Zeuxidamus, fifth-century Eurypontid king, 51, 53, 70, 170–71, 173, 192

Archilochus of Paros and Thasos, lyric poet, 87, 179–80

Ardys son of Gyges, seventh-century king of Lydia, 95, 182

Argos, Argives, xviii, 11, 33, 42, 68, 75, 93–96,
    101–6, 110–19, 123, 134, 151–52, 159,
    179–88
        Argolid (Argeia, Argive plain), 68–69,
            74, 90, 110, 179, 186
        hegemony within the Peloponnesus
            early on, 110, 186
Aristagoras of Miletus, 106, 110, 186
Aristocrates, seventh-century king of
    Arcadian Orchomenos, 94, 112, 182
Aristomenes of Messenia, 94–95, 112, 182–83
Ariston, sixth-century Eurypontid king, 70,
    115, 160, 188
Aristotle son of Nicomachus, philosopher,
    xiii–xv, 1, 4–6, 11, 14, 31, 38–41, 46–62,
    72–73, 79, 84, 88–92, 98–102, 110, 117,
    125–35, 145–50, 160–61, 164–65, 167,
    170–72, 179–81, 183, 190–91
        Lyceum founded by, 4, 91
        peripatetics (Aristotle and followers),
            4–6, 31, 55, 57, 60, 62–63, 99–100,
            180
        Politeía of the Athenians, 91, 127
        Politeía of the Lacedaemonians, 4, 6,
            49, 62, 72, 98–99, 127–28, 135,
            148, 150, 154–56, 162, 168–69,
            172, 174–75, 184, 188, 191
        The Politics, xiii–xv, 4, 36, 46, 98–99,
            125–27, 130–35, 150, 158–59,
            162–65, 172, 180, 183, 186, 188, 191
        The Rhetoric, 55–60, 63
Artemis Limnatis, sanctuary on western
    slopes of Taygetus, 74–75, 107–9, 175
Artemis Orthia, sanctuary at Sparta of, 18–19,
    74, 83, 154–55, 175, 177–78
Asia Minor (Anatolia), 66, 78, 106, 111, 172,
    177
Asine in Messenia near Cape Akritas, 75, 113,
    186
Asine in the Argolid, 75, 90, 110, 186
Assyria, Assyrians, 80, 87, 91, 177
Athens, Athenians, xi–xii, xvi, xviii, 1–4, 7,
    29, 31–32, 34–35, 38, 42, 46, 60, 65, 68,
    72–73, 91, 100–101, 103, 118, 126–27,
    132–34, 144–45, 147–49, 152, 157,
    161–62, 164–65, 167–68, 171, 179, 181,
    184–85, 187
Atreus son of Pelops, legendary king of
    Mycenae, 116
Aulon in Messenia, 107, 113
Australia, 26

Babylon, Babylonians, 80, 163
Belminatis region north-northwest of
    Laconia, 74–75, 109

Boeotia in Central Greece, Boeotians, xviii,
    66, 89, 92
Boreas, the north wind, 21
Burke, Edmund, 39, 164
Byzantium on the Bosporus, Byzantines, 187

Callicratidas the navarch, *móthax* (half-
    breed), 132
Callinus of Ephesus, lyric poet, 87, 179
Canaan, land of, 17
Caryae on border of Laconia and Arcadia,
    107, 116
Castor, legendary son of Tyndareus, 77
Cephisus river, 69
Chaeronea in Boeotia, Chaeroneans, 4
Chalcis on Euboea, Chalcidians, xviii, 89–90,
    179
        Hippobótai (Horse-Breeders) ruling
            order at, 89, 179
Charillos, eighth-century Eurypontid king,
    70, 74, 89, 98, 100–101, 105, 183–84
        seeks tyrannical power, 62, 101
Charondas of Catania, lawgiver, 62
Chilon the Spartan ephor, 117–22, 188–89
        Mēdèn ágan (Nothing too much), 117,
            120, 189
Chios off the Anatolian coast, Chians, 114,
    175, 188
Churchill, Winston, 2
Cicero, Marcus Tullius, xiii, 4–5, 48, 147
Cimon son of Miltiades, 40, 164
Cinyras, king of Cyprus, 21
Cleomenes (I) son of Anaxandridas, late
    sixth-century, early fifth-century Agiad
    king, 44, 50, 53, 70, 106, 110, 118–19,
    160, 166, 170–71, 189
Cleomenes (III) son of Leonidas (II),
    third-century Agiad king, 134–35
Cleomenes son of Pausanias, regent for
    Pausanias son Pleistoanax, 171
Cleonae in the Peloponnesus, Cleonaeans,
    133
Conon the mythographer, 79, 175–76
Corinth, Corinthians, xvi, xviii, 12, 38, 69, 71,
    101, 103, 117, 122, 133, 152, 182–85, 188
        Bacchiad aristocracy, 101, 184
        Corinthiad, 33
        Isthmus, 67–68, 173
Corinthian Gulf, 67–69, 71
Corneille, Pierre, 15
Crete, Cretans, 16, 67, 78–79, 101, 126, 149,
    153, 159, 176, 184
Critias son of Callaeschrus, 2–3, 5, 146, 155,
    157, 190
Croesus son of Alyattes, king of Lydia, 115

Cumae in Anatolia, Cumaeans, 4, 79, 131, 168, 176

Cynouria in the Peloponnesus, 33, 74–75, 80, 90, 93, 107, 110, 134, 175, 179, 186

Cyprus, Cypriots, 78, 177

Cypselid tyrants at Corinth and Ambracia, 117

Cyrene in Libya, Cyreneans, 78, 101, 103, 184–85

Cythera, island off Laconian coast, xviii, 75, 78, 110, 186

Damagetus, seventh-century king of Ialysos on Rhodes, 95, 182

Dante Alighieri, 15–16

Delphi in Central Greece and oracle of Apollo, xviii, 17, 32, 44, 50, 74, 90, 95, 99, 104, 115, 161–62, 166, 175–76

Delphos the Lacedaemonian, 79

Demaratus son of Ariston, late sixth-century, early fifth-century Eurypontid king, 28, 70, 86

Demosthenes of Sparta, 54

Demosthenes son of Demosthenes, Athenian orator, 35, 53–54

Dentheliatis on western slopes of Mount Taygetus, 107–8

Derveni Pass between Arcadia and Messenia, 75, 107, 109–10

Diagoridae, descendants of Damagetus of Rhodes, 95, 182

Dicaearchus of Messana, xiii, 4–5, 135, 147, 149, 187

Díkē (justice as goddess), xv, 93

Dio Cassius (Lucius Cassios Dio), xiii

Diodorus Siculus, xiii, 79, 131, 137

Dionysius of Halicarnassus, xiii, 24–25, 29–31, 52–53, 161

Dipaea, 131

Dorian, Dorians, 17, 42, 65–72, 77–80, 102–5, 116–19, 174, 176, 184, 189
    Hylleis, Dymaneis, Pamphyloi constituent tribes, 77
    invasion by, 67–69

Dorieus son of Spartan king Anaxandridas, 118–19, 133, 189

Doris on the Cephisus River in Central Greece, 69, 132

Dyrrachi on western slopes of Taygetus, 107, 109

Eckermann, Johann Peter, 15, 154

Egypt, Egyptians, 7, 78–81, 91, 96, 129, 177

Eira, Mount, on border of Messenia and Arcadia, xviii, 75, 94–95, 107, 112, 182

Elis in the Peloponnesus, Eleans, xviii, 52, 75–77, 171

Epaminondas son of Polymnis, Theban statesman, 94, 109–10, 113, 182, 186–87

Ephesus in Anatolia, Ephesians, 87

Ephorus of Cumae, historian, xiii, 4–6, 79, 101, 126–31, 135, 143–47, 153, 157–60, 166, 168–69, 173, 175–76, 179, 184, 191

Epidaurus in the Argolic Akte, Epidaurians, xviii, 110, 186

Epitadeus, ephor, 32, 46–47, 126–29, 134, 162, 167, 191

Eretria on Euboea, Eretrians, xviii, 89, 103, 179, 185
    early on *Hippeîs* the ruling order, 89, 179

Erineos on the Cephisus River in Doris, xviii, 17, 69

Eros (Cupid), 27, 159

Etruria in Central Italy, Etruscans, 152, 172–73

Euboea off the coast of Boeotia and Attica, Euboeans, xviii, 89, 103

Euclid, 36–37

Euhesperides in Libya, 78, 101, 184

Eupatrid aristocracy in Athens, 101, 184

Euripides son of Mnesarchus, tragedian, 86, 93, 98, 181

Eurysthenes, supposed scion of Agiad royal line, 69

Evans, Sir Arthur, 67, 173

Ferguson, Adam, 6, 39–40

Finley, Sir Moses, 67, 144–45

Gardiki fortress in Messenia, 109

Georgitsi on eastern slopes of Taygetus in Laconia, 107–9

Geronthrae in Laconia, xviii, 74–75, 102, 107, 175, 184
    three ephors, 102

Goethe, Johann Wolfgang von, 15–16, 154

Gorgo, daughter of Cleomenes son of Anaxandridas, wife of Leonidas, 106, 160, 170

Gortyn, Spartan colony in Crete, 78–79, 93, 98, 103, 150, 167, 176, 182

Great Britain, 37, 55
    Charles II, 45
    House of Lords, 55, 171

Grote, George, 172

Gyges, seventh-century king of Lydia, 95, 182

Gylippus son of Cleandridas, *móthax* (half-breed), 131

Gytheion on the Laconian Gulf, Spartan port, xviii, 75–76, 107–8

Hagnagora sister of Aristomenes of Messenia, 95, 182
Hagnon of Tarsus, 159
Hamilton, Alexander, xiv, 55
Harrington, James, 37
Hegesicles, sixth-century Eurypontid king, 70, 115, 188
Hellenic League, 34, 37–38, 52, 83
Helos in south-central Laconia, xviii, 75, 107, 110, 128, 175, 186
Hera, consort of Zeus, 16
Heracleides of Lembus, 4–5, 127, 147, 191
Heracles of Tiryns, legendary son of Zeus, 16, 20, 42, 67–69, 73–74, 154, 165–66
    Heraclids putative descendants of, 4, 17, 42–43, 60–61, 67–80, 90, 101, 116, 150–56, 161, 165–66, 168–69, 183–84, 189
        Aristodemos (or sons) awarded Laconia, 69
        Kresphontes awarded Messenia, 69
        reacquisition of the Peloponnesus, xiii, 4, 69, 79
        Temenos awarded Argos, 69
Herculaneum in Campania in Italy, 96
Herodotus of Halicarnassus, author of the *Historíai* (*Inquiries*), xii–xv, 7–8, 28, 65–66, 69–73, 77, 98, 106, 110, 115, 117, 121, 125, 127, 129, 136, 143–44, 148–49, 160, 165–67, 170, 173–75, 180, 188
Hesiod of Thespiae, xv, 92, 121, 180
Hetoimaridas, member of the Spartan *gerousía* (council of elders), 60, 171
Hieronymus of Rhodes, 98, 183
Hittite, 177
Hobbes, Thomas, 37, 163
Homer, xv, 2, 16, 20, 22, 42, 66, 80–82, 87–89, 106, 116, 121, 154–55, 173–81
    Iliad, 16, 80–82, 87–89, 92, 176–77
        Achilles son of Peleus, 20–22, 80, 176
        Agamemnon son of Atreus, king of Mycenae, 80, 115–16, 123, 176, 188
        Glaukos son of Hippolokos, 81–82, 92
        Hector son of Priam, 21
        Helen daughter of Tyndareus, 77
        Menelaus son of Atreus, king of Sparta, 13, 106, 116, 153
        Patroclus son of Menoetius, 177

        prómachoi (forefighters), 81–82, 87, 92
        Sarpedon son of Zeus and Laodamia, king of Lycia, 81–82, 92, 177
        Thersites, 92, 180
    Odyssey, 16
        Cyclops, 21
        Odysseus son of Laertes, 20–21, 92, 106, 174
        Peisistratus son of Nestor, 106
        Telemachus son of Odysseus, 106
Hume, David, 2, 37, 145
Hysiae on the border of the Argolid, xviii, 75, 90, 93–96, 104, 179–80, 182, 185

Imbros off the Hellespont, 79, 176
Ionia in and off the coast of Anatolia, Ionians, 16, 65, 154, 170, 189
Isocrates of Athens, teacher of oratory, xiii, 7, 32, 35, 55, 126–27, 152, 162, 169, 173
Israel, 17
Italy, 78–79, 96, 100, 172, 185
Ithome, Mount, in central Messenia, 75, 107, 110–11, 132

Jason and the Argonauts, 77, 177, 179
Jefferson, Thomas, 28, 159
Jews, 17, 154, 173
Josephus, Titus Flavius, 9, 26, 150
Justin (Marcus Junianius Justinus), epitomator of Pompeius Trogus, 150, 167

Kalamai above the Messenian Gulf, 107–8, 113
Kalathion spur of Taygetus into Messenian Gulf, 107–8
Kallisthenes of Olynthus, great-nephew of Aristotle, historian, 94, 182, 188
Kardamyle on Messenian Gulf, xviii, 75, 102, 107–8, 113, 184
Knossos on Crete, 67
Kopanaki in the Soulima Valley in Messenia, 107, 113
Kyparissia in Messenia, 107, 113

Laconia, Laconians, xviii, 10–11, 17, 23–24, 42, 45, 67–72, 75–80, 83, 89–90, 93, 100, 109–13, 119–22, 131, 133, 151, 157, 165–67, 174–76, 181–82, 186–90, 192
    Eurotas River and valley in, 11, 17, 72–75, 107–10, 149, 174–75, 192
Laconian Gulf, xviii, 75, 107–8
Langadha Pass over Taygetus, 75, 107–8
Las in Laconia, 75, 107–8

Lechaeum on the Corinthian Gulf, 33, 162

Lelantine plain in Chalcis, 89–90

Lemnos off the Hellespont, Lemnians, 77, 79, 176

Leobatas, ninth-century Agiad king, 70, 98, 100, 103

Leon, sixth-century Agiad king, 70, 115, 188

Leonidas (I) son of Anaxandridas, fifth-century Agiad king, 20, 32–33, 51, 69–70, 73, 160, 162, 170

Leotychidas (I) son of Anaxilas, seventh-century Eurypontid king, 70, 113, 174, 187

Leotychidas (II) son of Menares, fifth-century Eurypontid king, 50, 69–70, 73, 187

Lesbos off the Anatolian coast, Lesbians, 14, 93, 98, 103, 181

Leuctron (modern Leontari) in Arcadia north of Taygetus between Laconia and Messenia, 75, 107, 109, 116, 186

Leuctron on the Messenian Gulf, 107–8

Libanius of Antioch, 5, 154

Libya, 103

Lichas the *agathoergós* (doer of good deeds), 115, 188

Livy (Titus Livius), xiii, 145

Locke, John, 37

Luther, Martin, 15–16

Lycia in Anatolia, Lycians, 81–82
    Xanthos river, 82

Lycurgus, Spartan lawgiver, 3–6, 16, 43, 62–63, 98–105, 125–28, 135, 147, 154, 157, 161, 168, 171–72, 174, 183–85, 190–93

Lycurgus son of Lycophron, Athenian orator, 32

Lydia in Anatolia, Lydians, 95, 115, 182

Lyktos, Spartan colony in Crete, 78–79, 101, 176

Lysander son of Aristocleitus, *móthax* (half-breed) and navarch, 131, 164, 166

Macaulay, Thomas Babington, Lord, 7, 45, 148, 167

Macedonia, Macedonians, 44, 143, 160, 166, 178

Machiavelli, Niccolò, 1, 163

Madison, James, 8, 10, 28, 37

Magna Graecia, 103

Makaria, plain along Pamisos river in southern Messenia, 75, 107–8, 113

Malea, Cape, southeastern tip of Laconia, xviii, 75, 107, 110, 186

Mantineia in Arcadia, Mantineians, xviii, 52, 75, 130, 133, 171, 192

Medes, 144

Megalopolis in Arcadia, xviii, 107, 110, 186

Megara, Megarians, xvi, xviii, 38, 103

Melanesia, 26

Melos, Melians, 78–79, 176

Meltas, last Heraclid king of Argos, 115, 188

Menelaion, sanctuary near Sparta, 83

Mesopotamia, Mesopotamians, 81

Messene at Ithome in Messenia, xviii, 75, 89, 107, 110, 182–83

Messenia, Messenians, xviii, 11, 17–19, 24, 32, 42, 45, 65–69, 74–80, 89–122, 128, 149–52, 157, 166–67, 172–74, 179, 182–88
    nation in bondage, 96, 119, 122, 151, 187
    Pamisos river and valley in, 75–76, 80, 107–11, 119

Messenian Gulf, xviii, 74–76, 106–8, 113

Midas, king of Phrygia, 21

Miletus, Milesians, 106, 110, 186

Mill, John Stuart, 62, 172

Milton, John, 15

Minos, legendary king of Knossos in Crete, 101

Minotaur, 67

Montesquieu, Charles-Louis de Secondat, baron de La Brède et de, 1, 28, 36–37, 99, 152, 159

Moses, 17

Mothone near Cape Akritas in Messenia, 75, 107, 113, 187
    Spartans settle Nauplian refugees in, 113, 187

Murdoch, Iris, 64

Mycenaean, 66–71, 77–79, 108, 111, 173, 176–77, 182

Myron of Priene, 154, 169

Mytilene on Lesbos, Mytileneans, 37

Namier, Lewis, 36–39

Napoleon Bonaparte, 15

Nauplia in the Argolid, Nauplians, 75, 113, 187

Neda River, boundary between Messenia and Arcadia, 75, 94–95, 107, 112–13, 182

Nedon River on western slopes of Taygetus, 74–75, 107–9, 113, 175

Neochori on western slopes of Taygetus, 108–9

Nicomedes son of Cleombrotus, regent for Pleistarchus son of Leonidas, 132

Nikandros, eight-century Eurypontid king,
  xiii–xv, 70, 76, 89–90, 110, 176, 179

Ockham, William of, 69, 196
Oedipus son of Laius, legendary king of
  Thebes, 77
Oitylos on Messenian Gulf, 75, 107–8
Olympia in the Peloponnesus, site of Olympic
  Games, xviii, 50, 75–76, 83, 95, 176
Orchomenos in Arcadia, Orchomenians,
  xviii, 94, 96, 112, 114, 188
Orchomenos in Boeotia, Orchomenians, 66
Orestes, legendary son of Agamemnon,
  115–16, 188
Oresthasion in Arcadian Maenalia, xviii, 75,
  95, 107, 109, 112, 116, 182, 186, 188
Oxyrhynchus in Egypt, 96

Page, Denys, 67
Parnon, Mount, on border between Laconia
  and Cynouria, 74–75, 93
Pausanias son of Cleombrotus, regent, 50,
  160, 170
Pausanias son of Pleistoanax, Agiad king, 3,
  50, 146, 171
Pausanias the geographer, 4, 69–79, 94–95,
  110–15, 133, 152, 155, 162, 175–76, 182,
  186
Peloponnesus, Peloponnesians, 3–4, 11–12,
  17, 30, 32, 42, 45–46, 52, 66–69, 71,
  76–77, 83, 90, 93–94, 110, 115–34, 151,
  165, 167, 170, 176, 180–81, 187, 189, 192
  isle of Pelops, 17
Pelops, legendary son of Tantalus, 17, 21
Pephnus on Messenian Gulf, 108
Periander son of Cypselus, tyrant of Corinth,
  182
Pericles son of Xanthippus, 35, 40, 160, 162,
  164, 190
Persia, Persians, 7, 28, 32–33, 72, 82, 110, 129,
  144, 155, 165, 173, 177
  Great King (King of Kings), 15–16
  Ten Thousand Immortals, 153
Pharis in Laconia, 74, 175
Pheidon, Heraclid king of Argos, 90, 101,
  179–80
Pherae (modern Kalamata) on the Messenian
  Gulf, xviii, 74–76, 106–8, 113, 175
Phigaleia on the Neda River in western
  Arcadia, xviii, 75, 95, 107, 112, 133, 182
Philachaios, 118, 189
Philip of Macedon, 44, 166, 178
Phlius in the Peloponnesus, Phleiasians, 14,
  52, 171
Phocis in Central Greece, Phocians, 132

Phoenicia, Phoenicians, 77
Phylarchus the historian, 135, 193
Pindar of Thebes, xv, 14, 41, 65, 71, 73–74,
  77, 154, 164, 172–74, 182
Plataea on Cithaeron in Boeotia, Plataeans,
  xviii, 33, 103, 130–32, 184
Plato son of Ariston, philosopher, xiii–xv, 1,
  4–7, 12, 16, 30–31, 46, 51, 55, 60, 62, 92,
  102, 126, 129, 134–35, 146–50, 153–54,
  157, 159–61, 164, 170–72, 180, 191
  The Laws, 1, 4, 55, 126–27, 144–49,
    153, 172
  agronómoi, 157
  Nocturnal Council, 55
  The Republic, 4, 30, 144, 150, 164
Pleistarchus son of Leonidas (I), fifth-century
  Agiad king, 51, 70, 170
Pleistoanax son of Pausanias, fifth-century
  Agiad king, 50, 170–71
Plutarch of Chaeronea, biographer, xiii, 4–9,
  12–14, 16, 23, 26–29, 32, 40, 49, 53–54,
  59, 79, 94, 98, 101, 117, 121, 125–28,
  134–37, 146–48, 152, 154–57, 161, 164,
  168, 171, 174, 183–85, 190–93
  Life of Agis, 125–28, 134
  Life of Cleomenes, 128, 134
  Life of Lycurgus, 5–6, 16, 98, 101, 125,
    127–28, 135, 147, 154, 157, 168,
    171, 174, 183–85
Pollis the Lacedaemonian, 79
Pollux, legendary son of Tyndareus, 77, 150,
  170
Polyaenus of Macedon, 79
Polybius of Megalopolis, historian, xiii–xiv,
  26, 35, 51, 94, 126–27, 134–36, 154, 170
Polydorus son of Alcamenes, seventh-century
  Agiad king, 53, 70, 98–99, 104–6, 113,
  125, 183, 185
Polyneices, legendary son of Oedipus and
  Jocasta of Thebes, 77
Pratinas of Phlius, lyric poet, 14, 154
Prokles, scion of the Eurypontid royal line, 69
Prytanis, legendary Eurypontid king, 70, 73
Ptolemy I, Macedonian king of Egypt, 129
Pylos (Koryphasion) on west coast of
  Messenia, xviii, 75, 96, 106–7, 111–13,
  187
Pythagoras of Samos, 8, 149

Rhodes in the Dodecannese, 95, 182–83
  Ialysos on, 95, 182
Rome, Romans, xiv, 4–5, 29, 43–44, 48, 52,
  61, 64, 103, 137, 144, 152, 168, 184–85
  Brutus, 52, 171
  tribunes of the plebes, 48, 168

Rousseau, Jean-Jacques, v, 1, 7, 29, 35, 39–40, 48, 153, 161–62, 168
Russia, 2

Sallust (Gaius Sallustius Crispus), xiii
Samos off the Anatolian coast, Samians, 8, 103, 185
Sardis, capital of Lydia, 95
Schliemann, Heinrich, 66
Scythia north and east of the Black Sea, Scythians, 7
Shakespeare, William, 15
Sicyon in the Peloponnesus, Sicyonians, xviii, 110, 117–18, 186
Simonides of Ceos, 29, 98, 100, 105, 161, 183, 185
Socrates son of Sophroniscus, philosopher, 3, 5, 135
Solon of Athens, 62, 144, 150, 181
Sophocles son of Sophilus, tragedian, 13, 27, 89, 164
    Antigone, 27, 89, 159, 164
Soulima valley in Messenia, 75, 94, 107, 111–13
Spendon the Laconian, lyric poet, 11
Sphacteria, isle near Pylos, xi, 34, 130, 162
Sphaerus of Borysthenes, xiii, 4–5, 135, 147, 193
Stenyklaros, plain along Pamisos river in northern Messenia, 75–76, 79–80, 89, 104, 107, 109, 111–13, 119
Sthenelaidas the ephor, 53, 171
Styphon son of Pharax, xi–xii

Tacitus, Cornelius, historian, xiii, 61, 155
Taenarum, Cape, between Laconian and Messenian Gulfs, 75–76, 107
Taenarum, village of *períoikoi* (free "dwellers-about"), 102, 184
    three ephors, 102, 184
Tanagra, 132
Taras, Spartan colony in Magna Graecia, 78–79, 100–102, 176, 184
    king and three ephors, 100–102, 184
Taygetus, Mount, between Laconia and Messenia, 11, 19, 74–76, 93, 106–10, 113–14, 121, 187
    roads built over and around, 75, 106–10, 186
Tegea in Arcadia, Tegeans, xviii, 3, 75, 107, 114–16, 118, 131–32, 171, 188
Teisamenos, legendary son of Orestes, 116, 188
    bones of, 115–16, 188

Teleklos, eighth-century Agiad king, 70, 74–75, 89, 108, 175
Terpander of Lesbos, lyric poet, 11, 14, 93, 98, 103, 105, 154, 181, 183
Thalamai on the Messenian Gulf, 75, 107–8
Thaletas of Gortyn, lyric poet, 93, 98, 103, 105, 182–83
Tharyx of Phigaleia, 95, 112, 182
Thebes in Boeotia, Thebans, xviii, 11, 27, 77, 89, 111, 144, 151, 159, 179, 193
    charioteers and footmen, 89, 179
Themistogenes of Syracuse, 146
Theophrastus of Eresus, xiii, 4–5, 51, 135, 147, 169–70, 192
Theopompus of Chios, 114, 175
Theopompus son of Nikandros, late eight-century, early seventh-century Eurypontid king, 53, 70, 76, 89, 94, 98–105, 113, 176, 183, 185, 188
Thera, Spartan colony in the Cyclades, Theraeans, 77–79, 100–102, 176, 184
    king, three ephors, *gerousía* (council of elders), and perhaps helots, 100–102, 184
Thermopylae, xviii
Theseus, legendary king of Athens, 67, 147
Thessaly in Central Greece, Thessalians, 33, 90, 131, 159
Thibron of Sparta, harmost, 3, 146
Thouria in Messenia, 107, 113
Thucydides son of Olorus, historian, xiii–xv, 2, 7, 11, 34–35, 40, 71–72, 79, 86, 114, 125–33, 143–44, 151–52, 160, 162, 165–66, 169, 174, 184, 187, 192
Timaeus of Tauromenium, historian, 99, 183–84
Tiryns in the Argolid, Tirynthians, 66, 90
Tithonos, legendary son of Cephalus, 21
Tocqueville, Alexis de, 10, 181
Tourkoleka on western slopes of Taygetus, 109
Triphylia in the Peloponnesus, 75, 77, 95, 176
Troezen in the Argolic Akte, Troezenians, 133
Troy in Anatolia, 22, 66, 80–81, 111, 173
Tyndareus, legendary king of Sparta, 77, 16
Tyrtaeus, lyric poet at Lacedaemon, xv, 16–23, 33, 76, 87–88, 94, 96, 104–5, 111–12, 121, 144, 152–55, 166, 173, 176, 179, 182–87, 190

United States of America, 8, 36–37, 39–40, 145

Vasilikò in the Soulima valley in Messenia, 113
Vlachs, 71

Xenophon the Socratic, xiii–xiv, 3–5, 7, 11,
    25–26, 30–35, 43, 48, 51, 62, 73, 125–29,
    134–35, 137, 145–48, 156–62, 166, 168,
    172, 183

Politeía of the Lacedaemonians, 3–5, 7,
    11, 25–26, 30, 32, 43, 51, 62, 129,
    134–35
Xerxes son of Darius, Achaemenid, Great
    King of Persia, 28

Zeus, 16, 42, 60, 69, 76, 165